PENGUIN BOOKS

RUSSIAN STUDIES

Leonard Schapiro was born in Glasgow on April 22, 1908, and spent his childhood years in Riga and St. Petersburg, where he witnessed the Russian Revolution. At the age of twelve, he returned with his parents to London, where he attended St. Paul's School, University College, London, and Gray's Inn. In 1955, after practicing law for sixteen years, he joined the Department of Government at the London School of Economics, and in 1963 became Professor of Political Science there. He became a Fellow of the British Academy in 1971; in 1980 he was made an Honorary Fellow at the London School of Economics and a CBE.

His books include *The Origins of the Communist Autocracy* and *The Communist Party of the Soviet Union,* still the best accounts of the formative years of Soviet Russia; *The Government and Politics of the Soviet Union; Rationalism and Nationalism in Russian Nineteenth-Century Political Thought;* and *Turgenev: His Life and Times.* Leonard Schapiro died in London in November 1983, after completing work on his last book, *1917: The Russian Revolution and the Origins of Present-Day Communism,* which was published posthumously.

Ellen Dahrendorf was a student of Leonard Schapiro at the London School of Economics and later his colleague there.

Harry Willetts is a fellow at St. Anthony's College, Oxford.

RUSSIAN STUDIES

Leonard Schapiro

Edited by
Ellen Dahrendorf
with an Introduction by
Harry Willetts

PENGUIN BOOKS

PENGUIN BOOKS
Viking Penguin Inc., 40 West 23rd Street,
New York, New York 10010, U.S.A.
Penguin Books Ltd, 27 Wrights Lane, London W8 5TZ
(Publishing & Editorial) and Harmondsworth,
Middlesex, England (Distribution & Warehouse)
Penguin Books Australia Ltd, Ringwood,
Victoria, Australia
Penguin Books Canada Limited, 2801 John Street,
Markham, Ontario, Canada L3R 1B4
Penguin Books (N.Z.) Ltd, 182–190 Wairau Road,
Auckland 10, New Zealand

First published in Great Britain by William Collins Sons & Co. Ltd 1986
First published in the United States of America by
Viking Penguin Inc. 1987
Published in Penguin Books 1988

LIBRARY OF CONGRESS CATALOGING IN PUBLICATION DATA
Schapiro, Leonard Bertram, 1908–1983.
Russian studies / Leonard Schapiro; edited by Ellen Dahrendorf;
with an introduction by Harry Willetts.
p. cm.
Includes index.
ISBN 0 14 00.9376 1
1. Soviet Union—Politics and government—1894–1917.
2. Liberalism—Soviet Union—History. 3. Socialism—Soviet Union—
History. 4. Authors, Russian—Political and social views.
I. Dahrendorf, Ellen. II. Title.
[DK262.S317 1988]
947.08—dc19 87-18625
CIP

Printed in the United States of America by
R. R. Donnelley & Sons Company, Harrisonburg, Virginia
Set in Sabon

Thanks to the generosity of
Leonard Schapiro's many friends and admirers
a graduate studentship to honour his memory
has been established at
the London School of Economics.
All royalties from this book will be added
to that fund.

CONTENTS

EDITOR'S NOTE

The pieces in this volume were written at different times and for diverse audiences. They reflect Leonard Schapiro's wide-ranging interest in history, politics and literature. Some have never before been published while others are no longer readily accessible. Writings on the contemporary Soviet scene have not been included, since even the most acute analysis of current political affairs inevitably loses force in the light of subsequent events. Editorial changes have been minimal and minor; all footnotes are those of the author, except where otherwise indicated.

At a very early stage, Harry Willetts was kind enough to read the proposed selections. I am extremely grateful to him for his suggestions and his encouragement. I would also like to thank Howard White for his most helpful comments about the project, and Christopher MacLehose for his support and enthusiasm. Catriona Luce has seen the book through to the printer with efficiency and dedication.

I was exceptionally fortunate to have been Leonard Schapiro's student at the London School of Economics, and later his colleague and friend. It is my hope that *Russian Studies* will give stimulation and pleasure to a variety of readers and to another generation of students.

Ellen Dahrendorf
London, 1986

INTRODUCTION

It is not at all sure that Leonard Schapiro would have wished to see a miscellany of his occasional pieces brought together in a single volume. Everything he produced – whether it was a book or an after dinner talk to a small student society – was painstakingly worked and reworked until he was satisfied that it had the right weight and shape for its particular purpose. There are items here which he would have wished at least to re-write before circulating them, and he would have wanted to give the collection a more obvious unity.

If we have overruled our late friend it is not because he stands in need of a memorial volume. He has erected his own monument: two of his major works – *The Origins of the Communist Autocracy* and *The Communist Party of the Soviet Union* – are indispensable to all who hope to understand the USSR, and others of his books, especially his biography of Turgenev, will continue to find appreciative readers. But we are equally confident that anyone interested in Russian history and Russian culture will find not only enjoyment and instruction in these small pieces, but the vivid imprint of a remarkable personality.

There is of course an essential unity, and not just in the sense indicated by the title of the book. Everything that Leonard Schapiro wrote and said about Russia was informed, but never distorted by beliefs, passionately held but calmly and patiently expounded, which should be called philosophical, rather than political. He believed above all in the rule of law as the essential condition of a decent and dignified human existence: and he was even more concerned with legal safeguards against the encroachment of the overbearing state on the rights of the individual than with society's need to set limits to the disruptive activities of individuals. A persistent theme in his writing on Russia is the historically conditioned weakness of the sense of legality in that country and the consequent tragic impotence of late-born liberalism in face of fierce and impatient political creeds.

His feeling for the tragic essence of Russia's history never degenerated into facile pessimism. He believed in the healing and redeeming powers of the Russian cultural tradition. He looked for, and made the most of, hopeful signs in the present. His was an awesomely busy working life: his habitual reading embraced nineteenth and twentieth century Russian literature, the notoriously uneconomical writings of Russian political thinkers (the grim systembuilders as well as the coruscating dilettanti), and mountains of books, theses and articles on the Soviet Union. He wrote almost daily, alleging that he found it very difficult and dare not pause. He was a diligent and inspiring teacher, and he very rarely refused to give a talk to an outside audience. Yet in the middle of all this he conscientiously scanned the grey wastes of the Soviet press, making sure not merely that he was well-informed but that he was *fair* in what he said about the USSR. He condemned harshness and injustice in the USSR, or indeed wherever he saw it – but he was ready and glad to acknowledge improvements in Soviet legal codes and judicial practice, and of course in the conditions of life generally, since Stalin's death. His fairmindedness and scholarly detachment are strikingly exhibited here in his masterly pieces on two historical figures, intellectually and politically uncongenial to him – Lenin and Plekhanov – and no less in his defence of Alexander Solzhenitsyn, whom he greatly admired, but with whom he often disagreed, against absurd charges of anti-semitism.

Those of us who were privileged to be his friends, colleagues or pupils benefited of course from his great and generously shared erudition, but even more perhaps from his example: his relaxed yet unrelenting pursuit of the facts, the unemphatic but irresistible lucidity of his exposition, his restrained and objective examination of phenomena which he knew to be detestable. These qualities, we believe, will not escape readers of the pieces offered here.

H.W.

My Fifty Years of Social Science

This essay first appeared in *Government and Opposition*, vol. 15, summer/autumn 1980.

In strict truth, the first twenty of the fifty adult years of my life were spent either in practice at the Bar, or in military intelligence. The latter, and especially in wartime, is, of course, geared to the overriding practical objective of winning a war, though since I was involved with assessment of the Soviet Union's military strength and achievement, my work provided me with some kind of an introduction to the study of the Soviet Union to which, after the mid-fifties, I was to devote most of my time. But the Bar is far too egocentric an occupation to leave much time for interest in political issues, at most permitting time for the narrow practical pursuit of domestic party politics. For party politics I have never had much appetite – though I did campaign for the Conservative Party in one election.

I have been conservative by inclination, in the broad sense, as far back as I can remember. As an undergraduate and for some time after I was strongly drawn towards the right, much influenced by such critics of the then (as now) fashionable materialistic, egalitarian and rationalistic doctrines of society as T. S. Eliot and Maritain. I also recall that I was much impressed at the time by some of the writings of the American poet John Crowe Ransom. I believed then (as I still do, to a large extent) that the first requirement of a civilized society is order; and that the achievements of human culture are always produced by an elite (but certainly not necessarily by a class) and that the preservation of this elite is more important for human values than social and economic equality. Looking back as best I can on this remote period in my life, I believe that two influences were most potent in this phase of my intellectual development. One was the impact of Ortega y Gasset's *Rebelión de las masas*, published in 1930, translated into English in 1932. This book opened my eyes to the fact that we were entering an era in which the established hierarchies were breaking down before the onslaught of the rude and unlettered mass (what the late S. L. Frank called "the advance of the inner barbarian"), whose values and standards are gradually being imparted to our society. The other influence was that of a friend, an anthropologist and sinologist of outstanding intellectual force, George Pal. Pal, who hardly published, is quite unknown and died before completing the work to which he devoted his whole active life, argued on the basis of meticulous and far-reaching study of the genealogies of the leading families of Europe and China that the progress and regression of human culture was directly related to the rise or decline of the best breeding in these leading families at a particular time or place. (Many years later, long after Pal's death, I was excited to discover that the distinguished geneticist, C. D. Darlington, had arrived at a very similar conclusion by a quite different method, in his *The Evolution of Man and Society*, published in 1969.)

This *Neigung* to the right, which for me occurred in the late twenties and early thirties, did not last long. I don't think Italian fascism affected it very much. Mussolini was obviously no more than a mountebank, and Italian politics in any case were not something that one took seriously. (I did not incidentally read the shoddy rubbish that Gentile produced until many years later, when I was working on a book on totalitarianism.) What cured me of right-wing leanings were the Spanish Civil War and the rise of Hitler. So far as the civil war was concerned one side was as repellent to me as the other. (As regards Franco's side, the deepest impression made on me at the time was by Georges Bernanos's *Les grands cimetières sous la lune*. The cross and the sword in action was more than I could stomach.) Hitler's rise to power proved that the worst aspects of mass democracy could easily be combined with a pseudo-elitist political doctrine, as indeed Ortega had already stressed. The civil war taught me that the greatest disaster that can befall a society is to find itself in the grip of an all-embracing, all-resolving doctrine, whatever its nature. Henceforth I rejected all systems without exception as a solution for our ills, all preconceived formulae deliberately devised and then imposed. I think it must have been then that I became convinced that the only sure way is by a slow process of adaptation and evolution – in other words, by the organic growth eulogized by Burke, or by adopting the "piecemeal engineering" advocated by Popper in *The Open Society and its Enemies* after the war. (I suppose violent revolutions are sometimes unavoidable. But I recall a remark of Salvador de Madariaga that it is as inane for a country to glorify a revolution as it would be for an individual to take pride in an operation for appendicitis.) I have never changed my opinions about the evils of mass society, the merits of an elite of whatever social origins, but with aristocratic standards, or on the need for order above all. But I reject the view that the evils can be mitigated or the merits attained by the imposition of any kind of system. I also believe that societies reach a point of no return. When once we have reached a certain stage whether we believe that stage to be right or wrong, there is nothing for it but to seek adaptation or change within the terms of that development, and make the best we can of it. One cannot in politics turn back the clock.

One thing the rise of fascism did not do to me: incline me towards communism. I knew much too much about Stalin's Russia for that – and it is often forgotten when excuses are made for the traitors who entered the service of communism allegedly because they feared the onslaught of fascism, how much information there was available on the Soviet Union and on Lenin's Russia if one chose to look for it – and did not take transparently dishonest propaganda like the Webbs' *Soviet Communism. A New Civilization?* at face value. I may add that my critical attitude to Soviet Russia was in no way due to the fact that I had spent my early boyhood in Petrograd during the revolution and the civil war. On the contrary, these years, for all the hardship and brutality which characterized them, remained in my memory as a time of exhilaration – new art forms, the elation of watching a new society in the making, in fact a period of great romance. It was only many years later, when I came to study Lenin's period of rule and rise to power in detail, that the reality of the revolution (or what I concluded had been the reality) became clearer to me.

Our alliance with the Soviet Union during the war produced two results, one transient, the other not so ephemeral. One consequence, for many of us, was the refusal during wartime to accept the horrors of the Soviet regime as they emerged into the light of day as relevant, or deserving of attention. It is difficult to explain this attitude to anyone who is not old enough to remember the war – I constantly find various signs of this inability to understand the mood of the time in the writings of young historians of the war. But such was the overwhelming sense of the urgency for the need to see Germany defeated, and so great the contribution which the Soviet Union was making to this aim, that any criticism of Soviet conduct was resolutely stifled under the impact of this all-compelling urge. I can recall vividly (with no particular pride) my own reaction to the news of the Katyn discovery, for example. The responsibility for the massacre was even then plainly that of the NKVD – O'Malley's report alone to which I had access at the time made this absolutely clear. Yet I fully shared the official government view that the Poles must be discouraged from raising the issue for fear of endangering the Soviet alliance.

This was, no doubt, a transient mood, dictated by the exigencies of the period. But there also prevailed a second widespread attitude to the Soviet Union which has proved less transitory – the illusion that the Soviet Union, under the impact of the war, had recovered from the worst excesses of ideological commitment, and that once the war was over one could expect rational co-operation in building the future peace. This illusion that at bottom the Soviet Union is reasonable and basically motivated by the same aims as the Western nations – such as security, extension of its influence, trade and co-operation – persists to this day, and has at times influenced US or British policy. It is, I believe, the most dangerous illusion that Western statesmen can suffer from, and is caused by ignorance of Soviet history, by failure to attach any importance to Soviet party literature and by an underestimation of the influence of ideology on Soviet aims.

So far as I was concerned, the most powerful single factor that cured me of any illusion that the Soviet Union might have changed after the war was the Nuremberg trial, and the way in which it entered into the fabric of international relations. Nuremberg was both an appalling travesty of international law, and a craven acquiescence in and tacit acceptance by the Western powers of the principle that the grim record of the Soviet Union in its treatment of its population was beyond criticism. International law was traduced by the introduction of the new principle of law which certainly did not exist at the time the acts were committed, that waging an aggressive war is an international crime. As regards the violation of human rights, the Western allies acquiesced in a Soviet demand for an amendment to the agreement setting up the Tribunal. This consisted in the removal of a comma, and this had the result of placing it beyond doubt that violation of human rights was only an international crime when it was committed in furtherance of acts of aggression, but not otherwise – thus precluding even the possibility that Stalin's atrocities might one day be condemned by the international community. There were, of course, other instances of Western acceptance of Soviet hypocrisy – the ratification of the treaties with Eastern Europe, for example, or indeed the acquiescence in the gradual incorporation of the countries of Central and Eastern Europe into the Soviet empire by means of the "salami tactics" so admirably described by Hugh Seton-Watson in his *The East European Revolutions*. For the most blatant exercise in international cynicism it is unnecessary to go further than the Charter of the United Nations itself: "We, the Peoples of the United Nations, . . . determined to reaffirm faith in fundamental human rights, in the dignity and worth of the human person . . ." signed by the USSR, Belorussia and the Ukraine. But the Nuremberg trial was the worst, and was not made any better by the zeal with which many distinguished British lawyers rushed to defend its propriety and legality. For me the trial was a significant milestone in my perception of communism, and the realization of the hypnotic influence which Leninist tactics could exercise over the democracies. The subsequent bombshells in the communist world did not in any way add to my understanding of communism – I mean the suppression of the Hungarian and Czechoslovak revolutions, or Khrushchev's denunciation of Stalin. By then I was devoting myself almost entirely to the study of the Communist Party and its history, and none of these events, though obviously of interest and significance, suggested any departure from the standard behaviour of a communist power, or (in the case of Khrushchev's famous speech) produced information that was not already largely familiar.

But there was one consequence of the toppling of Stalin's reputation that really did surprise me, and which should perhaps be regarded as the most significant development of the past decades in the area of the social sciences with which I have been mainly concerned – Soviet and communist studies. What surprised me was that instead of, as I expected, weakening, even finally exploding, marxism as a desirable or convincing doctrine, the exposure of Stalin served to give marxism a new and more vigorous lease of life. It was as if, having thrown off the horrifying practical consequences of Marx as interpreted by Stalin, it was at last possible to return to the pure stream of wisdom and nobility expounded and practised by Lenin. The egregious Sartre, who had for years acted as the apologist of Stalinism, even discovered, to quote his own peculiar language, that it was only in the post-Stalinist period that the critique of dialectical Reason (by which he meant the pure stream of revolutionary theory) could appear. It could not "occur *before* the *abuses* which have obscured the very notion of dialectical rationality . . . Critical investigation could not occur in our history before Stalinist idealism had sclerosed both epistemological methods and practices. It could take place only as the intellectual expression of that reordering which characterized the post-Stalin period" (*Critique de la Raison Dialectique*, Paris, 1960; p. 50 of the English translation published in 1976). Whatever the reason for the "reordering" there is no doubt about the fact: liberated from the stigma of Stalin's concentration camps and mass murders, marxism in various "New Left" guises flowed into scholarship and into politics, enjoying a phase of intellectual respectability which the former slavish obedience to Moscow (via King Street) could never hope to achieve. In some Western European countries shrewd communist leaders cashed in on the "reordering which characterized the post-Stalin period" and tried to give communism a novel respectability in the guise of "Eurocommunism".

My own preoccupation with communism had antedated all this. In 1955, after years of research, I published a book entitled *The Origin of the Communist Autocracy* which dealt with the early years of the Soviet regime when Lenin was in charge. I see no reason today, nearly a quarter of a century later, to depart in the slightest degree from the conclusions which I came to, namely that it was Lenin who created the instruments which Stalin put to even more terrible use; and that Lenin, while a great revolutionary, had none of the attributes of a statesman. My approach to the study of Soviet history and politics was very much influenced by the two books, which I still consider to be in a class by themselves in this field: Boris Souvarine's biography of Stalin, published in 1935, and Merle

Fainsod's superb *How Russia is Ruled*, of which the first edition appeared in 1953. Both these books taught me to study Soviet Russia as a society characterized by a regime which sought to exercise total power; and which in pursuit of this total power rode roughshod over all institutional forms, and in particular used the courts and judges as instruments of that power, thus depriving the individual of any means of protecting himself. Broadly speaking, this still seems to me the only valid approach to the study of Soviet government today.

There have, however, been far-reaching changes in the study of Soviet Russia, especially among American scholars, since Fainsod's masterpiece appeared, and most notably since the second revised edition appeared in 1963. In particular, the notion of totalitarianism has fallen into disfavour, felled by twin blows: it is denigrated as a "cold war" term, which should not be applied to Soviet Russia; and in any case, since interest and pressure groups operate inside the Soviet Union, the term "totalitarian" is deemed inappropriate. I suspect there is a good deal of the guilt which often seems to characterize intellectuals, perhaps particularly American intellectuals, about this line of reasoning. (A very striking example of this self-flagellation was recently provided by George Kennan who roused much controversy by arguing that the moral record of the United States was so bad that Americans had no right to criticize the Soviet Union.) Another recent fashion which has developed in some writing about the Soviet Union is calling in aid the specialized jargon of sociological analysis and applying it to Soviet society, with the result that all perception of the real nature of that society is lost in a welter of meaningless technicalities – meaningless, that is, in the Soviet context, where the basic data for sociological analysis are absent. In the writing of the history of the triumph of Bolshevism and the early development of communist rule there has been much emphasis on development at the "grass roots", based on archival research, probably motivated in some cases by a desire to show the extent of popular support enjoyed by the Bolsheviks and to counter the view that the October revolution was little more than a *coup d'état* by determined conspirators.

These developments in the writing of modern Russian history are sometimes valuable as a corrective, though in some cases I find that historians fail to distinguish between support for the

Bolsheviks and support for the soviets – it was an aspect of Lenin's genius to create this confusion between the two in the public mind. But the other developments seem to me entirely misguided. It is not historically true that "totalitarianism" is a "cold war" term – it was used long before the "cold war" began. (Even if it were, a political term does not cease to be valuable merely because it is abused by politicians.) And if one ignores the totalitarian nature of Soviet power, and in particular the way in which the ruling elite exercises power by ignoring, circumventing and manipulating all institutions, one is writing about a product of one's imagination, not the Soviet Union. The fact that terror has been substantially reduced since Stalin's day is also not relevant. The possibility of benevolent totalitarianism was foreseen already *inter alios* by Diderot and Tocqueville (if benevolent is the right term to apply to present-day Soviet Russia) and control of jobs and privileges has been proved by Stalin's successors to be a very effective substitute. On the other hand, the partisans of the "interest group" analysis of the Soviet Union seem to me to fail to take account of the extent to which interests are in fact prevented from acting as a group, but are on the contrary manipulated and at times even controlled (by the selection of spokesmen, for example) by the party apparatus. In the sphere of the "pressure group" interpretation of Soviet society, Professor Jerry Hough has even argued, not very convincingly, that the Soviet system of government is one of "institutionalized pluralism". His fullest analysis of Soviet government on these lines is to be found in a book which purports to be a "revision" of Merle Fainsod's masterpiece. Mr Hough is entitled to write what he pleases. But it is regrettable that reputable publishers should have allowed a work which is little related to Fainsod's in outlook or in merit to share the lustre of his name.

I have drawn attention to some of the aberrations, as they seem to me, which have been taking place in my field of study. There have, of course, been a great many fine, and some superb, works published on nineteenth-century Russia, on the Soviet period and on communism – though it is a strange fact that in spite of the great quantity of new sources which has since become available Chamberlin's history of the revolution, published in 1935, has not yet been superseded. I single out two books in the Russian field which, so far as I am concerned, fall into the category of those milestones in one's reading which permanently transform the way in which one henceforth perceives a subject. One is Victor Leontovitsch's *Geschichte des Liberalismus in Russland*, published in 1957. This book opened my eyes to the extent to which the legal structure permeates and dominates society – even where the law is as frequently violated as it was in nineteenth-century Russia. This book also underlined the contrast between imperial Russia, and Soviet Russia where there is no legal structure, because the law is purely an instrument in the hands of the ruling elite. In nineteenth-century Russia, however much violated by the government, law still served to shape society. Leontovitsch also showed the progress which liberalism – in the sense in which he uses the term, i.e., *Abschaffung*, or dismantling of absolute power – was fast making in Russia. The other book in my category of "milestones" is Wittfogel's *Oriental Despotism*, published in the same year, 1957. This illuminated for me, as no other book had done, the contrast between Russian society and the feudal societies of Western Europe out of which our common law and, to a large extent, the systems founded in Roman law, evolved. Wittfogel's book also made clear to me, more than ever before, that Marx's analysis of the development of industrial societies has no application to Russia to which not feudalism but his category of the "Asiatic mode of production" applied. For me, at any rate, this threw new light on the totalitarian nature of Stalin's regime and helped to strip it of the irrelevant marxist analysis with which politicians and historians have encrusted it.

I ought, while on the subject of these "milestones", also to refer to Norman Cohn's *The Pursuit of the Millennium*. This work taught me that totalitarianism is not only the product of social trends and the will of determined tyrants, but is something rooted deeply in human consciousness, and therefore liable to break out periodically in any human society.

As I look back over the past fifty years of my adult life, I am struck by the influence which my undergraduate study of law – and particularly of the common law – has had on my attitude to politics. If Ortega's masterpiece first made me aware of the deficiencies of mass society, the systems of banditry masquerading as regimes of the right soon showed that the solution did not lie in that direction, nor indeed in any "system". Ortega, of course, was in no conceivable sense an advocate of right-wing regimes – or any regimes for that matter. Mass society, as he saw it, operated through the state, and he hoped for the regeneration of the world in the growth of internationalism. He was probably right, but I have always found it difficult to believe in the reality of internationalism – there was room for idealism in the League of Nations, at any rate in its early years, but the United Nations, founded on a lie, was a fraudulent mess from the start. If internationalism is ever to be attained, it will come about through the regeneration of individual societies, and not through the attempt to simulate union among a congress of barbarous and nationalist entities. What the common law taught me is what I have believed for years – that a society can only progress by evolution, and not by convulsions, by growth and not by surgery dictated by belief in some system. And further, that the only safeguard against convulsion, and the only condition for ensuring organic growth, is a well-rooted legal system and a strong and independent judiciary to safeguard it. Never must these primary requirements of a civilized society be sacrificed to the demands of the uncultured masses which will readily yield to the blandishments of demagogues in the hope of achieving their material aims. In my excursions into a very different society from England – nineteenth-century Russia – I have tried to find traces of that belief in gradualness and rejection of systems which is very rare among Russians. But there were a few who held to this faith: Pushkin, Granovsky, Chicherin, the novelist Turgenev, perhaps some more, but the list is very short.

It is difficult in the midst of the increasing barbarism in which the world is rapidly becoming engulfed to see grounds for optimism. I can only think of one tiny ray which has pierced the descending gloom in the last twenty-five years. This is the recognition which is gradually taking shape in international society that the way in which a government treats its population is no longer solely a domestic issue but a matter of concern to the whole community of nations. The policy of the United States has played a decisive role here, but so have the various international conventions to which the Soviet Union is a party, and which, in spite of all its efforts, it has not been able entirely to dismiss as the exercises in hypocrisy which it originally intended them to be. This change is, of course, a very modest one – it has had little effect on the conduct of the innumerable tyrannies which exist in the world. But it marks at any rate some progress from the day when the Western Allies agreed to that comma being removed from the Statute of the Nuremberg Tribunal for fear that someone someday might call Stalin to account for his twenty million victims. It must always be reckoned as progress if international relations are based on the recognition of reality rather than wrapped up in elaborate hypocrisy and self-deception.

LIBERALISM AND THE LAW

The Importance of Law in the Study of Politics and History

This essay has not been previously published and was originally delivered as a lecture to the Carlyle Club at Trinity College, Cambridge, on 21 October 1972.

It is now sixteen years since I left the practice of the law in order to teach and study political institutions and modern and contemporary history. In this study my experience of the law has been a constant guide and inspiration, and I have repeatedly found myself searching the legal theory and structure of the countries with which I have been concerned for explanation which the examination of institutions alone did not provide.

In my somewhat random selection of topics I should like to draw on my study of contemporary history, but especially in regard to what has proved the major political problem of our time, in practice as well as in theory – the emergence of what is usually called totalitarianism in National Socialist Germany and in Soviet Russia. We often like to think – and I hope we are right – that we are immune in this country from that most terrible scourge of contemporary democratic society. I believe that if we are immune, or at all events have remained immune so far, then this is intimately interwoven with our common law and in the contrasts which it presents with the legal systems of all the countries of continental Europe. By this I mean not so much the legal systems themselves, both substantive and procedural, as the evidence which they afford of what, in the jargon of modern political science, is called "political culture" – a kind of amalgam of habits, traditions and attitudes which gives its character to a political system.

I should like to choose my first example from our criminal law – the nature of our criminal trial. Although our criminal procedure did not assume its present form until perhaps one hundred years ago, there is one feature of it of vital importance which goes back to the Middle Ages – the non-inquisitorial role of the presiding judge. As Pollock and Maitland tell us, the medieval trial reminds one of a cricket match: "The judges sit in court," they write, "not in order that they may discover the truth, but in order that they may answer the question 'How's that?' This passive habit seems to grow upon them as time goes on." I am not so sure that the passive habit has survived to that extent to the present day. But the contrast with the continental systems of inquisition by the judge remains as valid as it was. Our trial retains its essential feature of a contest between two sides – the prosecuting authority which has to prove its case *prima facie* before the accused is called on to make his defence; and the presiding judge ensuring justice for both sides as required by strict rules of evidence, and directing the jury. In the inquisitorial system, which was adopted in the countries of the European continent after the twelfth century, and which was regarded as a great advance on the system which derived from trial by contest, the accused is at all stages subject to inquisition by the court. So far from holding the ring, as it were, the court has the function of discovering, by means of the very extensive powers of enquiry conferred upon it, the full truth of the matter before it. It may be observed, in parenthesis, that the new continental fashion was adopted in England in the sixteenth and seventeenth centuries in the ecclesiastical courts and in the Star Chamber – but happily did not survive. My reason for stressing this particular contrast in the law is not so much because of its direct influence – though I should think that that has been considerable – but because I think it is typical of our proceedings in areas which extend far beyond the law – in Parliament, for example, with the government and opposition locked in battle under the rule of an impartial Speaker; and below Parliament in countless deliberative bodies, from a local council to a school or university debating society. It is indeed a way of conducting our affairs which is appropriate to a polity which lacks, to anything like the extent to which it is to be found in France, say, or in Germany, the notion of the all-pervading *state* not only as the sole fountain of all authority, but as a permanent, corporate body in society. This brings me to my second main example of the contrast between England and the continental European countries.

This second contrast has, of course, often been studied and

described and is very familiar, if only because of the stress that was laid on it by Dicey. The great authority on French administrative and constitutional law, Maurice Hauriou, put it something like this. In the English common law concept of government, government is seen as a trustee. Government officials bear responsibility for their acts as individuals in accordance with the principles of the common law. In this process a vital part is played by law, and by judicial interpretation. But this interpretation, so long as it is based on the common law, cannot depart from certain inherent principles of law which are enshrined in custom. However, by reason of the important role played by judicial interpretation, the function of the judge is always a creative one, he remains the guardian of a living and growing body of traditional wisdom. So far Hauriou. One could add two glosses on his summary. In the first place the notion of government as a "trust" derives from Locke, whose *Second Treatise on Government* was described by Sir Frederick Pollock as "probably the most important contribution ever made to English Constitutional Law by an author who was not a lawyer by profession". But, lawyer or not, Locke derived his notion of "trust" from the law, and made use of it in two ways which laid the foundations of our modern political order. First, he adapted the notion of government power being held and exercised in trust for the governed, just as the common law owner was compelled by the Court of Chancery to exercise the beneficial ownership for the benefit of the *cestui que* trust; and secondly, just as the trustee can be removed by the court, and replaced, yet the trust endures, so a government may be replaced if it fails in its trust, without beheading a king, or winding up a commonwealth. My second gloss is that, since Hauriou wrote in 1929, changes in our law have come about which make something uncommonly like the state, or at all events government departments, directly responsible out of public funds in certain kinds of actions. We are, perhaps, creeping nearer to the continental notion of the state: but I hope we still have some way to go, and that the common law may yet save us.

The whole of the European continent, Hauriou continues, holds to the concept of the state as a corporation, with both rights against and duties towards its subjects. Hence the most basic notion of public law is that of administration. This, it will be recalled, was the contrast between the common law and French law so severely censured, in favour of the common law, by Dicey. But again, time has not stood still. The efforts of the *Conseil d'Etat* in France, and the influence of administrative lawyers like Hauriou, have resulted in a system of French administrative law which offers very substantial safeguards to the individual in his conflicts with the state; and in this country the rapidly growing administrative powers have sometimes been able to escape the jurisdiction of the common law and the judges. But enough of the contrast remains. This becomes particularly apparent when one looks at some aspects of the rise and triumph of National Socialism in Germany in which notions of state and law seem to me to have played an important part.

The strength of the common law lies in the fact that it does not raise any particular need for enquiry into the source of its validity: it is rooted in immemorial practice, it is there, it has always been there, and the judges in their wisdom know it and apply it. Its validity does not, for example, rest on natural law, which so easily fell a victim to the rationalism and scepticism which emerged from the Enlightenment. But, in the absence of common law, the source of the validity of the law for the rationalists of the German nineteenth century became the state; and the dominant doctrine in German law, right up to the advent of National Socialism, was positivism. One can take Georg Jellinek as the most influential exponent of the doctrine, since he occupied for many years the Chair of Law at Heidelberg, and through the medium of his *Allgemeine Staatslehre* (first published in 1900) educated generations of judges and administrators who were active in the Weimar Republic and after. For Jellinek the force of law derives from the fact that it is enacted by the state. But the state at the same time enacts rules which bind itself: it thereby becomes a *Rechtsstaat*, a state based on law. Now, the obvious weakness of the *Rechtsstaat*, as we know from the bitter experience which Jellinek could not ever have imagined, is that the state will only remain founded on law as long as it chooses to do so: or, to put it another way, that it retains the authority to enact the kind of emergency powers and the like which Hitler used to destroy the tottering Weimar Republic – legislation which, though a travesty of the law, will nevertheless be valid and enforceable. It is true that Jellinek's doctrine retained certain natural law elements, such as his theory that the force of the law did not lie in the physical might of the state which lay behind it, but in what he called the "conviction that it is valid. The whole legal order," he writes, "is built upon this purely subjective element." But events proved him cruelly wrong. He did, it is true, envisage certain other safeguards – they are listed in a short chapter at the very end of a book which runs to all but 800 pages. These included such social factors as morality, religion and custom; administrative control systems; legal actions by individuals against officials; and judicial decisions. But – and this is the essential nature of positive, enacted law – the function of the judge is solely to test the validity of a law by examining its conformity to the enacted legal order. Of course, Acts of Parliament are likewise binding on our courts. But our law does not consist solely of Acts of Parliament. Moreover, judicial interpretation in England is a creative process far more extensive than in Jellinek's conception; in the words of Hauriou, it is an art, and not a science. In time of crisis it can be hoped that it might provide a safeguard, or at the very least ensure a period of delay, which the German judiciary proved unable to provide, since Hitler – as he repeatedly boasted – was most careful to clothe his assumption of unlimited powers with the semblance of conformity to the legal order.

The story of German positivism in its relation to the victory of National Socialism does not, however, end there. It was to undergo two further stages of transformation in influencing the collapse of legal order in Germany. The first was the refinement introduced by Hans Kelsen's pure theory of law. The second was the transformation of positivism into a kind of grotesque travesty of natural law in the hands of the main legal ideologist of National Socialism, Carl Schmitt. At first sight Kelsen's pure theory of law which exercised enormous influence on German lawyers before the First World War, and especially during the Weimar Republic, appears to go even further than Jellinek's positivism in clearing the way for the acceptance of every enacted law, however monstrous, as valid and beyond question. He rejects even the fragile limitations accepted by Jellinek – the recognition of a law's legitimacy by the public, traditional morality and ethics, the self-imposed limitations on the powers accepted by the state, and the like. For Kelsen, law is a binding norm, and nothing more: it has no ethical or moral content so far as the lawyer is concerned, its validity derives purely causally from the fact that it is enacted with the power of the state behind it. The positivist *Rechtsstaat* appeared to Kelsen to be drawing a distinction in favour of the latter between a state based on force and a state based on law: for Kelsen the two are identical, since state and law are for him identical. The state is the sum total of laws, and laws are the state in action, the legal order. Every state, therefore, which has a legal order is of necessity a *Rechtsstaat*, a state based on law.

Kelsen was a staunch opponent of National Socialism, and has remained ever since an adherent of liberal values. His object in devising his theory of law was to divorce law from all ideology and thereby to strengthen its role in society, and to prevent its abuse by the enemies of liberty. It is, however, easy to see how much more judges reared on the pure theory of law would have been ready to give effect to National Socialist legislation than, say, judges brought up on the common law of England. The defence of "superior orders", so much relied on at the Nuremberg trial, is also a possible logical extension of Kelsen's doctrine. Yet, in spite of this, positivism and the pure theory of law were swept aside by the legal ideologists of National Socialism, and particularly by Carl Schmitt. There can, of course, be no comparison between the two men. Kelsen is a scholar of great intellectual distinction and integrity, whereas Schmitt prostituted his talents in order to bolster a vile tyranny of which one object was the destruction of all legal order in Germany in favour of arbitrary rule glorified as "the higher law", and the like. But the very nature of Schmitt's attack on classical German positivism illuminates the way in which any kind of legal order, even one like Kelsen's, stripped even of the residues of tradition and ethics which Jellinek was prepared to allow, was an obstacle to the aims of National Socialism. Schmitt rejects both the positivism of Jellinek and Kelsen and the traditional view, deriving from Hegel, of the division of a political entity into the state, society and the individual. Positivism, he said, was appropriate to the period when this division was still accepted, and served its purpose so long as "the political entity alternated between conditions of legality and conditions of emergency, and suspension of legality". But in the new order the old division into state and society has been superseded by the division into "State, the Movement and the *Volk*. The state," he wrote in 1934, "as a special category within the political unit no longer enjoys its monopoly of political force, but is only one organ among several at the disposal of the Leader of the

Movement." The new order, he concludes, demands new forms of legal thought "which are lofty enough for the manifold new tasks of the situation of Germany, the new forms of its community, its new political, national, economic and world outlook".

The concrete meaning of this gibberish was quite simply that the Führer and his minions were not going to let any mere legal obstacles stand in their way. The ample emergency powers with which Hitler was endowed after the fire in the Reichstag offered very wide scope for the exercise of arbitrary rule under the thin disguise of law: I have already suggested that long training in positivist theories of law had made German lawyers particularly vulnerable to this kind of assault. However, what is more interesting in my context is the way in which National Socialism, in spite of all the powers at its disposal, nevertheless had to wage continuous war on the existing legal order, or invent obligations falling outside the legal sphere in order to achieve its policies. One index of the resistance of the legal order to the onslaught of the new regime is to be found in the large-scale dismissals of judges which took place in the early years of the regime, as well as in the intimidation and coercion of those who were likely to resist the demands of the new order that the law should be made subservient to its aims. There were cases of courageous resistance, even of executions, among the German judges too. But the judges were in the end powerless against the naked force which was brought to bear against them. Some of the new legislation was indeed so drafted that its implementation in fact invited, indeed demanded, continuous interference and influence by the party and its executants in the government offices over the course of justice. I will quote only one instance – paragraph 2 of the new criminal code adopted in the early part of the regime. It runs as follows:

> Anyone who commits an action which the law declares to be liable to a penalty shall be punished, as shall also anyone who deserves punishment in accordance with the principles underlying a penal law, as well as anyone who deserves punishment according to the sound and healthy instincts of the *Volk*. If there should be no definite criminal law enactment applicable to the action in question, then the action in question shall be punished in accordance with that law of which the basic principle seems most appropriate in the circumstances.

Who but the party, after all, can pronounce on the "sound and healthy instincts of the *Volk*"?

I am, however, less concerned with the intimidation and influencing of the judiciary which are, after all, features of most police states, and throw no particular illumination on the phenomenon of totalitarianism, as illustrated by National Socialist Germany. In fact, the subjugation of the law in Germany during this period, both in theory by Carl Schmitt and those like him of whom there were too many, and in practice, seems to me to illustrate the essential nature of totalitarianism; and moreover to do so in a way which throws doubt on the work of some students of politics who have neglected this aspect. For example, many writers on totalitarianism have seen this phenomenon as a process whereby "the state" extends its area of control over "society" almost to the point where the two become one. This seems to me to be a misunderstanding of both the theory and the practice. Schmitt, whom I have just quoted, quite rightly pointed out that "the state" under National Socialism becomes merely one of *several* instruments at the disposal of the Leader – thus quite correctly emphasizing that there is a power above the state to which the state is subordinate, namely the Leader. Exactly the same applied to the law. From one aspect this is illustrated in the type of enactment, only one of countless such enactments, relating to the punishment of crime which I quoted before: clearly, the legal order, indeed the very principle of legality – *nullum crimen sine lege* – is replaced by a subjective, discretionary device of oppression, in which the judges are forced to co-operate. But this is only one aspect of the way in which the totalitarian apparatus of rule – the Leader and his agents – eats like a cancer into the body of *both* the state and the legal structure. The history of National Socialism in this respect illustrates the other aspect: the conflict in the formative years between the remnants of legal order, humiliated, battered, invaded and circumscribed, but nevertheless some kind of legal order, on one side; and a "superior law", the ideological mission of the Führer or some other circumlocution for pure arbitrary violence, on the other. It is strange that where there was so much power to change or sweep aside the existing law with the minimum of formality there should have been any need for any such conflict: there is no doubt about the fact. Perhaps it is one of the mysteries of the psychopathology of a nation possessed by madness. One example must suffice to illustrate the way in which even a subjugated and cowed legal order still presented too much of an obstacle to the kind of freedom of action which the Führer demanded. As is shown in Dr Hans Buchheim's masterly study of the SS, it required some years before that armed instrument of the party was able completely to take over the existing police machine. The appointment of Himmler to the party post of Reichsführer SS "was the all-important step in the transformation of the German police into an instrument of the Führer's authority". But, as Buchheim shows, "time was required for the official character of the police and its internal and organizational regulations to be adapted to the very different forms and rules operative in the SS. Many aspects of police administration therefore remained unaffected . . ." It was not really until the war, or at any rate the preparatory stages towards war on the German side, that the arbitrary principle finally took over from what was left of the law. Thus, for example, the authorization to Himmler in 1938, after the incorporation of Austria and Sudetenland, to take all necessary steps "even if these transgress the legal limits hitherto laid down for this purpose" was extended both to new territories incorporated after 1939 and to Germany itself. In similar manner, the extermination of the Jews was based not on legal enactments but on arbitrary and secret orders issuing from Hitler and Himmler: apparently even the orderly Germans could not be trusted to carry out such horrendous instructions within the make-believe of some legal framework hatched up for the purpose. Indeed, as Buchheim rightly points out, the Nuremberg Laws, for all their oppressiveness, represented a measure of progress in the direction of legality: they were, he says, "calculated to bring to an end the previous legal uncertainty which had provided a fruitful field for terrorism of all descriptions". When the mass extermination began, it was, as it were, in violation of the Nuremberg Laws. "The murderers could not . . . quote the Nuremberg Laws as even partial legal justification for their actions: these laws were not a link in the chain of non-official terrorism; instead they formed a temporary break in it."

The case of National Socialist Germany is particularly instructive in this respect because Germany, in spite of the inroads made by positivist theories, had a long tradition of legal order, of the *Rechtsstaat*. Germany therefore provides a particularly good illustration of the view, which I hold to be the right one, that totalitarianism is not a new kind of state: it is a negation of the whole idea of the legal order, state and all; it is, in full operation, nothing more than naked, arbitrary power struggling for supremacy against any part of the legal order which survives.

We find an entirely different situation in the case of Soviet Russia, if only because there was no legal order in existence for Stalin to sweep away. To be sure, after 1864 Russia had created and developed a Bench and a Bar of the highest standards, and a modern legal system in no way inferior to that of any country of the European continent – save that this legal system was only too frequently set aside or circumvented by martial law, by executive powers and the like. But the whole of the law, along with the whole of the Bench and the whole of the Bar, was swept out of existence by the Bolsheviks within weeks of their taking power. Of course, a legal system of courts, codes and procedures was gradually re-created: no complex society can live without law for the ordering of the daily affairs of the men and women who compose it. The Soviet legal system has also been improved in 1958 and again in the early sixties in many important respects. But the new courts have never been able to assert their independence against the party; indeed I know of no case in which they have tried to do so, though there may well have been such cases, and certainly some academic lawyers paid with their lives and liberty for attempting to do so in 1936 and 1937. It is thus true to say that until quite recent years the Soviet legal system proved no kind of obstacle to the Communist Party leaders in any kind of policy, however arbitrary and however oppressive, which they wished to put through; and the kind of rather bizarre conflict between the arbitrary and the legal which took place in Germany was inconceivable in the Soviet Union.

The law has always been and, I believe, always must be the acid test of a free society. It is therefore not surprising that the slender signs of evolution of totalitarianism towards something less oppressive and less total in some of the communist countries have been accompanied by changes in the nature of their legal system. Yugoslavia is the one case where the process of evolution has gone some slight way. This has become evident in two main respects in the past eight or ten years. First, in the reform of the law itself both criminal and civil. New codes have replaced the old – new codes more reminiscent of Austrian and French law, and less slavishly identical with Soviet law. This has meant among other things that crimes, rights and duties are now defined with some degree of precision; and that the vague generalities characteristic of the Soviet codes of law, which (like the National Socialist criminal code) leave much room for party-guided interpretation, have been greatly reduced in number. The second change which is beginning to be discernible in Yugoslavia is the emergence of judicial independence. Observers are not agreed on the extent to which the Yugoslav judges are really acting independently of party pressure and party policy. But I think it is true to say that all observers are agreed that there are many more signs of judicial independence to be found in Yugoslavia than in the Soviet Union. Yet, even in the Soviet Union time has not been standing still since the death of Stalin in 1953. I think it is still the case that in any Soviet criminal trial involving a conflict between the individual and the ruling machine the party and security forces can influence the courts and ensure a conviction, whatever the evidence may be. But a curious thing is happening in the Soviet Union, where a very different policy has always been pursued, so far as the law is concerned, as compared with that pursued by Hitler. The National Socialists were not content to pervert the law and subjugate the courts. It was necessary for them, at any rate by the time the war started, to place themselves openly above the law, to act in the name of ideology, or history or the *Volk* or whatever other expression might be chosen to hide the realities of violent gang rule. Not so Stalin. Stalin, and indeed his successors, and for that matter his predecessor, Lenin, have always maintained an attitude of scrupulous respect for the law, while making quite sure that they could circumvent, disregard or twist it whenever it suited them to do so. This system worked quite well for a long time, and with a flexibility which reflected changes in policy laid down by the ruling party leaders. Thus, the procurators, the official guardians of legality, did not even go through the motions of doing their duty during the purge years of 1936 to 1938 and in the somewhat comparable period of the years after the end of the war. Yet, since Stalin's death, when greater observance of the law began to be encouraged from above, they have shown considerable zeal in ensuring that the laws are observed. This phenomenon of "tolerated legality", as I have called it in the past, clearly shows the extent to which the legal order in the Soviet Union is controlled and manipulated by the ruling elite, and is therefore, in the view of many students of the subject, not to be properly regarded as law at all. But I think some recent developments are tending to show that if you go on pretending for long enough that your rule is based on law and not on arbitrary and unpredictable will, someone someday will take you seriously. Something of the kind is happening in the Soviet Union, if only on a small scale. The small, but not uninfluential, dissent movement which has grown up, persisted and expanded among scientists and intellectuals, variously described as the democratic or the human rights movement, demands no changes in Soviet law or theory: all it demands is that the existing laws should be observed, and that those things which are not forbidden by the law should be freely tolerated. This is something new, and there are some signs that the "revolutionary" demand that the law should be complied with is having some effect – at any rate to the extent of making the authorities a good deal more careful than they have shown themselves to be in the past: the police have become more circumspect in exercising their vast powers, defence counsel have become a little more courageous, and the authorities are thinking twice before launching prosecutions which on the evidence would be impossible to sustain, but which formerly would have undoubtedly ended in convictions simply because of party pressure. These are important cracks in the totalitarian armour, however small they may appear to be. For if there is one thing which is incompatible with the totalitarian way of rule it is legal order of any kind – and a legal order, however severe, however repressive, however illiberal, nevertheless recognizes some limits to the powers which the rulers can exert over the ruled, and is to that extent better than totalitarianism.

I hope I have indicated some of the ways in which the legal factors can enrich and clarify the study of totalitarianism. In the case of Germany I was concerned to show how the National Socialists entrenched themselves in office by exploiting the positivist traditions in which German lawyers were educated; and, having done so, waged war against the very legal order which they had made use of on their rise to power. The story in Russia before the rise of the Bolsheviks to power in November 1917 is very different. It is one of the failure of legal order to take deep enough roots in Russian society; and of the exploitation by the Bolsheviks of this all-important factor at a decisive moment in their bid for power. I have already referred to the excellence of the law and the lawyers in imperial Russia – when, and if, they were allowed to function. In particular, Bench and Bar displayed a determination to defend their independence which has had no kind of equivalent in Soviet Russia. Yet, except in a very narrow circle, the tradition of law and legal principles was very weak in Russia, even among the educated class – both among those of more traditional outlook, and among those who considered themselves progressive, if for different reasons. Those who looked primarily to what they regarded as the real, historical Russian tradition, the Russian way of life – of whom Dostoevsky is typical – rather despised law as a mark of an inferior society. They rejected constitutionalism in favour of the traditional Russian autocracy, and regarded Russia as fortunate in having escaped both Roman law and the rigid formalism, as they saw it, of the Roman Catholic Church. These Slavophiles, as they were called, or some of them at all events, regarded constitutional guarantees as an infringement of the trust and confidence that ought to exist between an Orthodox Tsar and his Orthodox people; and sought for the just life in sanctity, monastic asceticism and the practice of Orthodox devotion rather than in the law and the courts. They were, incidentally, very critical of the existing autocracy, regarding it as a bureaucratic perversion of true Muscovite Tsardom, before it had been corrupted by Peter the Great; and they fell foul of the police by demanding freedom of speech and press, so that the Tsar could hear the voice of his people. At the other extreme, the other camp of dissidents, the radicals and the revolutionaries despised and rejected all forms of constitutionalism on the grounds that this was of no interest to the people, but only to the gentry. Even the social democrats in Russia, unlike some social democratic movements elsewhere, had little time for law and order, and thought mainly in terms of the social revolution which would of itself render all law and all coercion superfluous. Nor did the autocracy, and its close supporters – with some very remarkable exceptions – do very much to promote the growth of legal order in Russia. The reform of the law and of the courts and procedure was indeed put through with the encouragement of Alexander II in 1864. But Russia remained a police state – though not, of course, a totalitarian society; and the needs of a police state so often fall foul of the legal system that it soon finds itself either circumventing the legal system, or finding others ways of bypassing it. Besides, there can be no well-founded system of the rule of law without some kind of constitutional or traditional limitations on the absolute and unlimited powers of the monarch: this Russian monarchs resolutely refused to concede, or even to discuss – until 1905, when the violence of the revolutionary year forced the last Emperor, Nicholas II, to concede much too much – and much too late.

With this background in mind, it is easy to see that the voices of the few real liberals which nineteenth-century Russia produced remained largely unheeded. These liberals, whether writers or incumbents of high office under the Emperor, regarded Russia's failure to come under the influence of Roman law, the fact that Russia had never been through the salutary experience of feudalism, the absence for many centuries of any real legal order – for it is a curious fact that Russia, which inherited so much from Byzantium, received little legal structure along with the inheritance – these liberals regarded all these factors which placed Russia apart from the rest of Europe as a tragedy. They believed that the creation of a proper legal framework and order was Russia's first and foremost need if liberty were ever to be assured; and they believed that legal order had to precede any constitutional transformation of the autocracy if firm foundations for liberty were ever to be built.

It was here that the liberal reformers came up against the hard reality of the consequences of the form which the emancipation of the peasant serfs in 1861 had assumed – like so many Russian developments, probably as much by accident as by design. For the emancipation had resulted in the preservation of the primitive, traditional peasant commune. Within this commune the peasants were preserved in a status which set them apart from the rest of society. Their property rights, when they acquired land, were rights confined within the commune which was charged with the duty of periodical redistribution of the land. Their criminal responsibility was in the main left outside the ordinary operation of the law and of the new reformed courts. Subject to special courts and special law, euphemistically called customary law, and in practice often little more than arbitrary rough and ready paternal management, the Russian peasant remained largely untouched by the newly established legal order. The peasants' contractual relations did not usually fall within the ambit of the civil code. Now this system was convenient to the fiscal authorities since the commune as a whole was responsible for taxes; it also corresponded to the paternalistic attitude towards peasant welfare which some statesmen sincerely believed to be best. But it had the result that the great majority of the population of the country remained largely untouched by the new legal system, failed to come under its educative influence, and indeed remained in a permanent state of second-class citizenship. There were a number of attempts at the turn of the century to put an end to this state of affairs on the part of statesmen, who realized that unless the peasant was fully emancipated in a way that he had not been emancipated in 1861, then any attempt to build legal order in Russia would fail. The long-delayed reform eventually came about in 1906, through the energy of Stolypin, the Prime Minister. But it was too late. Stolypin was assassinated in 1911; and the First World War broke out in 1914 with the reform (which Stolypin had envisaged would take at least twenty years) scarcely beyond its early stages.

This chain of events seems to me the most momentous factor in the whole history of events which led to the eventual triumph of the Bolsheviks. When the monarchy collapsed in March 1917 it soon was clear how slender were the foundations on which institutions rested; and how easily they could be overthrown by any conspiracy resolute and determined enough to do so. When Nicholas II abdicated on 15 March the Duma, the legislature set up in 1906, which had been freely – or more or less freely – elected on a reasonably wide franchise, should have been ready to take over government. It failed to do so; and the Provisional Government which emerged was neither appointed by the Duma nor responsible to it. High on the list of its many inadequacies was the fact that it lacked any visible legitimacy. Historians, or some historians, are apt to dismiss legitimacy as a mere "lawyer's quibble" – the phrase comes from one of our leading historians of Soviet Russia. But it is not a lawyer's quibble when it comes to serious questions like the confidence which a government has in its own right to govern, and the sense which the population at large acquires of the basis of its right. And it can come about, as it did come about in Russia in November 1917, that one government without much claim to legitimacy, but more determined, better armed and better financed, can sweep away another whose claim to legitimacy is equally slender – with a neutral army and an indifferent population looking on.

These, then, are some examples of the way in which I have found the legal factors in political situations which I have been concerned to study of prime importance. Historians, I find, are in general aware of this importance – though, so far as the history of Russia is concerned, not always to the extent which I think is necessary. My colleagues in political science, however, have, I am sorry to say, rather reacted against law in favour of modern methods of analysis of government which are said to be more scientific. In some ways their reaction is to be explained by the excessive concentration on legal structures alone which characterized the study of politics in the past generation. The reaction is healthy in so far as it leads to the realization that one must look at a government not only in terms of what it claims to be, but what it actually is. But all government, in the end, comes down to the question of the relationship which subsists between those who rule and those who are ruled. In the study of this question the nature of the legal system is not only relevant; it is, in my view, indispensable. It would, I believe, be very regrettable if the fashionable sociological approach to the study of government should ever lead to a gulf between the work of the political scientist and the work of the lawyer which could no longer be bridged.

Liberalism in Russia

This review of Victor Leontovitsch, *Geschichte des Liberalismus in Russland*, Vittorio Klostermann (Frankfurt am Main 1957), originally appeared in the *Times Literary Supplement*, 10 January 1958.

When some thirty years ago Professor Guido de Ruggiero wrote his masterly *History of European Liberalism* he omitted both Russia and Spain from his survey. This was a justifiable decision, at any rate so far as Russia was concerned. Not, as some might think, because there was nothing to say, for the Professor of Russian History at the Johann Wolfgang Goethe University at Frankfurt am Main has now shown what a rich field of enquiry lies open. Professor Leontovitsch has done very much more than supply a missing chapter to Ruggiero. The legend still persists that there was never any choice in Russia between dark reaction and red revolution, and that liberal order was an alien plant which could never have taken root. The legend has, of course, been much fostered by marxist historians and by the many historians of the end of the Russian empire who have been influenced by marxism. Professor Leontovitsch, whose work will assuredly come to be recognized as one of the most important contributions made to the study of the origins of Bolshevism in this generation, has done great service by restoring some of the true perspective. There were good reasons why liberalism failed in Russia; but they were neither those of Marx nor those of Lenin.

Professor Ruggiero's purpose was to study liberalism in Europe as a whole, to see the pattern which emerged from the many strands of political thought and activity which all put liberty first. It was therefore necessary for him to select for treatment only those countries of Western Europe whose traditions could look back to centuries, if not of enjoyment of liberty by all or wide sections of the population, then at any rate of continuous recognition that there existed certain guarantees of life and property which it was the function of every government to provide. Madame de Staël was the first to point out, after the French revolution, that liberty was the ancient tradition in France, and despotism the innovation. But the tradition of liberty in Western Europe, of which Professor Ruggiero traces the origins to feudalism, was not, of course, a tradition of what would now be called democracy.

It was more concerned with the safeguarding of individual or corporate rights of property or person against all encroachments. It was thus more a tradition of civil liberty than of political liberty. The distinction is important, because civil liberty can exist and often has existed without political liberty, the right to participate in government. Charles I, in his speech from the scaffold, was not entirely wrong according to his lights when he asserted that the people's "Liberty and Freedom consists in having the government of those Laws, by which their Life and their Goods may be most their own: 'tis not for having share in Government that is nothing pertaining to 'em. A Subject and a Sovereign are clear different things . . ." In terms not unlike those used by Charles, Napoleon is reported to have described liberty as "*un bon code civil*".

But what happens if the sovereign, be it monarch or parliament, will not abide by or extend the protection of the laws to all those who are in need of it? This was the problem which in one form or another began to preoccupy English and French liberals in the nineteenth century. In England, where political liberty had long been grafted on to the traditional civil liberty, the answer was found in the gradual assertion by new classes of their claim to an increasing share of power. In France the nature of the problem was different. Napoleon's grant of civil freedom at the price of political freedom had proved precarious because he did not keep to the bargain. Hence Constant turned to the problem of devising constitutional guarantees which would define and circumscribe the authority of the state in the interests of the individual. On the other hand, popular government had quickly turned to despotism between 1789 and 1794. Hence Tocqueville was mainly concerned to show how democracy could be reconciled with liberty.

It was taken for granted by Western European liberals that civil liberty was a citizen's right. In the case of England even political liberty had a long history. Burke's contention that the revolt of the American colonies was but the assertion by Englishmen of their traditional liberties was not far from the truth. The colonists had carried these liberties with them distilled in the common law – as Burke reminded the House of Commons, nearly as many copies of Blackstone's *Commentaries* had been sold in America as in England. But what would a Russian have said in 1776 if asked to sign the Declaration of Independence? "We hold these truths to be self-evident. That all men . . . are endowed by their Creator with certain unalienable rights; that among these are life, liberty & the pursuit of happiness . . ." Desirable, maybe, he might have replied, but self-evident? No more self-evident than the "unalienable" right to six hours' sunshine every day. One was lucky if one got it, one could do little or nothing about it if one did not.

In Russia the whole fabric of liberty still remained to be constructed at the turn of the eighteenth century. Uninfluenced by feudalism (at any rate after the Mongol invasion in the thirteenth century), Russia had developed in a manner resembling rather those oriental despotisms which Professor K. Wittfogel has lately described than any country of Western Europe. Even by the second half of the nineteenth century the process of safeguarding civil rights which had virtually been completed all over Western Europe had barely begun. Of political liberty there was no trace. The problems of guarantees, of the harmonization of democracy and liberty, or of the gradual extension of political liberty to new classes still lay ahead.

Of course there were many Russians in the nineteenth century who pleaded passionately for liberty. But not all who cry liberty are liberals, as Professor Leontovitsch very justly observes. The romantic exiles and the marvellous decade have hitherto usually enjoyed the centre of the stage. But in one form or another these exiles and intellectuals all dreamed of some short cut to freedom which would avoid the laborious construction of solidly based independent institutions such as had been slowly built up over the centuries in Western Europe. Some, like Herzen, pinned their faith to a largely imaginary, innate peasant socialism, and despised European liberalism, which they did not understand. The more violent Bakunin wished to conjure up from the depths of that hell where the oppressed and the poor cried for vengeance a conflagration from which, by some means hitherto unknown to history, universal liberty would arise, like a phoenix from the ashes. Their liberty was always but a means to an end – socialism – and, as Tocqueville reminds us, those who desire liberty for anything other than itself are destined to servitude.

Thus it came about that the only solid achievement of the libertarians of the nineteenth century was the murder in 1881 of Alexander II, a futile and retrograde act. For they halted thereby the programme of reforms which the Emperor had been steadily implementing: only two hours before his murder the Emperor had signed a rescript establishing a consultative, but nevertheless broadly representative, assembly. But the assassin's bomb also widened the gulf between the monarchy and the intelligentsia, served to polarize Russian society towards the extremes of revolution and reaction, crushed the moderates, and led eventually to the triumph of Bolshevism. The nineteenth-century revolutionaries were certainly moved by compassion, love of justice and impatience with the snail's pace of reform. But, as events showed, they were fomenting not freedom but a slaves' revolt. And a slave revolt has little to do with liberty, since it denies it to all but the liberated slaves, who are in turn incapable of safeguarding it even for themselves. Therefore, the moving story of the nineteenth-century libertarians rightly forms no part of the history of liberalism in Russia.

Professor Leontovitsch has strictly limited his enquiry to what he calls "conservative liberalism" or those developments in Russian social and legal history which were aimed both at safeguarding the fabric of the state from a revolutionary cataclysm and at encouraging the development of civil rights and political liberty within the framework of traditional institutions. He does not claim to have written a history of liberals but of liberalism, and within the limits of the exact definitions from which he sets out we ought not to be surprised to see some names included which have not hitherto been associated with the term "liberalism". No one will cavil at the inclusion of Catherine II – indeed "*cette princesse de Zerbst catherinisée*", as Joseph II described her, would with justice be deeply offended if news that she had been omitted were to reach her in the Elysian Fields. For Catherine was more than a dilettante of theoretical liberalism imbibed from Montesquieu and Blackstone. She not only created institutions, she did her best to make them work; she left behind her a tradition of a liberal approach; and above all she succeeded within the limits of the difficulties which confronted her in extending and consolidating the civil rights of at least one class, the nobility – the first necessary step towards a legal order. An enlightened absolutist, she was an advance on the Byzantine despots of the past. Speransky's place here will also not be questioned, but that of Karamzin might be. Professor R. Pipes, who has recently published a study of Karamzin which agrees very closely in many respects with Professor Leontovitsch's, classifies him as a conservative. But the difference is one of name – the borderline between conservatism and liberalism is not always easy to draw, as Professor Leontovitsch himself recognizes.

The hesitant steps towards civil freedom up to 1861 (of political freedom there was as yet little thought) are but the introductory part of the story. The real problems, to the study of which Professor Leontovitsch's scholarly analysis has made a remarkable and original contribution, were the peasant question and the belated development of constitutional government. The emancipation of more than twenty million serfs in 1861 has usually been examined from the point of view of its effect on the peasants and on the economy as a whole. Here it is treated from the angle of its relation to the development of civil liberty, and therefore to the progress of liberalism. For the Emancipation Statute, and more particularly its judicial interpretation by the Senate, freed the serfs from bondage, but did not give them full civil rights. The autocracy, from motives in which paternalism and fiscal convenience were mixed, wished to shore up the traditional commune. This meant that the peasant's right to the land was not protected by private law of property, but remained a part of public law: the peasant was not a full citizen; he remained, as it were, the ward of the state. Relations between peasants were largely governed not by the law of the land but by what in theory was customary law, and in practice was often arbitrary administration by bureaucrats – or, as Sir Paul Vinogradoff described it, "a kind of shifting equity tempered by corruption". Worst of all, the removal from the operation of the civil law and of the ordinary courts of so large a section of the population acted as a brake on the development of civil liberty, and therefore, argues Professor Leontovitsch, of liberty in general. Hence the Stolypin reforms of 1906, which were designed to break up the communal system and to place the peasant on a footing of legal equality with the rest of the population, were a most significant step on the road to liberty. For liberty cannot develop far where any one section of society remains permanently restricted in the enjoyment of its civil rights.

Stolypin's reforms are usually interpreted as primarily intended to create a solid block of rich peasants who could be relied on to protect their stake in the soil by supporting the monarchy. Professor Leontovitsch proves conclusively that Stolypin's aims went much further than this immediately practical end, and that he understood the importance of his reforms as a step on the road to moderate constitutional liberty. Those prepared to smile at the inclusion of Stolypin among the liberals would do well to reflect whether the Bolsheviks could ever have won if his reforms had been given time to come to fruition. Lenin never doubted that it was a race between him and Stolypin. And which, one may pertinently ask, was in the end the greater blow to Russian liberty – the determined measures (as they then seemed) with which Stolypin endeavoured to render harmless the revolutionaries, or the victory of the Bolsheviks?

The history of the pressure for political freedom was closely interwoven with the development of the organs of local self-government, the *zemstva*, which owed their origin to Alexander II's far-reaching plan of reforms. Once started, nothing could stop their growth. Although the monarchy rightly regarded them as a potential challenge to the principle of unlimited autocracy, and repeatedly tried to hamper their activities, some idea of their expansion can be gained from the fact that their expenditure increased by forty-five times between 1865 and 1912. It was from their midst that the two parties to which the name "liberal" is commonly applied in Western literature emerged in 1905 – the Octobrists and the Kadets. Once again, as in the case of the legal *apartheid* of the peasants, the history of the *zemstva* illustrated the principle that you cannot maintain at one and the same time institutions of contrasting content without their interacting upon each other. Thus, the legal tutelage of the peasants hampered the development of a full legal order. The self-governing *zemstva* in turn generated a ferment which undermined the absolutism of the autocracy.

The Russian monarchy met the challenge of the *zemstva* in a way which boded ill for the development of constitutional liberty. The first tentative demands for political freedom which emanated from the *zemstva* were modest – did not indeed go far beyond the consultative share in government which Alexander II had already decided to concede in 1881. But Plehve, the Minister of the Interior, one of a long line of those to whom the term "evil genius" of Russian liberty must be applied, rejected the demands when they were put forward shortly before the revolution of 1905. The effect of this blindly reactionary policy was to throw the incipient liberal movement increasingly into sympathy, if not alliance, with the growing revolutionary forces. When at the height of the revolutionary wave of 1905 the two new parties emerged, the majority of the *zemstvo* liberals found themselves on the side of the more left-wing Kadets, and only the minority among the Octobrists.

Professor Leontovitsch argues that it is only the Octobrists who should be regarded as liberals, and that the Kadets must properly be described as radicals. This is likely to prove the most controversial part of his case. But he is a lawyer by training as well as an historian, and his analysis will not be easily refuted. When the famous Manifesto of 17 October 1905 was followed in the spring of 1906 by the fundamental laws, which for the first time set up a constitutional regime, only the Octobrists made it the keystone of their policy to try to make the new constitution work. The Kadets from the very first rejected the constitution as inadequate: since it did not provide for a government responsible to the Duma, they determined to use the Duma solely as a platform from which to force the government to yield still more. (There was an echo here of what Herzen had written in 1851: ". . . whatever happens, we shall accept nothing from the enemy camp . . . Russia will never be *juste-milieu.*") Again, the Octobrists wanted full civil rights for the peasants, but at the same time respected the property rights of the landlords; the Kadets were in favour of forcible expropriation of land for the peasants' benefit at a compensation below the market value. This, argues Professor Leontovitsch, was socialism, not liberalism.

It was also true that the Kadets, though not avowedly republicans, let alone revolutionaries, felt closer to the revolutionary parties than they did to the monarchy and its ministers. They were at any rate prepared to use the revolutionaries on the principle of *flectere si nequeo superos, Acheronta movebo* (the analogy is V. A. Maklakov's, whose memoirs have thrown much light on this period). On the other hand not all Octobrists were liberals in any sense of the term. Again, with the benefit of hindsight it is easy to see that the policy of the Kadets contributed to the victory of the revolutionary forces. But at the time the gulf between Russian educated society and the monarchy was already very deep and not easy to bridge. The very thought of co-operation with the monarchy seemed an outrage to decency in the eyes of many Kadets. The historian is perhaps justified in looking at the results and in disregarding these psychological factors. They were very real at the time. They led to an inevitable clash between the monarchy and the Duma, which was resolved by Stolypin in 1907 by a *coup d'état* – the franchise was truncated in open violation of the fundamental laws, and a more moderate Duma, more prepared to co-operate with the monarchy, was elected. And yet, paradoxically, this unconstitutional act initiated a period of real constitutional progress, in the course of which liberalism might have taken firm root. But Stolypin fell to an assassin's bomb in 1911, with his work half finished, and with no one to carry it on. Liberalism, which, but for the revolutionary dreamers of the nineteenth century, might have been born in 1881, had come too late.

The Pre-Revolutionary Intelligentsia and the Legal Order

This article first appeared in *Daedalus*, summer 1960, and then in *Revolutionary Russia*, ed. Richard Pipes, Columbia University Press (New York 1961).

Contempt for the science and forms of law and a marked preference for moral principles as a guide to the good life did not, it would seem, originate with the radical intellectuals of the nineteenth century. In 1788, the dramatist Fonvizin, then aged thirty-three, made a journey to France. Writing to Count Panin of his impressions of the University of Montpellier, he noted with unconcealed delight that while the fee for lectures in philosophy was two rubles forty copecks a month, "Jurisprudence, being a science which in the present state of depravity of the human conscience is fit almost for nothing", cost very much less. Some months later he summed up his general view of France. France, he wrote, had taught him that one must distinguish liberty under the law from real liberty. The Russian, while lacking the former, was in many respects more able than the Frenchman to enjoy the latter. In contrast, the Frenchman, while enjoying legal order, on paper, in practice lived in a state of total servitude.[1]

Making a virtue of necessity is not peculiar to the Russian, and by the nineteenth century many thinking Russians were able to discern some grounds for consolation in the almost universal lawlessness which prevailed around them until the reforms of Alexander II. By the more romantic Slavophiles it was even regarded as evidence of the superior moral principle which underlay the Russian state. Writing about the middle of the century, Konstantin Aksakov contrasted the historical origins of Russia with those of the countries of Western Europe. The origins of the latter, he writes, were "violence, slavery and enmity". Russia, in contrast, owed her origins as a state to "willing consent, freedom and peace". From this Aksakov deduced that the forms of state order required in each case were entirely different. In the West, relations between government and governed could be founded only on force; in Russia, they rested on mutual faith and confidence. There was therefore no need in Russia for any kind of legal guarantee. Yet, he goes on to say, it will be objected that "either the people or the state power may prove false to the other", and therefore there is need for some guarantee. He immediately rejects this argument, however. "There is no need for any guarantee! Every guarantee is evil. Where it exists, there can be no virtue. It were better that life in which there is no virtue should collapse than that it should be shored up with the aid of evil."[2] (There is a parallel here to much modern communist thought on the subject of "guarantees", but it would perhaps be unfair to Aksakov to press it too far.)

Konstantin Aksakov was an extreme romantic, whom even his contemporaries were not always able to take quite seriously. But even a sober radical like Herzen, whose love of personal liberty, at any rate, cannot be questioned even if his discernment of the means to achieve it is at times open to doubt, could see grounds for optimism in the universal Russian misrule and lawlessness. His views were fundamentally not unlike those of Aksakov. Writing about the same time, he has the following to say, which may be taken as fairly representative of the views of a good many radicals of the nineteenth century:

> The lack of legal order, which has from the earliest times hung like a cloud over the people, has at the same time been something in the nature of a schooling. The crying injustice of one half of its laws has taught the Russian people to hate the other as well: the Russian submits to the law from force alone. Complete inequality before the courts has killed in him all respect for legality. A Russian, whatever his calling, evades or violates the law whenever he can do so with impunity, and the government does exactly the same. All this is distressing and hard to bear at present, but so far as the future is concerned, it is an enormous advantage. It proves that in Russia there is no ideal, invisible government lurking behind the visible government as some sort of apotheosis of the existing order of things.[3]

But while most early nineteenth-century intellectuals would have subscribed to this vision of anarchy engendered by despair, there were notable exceptions. Such was Chaadaev, whose pessimism for the future of Russia was unrelieved by any ray of hope. In his famous *Philosophical Letters*, written in 1829, he ascribed the past and present ills of Russia squarely to the fact that Russia had developed outside the influences which had done so much to shape the path followed by the countries of Western Europe – Roman law and the Renaissance, for example. All the peoples of Europe, save Russia, shared in a certain common heritage of "knowledge and habits" which they absorbed unconsciously from the cradle, "together with the air they breathe". This had created in the Western European a "moral essence even before he enters the world and society", of which the foundations are the ideas of "duty, justice, law and order". The Russian alone was denied this, and had nothing to put in its place. Hence the Russian could take neither pride in the past nor hope in the future.[4]

Chaadaev's pessimism was, of course, the opposite pole of Konstantin Aksakov's naïve optimism, with the added quality that it offended the national pride of most Russians. Pushkin, a close friend of Chaadaev, who (according to tradition, perhaps, rather than to any evidence provided by works of his which have survived) shared Chaadaev's respect for Western constitutional order, gently reproved him. He had done well, Pushkin wrote, to point out that ". . . our social existence, is a sad affair. The absence of public opinion, the indifference to all duty, justice and truth, the cynical contempt for the thoughts and dignity of man are something really desolating. But I am afraid that your historical opinions may do you harm."[5]

The publication of Chaadaev's essays caused an uproar that ended with his being officially declared a lunatic. But his views, if exaggerated, nevertheless contributed something towards the swelling of that small stream of Russian intellectual life which stubbornly clung to traditional constitutional and legal principles as they had developed in Western Europe, seeing in them the only solution to Russian problems. The *Vekhi* group, to which reference is made later, owed much to the rude shock to Slavophile complacency administered by the *Philosophical Letters*. But in the main, Chaadaev and Pushkin represented an already outdated trend in

Russian revolutionary thought. Under Western influence this trend had formed a part, albeit a small one, of the constitutional ideas of the Decembrists. When once the abortive rising which these young noble intellectuals in uniform attempted in 1825 had been severely repressed, the voice, though not the hope, of revolt was stilled for over a generation. And when revolutionary activity revived in the sixties, constitutional ideas no longer formed any part of its ideological baggage.

The problem of legal order took on new actuality in the sixties, when after the accession of Alexander II the whole social order of Russia was transformed by a series of far-reaching reforms. The emancipation of some twenty million serfs in 1861 was the first step in this revolution from above, to be followed by reform of the judicial system and by the establishment of limited but quite real local self-government. The condition of the peasant serfs had for long lain heavily on the conscience of all thinking Russians. The Emancipation Act did little so far as most of them were concerned to ease the intelligentsia's sense of shame and guilt. The provisions laid down in the Act for enabling the peasants to acquire land disappointed the peasants' hopes, even if its meagre concessions were sufficient to arouse opposition from many landowners. As the poet Nekrasov put it, when the great chain broke, one end struck the landowners, and the other the peasants. Almost immediately revolutionary conspiracies, led of course by intellectuals, began to form. The first conflict raised among the intelligentsia by the Emancipation was therefore between those who welcomed the reforms as a first step which would ultimately lead Russia along the path of the legal order discernible in Western Europe, and those (the great majority) whose impatience, disappointment, or moral fervour led them to see revolution as the only solution to the achievement of social justice.

For this majority of the intelligentsia, preoccupation with the social problem of land distribution became paramount, and, as will be seen, it obscured or eclipsed all questions of establishing society on the basis of legal order. In contrast, the minority (and it was a very small one) was beset with fear that the mere abolition of serfdom would not of its own accord bring with it abolition of the mentality which had engendered it, and which was itself the result of centuries of arbitrariness on the part of the state and the landlords, of patriarchal administration rather than of law. Among the few who were aware of this danger was B. N. Chicherin, the outstanding liberal jurist and philosopher of the Russian nineteenth century. For several decades Chicherin watched with apprehension the growing forces of socialism, which in his view represented a return to the mentality of serfdom and therefore presented a greater danger to the liberal principles in which he believed than did the autocracy. For the autocracy was now embarked on the road of reform, which would in time lead to the establishment of full civil, if not political, freedom; but the socialists, in his view, with their downright attack on private property, threatened the very principle of civil rights, and therefore all freedom, and could if victorious achieve only despotism.

The kernel of the division between the liberals of the type of Chicherin and those who saw the solution for Russia on quite different lines was the attitude adopted to the traditional peasant commune (the *obshchina* or *mir*).[6] As time went on this peasant institution for the communal tilling of the land and for the management of local village affairs became the subject of the most heated controversies. It was Herzen who first drew attention to an institution which had hitherto escaped the notice of the intelligentsia. Thereafter its champions were drawn from wide sections of society, whose motives for supporting the commune were very different. To the Slavophile of the type of Aksakov, the commune represented the traditional Russian form of patriarchal life, with all the virtues which anything rooted in Russian antiquity possessed for them. The populists (the *narodniki*) saw the commune as the germ of a future socialist society: for them this traditional form of primitive Russian communism could, if encouraged and extended, make it possible for Russia to develop into a full socialist society without going through the industrial phase, which was the path towards socialism embarked on by the socialist parties of Western Europe, and which the populists were anxious to avoid. Finally, the commune was supported by large sections of the official bureaucracy. They believed, if erroneously, that the commune was a bulwark of conservative support for the Emperor. Moreover, it was a convenient institution for the collection of taxes and dues, since responsibility for payment could be laid on the commune as a whole, and not merely on an individual. It also provided a convenient means for preserving the peasant as a kind of ward of the state, subject to separate administration, to separate laws and customs, and to a form of tutelage which the ordinary courts, as reformed after the Emancipation, were not equipped to provide. This view of the peasants' needs corresponded with the age-long tradition of serfdom and with the belief, often sincere, that a paternal regime was best for the peasant. It was this attitude above all which for Chicherin represented the survival of the mentality of serfdom.

The attitude towards the commune of those who were mainly responsible for framing the Emancipation Act can perhaps best be described as neutral: they did not intend to abolish it, but on the other hand neither did they intend to shore it up. N. A. Miliutin, the man most responsible for the form which the legislation of 1861 took, later described the intention at the time as follows:

> The lawgiver does not impose on the rural class any one form of property preferably to others: it may be individual or communal according to the custom prevailing in each region, and it will be left to the purchasers' own pleasure whether they will transform the lands acquired by the communes into private or individual property.[7]

Certainly it was the intention of the legislators and of the Emperor that "the status of the peasant, after the transitional period [required for the payment of compensation for the land acquired by them] was concluded should be the same in law as the status of free landowners".[8] It did not work out that way. Far from letting the commune live or die, as the natural inclination of the peasants dictated, the government shored it up by legislative devices of all kinds. The courts which were set up to replace the personal jurisdiction over the peasants hitherto exercised by their owners did not administer the criminal law of the land, but something which was in theory a form of customary law, supposedly better adapted to the traditional childlike nature of the peasant, but which in practice amounted to, in the words of the late Sir Paul Vinogradoff, "a kind of shifting equity tempered by corruption". A series of decisions in the highest court of appeal, the Senate, soon made it plain that the peasant owner was far from equal in status to the free landowner. The law recognized only the commune as the owner of land. The individual peasant had to look to his remedy within the framework of the "customary" law of his district, and within and against the commune. He could neither enforce civil rights on the basis of the law of contract nor protect his property under the general civil law applicable to those other than peasants.

Thus the emergence of a class of free smallholders with full civil rights and equal before the law, which some at any rate had hoped would be the result of the Emancipation, was made impossible. More serious, from the point of view of those who hoped that the Emancipation would be the first step towards the emergence of a universal legal order, a large class of persons in society was thus isolated and denied full civil rights. No greater obstacle to the development of general habits of law and order could have been imagined. The essentially "administrative revolution" which the shoring up of the commune represented was completed in 1889. The institution of the land captains, by introducing direct bureaucratic intervention and tutelage, undermined self-government in the villages.

The attitude of the intelligentsia to the question of legal order can only be understood against this background of the peasant commune. There were a few, a very few, of whom Chicherin was probably the most consistent, who were convinced that the most important aim for Russia was to develop along the constitutional lines discernible in the countries of Western Europe – towards civil freedom, legal order, and eventually, though this would necessarily take a long time, political freedom and a constitutional order. They rejected out of hand any special Russian solution which did not partake of the same features as those obtaining in the countries of the West – in so far as Russia at present lacked those features, it was necessary for her to acquire them. For Chicherin, the peasant commune was a drag on the development of private property in the villages, which was in his view essential for the development of civil freedom. He believed that the commune should be allowed to disintegrate, as he believed it would if full rein were given to the private property instincts of the more industrious peasants by allowing them freedom to own land as individual bearers of normal civil rights. (Some years before the Emancipation Act Chicherin had already thrown a bombshell among the Slavophile admirers of the commune as a traditional and specifically Russian institution in a series of historical essays designed to show that it was neither traditional nor peculiarly Russian, but largely the result of comparatively recent fiscal policy.[9]) Chicherin also wished that all the patriarchal legal *apartheid* under which the peasant still lived should be swept away, regarding it as a survival of the serf-owning mentality and inconsistent with legal order.

At the time of the reforms of the sixties and until 1868 Chicherin was Professor of Public Law in Moscow University (after that he retired to private scholarship and to active work in the local councils, or *zemstva*). In a series of pungent polemical articles, published in collected form in 1862,[10] he argued the case for legal order in the light of the new hope opened up by the accession of an Emperor whose heart was set on reform. In 1858 he caused a storm among the radical intelligentsia by attacking their idol, Herzen's paper *The Bell*, in an open letter in which he argued that the responsible course for those who genuinely desired reform in Russia was to support the new liberal efforts emanating from the throne, and not to encourage revolt and violence. Writing about this letter a few years later he said: "It seemed to me that there was a need of drawing attention to two factors forgotten in our literature – state power and law – which are just as necessary to a society as freedom itself."

The interdependence of freedom and order is the keynote of all Chicherin's writings of this period. Order depends on a strong state. But if such a state is not to be despotic, its power must be based on legal order, and legal order can only be acquired by the constant practice and observance of the law. Later he returns to the subject:

> The liberation of the peasants and the development of a society standing on its own feet demand the safeguarding of rights and a solid legal order . . . Legality does not fall suddenly from the skies . . . Respect for and confidence in moral force become rooted only after age-long habit. The main task here belongs to the government. By refraining from arbitrariness, by hedging itself in with legal forms, by resolutely adhering to the established legal order, the government points the way, and makes society discern norms and guarantees where before it only saw force and oppression.

Thus Chicherin recognized that the duty was a double one: both society and the state had to show the necessary restraint. He believed, however, that the foundation had been laid in the reforms.

What was needed now was moderation and honesty on both sides. The cause of liberalism could now best be served by preserving and nurturing the first fruits: since 19 February 1861 (the date of the Emancipation Act) liberalism and conservatism had become one.

Chicherin offered no short cut to utopia, no immediate solution for the peasant's hunger for land, and no immediate remedy for the many social injustices which marred Russian life. What he provided was a reasoned argument against a too precipitous attempt to achieve the solution of these social problems without the solid foundation of legal order, and a warning that such an attempt, if made before the consequences of serfdom had been eradicated from the body politic, could only result in a despotism more dangerous than the existing autocracy. If reason alone determined political convictions, Chicherin's influence and that of the few who thought like him might have been greater. But emotion and passion are quite as important in forming opinion as is reason, and there were many emotional reasons which made this liberal approach repellent to the intellectuals.

There was first the fact that this approach was frankly Western European in character. It deliberately turned its back on everything specifically Russian, it offered no sop to Russian pride. It squarely assumed that Russia must go the same way as France or Britain – or else remain sunk in barbarism. Besides, to put all hope for the future in constitutional development on the French or British model was an act of faith which was difficult in the nineteenth century. The July Monarchy was detested among the great majority of enlightened Russians. The critic and writer of memoirs, P. V. Annenkov, records as the general opinion of his contemporaries that the July Monarchy was a betrayal of the old, real, traditional France, a kind of "ghost which had, like a usurper, substituted for the natural physiognomy of the country a repulsively smooth and stupid mask".[11] Somewhat later, Herzen, during the long years of his exile in England, castigated the social injustice he saw behind the façade of Victorian liberalism.

Further, to the majority of the intelligentsia, the long-term liberal constitutional solution for Russia often appeared as a cold and selfish policy, of interest to no one except the small privileged upper class, and of no ultimate benefit to the great majority, the peasants. K. D. Kavelin, a liberal-minded lawyer, who at the same time had strong Slavophile leanings, in 1875 stated the case against constitutionalism:

> A constitution can only have some kind of sense when those who put it into effect and safeguard it consist of strongly organized rich classes, enjoying authority . . . Many among us dream of a constitution . . . and it is mostly those who hope with its help to seize power for themselves over the government, on the French Napoleonic model, to keep it in the hands of a few families, and exclude the people as a whole.[12]

As a criticism of such a view as Chicherin's, this was unfair. Nevertheless, it represented the genuine moral repugnance which constitutionalism, or indeed the advocacy of legal order in general, evoked among many members of the intelligentsia. Chicherin and those who thought like him were forced to advocate a form of order which in the first instance would have benefited their own class. Had they been better historians, Chicherin's critics might have recalled that civil and political liberty was in the first instance usually asserted by one class for its own benefit, and then only gradually extended to other classes as well – from the barons of Magna Carta to the industrial magnates of nineteenth-century England. But they did not reason in this way and were inclined to be carried away by moral indignation.

The philosophy of moral indignation was perhaps best voiced later in the century by the populist writer Mikhailovsky. Writing in 1880 (when the policy of reform had failed and the revolutionary society, the People's Will, with a certain amount of secret support from Mikhailovsky, was actively planning the death of the Emperor), Mikhailovsky said, "Freedom is a great and tempting thing, but we do not want freedom if, as happened in Europe, it will only increase our age-long debt to the people."

In a general review of the thoughts and aspirations of the radical intelligentsia over the past generation, he goes on to say:

> Since we were sceptical in our whole attitude to the principle of freedom, we were ready to refrain from demanding any rights for ourselves: not only privileges – that goes without saying – but even the elementary rights that were in the old days called natural rights . . . And we did all this for the sake of one possibility into which we put our whole soul: the possibility of immediate transition to a higher order, leaving out the middle

> stage of European development, the stage of bourgeois government.[13]

These two elements in all nineteenth-century radical thinking – moral indignation, and an intense faith that Russia could progress by some separate path to a higher state than Europe had achieved, without the intermediate European stage of bourgeois capitalism – are most graphically illustrated by a famous controversy in the sixties between two very different representatives of the intelligentsia, Turgenev and Herzen. Turgenev, whose acute political insight has perhaps been eclipsed by his genius as a novelist, and distorted by the hostility of the radical intelligentsia, was one of the most consistent advocates of the need for legal order. His acumen in discerning the basic ills of Russian society was already apparent in a memorandum on the peasant question, written in 1842, when at the age of twenty-four he made application for employment in the Ministry of the Interior. The views expressed there anticipate by some twenty years the analysis later made by such experts as Chicherin.

Turgenev's main argument is that a healthy development of civil order in Russia is impossible unless the entire patriarchal structure of Russia is swept away, with the emancipation of the serfs as the first step. Relations between landowners and peasants must be based on law, not on arbitrariness. However enlightened some landowners may be, benevolent despotism is no substitute for the certainty of a legal order. The peasant must be made to feel that he is a citizen and a full participant in that legal order. The landowner in turn must develop a sense that his relations to the peasants must be based on law, not on will. This is necessarily inconsistent with serfdom, which must be abolished. Turgenev ends with a tribute to Russian traditions and virtues, but remarks, "God forfend that we should fall into blind worship of everything Russian only because it is Russian: God preserve us from limited and, to be frank, ungrateful attacks on the West, and especially on Germany . . . The most certain sign of strength is to know one's own weaknesses and imperfections".[14]

In contrast, Herzen could never bring himself to accept the view that Russia must either follow the broad lines of development towards law and order upon which Western Europe had embarked, or else remain in her pristine state of barbarism. Russia's salvation, according to him, lay in the Russian peasant, who was uncontaminated by the corruption of modern society, and who in his traditional commune preserved the germ of a future, higher form of society that would avoid the evils accompanying the bourgeois development of the West. The idea of the "separate path" for Russia, the devotion to the peasant commune, the hope of avoiding the evils of bourgeois capitalism – all these basic tenets of populist philosophy which exercised so enormous an influence on the intelligentsia stem from Herzen. In a series of articles entitled "Ends and Beginnings", which appeared in his paper *The Bell* between July 1862 and January 1863, Herzen again expounded these already familiar ideas.[15] Turgenev, in a series of letters written in the light bantering vein of which he was master, took Herzen to task. The doctrine that any one country could travel by a "separate path" was an illusion. The development of Russia must necessarily follow the broad lines followed by other countries. Since those countries had developed freedom and a legal order in the first instance through the efforts of the middle class, this was the only way in which such a development could take place in Russia. To put faith in some peculiar virtue of the Russian peasant was not only unhistorical but also illusory: the Russian peasant, like peasants the world over, was conservative and bourgeois by nature, without the instincts for socialism which Herzen believed him to possess. (Turgenev, incidentally, had had a good deal more practical experience of life among the peasants than had Herzen.) This correspondence contributed to the rupture between the two lifelong friends which soon followed.[16] The argument may be taken as an apt illustration of the deep emotional gulf between those few courageous enough to embrace the unpopular view that there were no short cuts for Russia if she was to escape from her long tradition of despotism, and the more emotional majority who hoped against hope for some peculiarly Russian miracle.

Such, then, was the background which produced a climate of opinion that regarded the advocacy of law and order as cold, calculating, immoral, selfish, un-Russian, or unpatriotic. It was therefore not surprising that the influence of men like Chicherin was in the end very slight. Such influence was probably most clearly felt in the views of a small intellectual group, which included a number of former marxists like Struve and Bulgakov, and outstanding thinkers like Frank, Izgoev, and Gershenzon. This group published in 1909 a collection of essays on the Russian intelligentsia under the general title of *Vekhi* (Landmarks).[17] The *Vekhi* group believed in the primacy of moral and religious principles, and the volume they published was essentially a call for the regeneration of the intelligentsia and a plea for the recognition of the need to work *with* the social order, not against it, in an endeavour to transform it along the lines of morality, law, and justice. The failure of the intelligentsia to realize or understand the need for legal order was the subject of one of the essays (by B. A. Kistiakovsky), from which some of those illustrations of the attitude of the nineteenth-century intelligentsia to law and the state discussed above have been drawn. The violent reaction produced by the publication of *Vekhi* showed how far the Russian intelligentsia still was from accepting legal order as a basis for progress. Opposition to the views of the *Vekhi* group was strong, not only among avowed radicals such as the socialist revolutionaries, the heirs of the nineteenth-century populists, but even more so among the Kadets, a party with an avowedly liberal programme.

In the end it was not the intelligentsia – at least, not in the generally accepted use of this term – but the government bureaucrats who became the real advocates of legal order. It was from this group that two outstanding men emerged, Witte and Stolypin, who sought to attack the problem at its roots – in the peasant commune. Both men realized that without destroying the commune no secure legal order could ever come about in Russia. The failure of their policy (in the case of Witte, he never succeeded even in getting it started) is not a part of the present story. What is significant for our investigation is the fact that their policy had to face the opposition of almost the entire thinking class of the country. The conclusion can best be expressed in the words of Professor K. Zaitsev:

> If one disregards a few isolated voices which never exercised any direct influence, one observes with a certain astonishment how political figures of various views, from the most extreme reactionaries to the most passionate revolutionaries, how scholars and writers of all trends of opinion, often urged on by the most different motives, all were committed to the idea of a peculiarly Russian, separate, peasant land law. Populism so

called cannot merely be represented as a narrow revolutionary party dogma . . . It is usually assumed, and quite rightly, that one of the causes of the revolution of 1917 was the gulf between government, intelligentsia and people. But one should not lose account of the fact that populism in its widest sense, the agrarian ideology of the Russian intelligentsia, was nothing but a refined transposition of the legal outlook of the peasants, which to a certain extent was anchored in government decrees and bolstered by government legislation. Government, society and people were therefore at one on this question, the unhappy solution of which led to the collapse of the Russian Empire.[18]

1. *Polnoe sobranie sochineniy Denisa Ivanovicha Fonvizina* (St Petersburg 1893), pp. 198, 216.
2. *Polnoe sobranie sochineniy Konstantina Sergeevicha Aksakova*, vol. I, ed. I. S. Aksakov (Moscow 1861), pp. 8–9.
3. Quoted by B. A. Kistyakovsky in *Vekhi: Sbornik statey o russkoy intelligentsii* (2nd edn. Moscow 1909), p. 130.
4. *Sochineniya i pis'ma P. Ya. Chaadaeva*, vol. II, ed. M. Gershenzon (Moscow 1913), pp. 113–14.
5. A. S. Pushkin, *Polnoe sobranie sochineniy v desyati tomakh*, vol. X (Moscow-Leningrad 1949), p. 597. For an analysis of Pushkin's political views see S. L. Frank, *Etyudy o Pushkine* (Munich 1957), pp. 28–57.
6. On the whole question of the importance of the commune and the developments in agrarian legislation generally, and for the evolution of the attitude to legal order in the nineteenth century, see V. Leontovitsch, *Geschichte des Liberalismus in Russland* (Frankfurt am Main 1957), Part II *passim*. This study is indispensable for the understanding of the intellectual development of the century, but unfortunately is not yet available in English. [In 1980, a Russian translation was published in Paris: *Istoriya liberalizma v Rossii. 1762–1914*. (Paris, 1980). (ed.)]
7. From a speech in 1863, quoted in Anatole Leroy-Beaulieu, *The Empire of the Tsars and the Russians*, translated from the 3rd edn by Zenaide A. Ragozine, vol. I (New York 1893), p. 485 n.
8. V. Leontovitsch, *op. cit.*, p. 149.
9. See B. Chicherin, *Opyty po istorii russkago prava* (Moscow 1858).
10. B. Chicherin, *Neskol'ko sovremennykh voprosov* (Moscow 1862).
11. P. V. Annenkov, *Literaturnye vospominaniya* (Leningrad 1928), p. 299.
12. *Sobranie sochineniy K. D. Kavelina*, vol. II (St Petersburg 1898), pp. 894–5.
13. *Sochineniya N. K. Mikhaylovskago*, vol. IV (St Petersburg 1897), pp. 949, 952.
14. I. S. Turgenev, *Sobranie sochineniy v dvenadtsati tomakh*, vol. XI (Moscow 1956), pp. 420–33.
15. A. I. Gertsen, *Polnoe sobranie sochineniy i pisem*, edited by M. K. Lemke, vol. XV (St Petersburg 1920), pp. 242–310, where Turgenev's letters are also reprinted.
16. For a more detailed account of this quarrel, due not only to this particular disagreement, see also Henri Granjard, *Ivan Turguénev et les courants politiques et sociaux de son temps* (Paris 1954), Ch. IX. [See also pp. 321–337, below. (ed.)].

17. *Vekhi: Sbornik statey o russkoy intelligentsii*, N. A. Berdyaeva, S. N. Bulgakova, M. O. Gershenzona, A. S. Izgoeva, B. A. Kistyakovskago, P. B. Struve, S. L. Franka, 2nd edn. (Moscow 1909). For a fuller discussion of this group, see the writer's "The *Vekhi* Group and the Mystique of Revolution" [see pp. 68–92 below. (ed.)].

18. Quoted in V. Leontovitsch, *op. cit.*, p. 153.

The *Vekhi* Group and the Mystique of Revolution

This article first appeared in *The Slavonic and East European Review*, XXXIV, December 1955.*

This is the story of a debate which engaged most, if not all, of the best intellects of the present century in pre-revolutionary Russia. It started some time before the 1917 revolution as an argument about the Russian intelligentsia. It continued in exile, after the revolution, as a dispute on the historical meaning of the revolution. Every one of the main participants in the debate is now dead, and its subject matter belongs to history. But some of the issues involved may still be of importance today.

The general character of the *intelligent* of the opening of this century is familiar to all. His outlook was still moulded by the radical heroes of the generation of the 1860s and 1870s – Chernyshevsky, Pisarev, Mikhailovsky. At the end of the nineteenth century the influence of Marx and Engels had also made itself felt. The Russian *intelligent* believed passionately in progress, in utilitarianism, in the perfectibility of human society – if the right formula could be found. The autocracy and its supporting bureaucracy were anathema – not to be against them in spirit, if not in action, was a betrayal of all that was noble in man. This radicalism of outlook, though not without its naïve side, which was born of the fact that most of the intelligentsia had had virtually no experience of practical government activity, certainly had the appeal of nobility. But there was some truth in the reproach later to be made by S. L. Frank[1] that it also had something of the slave mentality about it in its attitude to the government: all ills spring from the government, which is no part of us, and with which we have no concern except to revolt against it.

Early in the century a group of young philosophers, most if not all of whom had been much influenced by marxism, broke both with marxism and with some of the main philosophical and social foundations inherited from the radical thinkers of the 1860s and 1870s. This group, which included S. N. Bulgakov, N. A. Berdiaev, S. L. Frank, P. I. Novgorodtsev and B. A. Kistiakovsky, joined together to publish a volume of essays under the title *Problemy Idealizma*[2] (Problems of Idealism). The ideas of this volume, though they ran directly counter to the sacred beliefs of the radical intelligentsia in that they were critical of both positivism and materialism, were expressed on a sufficiently academic plane not to arouse either violent controversy or very wide attention. As Frank wrote many years later,[3] although regarded as heretical, "they were nevertheless condescendingly forgiven by radical public opinion as a relatively innocent piece of crankiness, even if not without its dangers". In the Preface to *Problemy Idealizma* the editor, Novgorodtsev, drew attention to the fact that philosophical idealism was not a novelty for the Russian public. At the height of the development of positivism, this doctrine had been boldly assailed both by Vladimir Soloviev and by Boris Chicherin.[4] The volume included essays criticizing the historical theories of Marx and Engels, criticism of Auguste Comte and of Mikhailovsky, and an essay on the revival of natural law doctrines.

But, although unobtrusive, this volume, which already signalized a break with marxism by a number of its former adherents, was to prove the forerunner of a much more dramatic attack. The main influence in this development came from Petr Berngardovich Struve. Struve, seven years older than Frank, with whom he was closely linked in friendship, was the most prominent of the renegades from marxism, if only by reason of the fact that it was he who in 1898 had drawn up the Manifesto of the Social Democratic Party. He parted company with marxism in 1901, and in 1902 founded a paper in Stuttgart, *Osvobozhdenie* (Liberation), which became the leading influence in the formation of the Party of National Liberation (Kadets) in 1905. Struve became a member of the Kadet party, and sat as a deputy in the short-lived Second Duma in 1907. After the dissolution of the Duma he retired from politics to academic work, and to work on *Russkaia Mysl* (Russian Thought), first as joint editor with the historian Kizevetter, and after 1911 as sole editor. Already by 1907 a vast gulf separated Struve from the party which he had done so much to create. Before 1905 Struve had urged in

Osvobozhdenie that Russian liberalism should express its solidarity with the revolutionary tendencies. After the revolution of 1905 he believed that the time had come for liberalism to break with the revolutionary tradition from which the party had in large measure drawn its inspiration. This the Kadets were unable or unwilling to do. In his memoirs of the period of the First and Second Dumas V. A. Maklakov traces the victory of Bolshevism to this factor above all, and Struve would probably have agreed with this judgement. But in 1907 Struve was almost alone in his belief that the primary duty of the liberal forces was to strive for some sort of working agreement with the monarchy, so that reform could take place on the solid foundation of order. In order to appreciate the originality of this outlook one must see it in the psychological setting of the radical intelligentsia of the period, and nothing could show this better than the following passage from Frank's unpublished memoir of Struve.[5] Struve, writes Frank, brought a new note into the typical outlook of the intelligentsia of his day. Frank continues:

> This note I can only describe as government consciousness. Oppositional and particularly radical public opinion felt itself oppressed by the government and completely estranged from it. State power was "they", a strange and inaccessible compound of court and bureaucracy, pictured as a group of corrupt and mentally limited rulers over the real "national and public" Russia. To "them" were opposed "we", "society", the "people", and above all the "caste" of the intelligentsia, concerned for the welfare of the people and devoted to its service, but by reason of its lack of rights capable only of criticizing the government power, of arousing oppositional feelings, and secretly preparing a revolt. Petr Berngardovich had within him, and displayed from the very first, the embryo of something quite different . . . from the usual – *tranchons le mot*! – slave consciousness (which was alas! destined in practice to triumph and to determine the fate of Russia). He always discussed politics, so to say, not from "below", but from "above", not as a member of an enslaved society, but conscious of the fact that he was a potential participator in positive state construction.

This new outlook took shape, mainly in the columns of *Russkaia Mysl*, after 1907. In his reflections on the 1905 revolution, written after the dissolution of the Second Duma, and in later articles, Struve urges compromise, and denounces hatred and vengeance as political motives so far as liberals are concerned. He emphasizes throughout that what is needed is not a question of tactics, but of a "political and moral re-education of the Russian intelligentsia", to emancipate it from its outworn heritage of the period before 1905. But at the same time, the government must be founded on the idea of law, "which excludes all absolute power, however disguised and however justified". The only solution is for the "state and the nation to grow organically into one".[6]

These three ideas – the need for a moral re-education of the intelligentsia, for a legal order as the foundation of government, and for the fusion of state and nation – became the foundation for a volume of seven essays published in 1909 under the title *Vekhi*[7] (Landmarks) by a group of thinkers whose views were both close to those of Struve and influenced by him. Some of them had already contributed to *Problemy Idealizma* in 1903: N. A. Berdiaev, S. N. Bulgakov, S. L. Frank and B. A. Kistiakovsky. The newcomers were M. O. Gershenzon and A. S. Izgoev. We have it on both Struve's and Frank's authority that *Vekhi* was not in any sense a joint effort – each author wrote independently, and without consultation with the others. The publication of this slim volume of essays was a bombshell. It ran into five editions in a short time. It provoked violent attacks from the Kadets, from the Socialist Revolutionaries, from Lenin, from a whole number of outraged individuals, in books and in articles. The leader of the Kadets, P. N. Miliukov, toured Russia for a series of public meetings organized by his party for the denunciation of *Vekhi*. The violence of the reaction is sufficient indication of the fact that emotions were engaged as much as, if not more than, intellects. In his memoir, to which reference has been made, Frank gives the following explanation: in contrast to the mild and academic *Problemy Idealizma*, he writes, *Vekhi* embodied "criticism of the basic sacred dogma of the radical intelligentsia – the 'mystique' of revolution. This was regarded as an audacious and quite intolerable betrayal of the age-old sacred testament of the Russian intelligentsia, the betrayal of the tradition handed down by the prophets and saints of Russian social thought – Belinsky, Granovsky, Chernyshevsky, Pisarev – and a betrayal of the age-old striving for liberty, enlightenment and progress, and a going over to the side of black reaction."[8] He adds that it was not only the revolutionaries, but also the more moderate liberals who rose up against *Vekhi*. This was not surprising, since the liberals were quite as much the target of criticism as the revolutionaries and were often little behind the revolutionaries in "revolutionary mystique".

Let us examine the contents of this explosive volume. The Preface, by M. Gershenzon, from whom incidentally the suggestion to publish the volume had emanated, stresses that the only platform common to all the seven authors is "the recognition of the primacy both in theory and in practice of spiritual life over the outward forms of society, in the sense that the inner life of the individual . . . and not the self-sufficing elements of some political order is the only solid basis for every social structure".[9] It is indeed the case that an acceptance of the religious basis of life is common to all the authors of *Vekhi* – a fact which, no doubt, contributed to earning them the charge of being "reactionary" from their radical and rationalist opponents. In the first essay, N. A. Berdiaev examines the attitude of the intelligentsia to philosophical systems. His main thesis is that the value of the different philosophies, from the point of view of their absolute truth, has been subordinated in Russia to the utilitarian and social purposes which it was considered those systems could serve. This attitude, although inspired by the noblest of motives, has led to a general failure to seek and recognize truth for its own sake, and those who devote themselves to this pursuit fall under the suspicion of being reactionaries. (In a footnote to the second edition of *Vekhi* Berdiaev points out that the accuracy of his criticism has been confirmed by the character of the polemics evoked by his article.[10]) Owing to historical reasons, says Berdiaev, the following misfortune has befallen the Russian intelligentsia: "Love for egalitarian justice, for the general good and national wellbeing has paralysed love of truth, has almost destroyed any interest in truth."[11] But love of truth in the absolute is the *sine qua non* of all real philosophy. Even economic materialism, he argues, when transplanted onto Russian soil, has lost its objective analytical character, which had a grain of truth in it, and has suffered a change, whereby the subjective element of class warfare has been elevated to first place. As against that, the truly Russian thinkers such as Chaadaev, Dostoevsky, or Soloviev have been misunderstood or ignored. The reason for this is that the systems of these philosophers do not lend themselves to adaptation for use in the fight for socialism. "We only recognized that philosophy as true," says Berdiaev, "which helped us to fight the autocracy in the name of socialism."[12] His conclusion is that the intelligentsia must cure itself of its "inner slavery", for only thus can it free itself from the external oppression upon which it is accustomed to throw all the blame for its own *malaise*.

S. N. Bulgakov, writing on "Heroicism and Askesis", examines those elements in the outlook of an essentially atheistic intelligentsia which are derived from religious traditions, in order to point the contrast between these elements and the true Christian tradition. Puritanism in living, self-denial, a sense of guilt and repentance – not, of course, before God, but before the people – are all relics of Christianity. But their spiritual character is set at naught by the atheist materialism which has been slavishly copied from the West, along with socialism and belief in progress. For in adopting these Western beliefs, the intelligentsia has ignored the essentially Christian heritage in the West of the Roman Church and of the Reformation, which does not exist in Russia – freedom of person, and of speech, and the rights of man. In the result the Russian intelligentsia is propelled by an unrestrained passion for the betterment of mankind, which is essentially hubristic, and which sacrifices the means to the hoped-for end. This is the "heroicism" of the intelligentsia in contrast to the true humility of Christian "askesis". S. L. Frank, in a much more profound and brilliant essay, "The Ethics of Nihilism", is also concerned with the problem from the religious aspect. He sees the main characteristic of the intelligentsia as "nihilistic morality". Like Bulgakov he recognizes the pseudo-religious morality of the *intelligent*. But this morality is based on nihilism, in other words on the denial of any absolute values. Hence, it seeks its foundation outside absolute values, and finds it in the *narodnik* mystique of "the people", in the idea of service and devotion to the welfare of "the people". In a passage of quite extraordinary perceptiveness, especially if one recalls the date when it was written, Frank points out that the conflict between marxism and *narodnichestvo* is really illusory. In fact, he says, "the victorious and all-devouring *narodnik* spirit has swallowed and annihilated marxist theory and at the present time the difference between avowed *narodniki* and *narodniki* who profess marxism is reduced at most to a difference in political programme and sociological theory, and has no significance as a difference of a cultural and philosophical nature".[13] Today, forty-six years later, in the better perspective which the passage of time has brought, it is easy to see that the victory of Bolshevism in 1917 was at least as much a victory of *narodnichestvo* as of marxism. Developing his idea, Frank, with equal foresight, traces the spiritual odyssey of the nihilist-moralist. The love of man yields in him to the love of an idea – an abstraction, human happiness. "Ready to sacrifice himself for this idea he does not hesitate to sacrifice others."[14] He sees his contemporaries either as victims or as enemies. Out of great love for mankind is born great hatred for men – and the believing *narodnik*-socialist has become a revolutionary. The *intelligent*, Frank writes, must seek escape from the danger of nihilistic moralism in creative religious humanism.

The remaining essays are less directly religious in their main ideas, though the acceptance of a religious belief is common to all of them. B. A. Kistiakovsky, who for some years edited in Moscow a periodical called *Kriticheskoe Obozrenie* (Critical Survey), in which ideas akin to those of *Russkaia Mysl* found an outlet, writes "In Defence of Law". He sees the main vice of the Russian intelligentsia in its failure to acquire any consciousness of the importance of law and legal order. Russia has made no contribution whatever to the development of legal ideas, while the absence of legal order in daily life has in turn led not only to an ignorance of the nature of a state founded upon law, but even to an illusion that the Russian people through some innate sense of truth has found a superior form of social life to that provided by the external truth of a legal order. Kistiakovsky quotes from the witty satire of B. N. Almazov on the views of Konstantin Aksakov, of which the following is a rather lame translation:

For reasons entirely organic
We have not been endowed with at all
That quality wholly satanic –
Common-sense in the matter of law.

Russian natures broad and wide
Seeking truths eternal,
Cannot be constrained inside
Lawyers' rules infernal.[15]

Such views, says Kistiakovsky, are not, however, confined to the Slavophiles. He quotes tellingly from the works of Mikhailovsky; and also the famous passage from Plekhanov's speech at the Second Social Democratic Congress to the effect that if the parliament freely elected after the revolution should prove to be a bad one, it should be dispersed. Our principle must be, said Plekhanov, with more enthusiasm than latinity, *salus revolutiae suprema lex.* (It should be added that in the last article which he wrote Plekhanov bitterly deplored the attempts made in January 1918 to justify the dispersal of the Constituent Assembly by references to this speech.[16]) The main moral of Kistiakovsky's essay is that in the absence of a sense of the importance of legal principles among the radical intelligentsia, it is impossible for the courts of law to acquire their proper place in the life of the country.

Of the remaining essays, A. S. Izgoev's on the youth of the intelligentsia paints a fairly deplorable picture of the moral life of university students. The progressive views of the fathers, he says, have led to a breakdown of family influence, which in turn has led to a decline in moral standards among the sons. As evidence he adduces the results of a questionnaire submitted to over 10,000 Moscow students on their sex life, which are certainly somewhat staggering. Much of the rest of what he criticized was, as Izgoev recognized, at least to the same degree the fault of the authorities as of the students. As the result of restrictions on freedom of ideas, the student had become suspicious, conspiratorial and over-interested in politics to the detriment of his studies. His ideal was the revolutionary, his enemy the state. The further to the "left", the nobler he felt himself to be; the nearer to the shadow of the gallows, the more he believed he was fulfilling his holy duty. In consequence, says Izgoev, "the great majority of the deputies in the Dumas, with the exception of thirty to forty Kadets and Octobrists, have not displayed any of the knowledge which is necessary for the government and reconstruction of the country".[17] M. O. Gershenzon's essay on "Creative Self-Knowledge" is the wittiest, but least profound in the volume. Gershenzon, who was in some respects out of tune with the other six contributors, does not add much to the ideas developed in the other essays, but perhaps his attack was more telling because of the popular nature of the style. At all events, it was Gershenzon's essay that aroused the most violent reactions. His main thesis is that the intelligentsia, carried away by romantic notions, has lost all touch with reality and all capacity for concrete work. For the past half century, he says, "A handful of revolutionaries has been going from house to house, knocking at every door, shouting 'Out into the streets, everyone. You ought to be ashamed of sitting at home.' And all living creatures poured into the town square, the lame, the blind and the halt, not one of them stayed at home. For half a century they have remained in the square, jostling one another and exchanging abuse. At home there is dirt, beggary, and disorder – but what does the householder care about that? He's out in the world, saving the people – and of course that is easier and more entertaining than doing the household chores at home."[18] Meanwhile, these revolutionary *intelligenty* remain oblivious of the fact that between them and the people is a vast gulf. In fact, the people hate us with a deep hatred, says Gershenzon. "Such as we are, so far from dreaming of union with the people we ought to fear the people more than any executions by the government and bless this government which alone, with its prisons and bayonets, still protects us from the people's fury."[19] This last sentence aroused a special storm of protests. Struve was also later critical of it, pointing out that it was not the intelligentsia but the propertied classes which had to be protected with prisons and bayonets from popular fury.[20] In a note to the second edition of *Vekhi*, Gershenzon explained that what he had meant was not that the intelligentsia *ought* to bless the government, but that it is in the circumstances *compelled* to do so, i.e. *müssen* and not *sollen*. (The word used by him in Russian was *dolzhny*.[21]) In a later reprint of the article he omitted the whole sentence. "Better late than never" was Struve's comment,[22] though in the light of later events Gershenzon does not appear today to have been so very wide of the mark. In contrast to the remaining authors, it is fair to say that there is a bitterness about Gershenzon's essay which is completely absent in the others. There is less charity, more censure, less recognition of the fact that the plight of the radical intelligentsia was not so much a moral fault as a tragedy of history. Gershenzon, incidentally, was the only one of the *Vekhi* group to remain in Russia after the civil war – all the others, except Kistiakovsky who died at the end of the civil war, went into exile. He enjoyed a high reputation as a literary critic, and was allowed by the Soviet authorities to publish several volumes, some of a deeply religious content, before his death in 1925. A selection of his letters to his brother was published posthumously in 1927. He was allotted a substantial article in the first edition of the Great Soviet Encyclopaedia, which has not survived in the current edition.[23]

Struve's article, "The Intelligentsia and the Revolution", is the most remarkable in the volume, and one of the best from Struve's pen. The ideas developed in it had first been jotted down by him in 1907 as notes for a chapter of a book. That they represented a very fundamental part of Struve's outlook is evident from the fact that echoes of them are to be found both in his earlier writings in *Russkaia Mysl* and in his later work. The intelligentsia, he argues, is the social element which in contemporary Russian society has taken up the role once played by the *kazachestvo* in the seventeenth and eighteenth centuries – that of an anti-government jacquerie. Not all intellectuals are *intelligenty*: the essence of the *intelligent* is his "standing apart" (*otshchepenstvo*) in relation to the government, and, as an expression of the same "standing apart", his irreligious nature. The beginning of the intelligentsia can be dated from the taking over from the West of atheistic socialism – the first *intelligent* was Bakunin. Thus Radishchev and Chaadaev are not forerunners of Bakunin and Chernyshevsky – they belong to two quite different and quite irreconcilable spiritual orders. In this sense, the great nineteenth-century writers were not *intelligenty*. In the atheism and in the "standing apart" of the *intelligenty* from the state lies the key to the understanding of the results of the revolution of 1905. The Manifesto of 17 October 1905 marked the most fundamental change in the political structure of Russia for centuries; it should, but for the intelligentsia, have marked the consummation of the revolution. But the intelligentsia failed at this point in its duty. Instead of co-operating with the government, it tried to rouse the masses to revolt. Because of its irreligion, the intelligentsia failed to realize that its real moral duty to the people was to educate them, not to arouse them. This left the alternatives of despotism or mob rule. In defence against mob rule, the autocracy inaugurated the present (1909) despotism (for such it then seemed). But the mistake of the intelligentsia was not one of tactics: it was a moral mistake. As Struve says: "Fundamentally it was due to the conception that the progress of a society is a stake to be won at the gambling tables of history by appealing to the aroused masses, and not the fruit of the perfection of individual men."[24] These words sum up the essence of the idea which inspired the publication of *Vekhi*. Economic development, Struve concludes, will in part lead to the *embourgeoisement* of the intelligentsia and thus in time bring about its reconciliation with the government. But equally important remains the moral duty in the realm of ideas, man's mastery over himself.

It should be apparent by now that in their criticism of the intelligentsia the *Vekhi* group were appealing to what they believed was the real, Russian, tradition. Indeed, as Bulgakov puts it, one of the main complaints of the *Vekhi* group against the radical intelligentsia was that they had borrowed the empty shell of atheistic socialism from the West, without its important Christian substratum or heritage of law, order, and social morality. The Russian tradition to which *Vekhi* appealed was, first, that of the sombre pessimist, Chaadaev, who was the first to analyse the consequences to Russian society of the fact that Russia had never experienced either the Christian social order of the Roman Church, or the humanistic revolt of Reformation and Renaissance. The ideas of duty, justice, law and order which in Western society were the "ideas which are breathed in with the very air" had in consequence never taken root in Russia.[25] Next Pushkin, who combined love of liberty with love of order, and who was both conservative in recognizing the importance of preservation, and liberal in seeing the need for reform, who could remain personally attached to the Emperor without being blinded by the nature of the society around him. His well-known letter to Chaadaev of 19 October 1836 is much quoted by members of the *Vekhi* group. (In 1937, Frank published an essay of great penetration on Pushkin as a political thinker, for which Struve wrote an introduction and some addenda.[26]) Another influence on *Vekhi* was Boris Chicherin, the legal philosopher, and particularly his collected essays, published in 1862, which included the famous letter of protest to Herzen on the policy of *Kolokol*.[27] In the Preface he speaks of the necessity of "pointing to the elements of power and law, forgotten in our literature, but just as necessary to society as freedom itself. Sensible civil life is only possible when freedom is united to these principles". Soloviev was another obvious influence, and so was Dostoevsky.

Dostoevsky's genius is so manifold that no doubt many sides of it were influential at different times. But at least two aspects of his thought can be singled out in this context. First, his opposition to all forms of utilitarian philosophy as a basis for the social order. Secondly, his profound analysis of the mystique of the revolutionary, and his foreboding of the terrible danger implicit for Russia in the revolutionary philosophy. As for Soloviev, it was not only his philosophical idealism which influenced the *Vekhi* group. Its members saw in Soloviev's teaching a revival of the Christian humanism of Erasmus and St Thomas More: Soloviev had recognized the essentially Christian nature of humanism – so long as it was not atheistic humanism – as a corrective to the defects of the Christian past. Another reason why Soloviev was influential was because, like Dostoevsky, he shared that vision of impending doom which obsessed so many of the non-socialist intellectuals of the early twentieth century.[28] It would seem natural to add Turgenev, not only the Turgenev of *Fathers and Sons*, but more especially of the *Letters to Herzen* published in Geneva in 1892.[29] But there is little direct trace of Turgenev's influence among the *Vekhi* group – though Gershenzon wrote about him, mainly from the literary aspect. Perhaps the *Vekhi* authors felt something of that hostility which Turgenev aroused, and still arouses, in so many Russians, for his unashamed adoption of Western European life, in the train of Madame Viardot. Dostoevsky's feelings for Turgenev spring immediately to mind. And, after all, the *Vekhi* group were first and foremost nationalists and patriots.

If one had to attempt a rough summary of the position of *Vekhi*, one could say that they stood midway between the Slavophiles and the Westerners. They accepted the Slavophile veneration of Russian national tradition, while rejecting their romantic idealization of innate Russian virtues as a substitute for the more usual civic virtues. They accepted the Westerners' desire to learn from the countries of the West, while rejecting their atheism, their socialism, and their utilitarianism.

It was suggested above that the very violence of the reaction to the publication of *Vekhi* shows that emotions were engaged as much as reason. The quality of the rejoinders rather confirms this. Since the extreme right-wing welcomed what it regarded as a useful attack on the revolutionaries, it was easy for the revolutionaries to say in one voice: "The liberals have joined up with the reactionaries." This, in the main, was the burden of the Socialist Revolutionary reply to *Vekhi*, which was published in the form of a volume of essays. Ivanov-Razumnik in a very witty pamphlet[30] summed up the *Vekhi* position as: '*pereat mundus fiat iustitia*'. (The authors of *Vekhi* might well have replied that there is quite a strong case to be made for this maxim.) Lenin, in characteristic fashion, made political capital out of the split in the liberal ranks. *Vekhi*, he wrote, with less regard for truth than was usual even for Lenin, was typical of the whole Kadet outlook. It showed that Russian liberalism, under the guise of attacking the intelligentsia, was really attacking democracy, and was thus identified with *Moskovskia Vedomosty* and Pobedonostsev. Then, as an afterthought, he added that the Kadet leaders' attack on *Vekhi* was just hypocrisy.[31]

The Kadet reply appeared as a volume of eight essays, edited by I. Petrunkevich.[32] Apart from the longest essay, that of P. N. Miliukov which takes up nearly half the book, it cannot be said that the intellectual level is very high. The appeal is rather to the emotions than to the head. "The authors of *Vekhi*," writes Professor N. A. Gredeskul (who was later to co-operate with the Bolsheviks), "have left out nothing more nor less than the main actor on the historical scene – the people . . . The intelligentsia is only a superstructure upon the people."[33] Miliukov's essay is witty, a brilliant piece of advocacy in the sense of scoring debating points against an adversary, but somewhat devoid of political realism. It was Miliukov's tragedy that he believed that he was a liberal, when he was in reality a radical. He ends his essay with numerous quotations from Graham Wallas's *Human Nature in Politics* and with a plea for a "scientific spirit in politics". The *Vekhi* plea for the moral rearmament of the *intelligenty* is reactionary and dangerous. "Just imagine," he says, "such words as 'purification' or 'repentance' on the lips of a European intellectual."[34] It was in all sincerity that Miliukov, a highly civilized historian, saw himself in 1909 as the equivalent of a Western European liberal politician. Yet it was Miliukov who, in 1905, at the foundation congress of the Kadets, had welcomed the revolutionary parties as "our allies on the left"; and it was his Kadet party in the First Duma which refused to vote even moral censure on terrorism as a method of political struggle.

Perhaps the emotional nature of the opposition to *Vekhi* is best illustrated by a pamphlet written in reply by a passionate disciple of Chernyshevsky. "The name of Chernyshevsky," he writes, "brings to us the spirit of unconquerable courage, creative energy and plans for widespread reorganization. His spirit exudes refusal to bow before the present in the name of a better future. The volume *Vekhi*, on the contrary, smells of a kind of elderly impotence, preaching moderation and meticulousness; it is steeped in the love of quiet and order."[35]

So ended the great debate of 1909 and 1910, and passed into history. But the voice of some members of the *Vekhi* group was to be heard again for a fleeting moment, and in rather dramatic circumstances. In the course of 1918, after the revolution, on the initiative of Struve, the main participants in *Vekhi* – Struve, Frank, Berdiaev, Bulgakov and Izgoev – joined with six others, including Viacheslav Ivanov and Novgorodtsev, to publish another volume. The publication was fraught with difficulty – Struve, who had by then joined the side of Denikin, was living illegally in Moscow; Frank was in Saratov. But the difficulties were overcome, and the volume was completed, set up and printed in Moscow by the autumn of 1918, when Struve left for Finland. The title, *De Profundis (Iz Glubiny)*, was chosen by Frank. But though printed, the volume was not published; it was overtaken by the renewed wave of Bolshevik repressions which followed upon the attempt on Lenin's life in the summer of 1918. The printed copies remained lying in the printing office of *Russkaia Mysl*. Three years later, in 1921, apparently around the time of the Kronstadt revolt, the printers of their own accord "published" the book, by putting it out for sale in Moscow. It is to be presumed that most of the copies were confiscated – at any rate it is unlikely that more than two copies ever reached the outside world.[36]

It could not be expected that this volume, written under the terrifying impact of the revolution, should contain the mature wisdom which distinguished *Vekhi*. The authors would not have been human if they had not pointed out, as Struve does in his preface to *Iz Glubiny*, that *Vekhi* had foreseen the catastrophe, but that the warnings were ignored. It is worth pausing for a moment to consider to what extent the mystique of revolution, which *Vekhi* set out to combat and which afflicted the radical intelligentsia, in fact contributed to the victory of the Bolsheviks. V. A. Maklakov, for example, blames the liberal constitutionalists of the Duma for persuading the Grand Duke Michael to abdicate, and implies that they were infected with the revolutionary virus.[37] This is a somewhat doubtful judgement: the temper of February 1917 was incompatible with monarchy and probably no amount of political wisdom on the part of the Duma could have saved it. But the revolutionary mystique played its part in the Bolshevik victory in two other respects. First, if it had not been for this mystique, with its concomitant inability to see reality separately from the preconceived theoretical idea of that reality, Lenin would possibly not have been the extremist he was. Revolution, which after all is at best a painful necessity, was to Lenin an obsession. His standard of judgement of men was, even after the revolution was over and done with, according as to whether they were more or less "revolutionary" – a completely meaningless judgement charged with emotional overtones. Hence, he could only feel safe with the most "revolutionary" of men around him. And hence, the disastrous decision to ensure monopoly of power for the Bolsheviks, from which most of the consequences of the Soviet form of dictatorship flowed. It had little, if anything, to do with marxism: it was the result of obsession with a mystique, and a mystique which was much more *narodnik* than marxist in character.

The second way in which the revolutionary mystique led to Bolshevism was in making co-operation between the so-called bourgeois parties and the socialists, after the February revolution, a forlorn hope. It was a two-way process. On the one hand the majority of the Kadets, but no longer Miliukov himself, who still regarded themselves as the heirs of the revolutionary tradition, were quite unable to perceive that those rather rough and absurd Bolsheviks were not, in their hearts of hearts, still "the allies of the left" that they had appeared to be to Miliukov in 1905. On the other hand the socialists, even when they were capable of understanding the necessity for co-operating with the "bourgeois" parties for the maintenance of order, were swayed more by their hearts than by their heads – with the disastrous consequence that they actively helped to increase the state of anarchy in the country (which they themselves, when their heads were in control, feared), from which Lenin alone could emerge the victor. The memoirs of Sukhanov, for example, fully bear out this view – in fact, Sukhanov himself was the most typical *intelligent* that ever lived.

Thus, the authors of *Iz Glubiny* could scarcely be blamed if they were tempted to say: "We told you so." In fact this forms a very small and incidental part of the book, which is deeply religious in tone – markedly more so even than *Vekhi* was. As in *Vekhi*, the authors emphasize again and again the need for moral self-perfection, for repentance, and the incompatibility of materialistic socialism and egalitarianism with the Christian way of life. The consolations of religious faith are the main solution which they offer for the catastrophe which had befallen the country. In his Preface, Struve points out that in spite of differences of views, the one conviction common to all the authors is that "the positive beginnings of social life are rooted in the depths of religious consciousness". For the rest, the articles in the volume are in the main a restatement of the bases of the faith which ruled *Vekhi*, with, perhaps, an added concreteness, the product of bitter experience. Izgoev's article, "Socialism, Culture, and Bolshevism", is one of the most interesting. The main argument is that the cause of the Russian disaster was not so much Bolshevism, as socialism in the form which it took in Russia. "The Russian Socialists," he says, "had they found themselves in power, would either have had to remain simple chatterers, doing nothing to put their ideas into practice, or else to have done from A to Z everything that the Bolsheviks did."[38] This argument is of course a familiar one in the mouths of most marxist historians of Bolshevism, as a justification of Bolshevism. What Izgoev meant, one need hardly say, was an indictment of socialism. He went on to argue that the only hope was to retain a few healthy grains which were contained in socialism, and to renounce for ever all the rest. Berdiaev in his article on "The Ghosts of the Russian Revolution" emphasizes that the revolution had finally shattered the illusion of religious *narodnichestvo*, from which even Dostoevsky had suffered, that the religious spirit of the Russian people would provide a safeguard against the anti-Christ of socialism.[39] Novgorodtsev, writing on "The Ways and Tasks of the Russian Intelligentsia", also analyses Russian socialism and liberalism. Liberalism in Russia, he says, lacking the experience of long practical work in the business of government, was emotionally attracted to socialism, without realizing that Russian socialism was devoid of any liberal elements: it was in essence *narodnik*, and its father was Bakunin.[40] Novgorodtsev preaches conservatism, in the fine words of Burke, from his *Reflections on the Revolution in France*: "Our political system [Burke, of course, is referring to England] is placed in a just correspondence and symmetry with the order of the world and with the mode of existence decreed to a permanent body composed of transitory parts . . . The whole, at one time, is never old, or middle-aged, or young, but, in a condition of unchangeable constancy, moves on through the varied tenor of perpetual decay, fall, renovation and progression . . . In what we improve we are never wholly new, in what we retain we are never wholly obsolete."[41] Struve's essay, though not perhaps equal to his best, contains some penetrating observations. He points out, for example, that the idea of "class" in Bolshevik Russia is a purely emotional one, and does not correspond to objective realities. It is not classes which determine class enmity; it is enmity which creates division into arbitrary classes. Where the idea of "class" divides, the idea of "nation" unites. Therefore the ultimate regeneration of Russia must come from the idea of nationalism. Struve probably meant by this not the gradual evolution of Bolshevism into a national state, but the forcible overthrow of the Bolsheviks by the resurgence of a national movement. Struve never accepted the idea that Bolshevism could in time evolve into anything essentially different from what it started as. He regarded it as an usurpation by evil men of the rightful traditional powers of the state, and as such an usurpation something which could only be overthrown by force. Consistently with this view he – alone of all the *Vekhi* group – took an active part to the best of his powers in the physical struggle against Bolshevism.

So ended the first part of this debate, of which the second part was pursued in exile. Reassembled in emigration, after the vicissitudes of the civil war, some of the participants in *Vekhi*, and particularly Struve and Frank, posed the question: what attitude must we adopt to the revolution? A group of lesser spirits, mostly former Kadets, but whose views certainly did not represent Miliukov, or the majority of the Kadets, had answered this question with startling simplicity: accept it, and co-operate with the Bolsheviks. They expounded their philosophy of national Bolshevism in a volume of essays called *Smena Vekh* (A Change of Landmarks) published in 1921, and in a periodical of the same name which appeared in Paris from October 1921 until March 1922, and subsequently in a daily called *Nakanune* (On the Eve) published in Berlin. The choice of the name *Smena Vekh* was probably in part due to the fact that two of the members of the group, Yu. V. Kliuchnikov and G. Ustrialov, had at one time been close to *Vekhi.* The very nature of the arguments used by this group was a melancholy reflection on the total failure of some of the Kadet intelligentsia ever to understand what *Vekhi* was about. The intellectual level is not very high – about the same as, say, that of the arguments used by Vichy supporters to justify collaboration with the Germans. With the introduction of NEP, Bolshevism has now become a national doctrine. The longer we intellectuals oppose it, the more we encourage Bolshevik excesses. We bow to the will of the Russian people – and so forth. Inside Russia, *Izvestia* and *Pravda* welcomed the new movement in identical terms.[42] Meetings organized by Professor Gredeskul, another ex-Kadet, proclaimed the new doctrine. But five intellectuals, including A. S. Izgoev (who had not yet succeeded in leaving Russia), were courageous enough to publish a volume of protest, in guarded but unmistakable terms, against what they regarded as a betrayal of the ideas of *Vekhi.*[43] Meanwhile the Communist Party Conference in August 1922 showed beyond doubt that, whatever hopes might have been placed on Lenin, his successors, i.e. Stalin and Zinoviev, now that Lenin had virtually lost his influence through illness, had no intention of following up the economic concessions of NEP by any political relaxation.

Of course the simple political chicanery of *Smena Vekh* could not even become a debatable issue for men of the calibre of Struve or Frank, whose reaction was confined to regret that the name of *Vekhi* had been so unscrupulously abused for such a purpose. But there was between 1921 and 1923 a discussion of some moment between the two men on the meaning of the revolution in its historical perspective, which forms a fitting conclusion to this sketch of the controversies raised by the emergence of the *Vekhi* group. By 1921, Struve was in Sofia, and had revived his old periodical, *Russkaia Mysl.* This appeared for some years thereafter, first in Sofia and then in Prague. It was opened, of course, to a much wider range of contributors living in emigration than former supporters of *Vekhi*, but some of the original *Vekhi* names – notably Struve himself, and Izgoev after 1922 – reappeared in its pages. It was to be expected that a good deal of controversy should have developed on the historical meaning of the revolution, on the attitude which should be adopted to it, on prognosis of its future development. Struve's own position remained clear and uncompromising. "For me," he wrote in 1921, "idealization of the revolution which took place in 1917 and in the subsequent years is at one and the same time a religious and moral lie, and an historical and factual untruth, self-deception and deception of others." There is no hope of salvation in mystical faith in the "people" and its ability ultimately to transform the character of the revolution. The only real faith in the Russian people is the faith that it will ultimately overthrow the communist regime. He describes *Smena Vekh* as "the most monstrous phenomenon in the whole history of Russian spiritual development". It represents, he says, the exact antithesis of *Vekhi*, which was a denial of the validity of revolutionary ideology in the name of certain basic religious, cultural and social principles.[44] (A. S. Izgoev, in the pamphlet published inside Russia in reply to *Smena Vekh*, to which reference has been made, had also written: "We must judge this or that action of the government in the light of our conscience and our consciousness, and not change our conscience and consciousness according to whose hands happen to hold government power at the moment . . . Outside this principle there is neither freedom, nor human dignity, nor spiritual strength."[45] It must have been very nearly the last time that such words appeared in print in the USSR.) Struve further rejected arguments based on the analogy of the French revolution – that when the turmoil and violence of the revolutionary period is over the revolution will be seen to have accomplished salutary and necessary progress. The analogy between the two revolutions, he maintained, was false: the French revolution, for all its violent nature, in fact achieved the objects which it set out to achieve, and in fact put into practice its main ideas. In contrast, the Bolshevik revolution put into practice from the start the very reverse of what had been its avowed principles – not socialism, but inequality; not freedom, but dictatorship; not a militia, but an army; not nationalized land, but private peasant holdings. In one of his articles Struve concluded that pre-revolutionary Russia "was in all respects immeasurably nearer to a free and prosperous Russia founded on peasant ownership" than was Soviet Russia.[46]

The best of Struve's thought on the meaning of the Russian revolutions in historical perspective is contained in two lectures which he delivered inside non-Bolshevik Russia in 1919, and reprinted in 1921.[47] The theme running through these remarkable essays is that the only hope of salvation lies in the restoration of the state as a result of the rebirth of national consciousness. "State" is thus contrasted with Bolshevik rule, to which Struve would probably have denied the quality of a state, because it lacked order; while "national consciousness" is contrasted with the class hatred fostered by Bolshevism – the idea which was already developed in Struve's contribution to *Iz Glubiny*. The foundation for this idea of state *plus* nation Struve found in historical parallel, and particularly the parallel which he saw between the Russian revolution and the *Smuta* – the period of the troubles in Muscovy in the seventeenth century. (On this question, Struve, and probably all the *Vekhi* authors, had derived a great deal from S. Th. Platonov's great study of the period, which had first been published in 1899.[48]) The parallel Struve saw particularly in the importance in each case of a foreign interest in the trouble – Poland and Germany, respectively. The lesson he derived from the *Smuta* was the fact that order in the seventeenth century was restored by a national movement of the middle classes, supported by the only intelligentsia which then existed, the clergy, and guided by the idealistic motives of safeguarding the faith, and the Church, and of saving the state from ruin. Then it was the middle classes, and not the people, who had the necessary qualities to restore the state: so it would be again, if those who should be the intellectual leaders of this class, and who had failed in 1917, would realize their mission. The tragedy of Russia in 1917 was primarily due, according to Struve, to what he calls "the abnormal, the deformed attitude of the Russian educated class towards the state and its activities". After 1905 political freedom and democracy could have been possible, on two conditions: sincerity on the part of the government in putting reform into practice, and recognition by the Kadets of the greater danger from the left than from the right, and a consequent will to cooperate in reform. Neither condition was fulfilled: hence Lenin's triumph became possible. By 1921 at all events, Struve did not dispute that restoration of the old order was impossible. But he never swerved from his belief that without restoration of some moral and legal order by overthrow of the Bolsheviks there could be no development of reforms on the basis of order. "New life – old might" was the slogan he proposed, by which he meant a new, not entirely foreseeable form of government order, but one drawing national inspiration from the Russian past.

Two years later, in 1923, Frank published his criticism of Struve's views on the revolution, also in *Russkaia Mysl.*[49] It was wrong, argued Frank, to throw the main blame for the Bolshevik revolution on the intelligentsia. The very embitterment of the intelligentsia was itself but a symptom of the national disease. What was happening was the death of the Russia of the nobility, the *dvorianstvo*, and its replacement by a peasant Russia – the "advance of the inner barbarian". It was incorrect, argued Frank, to explain the collapse of the monarchy by such factors as the war, the faults of the Emperor, and the like. The only reason why the old Russian state had been able to stand up, in spite of the vast chasm between the peasants and the state, was because of the monarchy: the monarchy had been the only institution deeply rooted in the consciousness of the people, in contrast to institutions like the courts, or local administration. But after 1905 a loss of faith in the monarchy had occurred, the change that V. V. Rozanov described as "the collapse of the great fetish", and with this collapse the entire old order was doomed. Frank saw the essentially peasant character of the revolution precisely in its indifference to government and forms of government. (Chicherin had, incidentally, previously discovered this characteristic in the Russian people throughout history – indifferent to the nature of power and ready to submit, the Russian people, says Chicherin, "in cases of extremity, when the state was threatened by collapse, would rise as one man, restore order, and then once again abandon all power and all state activity to the government".[50]) The return of the old order, according to Frank, was inconceivable, if only because of the physical destruction of the very social and political material out of which it had been constructed. Therefore the revolution must be lived through as a purifying catharsis, accepting the fact that the peasant state has replaced the old state. Whatever the future may bring in the way of regeneration can only come as the result of the moral regeneration of the whole people, helped on by the bitter disappointment which it has suffered in reaping tyranny where it had hoped to reap freedom.

This summary only gives a very bald idea of the profound historical and psychological analysis which this fine article contains. The controversy between Frank and Struve is perhaps now more remarkable for its analysis of the situation than for the solution it offers to any practical problem. If one had to venture a judgement on the dispute after some thirty years one might say that perhaps Struve underestimated the actual physical destruction that Soviet rule would entail of the class upon which ultimately he placed his reliance. Equally, Frank may have underestimated in 1923 the extent of the moral corruption of a nation which communist rule would produce, and which makes moral regeneration appear difficult to conceive. The difference of approach to the problem by the two men was perhaps due to a difference of temperament; yet, each stressed a vital aspect of the philosophy of *Vekhi*. To Struve, the more practical man of action, the first requirement was a state order, without which there could be no freedom and no progress. For Frank, the deeply religious philosopher and mystic, the predominant idea was the primacy of moral and spiritual forces over material circumstances. But these two elements – freedom under order, and the primacy of spirit over material forces – together make up *Vekhi*.

The importance of *Vekhi* lies not in what it achieved, but in the light which it throws on Russian liberalism on the eve of the revolution. Our historical assessment of the Russian revolution is so much consciously or unconsciously coloured by the influence of marxist historians that there is a risk that we may view the entire Russian liberal movement merely as something that stopped halfway on the road to revolution for lack of courage or consistency or class consciousness, and thus fail to distinguish the very different strands of which it was in fact made up. There is a grain of truth in the marxist view when applied to the Kadets, in the sense that they may have been revolutionaries without knowing it. When the Russian Kadet called himself a liberal, he may have believed that he was using this term as meaning what, say, Gladstone meant by it. But in fact he was in spirit much more the liberal of 1848, in other words more a revolutionary, or a radical. The great service of *Vekhi* was to illuminate this fact for the first time, even if the illumination came too late, and the message fell on deaf ears. But, as well as being pioneers, the *Vekhi* group also symbolized a return to a tenuous but more truly liberal Russian tradition, which recognized that when once a major change in society has been accomplished, the more important ally of liberalism is conservation, and not revolution. Thus Chicherin had written on the morrow of the emancipation of the serfs: "True liberalism is now measured not by opposition, not by glorification of freedom, not by progressive movements, but by devotion to the manifesto of 19 February which has liberated twenty-three million Russians . . . Conservatism and liberalism are here one and the same."[51] Let us concede freely that it was as difficult to see the truth of this in the years which followed the Manifesto of October 1905 in Russia, as it had been in 1862. But it was the *Vekhi* group and they alone, of all the progressive intelligentsia, who had the courage and the wisdom to make the attempt.

* This article was originally read as a paper to the Soviet Studies Seminar at St Antony's College, Oxford, at Whitsun 1955. I am grateful to Mrs T. S. Frank for permission to quote from the unpublished memoir on P. B. Struve by her late husband; and to Mr V. S. Frank and Dr V. Leontovitsch for their helpful comments.

1. In an unpublished memoir on P. B. Struve, from which some extracts are quoted in *Sbornik pamyati Semyona Lyudvigovicha Franka*, ed. V. Zen'kovsky (Munich 1954), pp. 51–2. Cited hereafter as *Sbornik*.
2. *Problemy idealizma. Sbornik statey*, ed. P. I. Novgorodtsev (Moscow 1903).
3. *Sbornik*, p. 11.
4. *Problemy idealizma*, p. ix.
5. *Sbornik*, pp. 51–2.
6. P. Struve, *Patriotica. Politika, kul'tura, religiya, sotsializm. Sbornik statey za pyat' lyet (1905–1910 gg.)* (St Petersburg 1911), pp. 92–3.
7. *Vekhi. Sbornik statey o russkoy intelligentsii N. A. Berdyayeva, S. N. Bulgakova, M. O. Gershenzona, A. S. Izgoyeva, B. A. Kistyakovskogo, P. B. Struve, S. L. Franka* (2nd edn., Moscow 1909) cited from hereafter as *Vekhi*. [The essays have been published in an English translation: *Landmarks, A Collection of Essays on the Russian Intelligentsia, 1909*, eds. Boris Shragin and Albert Todd (New York 1977) (ed.)].
8. *Sbornik*, p. 11. It should be noted that Granovsky belongs to a somewhat different tradition from the other three.
9. *Vekhi*, p. ii.
10. *ibid.*, p. 4.
11. *ibid.*, p. 8.
12. *ibid.*, p. 17.
13. *ibid.*, p. 188.
14. *ibid.*, p. 193.
15. *ibid.*, p. 131.
16. G. V. Plekhanov, *God na rodine, polnoye sobraniye statey i rechey 1917–1918 g.* 2 vols, vol. II (Paris 1921), pp. 257–68.
17. *Vekhi*, p. 123.
18. *ibid.*, p. 80.
19. *ibid.*, p. 89.

20. *Patriotica.*
21. *Vekhi*, p. 89, n.1.
22. *Patriotica*, p. 478 n.
23. The following works of Gershenzon were published after the revolution (apart from several reprints of works published before): *Troystvennyy obraz sovershenstva* (Moscow 1918); *Mechta i mysl' I. S. Turgeneva* (Moscow 1919); *Perepiska iz dvukh uglov* (with V. Ivanov) (Moscow–Berlin 1921); *Klyuch very* (Petrograd 1922); *Sud'by yevreyskogo naroda* (Petrograd–Berlin 1922). Posthumously: *Stat'i o Pushkine. So vstupitel'noy stat'yoy Leonida Grossmana, Gershenzon pisatel'* (Moscow 1926); *Pis'ma k bratu: izbrannyye mesta. Vstupitel'naya stat'ya i primechaniya M. Tsyarlovskogo* (Leningrad 1927); *Arkhiv N. A. i N. P. Ogaryovykh . . . Redaktsiya i predisloviye V. P. Polonskogo* (Moscow–Leningrad 1930).
24. *Vekhi*, p. 170.
25. *Sochineniya i pis'ma P. Ya. Chaadayeva*, ed. M. Gershenzon, vol. 2 (Moscow 1913), p. 114.
26. S. L. Frank, *Pushkin kak politicheskiy myslitel', s predisloviyem i dopolneniyami P. B. Struve* (Belgrade 1937).
27. B. N. Chicherin, *Neskol'ko sovremennykh voprosov* (Moscow 1862).
28. On Solov'yov see three broadcasts by S. L. Frank, reprinted in the *Listener*, 28 April 1949, 5 May 1949 and 12 May 1949.
29. *Pis'ma K. D. Kavelina i I. S. Turgeneva k A. I. Gertsenu*, ed. M. P. Dragomanov (Geneva 1892).
30. Ivanov-Razumnik (pseudonym of Razumnik Vasilievich Ivanov), *Ob intelligentsii. Chto takoye makhayevshchina. Kayushchiyesya raznochintsy* (St Petersburg 1910).
31. V. I. Lenin, *Sobraniye sochineniy*, 20 vols (Moscow 1920–6), vol. XI, Part 2, pp. 515–22. Lenin's attack on *Vekhi* was recalled in a recent article in *Kommunist*, in which the writings of R. Hare, N. Lossky and V. Zen'kovsky, *inter alios*, are critically reviewed. See V. Malinin, N. Tarakanov and I. Shchipanov, "Protiv sovremennykh burzhuaznykh fal'sifikatorov istorii russkoy filosofii", *Kommunist*, no. 10, July 1955, pp. 62–76.
32. *Intelligentsiya v Rossii. Sbornik stat'yey. S predisloviyem I. I. Petrunkevicha* (St Petersburg 1910).
33. *ibid.*, pp. 48–9.
34. *ibid.*, pp. 186–7.
35. V. M. Fritshe, *Ot Chernyshevskogo k "Vekham"* (Moscow 1910), p. 4.
36. *Iz glubiny. Sbornik statey o russkoy revolyutsii S. A. Askol'dova, Nikolaya Berdyayeva, Sergeya Bulgakova, Vyacheslava Ivanova, A. S. Izgoyeva, S. A. Kotlyarevskogo, V. Murav'yova, P. Novgorodtseva, I. Pokrovskogo, Petra Struve, S. Franka. Russkaya Mysl'* (Moscow–Petrograd 1918). I am grateful to the Warden and Fellows of St Antony's College, Oxford, for their assistance in procuring for me the loan of this rare volume. On the history of *Iz glubiny*, see *Sbornik*, pp. 53–4 (Professor Gleb Struve's contribution).
37. V. A. Maklakov, *Iz vospominaniy* (New York 1954), pp. 377–8.
38. *Iz glubiny*, p. 145.
39. *ibid.*, p. 55.
40. *ibid.*, pp. 209–10.
41. *The Works of the Right Honourable Edmund Burke*, 12 vols, vol. III (London 1887), p. 275.
42. *Izvestiya*, 13 October 1921; *Pravda*, 14 October 1921.
43. *O smene vekh.* (1) A. S. Izgoyev, *"Vekhi" i "Smena Vekh"*; (2) I. Clemens, *Novyye vekhi i russkaya gosudarstvennost'*; (3) P. K. Guber, *Sud'by tretyego Rima*; (4) A. B. Petrishchev, *Chuzhiye zemlyaki.* Izdatel'stvo "Logos" pri Dome Literatov (Petrograd 1922).
44. P. Struve, "Proshloye, nastoyashcheye i budushcheye", *Russkaia mysl'*, vol. I–II (Prague 1922), p. 222.
45. *O smene vekh*, pp. 23–4.

46. P. Struve, "Oshibki i sofizmy 'istoricheskogo' vzglyada na revolyutsiyu. Po povodu stat'yi K. I. Zaytseva", *Russkaia mysl'*, vol. III (Prague 1922), pp. 158–63.

47. P. Struve, *Razmyshleniya o russkoy revolyutsii* (Sofia 1921).

48. S. Th. Platonov, *Ocherki po istorii smuty v moskovskom gosudarstve XVI–XVII vv. (Opyt izucheniya obshchestvennogo stroya i soslovnykh otnosheniy v Smutnoye Vremya)* 3rd edn (St Petersburg 1910).

49. S. L. Frank, "Iz razmyshleniy o russkoy revolyutsii", *Russkaia Mysl'*, vol. VI–VIII (Prague 1923), pp. 238–70.

50. B. N. Chicherin, *Neskol'ko sovremennykh voprosov* (Moscow 1862), p. 166.

51. *ibid.*, p. 181.

Stolypin – Most Controversial Russian Statesman

This review of George Tokmakoff, *P. A. Stolypin and the Third Duma: An Appraisal of the Three Major Issues*, University Press of America (Washington D.C. 1981) was written for the *New York Review of Books*, and will appear posthumously.

Petr Arkadievich Stolypin was the Prime Minister who dominated Russia's short constitutional period. Appointed on 7 July 1906, he was shot by an assassin on 1 September 1911, and died a few days later. Probably no other figure in the modern history of Russia has aroused so much controversy. By the left he is generally dismissed as the savage butcher who hanged peasants and workers. (A monument to him erected in Kiev in 1912 was destroyed in 1917.) To the extreme right he became an odious figure, whose policy of reform and attempt to work with the Duma, or parliament, were a threat to the sacred principle of autocracy (which the right continued to pretend still subsisted, in spite of the constitutional regime inaugurated in 1906). For his many admirers he has posthumously become the wisest statesman that Russia ever had, who could, had he been given time, have saved Russia from war and revolution, and have effected a peaceful transformation of the country on moderate and modern lines. His ministerial colleagues, and others who knew him, have recorded that he was a man of great courage, sincerity, and absolute integrity.

Yet, in spite of the passion which Stolypin arouses, no biography of him exists in English – it could be, of course, that scholars have experienced difficulty in obtaining access to the relevant archives in the Soviet Union. Dr Tokmakoff's book deals only with what was the main period of his career, that of the Third Duma, and then only with three of the major issues with which he was concerned. Even so, it is a most welcome addition to the very scanty literature on Stolypin available in English.

The First Duma to come into being as the result of the Imperial Manifesto of 17 October 1905 and the new Fundamental State Laws of 23 April 1906 was elected on a wide franchise, which produced a turbulent and radical body, determined from the start not to co-operate with the government, or with any government not responsible to it. Stolypin, who had been appointed Minister of the Interior a day before the Duma met, on 26 April 1906, showed that he was better able to stand up to the barrage of hostile abuse which the government faced than the weak Prime Minister, Goremykin. It soon became obvious that no common ground could be found between the government and the Duma (historians will, no doubt, long debate the question whose fault this was), so the Duma was dissolved on 9 July, with an announcement that it would reconvene on 20 February 1907. Just before the dissolution, Stolypin was appointed Prime Minister.

Stolypin faced the Second Duma with a vast programme, which had been set out in detail in a government communiqué in August 1906. The omens for any kind of harmonious co-operation between the government and the still radical (if somewhat chastened) Second Duma were not good. Efforts to persuade some of the liberal leaders to come into the government had failed. Moreover, the country was in a state of revolutionary turmoil: for example, 3,000 deaths were caused by terrorists in 1907. In August 1906 a terrorist bomb had exploded in Stolypin's house, wounding his children. The government retaliated with strong measures, including numerous executions by sentence of courts martial which succeeded in breaking the wave of terrorism, but shocked and antagonized radical and liberal opinion. But Stolypin's policy, as the communiqué made clear, and as he told the Second Duma, was based on the belief that for the government to call a halt to necessary reforms and to devote all its energies to the suppression of terrorism, was wrong. He therefore envisaged a comprehensive programme of reforms, aimed at ultimately removing the causes of social discontent. Apart from the land reform, which occupied Stolypin in the Third Duma, the programme included the following: reform of civil rights; improvement of workers' conditions of life; extension and improvement of local government administration; reform of local courts; reform of secondary education; and reform of the police. Not included in the programme of reforms submitted to the Second Duma was a proposal, which Stolypin had persuaded the Council of Ministers to accept in October 1906, for the removal of a great number of restrictions from which the Jews suffered. The Emperor refused to approve the proposal in response, as he put it, to "an inner voice (which) keeps on insisting more and more". The hostile reaction of the Duma astonished even Stolypin's critics – indeed, as one of the Kadet leaders later noted, it would have been incomprehensible to an Englishman. The social democratic leader Tsereteli actually spoke of "tossing us a few scraps of reforms . . . incapable of satisfying anyone".

What was central to the entire programme, in Stolypin's view, was putting an end to the separate legal status of the peasants, derived from the survival of communal ownership of land. Unless the majority of the population could be given equal status with the rest, and relieved of its legal *apartheid*, all the other reforms in his view would be no more than "cosmetics on a corpse" – to quote the graphic phrase which he used in conversation with a colleague. Unless this fundamental belief of Stolypin is understood (and Dr Tokmakoff seems to me not sufficiently to appreciate this issue) his political conduct in 1907, which aroused severe controversy, cannot be seen in perspective.

Since there was no hope of passing a complicated and comprehensive law which would enable the peasants to leave the commune and to become individual, legally protected owners of land with the co-operation of the Second Duma, a way had to be found of doing it without this co-operation. Professor Seton-Watson is probably right when he observes that Stolypin "was in favour of co-operating with the elected representatives of the people, provided that they did what he wanted. But when his policies met with opposition, he had no respect either for the electorate or the law." At any rate, this is what happened in June 1907.

Article 87 of the Fundamental State Laws provided that "while the Duma is not in session" the Council of Ministers could submit an urgently required legislative proposal for the Emperor to approve. But a bill had to be introduced for the endorsement of the Duma within the first two months of the next Duma session; and the proposed measure could not alter the laws governing elections to the Duma. In defiance of this last provision, Stolypin persuaded his cabinet not only to dissolve the Second Duma (on 3 June 1907) so as to enable him to introduce his agrarian reforms by decree, but also substantially to alter the rules and system of election to the Duma, so as to ensure that the Third Duma would be dominated by more conservative and moderate delegates than the Second. This *coup d'état*, as it is usually described (though Dr Tokmakoff does not dwell on this aspect at all), was vociferously condemned by the more radical liberals, for many of whom the Duma became "tainted". On the other hand, there was not the remotest possibility of passing the agrarian laws in the Second Duma, or in any Duma elected on a similar franchise. It is, at all events, arguable that in a country in which constitutional practice is still in its infancy the slow process of learning this subtle art must be helped along by the occasional rough jolt. But there were many moderate and responsible men who rejected this argument, and who is to say that they were wrong in maintaining that a result, however desirable, can never be achieved by illegal means? This issue became even more acute in the Western *zemstvo* crisis referred to later.

The famous land reform was embodied in three decrees, of 5 October, 9 November and 15 November 1907, which were debated at great length both in the Duma and in the State Council, and were eventually passed into law on 14 June 1910. This did not leave Stolypin much time for his other reforms, before his life was cut short. Dr Tokmakoff deals in a somewhat pedestrian manner with the debates in both chambers. I suspect that the omissions from his accounts of the debates (and inclusion of much of little interest) are to be explained by the fact that he does not really appreciate the main idea underlying Stolypin's land reform – the transformation of millions of peasants from the status of subjects of public law to that of subjects of private law; or, in other words, from persons whose needs are protected by the state by means of communal rights, to persons whose rights are rights of individual property, governed by the civil law.

There is, to take one of several examples of such an omission, no mention of Count Olsufiev's argument in the State Council (which was typical of the patriarchal attitude to the peasants which was still common among landowners) that the Russian peasant had no real sense of or desire for private ownership – in other words, the traditional populist and Slavophile image of the peasant. The fallaciousness of this view, which was widely held by opponents of the Stolypin reforms, was established beyond doubt, with a mass of evidence, by the late Dr V. Leontovitsch.[1] Another argument omitted is that of Kropotov, the Trudovik (agrarian socialist) deputy in the Duma, that the effect of the reform was to deprive a member of the commune of his traditional right, embodied in decisions of the Senate, to have land allocated to him for his subsistence. This argument, true in itself, which was left without a reply by the government, went to the very heart of the Stolypin reforms, which were precisely designed to replace a right under public law by a private law right of ownership.

According to Stolypin in 1910, given ten years of peace Russia would be "unrecognizable". Of course, there were only four years of peace left. Even so, most critics of the Stolypin reforms concede them a measure of success in revitalizing Russian agriculture – and it is often forgotten that Stolypin's concern for peasant welfare was genuine, and that he was not merely motivated in putting through his reforms to effect a "wager on the strong", and to remove a powerful source of revolutionary unrest. By 1916, the last years of the old regime, nearly two and a half million households, or around twenty-four per cent of the total number of households in forty provinces of European Russia, had obtained individual proprietorship, and there were nearly three quarters of a million applications pending. With the aid of the Land Bank, nearly ten million hectares were purchased by the peasants from the landed gentry between 1906 and 1915. Resettlement in Siberia, which was a part of the Stolypin land reform, was also successful, and resulted in the creation in new areas of a prosperous and independent-minded peasantry. The "wager on the strong" was well under way when the war interrupted it. Even Lenin was forced to concede that the effect of Stolypin's policy might make it necessary for the social democrats to discard hopes of rallying the peasant mass to their side and to rely on the wage labourers on the land alone. Yet, while it is true that, given some more years of peace, the prospects of revolution in Russia might well have receded, the effect of the Stolypin reforms, uncompleted as they were, perhaps made the collapse in 1917 the more likely. For revolutions seem to occur where growth and high expectation are combined, and where an unyielding political order stands in the way of demands.

The so-called Western *zemstvo* crisis was an even more extreme example of Stolypin's indifference to constitutional niceties. Expanding the scope and activity of the local elected councils was an integral part of his programme, and many restrictions on their powers were removed on his initiative in 1906. The question of introducing the *zemstvo* system to the six western provinces was complicated by the fact that, unless modifications were made to the existing system of elections, the better educated and economically stronger Polish inhabitants would predominate in the resulting councils at the expense of the Russian population. The matter was debated in 1910 and 1911. The bill was eventually passed in the Duma, but ran into strong opposition in the State Council which, combined with a right-wing intrigue to oust Stolypin from power, resulted in its defeat.

Dr Tokmakoff devotes a detailed and useful chapter to an analysis of this crisis. Once again Stolypin resorted to Article 87 to get the bill passed, but, although he had taken this action in the interests of a policy approved by the Duma, his flouting of the normal constitutional process alienated all his former supporters in the Duma, and led to a severe decline of his political influence. Moreover, his intemperate action on this occasion, which had less justification perhaps than the resort to Article 87 in 1907, was a reaction against underhand intrigue by leaders of the right in the State Council and of the ambivalent behaviour of the Emperor.

Six months later Stolypin was dead, shot in the presence of the Emperor at a performance in the Kiev opera house. His assassin was both a former police agent and a one-time revolutionary: the question whether the murder was plotted by the police at the instigation of right extremists, or was the act of a penitent revolutionary, has never been resolved – though Dr Tokmakoff inclines to the latter view. In any case, the murder was symbolic of the way in which those who reject all-encompassing doctrines and systems as the solution for all ills – and such political actors have been rare in Russia – incur the enmity of both the extremes, the right and the left.

The classification of Stolypin by the late Professor Leontovitsch as a "conservative liberal" is probably not far off the mark, though the view has won few adherents. This is no doubt because those who find it hard to apply the term "liberal" to a man who was both a repressive upholder of order and one who achieved reform by defiance of the constitution, have not paused to reflect on Leontovitsch's detailed analysis of the whole concept of liberalism. This, based on the views of Hauriou, sees the essence of liberalism as both preserving an existing type of government or social order, and developing and perfecting its features in the direction of liberty by dismantling institutions which hamper such liberty. Above all, liberalism does not consist of the replacement of one type by another, which was the aim of the main Russian liberal party, the Kadets, and of course of the revolutionary parties.

The policy of Stolypin lay precisely in completing the process started by the emancipation of the serfs by granting them the legal equality which the reform of 1861 had failed to provide. This lack of legal equality – of a status in private law as distinct from the protection of public law – Stolypin saw as the main obstacle to the development of legal order in Russia, which he often stated, and no doubt believed to be, his main aim. Can legal order be achieved by illegal acts? Unfortunately the change in the status of the peasants had not gone far enough by the time the collapse came for this question to be answered.

1. See his *Geschichte des Liberalismus in Russland* (Frankfurt am Main 1957), pp. 168–76.

The Political Thought of the First Provisional Government

This article is reprinted by permission of the publishers from *Revolutionary Russia*, ed. Richard Pipes, Harvard University Press (Cambridge Mass.), Copyright © 1968 by Richard Pipes.

The First Provisional Government was formed on 2 March 1917, on the day of the Tsar's abdication. It lasted until 5 May 1917, when it gave way to the first coalition Provisional Government. The coalition was inspired by a crisis which provoked the government to issue on 26 April a declaration explaining its own record and views and urging the broadening of its composition to include socialists. This declaration[1] forms a convenient starting point from which to approach the political thought of the First Provisional Government.

The crisis that led to the formation of the coalition government was the result of demonstrations on 21 April in Petrograd against the Provisional Government. These were ostensibly provoked by a note of 18 April by the Foreign Minister, P. N. Miliukov, prepared for transmission to the Allied Powers, setting out the principles of the foreign policy of the Provisional Government.[2] The roots of the crisis, however, lay deeper. They derived from the growing rift between the Provisional Government and the "masses" – in other words, the anarchical Petrograd garrison, the Red Guards, and the mob – elements the Petrograd Soviet itself at this stage was only barely able to control.[3]

The main points of the declaration were as follows:

(1) That the Provisional Government had assumed power with the "unanimous support of the people" and with a policy "unanimously" endorsed by the country.

(2) This policy comprised the following: convocation of a Constituent Assembly at the earliest moment; civil liberties and

equality for all; democratic local self-government; extension of civil rights to the army with the preservation of military order and discipline; and continuation of the war "in close union with our allies".

(3) An enumeration of the extent to which these aims had already been achieved or embarked on.

(4) An expression of the anxieties of the Provisional Government over the difficulties that "threaten to become insurmountable". The Provisional Government "believes that the power of the state should be based not on violence and coercion, but on the consent of free citizens to submit to the power they themselves created". But "the repudiation of past coercive methods" has led to the result that "the less conscious and less organized strata of the population threaten to destroy the [country's] internal civil cohesion and discipline" and to produce internal disintegration and defeat at the front, raising the spectre of civil war and of anarchy, with consequent "reaction and the return of despotism".

(5) An appeal for order, coupled with a promise "of expanding its [own] composition by drawing into responsible government work representatives of those active creative forces of the country who have not previously taken direct . . . part in the government of the state". The declaration was accompanied by personal appeals to the socialists from Prince G. E. Lvov and A. F. Kerensky.

Although the First Provisional Government included a predominant number of leading Kadets (Miliukov, Shingarev, Manuilov, Nekrasov, Tereshchenko), it was for a variety of reasons in no way predominantly Kadet in its outlook or policy, and indeed it often departed from the official Kadet platform. There were a number of reasons for this phenomenon.

In the first place, there had been for some years past a considerable lack of agreement on policy among the Kadets themselves. In the course of the war a strong left wing had grown up inside the Kadet party with a leaning towards a mass movement, as distinct from the parliamentary opposition within the Duma constantly advocated by Miliukov.[4]

Second, this mass-orientated trend, insofar as it involved cutting across parties and institutions, had been traditional to the *zemstvo* constitutionalist movement that had grown up early in the century under the aegis of the Union of Liberation movement – Prince Lvov was perhaps most representative of it. So, in a sense, was the Progressive Bloc in the Duma. For the Progressive Bloc (like the Liberation Movement) was a union of like-minded men, not a coalition of political parties. The Progressive Bloc cut across the programme of the parties, whose members had agreed to form the Bloc. The Liberation Movement had sought the widest possible agreement on the simplest formula: "Down with the autocracy." The Progressive Bloc sought and found the same wide basis of appeal in two policy demands: first, a government enjoying the confidence of the country; and second, a full legislative programme to bring into being civil freedom and the rule of law.[5]

As the war wore on there was a growing sense both among the Progressive Bloc leaders and among the *zemstvo* leaders like Prince G. E. Lvov that it was essential for the liberal leaders to try to assume leadership over the masses for fear that otherwise the latter would spill over into anarchy and disorder. At the time of the formation of the Progressive Bloc (August 1915), a Central Committee had been formed in Moscow for the promotion of the aims of the Bloc by mass means which were very reminiscent of those of 1905 – that is, by pressure on the Emperor by *zemstvo* congresses and deputations. This Central Committee included among its leaders Prince G. E. Lvov and another future member of the Provisional Government, Konovalov.[6] A Moscow *okhrana* report on the mood of society at the end of February 1916 stressed first that in general all were agreed on the need to do nothing about the Tsar until the end of the war and then "to settle the score"; and second, that there was strong feeling in *zemgor* (union of *zemstva* and municipalities) circles on the need to link up with the working class movement and to assert influence and leadership over it.[7] This was also essentially the view at this time of the left wing of the Kadets, of whom Nekrasov was typical.[8] The tactics to be adopted were outlined by Nekrasov in a *zemstvo* banquet speech on 13 March 1916: what he had in mind was in fact nothing less than the re-creation of the *Soiuz Soiuzov* of 1905 – a super-union of all kinds and shapes of unions, forming one national front united on the slogan "Down with the autocracy".

Although very little can be confidently asserted about it, some evidence has come to light suggesting that the members of the First Provisional Government were further divided by the fact that, with the exception of Miliukov, its leading members were bound by some form of Freemasonry, which revived in Russia after 1905. In her guarded letter on the subject to N. V. Volsky (Valentinov) of 15 November 1955, E. D. Kuskova significantly said the aim of this movement was "to restore in this form the Union of Liberation and to work in the underground for the liberation of Russia". Miliukov, she states, had refused to have anything to do with this organization. However A. I. Guchkov (the Minister of War in the First Provisional Government), although a member of this Masonic organization, "was repeatedly threatened with exclusion" from it, according to Kuskova. This was because Guchkov had been involved in conspiratorial activity aimed at a "palace revolution" – of which, it would appear, his fellow Masons disapproved.[9] Certainly, this account by Kuskova is borne out by the evident manner in which Miliukov and Guchkov (the only two monarchists in the First Provisional Government) fell more and more out of step with their colleagues and were forced to resign within two months. It may also help explain why the bond of common membership of the Kadet party was of so little importance in maintaining any solidarity of political outlook between Miliukov, on the one hand, and Nekrasov and Tereshchenko (who were Masons), on the other.

Finally the predominant traditions of the Liberation Movement had little to do with liberalism or constitutionalism in any normal sense of the terms. They were in fact much closer to a form of populism: faith in the perfectibility of the people, regarded as being corrupted only by its institutions; and the lack of any sense of a danger from the left – a danger many Kadets understood. The Union of Liberation, on the contrary, believed that all opposition in Russia necessarily had to be extreme and violent and that the most extreme and violent elements would become milder once the autocracy had fallen. Similarly, the sense of the importance of order and institutions, not only on paper but of a kind that could in Russian conditions work in practice, formed no part of the tradition of Liberation. In short, here was a tradition typical of the Russian intelligentsia, which Lenin was the first to challenge from the left.

It is therefore easy to see why the declaration of 26 April found it necessary to stress repeatedly the unanimous support of the people at the moment when the authorities were trying to deal with the anarchy that was eventually to engulf the whole Provisional Government. This attitude to "the masses" was quite consistent with the views of a Lvov, Nekrasov, or Kerensky – though not of Miliukov. The weakness of the situation of the Provisional Government was already evident in the nature of this declaration of 26 April. Such legitimacy as the government could claim was in reality based on the precarious support and good will of the Petrograd "masses": in theory and formally the position was very different.

The Provisional Government that emerged from the Temporary Committee of the State Duma on 2 March received formal legitimacy from the Grand Duke Michael in his act of abdication of 3 March where it was described as having "come into existence at the initiative of the State Duma and being endowed with full power until such time as the Constituent Assembly . . . gave expression to the will of the people".[10] This act of abdication was drawn up by two eminent lawyers, Baron B. E. Nolde and V. D. Nabokov. It was a valiant attempt to endow the new government with legitimacy, and therefore with authority, by stressing its continuity with both the Duma and the Emperor. Legitimacy, however, requires more than an ingenious formula if it is to exercise its function of bolstering authority. In plain fact, the new government had not come into existence at the initiative of the Duma. It was brought about by an agreement concluded, on the one hand, between certain individual members of the Duma who called themselves a "Temporary Committee of the Duma" but who had never been approved, let alone elected, by the Duma and, on the other, by the Executive Committee of the Petrograd Soviet. Moreover, neither the Duma nor the Grand Duke disposed of full powers in Russian constitutional law. The Duma merely enjoyed certain legislative powers in conjunction with the State Council and the Emperor. The Grand Duke – even if one assumes that he inherited the powers of Nicholas II by the abdication of the latter, which is open to doubt – could not have inherited "full power", but only the limited powers the Emperor enjoyed after 1906. The formation of the Provisional Government was therefore a revolutionary act from the start.[11]

The Provisional Government would have been in a more solid and independent position had it really been appointed by and had it owed responsibility to the Duma. The problem of continuity would to some extent have been resolved. At this time the Duma still retained considerable popular support. Had the Duma survived it would have provided the basis of a legislative assembly that any government claiming to be democratic has to have. Without such a link to the Duma, the natural tendency was for the Provisional Government to become in the eyes of the public an executive government responsible to the Petrograd Soviet.[12] There were several factors that made it improbable that the Duma could in any circumstances assume the leadership at the critical moment, however theoretically desirable this course might have been.

First, although there had been some attempts both before the collapse of the Tsar's ministry in February and immediately after it to turn the Duma into the leader of the revolution, in general the Duma leaders were at no time fired with any determination to do this.

Second, even Miliukov, for whom the Duma was theoretically the natural institution to lead and guide popular discontent, had doubts about the moral right of the "June 1907" Duma – a product of Stolypin's *coup d'état* – to claim leadership of the revolution. At any rate, writing later in exile he tended to treat the Progressive Bloc as having in some way expiated the "original sin" of the June 1907 Duma and of having thereby acquired (after transforming itself into the Provisional Government) a moral right to lead the revolution that the Duma had lacked.[13]

And, lastly, the Duma was overtaken to some extent even before the revolution by the mass organizations that had been forming within and outside it and that exercised the real political influence – the Progressive Bloc, *zemgor*, and the like – in a word: *Liberation redivivum*. The Duma died, therefore, with the revolution, for which it was not prepared and which it did not really, as an institution, desire.

In plain fact – as distinct from myth – the Provisional Government from the start owed its existence not to the Duma, but to an agreement made between certain individual members of the Duma who had long overthrown the Duma and who became the Provisional Government; and to the Petrograd Soviet, which even if it did not represent the "people", certainly acted under the pressure, and in the interests, of the mutinous garrison. This becomes quite evident from the comparison of two documents: first, the list of demands made by the Executive Committee of the Soviet on 2

March to the Temporary Committee of the Duma as a condition for its support of the new government; and second, the "guiding principles" of policy enunciated by the Temporary Committee of the Duma at the time when the Provisional Government was formed. The two documents are virtually identical.[14]

The "guiding principles" were much more than principles: they were concrete policies, laying down the course of action the future government would follow. It was these policies that predetermined the impotence of the government and laid the foundations for future anarchy. The two documents contained the same eight points, which can be summarized as follows:

(1) Amnesty in all cases of a political and religious nature, including terrorist acts and military revolts.

(2) The basic civil freedoms and the extension of political freedoms to persons serving in the armed forces.

(3) The abolition of all restrictions based on class, religion, and nationality.

(4) The immediate preparation for the convocation of the Constituent Assembly on the basis of universal equal direct suffrage and secret ballot, which would determine the form of government and the constitution of the country.

(5) Substitution of the people's militia for the police.

(6) Elections to the organs of self-government to be held on the basis of universal equal and direct suffrage and secret ballot.

(7) Military units that took part in the revolutionary movement to be neither disarmed nor withdrawn from Petrograd.

(8) Soldiers to be freed from all restrictions in the exercise of civil rights to which other citizens are entitled, while preserving military discipline on duty.

There is nothing to suggest any serious disagreement between the future ministers of the Provisional Government and the Soviet representatives – indeed, the basic attitude to authority that is implied in the "guiding principles" closely follows the main lines of the populist philosophy of Prince Lvov, Kerensky, and Nekrasov. It was an outlook more remote than that of Miliukov and Guchkov – though, according to Sukhanov, our main source for the meeting of 1 March at which this agreement took place, Guchkov was not present. Miliukov's efforts were mainly directed to settling the issue of the legitimacy of the new government, a point to which all other persons present seem to have been completely blind. His vain efforts were aimed at the hopeless task (in which no one else supported him) of preserving the Romanov dynasty. There had as yet been no abdication, and it was still conceivable that the Grand Duke Michael would consent to act as regent for the heir. Miliukov's chance of success on this issue was of course negligible. It was for the same reason – the desire to preserve continuity and therefore to invest the new regime with legitimacy – that he insisted that the Soviet should issue a strong appeal for the support of the Provisional Government and the maintenance of order.[15] On the main question, that of yielding to the mutinous and anarchical garrison, Miliukov apparently contented himself with pointing out the dangers and with inserting into the guiding principles some phrases on discipline.[16]

V. A. Maklakov maintains that the only hope of survival of the Provisional Government would have been to use the old machinery to keep order and to replace the garrison with loyal troops.[17] Although this evaluation is no doubt correct hypothetically, it was in practice inconceivable that any member of this particular government would for a moment have thought of it. It was indeed contrary to the very being of the Russian *intelligent* to take action of this kind.

The term "dyarchy", referring to the dual role by the Provisional Government and its rival, the Soviet, launched by Guchkov (whose relations with the Soviet were strained from the very first) and then taken up by Lenin, scarcely fits the facts. There was indeed little dyarchy in the sense of rule by two opposed and conflicting institutions. The real dyarchy was more in the hearts of men than in rival institutions. The Provisional Government and the Soviet were at one in many respects, at any rate during the First Provisional Government – a fact correctly symbolized by the presence of Kerensky in the government. They started out on their path that was to lead to anarchy and mob rule jointly, not because one forced the other onto this course, but because they both ultimately believed in some of the same things. There were, of course, deep latent divisions between the two bodies – on the issue of the war above all. But the effect of these divisions was to become apparent only at a later stage.

The amnesty, the civil freedoms, the removal of discriminatory legislation and the like were certainly fully carried out – too fully, perhaps, for a time of war and incipient anarchy. No one could doubt the intoxication of the First Provisional Government with liberty or deny it the right to its proud boast that no blood had been spilt. It deserves some credit for rescuing the ex-Emperor in the early stages from the bloodthirsty clamour raised against him by the mob. On the other hand, the failure to remove the royal family to safety in Britain has been blamed equally on the hesitations of the Provisional Government and on those of Lloyd George: the former is alleged to have been restrained in its efforts through fear of popular feelings against the ex-Emperor and Empress, whereas the English premier is accused of pandering to radical opinion in England. This debatable question cannot be resolved here.[18]

There was, however, one respect in which the Provisional Government showed lack of understanding of the elementary principles of justice, and that was the case of the Commission of Enquiry into the collapse of the monarchy. True, the Commission was not a trial. But persons brought before it were in effect forced to incriminate themselves; and though possibly secure so long as the Provisional Government lasted, the accumulated evidence assured their execution once the Bolsheviks took over. The legal foundation of the Commission is strange: in so far as the Provisional Government was a revolutionary government (which most of its members claimed it to be, even Miliukov, the one minister always most anxious to stress the need for continuity of legitimacy), it was entitled to exact vengeance on the officials of the fallen regime. But vengeance was expressly contrary to the very first point of the Government's "guiding principles": amnesty in respect of *all* political matters. Surely this could not have been intended to apply to revolutionary acts only? If, as indeed the Provisional Government claimed, this was a judicial inquiry in respect of breaches of the law and practice ("malfeasance in office")[19] as they were before the revolution, there can be no doubt that the enquiry went much further – to the extent of investigating and bringing into the open actions by ministers that had been perfectly legal and within their duties at the time. Among such actions were abuse of Article 87 of the Fundamental Laws, the use of police agents and provocateurs among revolutionaries, and the like. Much of the time spent by the Commission of Enquiry related precisely to such issues.

The Constituent Assembly was the keystone of the political arch. In so far as there was to be any legitimation of the Provisional Government the Constituent Assembly alone could provide it. Everyone realized the urgency for summoning the Constituent Assembly. But those concerned, impressed by the solemnity of the whole matter, insisted on the most detailed preparations in order to assure the most equitable franchise possible. With hindsight such scruples may appear a terrible mistake, but at the time they accorded with the cardinal principle of the sanctity of the people's will. In this respect the Soviet was perhaps more realistic than the Provisional Government, in perceiving the need for speed in convoking a Constituent Assembly: indeed, it was as a concession to the Soviet that the government agreed that the Constituent Assembly should be convoked "no later than the middle of summer".[20] A council was set up on 25 March 1917, the expert members of which were to elect a drafting commission from among their own number "for the preliminary technical study" of the complicated questions involved.[21] At the time the task seemed to require a few weeks: but two months elapsed before the Second Provisional Government fixed the first meeting of the council for 25 May.[22] The idealism and perfectionism of the Provisional Government were its own undoing: it never saw the Constituent Assembly as a device to secure its own legitimacy – indeed, there is nothing to indicate that, with the exception of Miliukov, any member of the Provisional Government from the outset entertained any doubts on the subject of the government's legitimacy. As Prince Lvov told the first meeting of the council called to draft measures for the convocation of the Constituent Assembly, they would lay the foundation of the future order: "The Constituent Assembly must be the essence of all the spiritual and mental forces of the people, it must be the spokesman of their mind and heart." No effort was considered too great for the achievement of this ideal; but the practical results of this attitude, as is now so obvious, were catastrophic. The council could have done the work faster, the chairman (Kokoshkin) told its members, by appointing a small commission of experts to draft the electoral law. But the Provisional Government would not allow this procedure: it took the view that "it was not merely a matter of technical or theoretical perfection of the electoral law". The law should conform to the wishes and interests of all sections of the population, and these had to be ascertained.[23] The rest of the story is outside the scope of this paper: the date for the elections was fixed on 14 June for 17 September, in the teeth of objections from the council members that November was the earliest possible date, since the compilation of the electoral rolls depended upon the completion of the *zemstvo* and municipal reforms which were then still in their early stages. On 9 August the date of the elections was postponed until 12 November. The course of history might have been different if the members of the Provisional Government had been swayed less by populist idealism and more by a sense of practical urgency.

Enough has been said to show that the cardinal axis around which the faith of the Provisional Government revolved was the belief that the new order must be based on co-operation and trust in the people, and not on force. So far as its members were concerned this was the purpose of the revolution (which they had, after all, not wanted to happen when it did). This outlook was reflected in the government's actions; and its political philosophy may be said to have directly influenced the three major acts that sealed the fate of the Provisional Government: its policy towards the Petrograd garrison, the reform of the militia, and the reform of the administration. The course of action of the Provisional Government in these matters can only be sketched in outline here, in order to illustrate its basic political outlook, resting on confidence in the people as its central concept of the government of men, and the initial rejection of force, which was soon to lead to the fatal sequence of anarchy followed by force – reluctance, inadequacy, and the fact of being too late.

The decision to leave the Petrograd garrison its arms and to guarantee it from being sent to the front was already sealed in the first days by the promise contained in the "guiding principles". There is nothing to suggest that this promise had been wrung from reluctant ministers by the Soviet. Indeed, the whole mood of euphoria which characterized the first chaotic days, when realization dawned that the revolution had actually happened, was not conducive to sober thinking. Anarchical, idle, and demoralized, the Petrograd mutineers were to become an important element in Lenin's strategy. It may be that in theory the replacement of the garrison by the better disciplined and more loyal groups from the area of the front could have saved the Provisional Government:

the question is academic, since the government rejected any such move in the first days of its existence. Subsequently, even if it had desired to take such action, it was too late.

Consequences equally grave flowed from the decision of the First Provisional Government on the nature of the new instruments of coercion that the government considered it right to create: the militia and the administrative machine. The legislation on these matters was put into effect under the direct control of the Prime Minister, Prince G. E. Lvov, who also held the post of Minister of the Interior. Lvov's somewhat sentimental populism was perhaps greater than that of his colleagues, but again the "guiding principles", as agreed on from the start, do not lead one to infer that Lvov met with any serious dissent from his colleagues. The details cannot be dealt with here: the main outline illustrates the political principles behind the actions. The immediate abolition of the death penalty (a sign of "genuine magnanimity" reflecting "the impulse of the popular soul", as Vladimir Nabokov wrote at the time) was a foregone conclusion, as were also a series of enactments designed to mitigate the severe and brutal Russian penal regime. The Department of Police was abolished on 10 March, and the gendarmerie on 19 March.[24] After a short period in which policing was entrusted to a temporary militia, a new militia was established on 17 April. It was placed under the *zemstvo* and municipal authorities, in contrast to the former police, which had been highly centralized; and its powers and responsibilities were carefully circumscribed in what on paper was a very liberal and fair police statute.[25]

But, unhappily, good intentions were not sufficient. The truth seems to be that the Provisional Government in the critical first days was more anxious to assert its good intentions than to give proof of any awareness of the danger of anarchy. Two documents, of 4 and 6 March respectively, illustrate this frame of mind most clearly. The first contains the decision of the Provisional Government to "remove temporarily from their duties governors and vice-governors" – the backbone of the existing administrative machine. Their powers were "temporarily" vested in chairmen of *zemstvo* boards; the question of their position in the provinces where *zemstvo* institutions did not exist was to be "left open for the time being". The second document, of 6 March, is an appeal by the Provisional Government to the population. After reciting how the failure of the constitution granted in 1905 forced the people to take power in its own hands in 1917, it records that "the unanimous revolutionary upsurge of the people" led to the setting up of the Provisional Government thanks to the resolution of the Duma. There then followed two new promises, as well as others that were in part already contained in the "guiding principles": to carry the war to a victorious conclusion and to observe all agreements entered into with the Allies (neither of these provisions had been included on 2 March in the "guiding principles"), civil liberties, amnesty, democracy, the Constituent Assembly, and the like. The appeal ends: "In carrying out these tasks the Provisional Government is inspired by the faith that in so doing it will be carrying out the people's will, and that the whole people will support it in an honest endeavour to ensure the happiness of Russia. From this faith it draws its courage. Only in the friendly co-operation of all in its efforts does it see the guarantee for the triumph of a new order."[26] There is not a word in the whole document about the need for discipline, order, and obedience to the new authorities.

The reform of the administration envisaged not only the abolition of the gubernatorial system, but also the extension and democratization of the whole system of municipal government. It was an ambitious and idealistic scheme doomed to failure in face of the anarchy that the Provisional Government had done so much itself to encourage. For in truth it placed its faith in a greater response from a free people than that people, after centuries of despotic government, was capable of giving.[27]

There were two topics on which the "guiding principles" agreed upon with the Soviet had remained silent: land and war. Their omission provoked criticism in the Soviet from the left-wing minority.[28] Because these were the topics on which most controversy was likely to arise, their omission from the original agreement was perhaps inevitable. In the case of the land question the Provisional Government could quite properly take refuge in the view that this issue was so momentous in its consequences for the future of Russia that only the Constituent Assembly could decide it. It was not until after the end of the term of office of the First Provisional Government that any broad principles of future agrarian policy were enunciated. The Central Land Committee, at its first session, on 20 May, stated its views on the "general direction" of the future land reform: these included nationalization of land for the benefit of the toiling peasants as a basic principle.[29] Since the villagers remained relatively quiet for the first few weeks of the new regime, this shelving of the question did not immediately raise serious difficulties. Such peasant disturbances as did arise, for example in Kazan Province, were dealt with by the Provisional Government not by force, which was rejected, but by persuasion and exhortation.[30] It was only after April, with the tide of agrarian disorders mounting, that the Provisional Government felt compelled to take more concrete steps towards the solution of the land problem. On 21 April a series of Land Committees (first promised on 19 March) were set up and charged with the task of collecting the information upon which the ultimate future of the land would be decided.[31] At that date it was still believed to be possible to hold off the assaults of the peasants.

The question of war and peace was to prove the key to the whole situation – though this was not yet apparent at the start of the First Provisional Government's term of office. Both the government and the Soviet majority were agreed at the outset on a broad policy of "war to victory", supported by a "democratized" army, liberated from the indignities which the old regime had inflicted upon it. But as time went on and the effects of Bolshevik propaganda and of impatience over the land problem grew in the army, the question of the war began to assume gigantic proportions. The whole issue as to whether the policy of democratization of the army also helped to bring about this aggravation is perhaps debatable; but there is no doubt that the policy had the effect of creating favourable conditions for the conduct of the anti-war propaganda to which the Bolsheviks were soon devoting their main effort and financial resources. The question of war aims is outside the scope of this paper. But the incident over Miliukov's note of 18 April, which caused the reshuffling of the First Provisional Government, illustrates the explosive nature of the whole problem. The note, by its omission of phrases renouncing the intention to annex foreign territory after victory, could be interpreted by the radical minded as an affirmation of Russian enthusiasm to exact after victory the territorial compensations agreed on with the Allies. Miliukov's views on war aims and on Russia's national interests were certainly closer to Kadet policy than to the views of his more radical colleagues, who were much more inclined to accept as their own the Soviet view of "peace without annexations". Of course, Miliukov could argue that the reference to the strict observance of the treaties made with the Allies included in the Appeal of the Provisional Government published on 6 March (which was discussed above) also included by implication Russia's claim to the Straits after victory. But such an argument (though no doubt correct) would have been really impossible to maintain in the atmosphere prevailing at the time in the capital. And so, although the text of Miliukov's note had been approved by the whole government, the same government considered it expedient to jettison Miliukov.[32] Miliukov's note was now "explained" in an explanatory note of 22 April, which embodied the hallowed renunciation of annexation, and the principle of a just peace based upon the self-determination of all peoples. Such was the success of the Provisional Government's political diplomacy that the explanation was accepted by the Soviet without qualification or dissent.[33] And yet, the harmony between the majority of the First Provisional Government and the Petrograd Soviet at this date probably reflected more accurately the realities of the situation than the incongruous presence in the government of Guchkov and Miliukov. When these two ministers resigned, a coalition cabinet including socialists was formed, and this change represented a recognition of what had been a fact from the start – that the First Provisional Government had never been a liberal government based (as it claimed) on the Duma, but a radical revolutionary government based on "the people".

What bound the members of the First Provisional Government together was not so much a political philosophy as an intellectual tradition. This was true of all, except for Guchkov and possibly Miliukov. They were the heirs of the Russian intelligentsia, alienated from all institutions of the old regime, leaning on "the people" with an almost religious faith, passionate for liberty without any strong sense that liberty can only exist within the framework of order. They had hated the old order, but they had also feared revolution. When it came they could not lead it because they were the slaves of their own vision of the people – a people only too easy a prey to extremism and anarchy. Because they rejected coercion, their only hope and indeed policy was to woo the people with concessions, exhortations, trust, and love – and they failed.

Writing in August or September 1915, Zinaida Gippius recorded this penetrating judgement in her diary:

> The right – they understand nothing, they are going nowhere, and they refuse to let anyone else go anywhere.
>
> The centre – they understand, but they are going nowhere, they stand and wait (for what?).
>
> The left – they understand nothing but are going like the blind without knowing whither or to what ultimate aim.[34]

So it came about that in March 1917 it was the blind who led the halt along to the final drama of October. This is not to condemn the Provisional Government, so much as to record that, being what they were, they could not have acted otherwise. The causes lie further back than in the period between March and May 1917, or March and October 1917. There are many stages in the story: the failure of the moderate *zemstvo* movement around the turn of the century to achieve that degree of co-operation between society and the monarchy that it sought and that the monarchy repeatedly rejected; the success of the more extreme Union of Liberation movement that, in the shape of the October Manifesto of 1905, won a constitution which was, in Russian conditions, unworkable; Stolypin's *coup d'état* of June 1907, which certainly made the Duma more workable, but which also alienated the more impatient and idealistic liberals from the Duma for which they had laboured; and then, finally, the turning away during the war of the liberals to the wider mass organizations as instruments of influence that had the effect of undermining the one institution that rightfully should have become the centre of authority when the monarchy fell – the Duma. These wider organizations – the Progressive Bloc, the *zemgor*, even perhaps the mysterious Masonic organization – provided a basis for unity that the more tightly knit institutions like the political parties could not provide. But it was a unity based on visions and on myths, rather than on concrete policies – "the people", "democracy", "government of confidence". There was danger in these visions, as events were to show. Pasternak most perceptively records the sense of "the people" in 1917. "The revolution burst forth against our will like a sigh that has been too long repressed. Everyone breathed again, was born again; all suffered transformation and complete change. One could almost say that there were two revolutions for each of us: one, the personal one, and the other the common one."[35] It would be quite untrue to say that the members of the First Provisional Government did not perceive the dangers inherent in this situation. But they obstinately believed, or persuaded themselves, or hoped, that the virtue and wisdom of the Russian people must triumph in the end.

As heirs of the intelligentsia the members of the First Provisional Government shared both its virtue and its main vice: the idealism; the innocent faith in the perfectibility of man; the detestation of violence and coercion; the love of freedom; the compassion for and the sense of debt to the people – but also the lack of practical sense in discerning Russian reality. "What right have we, the brains of the country, to insult with our rotten bourgeois distrust the wise, calm, and knowing revolutionary people?" – so wrote Alexander Blok in his diary on 19 June 1917.[36]

Two weeks later the Bolshevik dress rehearsal for October was in progress in the streets of Petrograd. It was Lenin, himself sprung from the intelligentsia (but who rejected, or who reinterpreted, the traditional virtues of the *intelligent*) who was soon to provide that discernment of Russian reality that his opponents lacked and to restore in a new form the overthrown autocracy.

Note: All dates in this article are given in Old Style.

1. Reprinted as doc. 1075 in *The Russian Provisional Government, 1917 – Documents*, selected and edited by Robert Paul Browder and Alexander F. Kerensky, 3 vols (Stanford, Calif. 1961), vol. III, pp. 1249–1251. Cited hereafter as Browder and Kerensky.
2. *ibid.*, II, doc. 964, p. 1098.
3. The report of the examining magistrate on the demonstrations of 21 April leaves no doubt at all that this was carefully organized as a move against the Provisional Government with the aid of the armed, Bolshevik-controlled Red Guards. The role of the Bolsheviks in planning the disturbance was evident, but the magistrate either could not or thought it more politic not to pin responsibility on any individuals. *ibid.*, III, doc. 1071, pp. 1242–1244. Lenin on 21 April called for the overthrow of the Provisional Government by demanding that the "handful of capitalists" be made to yield to the soviets. However, two days later, on 23 April, he had recognized the authority that the Soviet still exercised over the crowds, and he now called for strict observance by all Bolsheviks of the prohibitions against armed demonstrations that the Soviet had issued. See V. I. Lenin, *Sochineniia*, 3rd ed., XX, pp. 208 and 224–5.
4. See *Burzhuaziia nakanune fevral'skoi revoliutsii*, ed. B. B. Grave (Moscow-Leningrad 1927), doc. 62, pp. 145–8, reproducing a Moscow *okhrana* report on the October 1916 Kadet conference. See also docs. 77 and 78, *ibid.*, pp. 175–8, for similar left-wing trends on the eve of the revolution, in January 1917.

5. See Grave, *Burzhuaziia*, doc. 12, pp. 26–9, for their agreed policy programme published on 25 August 1915.
6. *ibid.*, doc. 14, pp. 33–8.
7. *ibid.*, doc. 32, pp. 75–81.
8. *ibid.*, doc. 33, pp. 81–3. See also doc. 64, pp. 152–4, dated 1 November 1916, that shows that Protopopov was aware of this policy and was trying to counteract it by the methods which had once been used by Plehve, the prohibition of *zemstvo* gatherings.
9. Kuskova's letter to Volsky was published, together with some other relevant letters, in Grigorii Aronson, *Rossiia nakanune revoliutsii – Istoricheskiie etiudy* (New York 1962), pp. 138–43. The evidence on the whole question has now been examined by G. Katkov in *Russia 1917 – The February Revolution* (London 1967), pp. 163–73. For A. F. Kerensky's account of the matter, see Alexander Kerensky, *Russia and History's Turning Point* (New York 1965), pp. 88–91.
10. Browder and Kerensky, I, doc. 101, p. 116.
11. For a full discussion of this question see S. P. Melgunov, *Martovskie dni 1917 goda* (Paris 1961), pp. 356–67; and Katkov, *Russia 1917*, pp. 409–15.
12. The popular attitude towards the Duma before and just after the revolution is far from clear. There is no doubt that, perhaps for lack of an alternative, many sectors of discontent at different times looked to it with hope and confidence. Even if confidence in the Duma was fairly low among the masses, according to the police reports for October 1916 quoted in Grave, *Burzhuaziia*, docs. 58 and 75 (pp. 136–9, 168–9), the vigorous attacks by the Duma on the government at the end of the year certainly raised its stock by January 1917. In the early period of the Petrograd Soviet there was apparently a tendency among the Mensheviks to look upon the Duma as a kind of brake that would "prevent the revolution from serving as a foundation for a bourgeois dictatorship". (See Marc Ferro, "Les Débuts du soviet de Petrograd (27/28 février 1917 ancien style)" *Revue Historique*, CCXXIII, April/June 1960, pp. 353–80.) Above all, among the troops of the army in the field, as contrasted with the garrison troops of the capital, during the first weeks after the abdication confidence in the Duma was high – see *Razlozhenie armii v 1917 godu*, ed. N. E. Kakurin (Moscow-Leningrad 1925), pp. 25–7. In this context it is worth recalling the argument of a right-wing defensist Social Democratic delegate to the First Conference of Soviets held in April that in effect an unwritten constitution had come into being under which the Provisional Government represented the ministry and the Soviet corresponded to the legislature or the legislative chamber, to which the ministry is responsible. This was not an unreasonable picture of the situation as it must have appeared to many at the time. See Melgunov, *Martovskie dni*, p. 401.
13. P. N. Miliukov, *Vospominaniia (1859–1917)*, vol. II (New York 1955), pp. 207, 215, 275, 303.
14. Browder and Kerensky, I, docs. 104 and 112, pp. 125–6, 135–6.
15. In the end the appeal was very lukewarm indeed and in qualified terms. See Browder and Kerensky, I, doc. 113, p. 136.
16. The extracts from Sukhanov are reprinted in Browder and Kerensky as doc. 102, I, pp. 117–24. Miliukov's account in his memoirs (*Vospominaniia*, II, pp. 306–9) differs in some respects from Sukhanov's. In particular he states that Prince Lvov was absent, while Sukhanov says he kept quiet. Miliukov also refers to a late appearance on the second day of Guchkov and says that Guchkov insisted on some expression of continuity between the Duma and the Provisional Government.
17. *La chute du régime tsariste. Interrogatoires des ministres etc. du Gouvernement provisoire de 1917 (Comptes rendus sténographiques)*, préface de B. Maklakoff (Paris 1927).

18. All the available evidence on the question was examined by S. P. Melgunov. See his *Sud'ba Imperatora Nikolaia II posle otrecheniia* (Paris, n.d. [1944]), pp. 51–8 and 162–90. Melgunov was inclined to blame the Provisional Government rather more than the British. This much-debated question should now be capable of final solution since the British Cabinet papers for 1917 are open to public inspection.
19. The act of 11 March 1917, setting up the Extraordinary Commission of Enquiry, is doc. 165 in Browder and Kerensky, I, p. 194.
20. Browder and Kerensky, I, doc. 401, p. 434.
21. *ibid.*, doc. 403, pp. 435–6.
22. *ibid.*, doc. 405, p. 437.
23. *ibid.*, doc. 407, pp. 438–41.
24. *ibid.*, docs. 196 and 198, pp. 216, 217–18.
25. *ibid.*, doc. 200, pp. 218–21.
26. *Velikaia oktiabr'skaia sotsialisticheskaia revoliutsiia. Dokumenty I materialy. Revoliutsionnoe dvizhenie v Rossii posle sverzheniia samoderzhaviia* (Moscow 1957), I, docs. 323 and 326, pp. 422, 424–6.
27. See Browder and Kerensky, docs. 219–272, I, pp. 243–316 for details of the municipal and *zemstvo* reforms and for details of the mounting chaos in the provinces.
28. A. Shliapnikov, *Semnadtsatyi god*, I, 2nd ed. (Moscow, n.d.), p. 197.
29. See Browder and Kerensky, II, doc. 476, pp. 538–44.
30. See *Revoliutsionnoe dvizhenie* (cited in note 26), I, doc. 35, p. 46, for a minute of a meeting of the Provisional Government of 9 March.
31. Browder and Kerensky, II, docs. 467 and 471, pp. 524–5, 528–32. See also *ibid.*, doc. 474, pp. 534–6, which shows that at that date the Soviet was in complete agreement with the Provisional Government on the question of leaving all the ultimate decisions until the Constituent Assembly met.
32. For the note of 18 April see Browder and Kerensky, II, doc. 964, p. 1098. The note of 22 April is reprinted as doc. 966, *ibid.*, p. 1100. For the reference to the Appeal of 6 March, see note 26 above.
33. *ibid.*, doc. 967, pp. 1100–1.
34. Z. Gippius, *Siniaia kniga. Peterburgskii dnevnik, 1914–1918* (Belgrade 1929), p. 32.
35. Boris Pasternak, *Doktor Zhivago* (Ann Arbor 1958), p. 148.
36. *Dnevnik A. A. Bloka, 1917–1921*, ed. P. M. Medvedev (Leningrad 1928), II, p. 26.

Struve, Liberal on the Left

This review of Richard Pipes, *Struve, Liberal on the Left 1870–1905*, Harvard University Press (Cambridge, Mass. 1970), first appeared in *The Russian Review*, July 1971.

Petr Berngardovich Struve (1870–1944) is regarded by many as the most luminous intellect of his generation in Russia. Certainly, there was no subject in the many fields of history, politics, or economics which he explored on which he failed to shed new light: to have read Struve on Marx, on the Russian revolution or on serfdom is to have acquired for life a new perspective on the subject. In this, the first of two volumes in which Professor Pipes plans to complete his biography of him, we first see Struve as a young marxist; then forsaking marxism for his own kind of radical liberalism which led directly to the revolution of 1905; and we leave him on the threshold of the discovery of a new, and different – some would say the only true – devotion to liberty combined with order which was to remain with him for the rest of his life. This was not a sign of inconsistency, for Struve was consistent in that the liberty of the individual remained for him the prime and guiding goal in politics: experience led him from one means of achieving it to another. In his first phase, as a marxist, Struve exercised a greater influence on his contemporaries than any other Russian writer – not excluding Plekhanov. From Plekhanov or Lenin one had to swallow whole a rather bizarre dogma, totally irrelevant for Russia. Struve's eclecticism, indeed his own transformation of marxism, is usually completely misdescribed in the terms "legal marxism", or "revisionism". In Struve's hands marxism becomes an appeal for Westernization rather than a theory of revolution. Capitalism is thus seen as a necessary preparatory phase of apprenticeship out of which liberty and order are inevitably born. With the aid of reason socialism will then be naturally created. There is no irrational and quite unconvincing mythology in Struve about "withering away" of the state: it is marxism adapted for traditional civilized Europeans, and not a blueprint for the victory of the proletariat in a class war. As he tells us himself, he forsook marxism when he came to realize that the defence of liberty was in no sense the prerogative of any one class. But the next label, "liberal", usually attached to Struve after 1900 is equally misleading. As used in Europe, at any rate, "liberal" means one whose devotion to order and well-established institutions is as great as his devotion to liberty, since he knows that the latter will inevitably perish without the former. This was the lesson that Struve had to learn in practice between 1902 when he founded the paper *Liberation* and 1905 when the leaders of the radical movement which developed out of the paper had unleashed chaos and disorder in Russia from which the semi-constitutional regime of 1906 resulted. By then, as we shall learn from Professor Pipes's next volume, Struve no longer believed in such popular radical myths as the one that liberty has no enemies on the left; or that Russia's problems could be solved immediately by instantaneous universal franchise, because "democracy" would grow from it. "I regard an *active*, *revolutionary* tactic to be the only sensible one for Russian Constitutionalists to adopt," he wrote on 5 (18) March 1905. But Struve had not as yet reckoned with the social democrats, from whom indeed the liberals of 1905 for the most part could hardly be distinguished, and to whose revolutionary tactics they opened the door then – as they would do in 1917. The realization came, somewhat belatedly, a few months later when he wrote on 12 October 1905, with Lenin in mind (as he disclosed years later): "Social Democracy wishes to overcome the reactionary violence of autocracy with the revolutionary power of the people. It has in common with its enemy the cult of power: it merely desires a different carrier of power and assigns it different tasks. In its world outlook, law is not the idea of the just but the command of the strong." He never swerved from this view again.

Professor Pipes has put us all in his debt by his lucid, enormously well-researched and documented and illuminating portrait of a great mind. Indeed, this biography will take the place of a history of liberalism in Russia – a subject which, since publishers obstinately refuse to translate Leontovitsch's *Geschichte des Liberalismus in Russland*, has not hitherto found a worthy historian in English. But just because Professor Pipes's biography is a history of liberalism in Russia it is necessary to challenge some of his judgements. It is quite untrue in my opinion to suggest as he does that Russian social democracy outside Russia was at any time dominated by "economism" – that is to say the doctrine that workers should never engage in political action. This eccentric view (which incidentally in practical terms was nonsense, since no boundary could be drawn between economic and political industrial action in Russian conditions) was only held by about three intellectuals at most. But the label "economism" was a convenient one for Lenin to stick on all social democrats who disagreed with him – and, like so many of Lenin's labels, it is still in position today. It is time it was dislodged. Professor Pipes has also failed to convince one reader that Lenin seriously contemplated a genuine alliance with Struve and the liberals at the outset of *Iskra*'s career. He was after the money which Struve could raise, certainly. But in the light of Lenin's whole thought after September 1899 any genuine alliance with liberals seems inconceivable: the whole purpose of *Iskra* in Lenin's mind was to divide not to unite. Finally, it is unfortunate that Professor Pipes did not devote some profounder analysis to the views of D. N. Shipov – one of the most significant and most underestimated figures in Russian liberalism, whose policy at the time around 1904 was a good deal wiser than Struve's.

This splendid book, for all these minor carpings, and the second volume as well as Professor Pipes's forthcoming edition of Struve's works will be awaited with eagerness and welcomed with gratitude. The mature Struve is indeed the more fascinating. For he discovered after 1905 that he was too sceptical and critical, wise one should say, to embrace any overall master-theory of society. As S. L. Frank wrote of him when he died: "His attitude to reality can be expressed in the words of Goethe, that life is set into a theory only as a live body is set in the cross on which it is crucified." A rare phenomenon indeed among Russian intellectuals; but then Struve was no run of the mill intellectual.

Struve, Liberal on the Right

This review of Richard Pipes, *Struve, Liberal on the Right 1905–1944*, Harvard University Press (Cambridge, Mass. 1980), first appeared in the *Times Literary Supplement*, 20 June 1980.

This is the second, and final, volume of Professor Pipes's monumental biography of Petr Berngardovich Struve – an enterprise to which he has devoted twenty years. The first volume appeared ten years ago, and was rightly acclaimed not only as a study of the first part of the career of one of the most remarkable men to emerge from modern Russia, but as a considerable contribution to the history of that tender plant, Russian liberalism. For although Struve started his intellectual odyssey as a marxist – he was, indeed, the author of the Manifesto of the foundation congress of the Russian Social Democratic Labour Party in 1898 – it was not the revolutionary element in marxism that attracted him. On the contrary, in his first book *Critical Remarks on the Question of Russia's Economic Development* he argued the plainly "revisionist" view that Marx's conception of social change was basically evolutionary, rather than revolutionary. He was drawn to marxism because it seemed to him to offer the hope of the kind of modernization for Russia on which in his view liberty depended. Liberty was, and remained, his main and constant preoccupation. Before long he had broken with the social democrats, and in 1903 helped to found the Liberation Movement, which more than any other political group influenced the emergence of the revolutionary year of 1905. When towards the end of that year the Constitutional Democrat (Kadet) Party came into existence, he joined it and was elected to its Central Committee at the beginning of 1906.

Professor Pipes was right to make the break between his two volumes in 1905 since this year proved a watershed in Struve's intellectual development. For, after the inauguration in Russia of a semi-constitutional order, Struve became increasingly alienated from the Kadets, who at times pursued a radical policy little different from that of the socialists. As he stated in December 1905: "Our slogan is the rights of individuals and the rights of the people. We are sworn enemies . . . of all coercion, regardless of whether it emanates from authority or from anarchy. For us only that revolution is sacred which is carried out in the name of law and freedom . . ." Before long, he withdrew from active politics and embarked on his criticism of the intelligentsia – that powerful section of Russian society before 1917 which has eluded definition, but which was certainly characterized by alienation from the official centres of authority.

One of the other causes of Struve's growing estrangement from the Kadet party was his advocacy after 1908 (in the pages of *Russian Thought* which he edited) of a vigorous, but realistic, policy of imperialism and Russian nationalism. But Struve never embraced the extremes of Great Russian nationalism: anti-semitism and the supremacy of the Orthodox Church. He advocated full civil rights for Jews, and regarded religion as a highly personal matter.

His main charge against the intelligentsia was that it had failed to grasp the changes wrought by the 1905 revolution and to adjust its political behaviour to the new order. At the same time he placed the greater blame on the autocracy which kept the intelligentsia in "a condition of unhealthy artificial separation and estrangement from life". (This criticism of the autocracy showed how far Struve was from that adherence to the right with which his left-wing opponents repeatedly charged him.) He blamed the intelligentsia for its unprincipled attitude to the law, and for believing that "every action is allowable if it is useful to the revolution". The intelligentsia, in his view, was anarchical, fearful of responsibility, incapable of compromise and unable to grasp that beyond the "government" which they opposed there was another entity, "the state", which they should support. The result was that the government combined with the illiterate masses in a joint attack on the educated class. Struve's assault on the intelligentsia culminated with the publication in 1909 of the celebrated symposium *Landmarks* (*Vekhi*)[1] in which he and six other contributors argued from different angles around the central theme that the individual precedes society and that spiritual re-education precedes political reform. In spite of the editor's (M. Gershenzon) denial, the volume was a trenchant attack on the intelligentsia, and produced a furore of protest from both the left and the right. *Landmarks* can be criticized in some respect – as Pipes does. But its main thesis was proved up to the hilt in 1917 when the intelligentsia failed to rally in support of law and order, and opened the way to the dark age of Bolshevism.

During the First World War Struve played an important part as chairman of the committee for limiting trade with the enemy. He visited England in 1916 (where his growing reputation as an economist and publicist had gained him an Honorary Ll.D. at Cambridge), returning to Russia in 1917 – the year in which, on the eve of the February revolution, he successfully defended his doctoral dissertation at Kiev University, and a few months later was elected a member of the Academy of Sciences.

The revolution of March 1917 did not fill Struve with elation – in contrast to virtually all other representatives of the "opposition camp". His anxiety stemmed from the fear that without a lawful transfer of authority from the bureaucracy to representatives of "society" Russia would collapse, since the intelligentsia's utopian aspirations disguised as "class struggle" would unleash destructive anarchy. After the Bolshevik coup in November 1917 Struve identified himself as closely and energetically as he could with the political side of the White movement of military resistance to Bolshevism. He believed that by so doing he was fighting for the cause of liberty in Russia. His last service was with General Wrangel, whom he did much to promote as the head of the final Russian anti-Bolshevik government. With the defeat of Wrangel, there began (in 1920) Struve's long years of exile, which lasted until his death in 1944.

Life in emigration was spent by Struve first in Paris, and then in Prague, where he became Professor of Political Economy at the Russian Juridical Faculty established at Prague University for the training of lawyers and civil servants for a future democratic Russia. After an unhappy period as editor of a monarchic periodical *Renaissance* (*Vozrozhdenie*) he settled in Belgrade in 1928, where he was to remain until 1942. The last years of his life were spent in German-occupied Paris. Throughout his years of exile he played a leading and energetic role in Russian émigré politics. He opposed with all his might both the facile optimism of the many, especially those who followed the Kadet leader Miliukov, who claimed to see evolution in Soviet Russia towards a nationalist bourgeois order, and the extremism of the monarchists. As has always been the case with the small band of Russian thinkers who have followed the middle road, Struve was abused as a rabid reactionary by the left, and as a dangerous red by the right.

Struve's literary output extended over a vast range of subjects. His main efforts were devoted to economics and history, but literature and sociological and political analysis, among other subjects, feature in the 663 items listed by Professor Pipes in his bibliography (quite apart from hundreds of newspaper articles). Professor Pipes provides an extended analysis of Struve's economic writings, but leaves judgement on their significance to some future economist. His historical writings display immense erudition and originality – it is much to be regretted that his major work, a comprehensive social and economic history of Russia, remained unfinished. He will probably be best remembered for his penetrating analysis of Russian politics in general and the Russian revolution in particular, and his tireless advocacy of liberty within the framework of legal order.

Struve described himself as a "liberal conservative" – a term first applied by Prince Viazemsky to Pushkin, whom Struve held in lifelong veneration. The list of Russian liberal conservatives is not long: apart from Struve, Viazemsky and Pushkin, the historian Karamzin, Admiral Mordvinov, the novelist Turgenev, the *zemstvo* activist Dmitry Shipov, Boris Chicherin and A. F. Koni, the jurists, Stolypin, and a few others. They are all distinguished by their belief that freedom, which is the prime human desideratum, can only flourish on a foundation of legal order and private property; that it can be achieved only by gradual evolution and not by revolution; and that it must be based on the foundation of recognizing the value of one's national heritage. But in this context Struve completely rejected the idea so dear to the Slavophiles and the populists (populism was for him "the syphilis of Russian thought") that Russia should pursue some separate path from Western Europe – national Russia was for him personified by Peter the Great and Pushkin.

Like so much of Struve's political writing, his analysis of the

Russian revolution has stood up particularly well. He rejected the frequently drawn parallel between the Russian and French revolutions, because the societies in which they took place were fundamentally different. The distinctive cause of the Russian revolution was the traditional non-involvement (for which he squarely blamed the autocracy) in the political process of Russia's two principal population groups – the educated elite and the peasant masses. The educated minority were, as a result of the denial of political participation, imbued with the "psychology and traditions of political apostasy", while the peasants, being denied until too late any sense of private property, and consequently the appreciation of legal order, were incapable of resisting the anarchy of 1917. Thus boldly stated this argument is perhaps open to some rejoinders. But the truth of its basic elements is discernible in Soviet Russia to this day, justifying Struve's contention that the Soviet regime had no potentiality for evolution towards freedom under the law.

Professor Pipes has achieved a major work of scholarship and his long years of labour on the career of this remarkable Russian (German on both sides incidentally – his mother was Baroness Rosen) put us all in his debt. His judgements of Struve are critical, but always perceptive. His analysis of his views, in all cases where I am familiar with the original, is scrupulously fair and accurate. Even those who cannot read Struve in Russian will be repeatedly struck by the penetrating originality of his judgements. (The reviewer who once wrote in this paper that "nothing that he – i.e. Struve – did or said remains memorable", must be grateful that at that date anonymity of reviewers still prevailed.)

Pipes's first volume was acclaimed as a history of the rise of liberalism in Russia as well as a biography. The second volume can equally claim to continue the story of the sad fate of liberalism in Russia and among émigré Russians. Pipes's biography will join the late Victor Leontovitsch's *Geschichte des Liberalismus in Russland* (which owes much to Struve) to form a fitting memorial to the endeavours of the few noble-minded Russians, however unsuccessful, to place liberty in Russia on the only foundation on which it could hope to flourish – legal order.

Of course, those who knew Struve (of whom I am not one) may miss in Pipes's account something of the extraordinary effect which this unique and remarkable man had on his contemporaries. A much more dramatic picture of Struve can be found in the late Semen Frank's memoir of him, published in 1956, in Russian, in New York. But Frank was an intimate and lifelong friend and could convey something of the personal impact of Struve – his phenomenal memory, the way in which his failure to complete any major work and the wide range of his interests reflected his inner spirit, his search in speech for the exactly right word, and much more. But Pipes as the good historian that he is has captured the one essential quality which set Struve apart from so many of his contemporaries – intellectual honesty and integrity. Not for him the inhibiting thoughts – "What will it do for me? Am I not better off keeping quiet?" He was tolerant of political and intellectual opponents, gentle, with a strong sense of moral duty, and an absolute refusal to compromise on moral issues. As Pipes records, "That total absence of *arrière pensée* and that utter intellectual openness struck observers as an almost childish quality – not childishly simple, of course, but rather childishly saintly." At the end of his book Pipes quotes, in Russian, some wonderful lines from Blok's long poem "Retribution" (*Vozmezdie*) on the nature of Russian life, with its potentiality for destruction: "The best of men – let's not conceal it/Are often powerless before it." Such a man was Struve.

1. [See pp. 68–92. (ed.)]

MARXISM AND THE REVOLUTION

Marxism in Russia

This article first appeared in *Varieties of Marxism*, ed. Shlomo Avineri, Martinus Nijhoff (The Hague 1977).

The use of the term "marxism" to denote a certain doctrine gives rise to complicated problems. For example, if "marxism" is used in its widest and most political sense as it is by the leaders of the Soviet Union then everything that has happened in the Soviet Union since 1917 could be brought under the heading of "Marxism in Russia", and a paper on this subject would amount to a history of Soviet power much more than to the history of certain ideas. The much more modest aim of this paper is to look at the views of Marx and Engels in their relation to Russia, both in the way in which, in the formative years of the Russian revolutionary movement, Marx and Engels understood this movement and in the way in which the Russian revolutionaries, when they first became acquainted with the ideas of Marx and Engels, were influenced by them and attempted to interpret them in relation to their own situation. This is not to say that all discussion of the writings of Marx and Engels that has taken place in Russia since those early years is irrelevant to the question of marxism in Russia. However, one cannot escape the fact that after 1903, for example, after the split between the Bolsheviks and the Mensheviks as the two factions of the party were to become known, interpretations of what Marx and Engels were supposed to have said or written became an integral part of the political struggle and therefore belong much more to the history of that political struggle than they do to intellectual history. Or to take some other examples of a rather more extreme kind. Stalin's propagandists in the thirties were able to find, or claim to find, justification in the writings of Marx for the view that the idea of a Leader, a supreme Leader such as Stalin became, was an integral part of the doctrine of marxism. They were also able to show that the repressive policy of Stalin, which resulted in the doing to death of many millions of innocent people, was somehow or other justified by doctrines which were supposed to derive from Marx. All this is very interesting for those who study the nature of totalitarian rule. It has nothing whatever to do with the intellectual history of a doctrine.

If one goes a little further back in time in the history of the Soviet Union, there are two periods where much turned or appeared to turn on the political scene on the interpretation of the doctrines of Marx or at any rate on the interpretation of Lenin's interpretation of the doctrines of Marx. Thus, during the period of the New Economic Policy from 1921 to 1928 or 1929, Bukharin developed a number of doctrines, based on the last writings and the last opinions of Lenin as orally expressed to him, which claimed to be a new interpretation of Marx in the conditions of Russia of the third decade of the century. What this doctrine amounted to in short was that the peculiar circumstances, in which the proletariat had been forced to seize power in Russia in October of 1917, dictated the need for a long period of reconciliation between the countryside and the towns, a period lasting generations; that during this period social peace had at all costs to be preserved; that the peasants had to acquire the social consciousness which they had lacked in 1917 before one could even think about socialism; and that the state with its ownership of the principal means of production must meanwhile encourage socialism by example and not by compulsion. All this, which also implied a more humane attitude than had been practised in the early years after the Bolsheviks had seized power, may or may not have been a reinterpretation or deepening of the views of Lenin. It is very difficult to see what it has got to do with Marx's analysis of the future of industrial societies. Similarly, while the debates between Trotsky and the right wing on the pace of industrialization and later on the relation of Soviet communism to world communism may present a great deal of interest for the history of Russia, it is once again very difficult to see them outside the context of the peculiar Russian circumstances, or indeed as related to the general study of a doctrine which is based on the writings of two men in the nineteenth century. It is for this reason that my topic must, in my view, be mainly confined to the first impact of the doctrines of Marx and Engels on Russia and to the part which they played in influencing the course of Russian revolutionary history.

Before the reforms of the sixties and particularly the emancipation of the peasants in 1861, the interest of Marx and of Engels in Russia was mainly confined to the effects of Russian policy on other countries, or to Russia's reactionary repression of revolutions. Marx and Engels saw Russia as the arch enemy of Europe in particular, and of progress in general. However, in spite of their apparent dislike for this bastion of reaction, Engels's interest in language and in the history of culture generally prompted him to start learning Russian as early as 1851. As far as Marx was concerned, it was not until much later that he began to take a detailed interest in the internal conditions of Russia. He began learning Russian in October of 1869 and mastered it very quickly indeed, though even before that date he had been reading a good deal of material on Russia in translation. After 1869 he appears to have read and abstracted voraciously from a large number of books on Russia, and an incomplete list which has been compiled on the basis of his library and of the published extracts from his notebooks runs to very many titles.[1] Marx obtained his material on Russia mainly with the help of the populist economist Danielson. It would seem that the first book which drew an enthusiastic response from Marx was Bervi-Flerovsky's account of the situation of the working class in Russia, which was published in 1869 and was regarded by Marx as the first work to tell the truth about internal conditions in Russia.[2] Whatever intentions Marx may have had – and it would seem that he did intend, if he had the time, to write comprehensively on the subject of Russia – he in fact was never able to carry them out. It is an interesting speculation to consider the effect which a complete analysis in depth by Marx of the future of Russia might have had on the development of the Russian revolutionary movement, particularly if one considers the important influence which his fragmentary and usually inconclusive remarks on the subject seem to have had inside Russia.

Although there is no analysis in depth by either Marx or Engels of the nature of Russian society of the pre-Reform period, there are sufficient occasional references to show quite clearly what their view was. They regarded the communal organization of Russia as an example of a primitive form of society which had occurred in every country at some period of its history; they regarded the absence of private property in the Russian village and what Engels used to refer to sarcastically as the primitive communism of Russia as the best foundation for despotism; and Marx, in particular, indulged in caustic diatribes against Herzen's plans for rejuvenating

Europe through the influence of Russian primitive socialism – which Engels on one occasion describes as the "pan-Slavist swindle".[3] So far as the commune was concerned, it is clear that neither Marx nor Engels regarded it as having anything to do with socialism. Indeed it seems to have been Bervi-Flerovsky's book which persuaded Marx for the first time that the germs of socialism had been sown by the emancipation of the serfs. According to Marx, as expressed in a letter to Engels, this had accelerated the loosening-up process in Russia, with the result that a great social revolution could be regarded as imminent.[4] Marx was drawn into a discussion of the question of the village commune and consideration of the possibility that it might be a distinctive Russian institution and not merely a primitive relic, as Engels believed it to be right to the end. Marx yielded sufficiently to the persistence of the populists to bring his great authority to bear on the burning question of whether the communal land organization and its primitive socialism offered an opportunity for Russia to develop on lines which would avoid the effects which capitalism had had. The best-known discussion of this problem was the result of a request by Vera Zasulich to Marx on the subject of the commune. Her letter was dated from Geneva on 16 February 1881. It therefore came at a period when Vera Zasulich, together with Plekhanov and others, had deserted the populist organizations inside Russia and moved to Geneva, and were on the way to their "conversion" to marxism if they were not already "converted". One of the reasons which most affected Plekhanov, and therefore presumably Zasulich, in their "conversion" to marxism was their belief on the evidence before them that the commune in fact was already disintegrating, and that reliance upon it for the future of Russian socialism was therefore a chimera. Thus, in this letter, Vera Zasulich implores Marx to express his opinion on the commune. Was it doomed to decay, as some people in Russia believed? In that case, surely there was no hope for any kind of separate development for Russia, and therefore nothing remained but to wait with resignation for the development of capitalist and proletarian organizations in Russia before there could be any thought of revolution. On the other hand, if the commune could be saved, then its development might be regarded as a favourable factor for the development of a peculiar Russian form of socialism.

Marx devoted considerable thought to this letter, as is revealed by a number of draft replies which indicate the care with which he directed his thoughts to this all-important question. Even so, his ultimate reply was not conclusive, although on the whole it did appear to give more comfort to the populist point of view than to the marxist point of view of Plekhanov and Zasulich. What Marx in effect wrote, after apologizing for his inability to prepare a really detailed and adequate reply, was first of all to emphasize that his analysis of society and of the course of its development was designed for societies in which capitalist production prevailed. He further emphasized that the basis of this capitalist process is the expropriation of land by the capitalists and the creation of a landless proletariat. Now this, Marx continued, bore little relationship to Russia, where it is not a question of one form of property being transformed into another, but, on the contrary, of the transformation of communal property into private property. However, Marx goes on to say that he had come to the conclusion that the commune could provide a basis for the social transformation of Russia, provided that it was safeguarded from the decay with which it was threatened by various factors and circumstances.[5] It may be doubted whether Marx's cautious support of the populist dogma would have been fully shared by Engels, at all events by the end of his life. It is true that Engels did join with Marx in 1882 in the Preface to the Russian edition of the *Communist Manifesto*, which also gave cautious support to the populist belief in a separate destiny for Russia which would enable it to escape the general fate of European countries. In this Preface, Marx and Engels wrote after quoting the great problem with which the Russian revolutionaries were concerned, that if the Russian revolution were to become a signal for a proletarian revolution in the West so that revolutions in the West and in Russia complemented each other, then indeed the present Russian communal landholding system might become a point of departure for a development of Russia along communist lines.[6] But whatever may have been Engels's view of the subject in 1882, it is quite plain that his views on the subject had undergone a pretty fundamental change by 1895, if not before.

Of course it is not only views which could have changed in that time but the conditions inside Russia, and in particular the continuing and all the time more evident decline of the village commune as well as the growth of industrialization and the development of a proletariat. In 1894 Engels's opinion seems clear enough that Marx's earlier view, if it could be taken to justify the populist hope for a separate path of development for Russia, had been overtaken by events and that Russia would have to go the way of the other European countries. This, of course, was the view which Plekhanov and Vera Zasulich had been propagating for a decade and during that time they had maintained fairly close contact with Engels and had been encouraged and sustained by him.[7] Whatever the reasoned and closely argued views which were expressed by both Marx and Engels on the subject of the future of Russian development, it would seem that neither of them ever really abandoned a kind of simple inner conviction that the first and foremost priority for Russia was a revolution – revolution of any kind, but above all a revolution which would destroy the influence of this reactionary force and thus might have a beneficent influence on revolutionary development outside Russia. It is clear, for example, that neither of them derived any particular satisfaction from the fact that their own ideas had actually prompted Russians to begin to apply them to Russian conditions, and they showed scant sympathy for Russian revolutionary theorists in general. When Marx heard that Plekhanov and other members of the Russian revolutionary organization Land and Liberty had left Russia and emigrated to Geneva in order to form an intellectual group, Marx's indignation found expression in a letter to Sorge in which he wrote (in his characteristic and quite untranslatable style) about those members of the revolutionary organization who have "*voluntarily* left Russia in sharp contrast with those who are prepared as terrorists to risk their own skins, in order to form the so-called party of propaganda (in order to make propaganda in *Russia* they move to *Geneva*! What a quid pro quo!)"[8] And not very long afterwards, on 23 April 1885, Engels wrote to Vera Zasulich in politer but very similar terms. While expressing his satisfaction that Plekhanov's ideas had been so much influenced by the theories of Marx and stressing how proud Marx would have been had he lived to see it, he nevertheless expressed some doubt as to the relevance of these theories to the present position in Russia. He argued that Russia is on the eve of a revolution and that this could be one of those exceptional circumstances when the "blanquist phantasy" might have some sort of foundation for its existence. He then proceeded to say that such a revolution in Russia might very well start a universal conflagration.[9] In a private letter from about the same time Engels expressed his view even more forcibly when he pointed out that what Russia needed was "not a programme but a revolution".[10]

The question of the future of the village commune and of Marx's views whether or not Russia could escape the evils of capitalism and progress towards an indigenous form of socialism, although of great importance to the Russian revolutionaries and to Russian populist thinkers generally, was not, however, the only aspect of Marx's ideas which appeared of importance to Russians at different periods. The most intense and indeed revealing discussion of Marx's ideas developed in Russia after the publication of the first volume of *Das Kapital* in a Russian translation in 1872. However, this was not the beginning of the influence and discussion of Marx's ideas in Russia and some of these earlier contacts and influences must be examined. The earliest open mention of Marx was in an encyclopaedic dictionary published in 1848.[11] It would seem that some of Marx's works were already available in Russia in narrow circles. At any rate, the library which was organized between 1845 and 1848 by Petrashevsky contained a copy of Engels's *Condition of the Working Class in England* and Marx's *Poverty of Philosophy*. Petrashevsky was the leader of a small group of young Russians, which included Dostoevsky, who met mainly for the discussion of socialist ideas and the future of Russia. It was only a revolutionary group in the fevered imagination of the Russian police, and was disbanded with many subsequent arrests in 1848. There was, however, no sign that the ideas of either Marx or Engels had any influence on this group and, as indeed Marx himself says in the *Poverty of Philosophy*, speaking of socialists and communists, that "as long as the productive forces have not yet been sufficiently developed among the bourgeoisie . . . which are necessary for the liberation of the proletariat and for the formation of a new society, these theorists will remain utopians who . . . will continue to think out systems . . ."[12] At about the same time, the literary critic and historian P. V. Annenkov, who is best known nowadays for his account of what he called "The Remarkable Decade", after correspondence with Marx met him on a number of occasions in 1847 and 1848. He has left a very fascinating account of these meetings, which include one occasion on which Marx delivered an all-out attack on Weitling. In the course of this attack he pointed out to Annenkov that Weitling's fantastic ideas for immediate revolution might have some sort of meaning in a country like Russia, but could be of no possible relevance in a country like Germany. When Weitling attempted to defend himself against this savage attack, and among other things pointed out that the great support which he received from humble workmen was perhaps more important than all the theoretical analyses of this study, Marx struck the table with great force, jumped up, and said, "Ignorance has never yet been of any help to anyone."[13]

Marx's contempt for Herzen has already been referred to and is in any case well known, as is his very high regard for the work of Chernyshevsky. There was no contact at any time between the two men, and, indeed, by the time Marx became familiar with his works Chernyshevsky was already exiled. There is also no evidence at all that Chernyshevsky had ever read any work of Marx. The main coincidence between their ideas is passionate devotion to atheism and materialism. Otherwise there could be little in common between the views of Marx and those of Chernyshevsky, because Chernyshevsky believed that Russia was destined to follow an entirely separate and non-capitalist path of development from Western Europe. Marx, on the other hand, approved of Chernyshevsky because he saw in his method of analysis a similarity to the historical materialist approach. Before the 1870s Marx also had friendly contacts with Bakunin and even with the redoubtable Nechaev – until the character of the latter was fully exposed to Marx by German Lopatin. Lopatin, a prominent populist and then quite a young man, had a very close relationship with Marx when he came to London in the summer of 1870 in order to work under Marx's direction at the British Museum while at the same time taking English lessons from Marx's daughter Eleanor.[14] There is no evidence of correspondence between Marx and Lopatin, but Marx's correspondence with Danielson dates from 1868, and Lopatin would have been well informed of Marx's views and interests through this leading populist economist. In order to complete this story one should also recall that Marx had a certain amount of correspondence with the Russians who were members of the Russian section of the First International whose representative

Karl Marx became at their invitation. This correspondence is not very revealing from the point of view of ideas, though we do learn from it of the very high regard which Marx, after he learned Russian, had acquired for the works of Chernyshevsky and Bervi-Flerovsky.[15]

The earliest work that appears to have influenced the populists in Russia was Engels's *Condition of the Working Class in England*. A number of articles, both critical and approving, were published on this work which seems to have been widely known in Russia. If for want of a better definition we adopt a description of "populists" as those revolutionaries and reformers in Russia who rejected the capitalist path of development for Russia's future, the most interesting early case of the influence of Engels is that of N. V. Shelgunov. Shelgunov was one of the most radical of the populists and was of particular importance as the co-author of a revolutionary proclamation addressed "to the younger generation" in 1861, in the very first flowering of Russian revolutionary activity after the emancipation of the serfs in February 1861. Shelgunov discussed Engels's work at length in an article on the position of the working class in France and in England. His main purpose in writing this article was, in fact, to illustrate the misery of the working class under capitalism, and to draw the moral that the capitalist path was something that Russia should at all costs avoid. Indeed, in his famous proclamation Shelgunov expressly says, "Who can assert that we must travel the same path as Europe, the path of some Saxony, or England, or France? . . . We believe in our own fresh powers; we believe that we are called upon to bring to history some new principle, to say our own word and not to repeat the past errors of Europe."[16] But perhaps the most important question of the influence of Marx is that of his supposed influence on the Russian Jacobin thinker P. N. Tkachev. Tkachev was a very distinctive Russian nineteenth-century thinker, whom it is in some ways difficult to identify as a populist, though he certainly shared the populist characteristic of wishing to avoid any kind of industrial development of Russia. The interest of discussing Marx's influence on Tkachev is at least threefold. In the first place he claimed that he was a marxist, whatever he may have meant by this, as early as 1865, asserting at the same time that in his opinion there could scarcely be any objection raised to any of the doctrines of Marx on the part of anyone of any intelligence at all.[17] The second reason why the influence of Marx on Tkachev is of particular importance is because quite a strong case can be made for the proposition that Lenin was influenced by the views of Tkachev.[18] The third reason is that Tkachev engaged in open polemics with Engels. Now in view of the extraordinary acceptance by Tkachev of Marx's views as self-evident and really beyond any contradiction, one is entitled to enquire what it is he understood by "marxism". One thing that is quite clear is that he never for a moment regarded, either in 1865 or in the following decade when his main activity took place, the work of Marx as having any relationship to revolution at all. The side of Marx's thought which appealed to Tkachev was therefore in effect irrelevant to his revolutionary doctrine. What appealed to him was Marx's materialist interpretation of history. One of the most significant and most "marxist" of Tkachev's publications, which did not see the light of day until long after his death, was a study of political ideas in their relation to their material base and viewed as a superstructure of their materialist base.[19] How remote Tkachev was from any interpretation of revolution which could in any way be associated with Marx's analysis of society is shown by his polemics with Engels in 1874, in which Tkachev argued that the Russian autocracy was without any support at that time, but that the moment the peasantry became more prosperous as the result of governmental efforts, the government would then acquire peasant support, and the chance of a revolution effected by a revolutionary minority, as always advocated by Tkachev, would then be gone for ever. Tkachev argued that Russia could not therefore afford to wait while the laws of history slowly brought about the desired revolution. In other words, for Tkachev the laws of history were not something to be regarded as inevitable, but were plainly subordinate to the voluntary action of man. Engels in his attack is mainly concerned to argue against Tkachev's view that the minority should seize power in the name of the people and then put socialist measures into force. But Engels also advanced the view that the autocracy was already then, in 1874 or 1875, supported by landlords and rich peasants, and he quoted figures to support his thesis.[20]

This debate prompts several observations. In the first place it would be difficult for a true follower of Marx to regard a revolution as postponed "forever" if it were not undertaken at the right moment, though it will be recalled that Lenin got perilously near to arguing this in his impassioned letters to the Bolshevik Central Committee in 1917 on the eve of the Bolshevik seizure of power. It is also true that Lenin was seriously disturbed by the thought that the Stolypin reforms might succeed and create strong support for the government, and that this would make revolution much less likely to succeed. It may also be observed, however, that Engels's somewhat superficial argument that the landlords and the rich peasants supported the government because they derived economic benefit from their privileged position is a good deal further away from the historical truth than the position adopted by Tkachev; it would be very difficult to argue that, whatever their economic position, landlords and rich peasants exercised any political influence in the Russia of 1875, or acted as a support that the government could rely on. For completeness, one must note the relationship between Marx and Peter Lavrov, from 1873 to 1876 the editor of *Vpered*, the leading Russian revolutionary paper of the period – if such it can be called. Lavrov's main influence on the Russian populist movement was in the direction of gradualism and evolution, and his was the voice that influenced those who believed in long-term peaceful propaganda among the peasants rather than in any kind of sudden revolutionary violence. Lavrov was indeed a great admirer of Marx, particularly of Marx's erudition as an economist, but it is difficult to see of what relevance a confirmed opponent of capitalism as far as Russia was concerned could have found in Marx's analysis of Western Europe. And it is indeed difficult to see in Lavrov's ideas any direct influence of Marx other than a belief in gradualism, if indeed this aspect of Lavrov's thought was influenced by Marx. As far as Marx was concerned, he seems to have tolerated Lavrov with a certain amount of condescension, and was probably flattered by Lavrov's deference.[21] Thus it would seem that the populist revolutionaries, who have hitherto been considered, valued Marx and Engels either because they offered a good object lesson of what Russia should avoid – a view which was shared both by Shelgunov and by Tkachev – or because of the exposition of the materialist interpretation of history. As far as making revolution was concerned, this was regarded as a Russian matter to which Marx's analysis of society and history was irrelevant for Russians. Certainly there is nothing in the writing of Tkachev to suggest that any of his *revolutionary* ideas was inspired by Marx; and we know that, as far as Engels was concerned, there was a violent collision of views between Tkachev and him.

None of this, however, prevented Marx from acquiring an enormous reputation as the leading economist of Western Europe among the populist economists, of whom Danielson became the most famous. Hence the somewhat surprising fact occurred that the first translation of the first volume of *Das Kapital* should have taken place in Russia. The translation was first mooted in 1868 and promoted by Danielson (with whom Marx would maintain an extensive correspondence until 1881 and Engels until his death in 1895). But the translation was, in fact, not published until 1872. One of the difficulties was that of getting through the Russian censorship. The import of all of Marx's previously published works had already been prohibited in Russia. But when they came to read *Das Kapital* the censors decided that the book was "abstruse" and "obscure"; that "few will read it and even fewer will understand it"; and that its attacks on the factory system in England were not relevant to Russian conditions where the government protected the workers.[22] The censors proved to be right in their prognosis, at any rate in one respect, namely that in the event no one who was associated with the venture of promoting the translation of *Das Kapital* in fact became a revolutionary (Lopatin never became a revolutionary; and Danielson became one of the main theoretical opponents of the relevance of Marxism to Russian conditions). Marx was particularly scathing about this popularity of his work among Russians. In a letter to Kugelman of 12 October 1868 he attributed his popularity, with characteristic sarcasm, to the fact that the Russian aristocracy brought up in the universities of Germany and Paris was always ready to chase after any kind of extreme doctrine produced in the West. "This does not prevent the very same Russians from becoming rascals the moment they have entered state service."[23] Marx was really somewhat unfair in this comment. The avidity for serious foreign literature among aristocratic or other Russian intellectuals in the nineteenth century could well be explained by the rigorous censorship which prevented them from easy access to the latest developments in Western European intellectual life. However, this still raises the intriguing question of why Marx, whose doctrines in 1872 still seemed somewhat irrelevant to Russian conditions, was so popular in Russia.

The reactions to the appearance in Russian of *Das Kapital*, which remained a subject of vigorous discussion, praise, and criticism for many years, suggest part of the answer. As far as the populist theorists were concerned, they saw in Marx's work, rather as Shelgunov had seen in Engels's *Condition of the Working Class in England*, a terrible warning against the evils of capitalism and a powerful argument for the populist view that Russia must at all costs avoid going the way of capitalist development. The most influential criticism of *Das Kapital* along these lines, or rather welcoming of it, was that of N. K. Mikhailovsky, the leading theorist of populism, in his article on *Das Kapital* published in 1872. According to Mikhailovsky *Das Kapital* was above all a warning to Russia not to rush into industrialization, but, indeed, to take steps to avoid it. The alternatives before Russia were either capitalist industrialization or a form of popular production based on the commune, and Russia must take steps to see that the commune did not disintegrate, and that popular production remained possible. This far Mikhailovsky was, in fact, on a more sophisticated level, echoing Shelgunov. However, Mikhailovsky now attempted by a misinterpretation of what Marx had written to suggest that this view had the authority of the great Marx. He appeared to construe some sentences from the preface to *Das Kapital* as meaning that it was possible for one nation to learn from another and thus avoid the fate which had befallen other countries; and, by inference, invoked Marx's authority for the populist faith in the Russian "separate path". Mikhailovsky's interpretation of *Das Kapital* in this article became in the course of time a powerful argument in favour of the populist point of view. It was not, however, shared by Marx, who wrote a rejoinder to Mikhailovsky which remained unpublished for some time, but which certainly circulated in manuscript. Marx's rejoinder to Mikhailovsky is characterized by the ambivalent or even ambiguous position on the subject of the future of Russia which seems to have characterized everything that Marx wrote on the subject. He vigorously objected to what he regarded as Mikhailovsky's unjustified attempt to recruit him as a supporter for the populist view that Russia could and ought to follow a path different from capitalist Western Europe. In fact, he maintained that his book was limited in its analysis to Western Europe and could not be used one way or the other as an argument for what would happen in Russia. Having said this, he then proceeded to express a view on Russia which, while ambiguous, nevertheless seems to lean to the populist side. Thus, he said at length that if Russia is to become a capitalist country (and certainly, according to Marx, the signs of that in recent years were pretty clear) then it will only achieve capitalism by transforming a considerable number of its peasants into proletarians. After that, having reached the sphere of capitalist structure, Russia will be like other unfortunate peoples, destined inevitably to suffer the rigours of capitalism. There are, however, some sentences which suggest that Russia could avoid this fate, as indeed Mikhailovsky argued. Thus he wrote that "if Russia will continue to follow the path which it has been following since 1861, then it will lose the best opportunity which history has ever offered to any people and will experience all the fatal evils of the capitalist regime". It is difficult to interpret this as meaning anything other than the fact that Russia had some kind of alternative, and indeed a desirable one, to capitalism in store for her if she followed the right policy.[24]

The Russian debates over *Das Kapital* were too extensive and too numerous to be summarized here in any detail, and the whole subject has already been extensively treated. However, there are certain trends which should be mentioned. First there were those who saw *Das Kapital*, with its portrayal of the horrors of industrial England, as a timely argument in favour of those who believed in factory reform. Then there were the out-and-out opponents of the argument on economic grounds, who challenged the whole theory of surplus value and other cornerstones of Marx's analysis. The most prominent among these was B. N. Chicherin, the leading liberal lawyer and legal historian of that time, whose criticism aroused much indignation from Marx's supporters in Russia and from Marx himself. Of greater interest for the present investigation are the arguments which were adduced by those who could be regarded as followers of Marx. One of them was the liberal Professor of Economics at St Petersburg, Kaufmann, who wrote the review which seems to have pleased Marx best of all the reviews which appeared in Russia. The point that distinguishes Kaufmann from other Russian reviewers is that he realized that *Das Kapital* represented a scientific investigation of the basic laws governing the transformation of one social order into another, and that it set forth the essential nature of the materialist interpretation of history.[25]

One of the most important exponents of Marx whose writings did more than those of anyone to make Marx's works known widely among the Russian intellectuals was N. I. Ziber, who at one time taught in the Economics Faculty of the University of Kiev. Ziber, who was born in 1844 and died in 1888, produced a number of substantial works during his lifetime, including a long study of the comparative views of David Ricardo and Karl Marx. He also contributed a number of articles to the controversy over *Das Kapital*, several of which became part of the regular reading of the Russian revolutionary circles of the eighties. The striking feature about Ziber, as indeed of every single one of the Russians whose views on Marx have so far been examined, is that there is no suggestion anywhere in his discussion of Marx that the doctrine of Marx is in any way related to revolution. In fact this is one of the faults which are laid at his door by Soviet critics who otherwise, quite rightly, regard him as having made a great contribution to the spread of the ideas of Marx in Russia. It is evident from Ziber's view of Marx that he regarded the social transformation foretold by Marx as an inevitable process, in which no voluntary activity of any kind by revolutionaries was required, and indeed there is no trace in Ziber of any kind of advocacy of revolutionary activity, nor was he at any time subjected to any kind of persecution by the police. This view, that marxism was quite unrelated to revolution and indeed did not call for any kind of action on anyone's part at all, was apparently not unusual in the seventies, according to the historian B. P. Kozmin. Kozmin recounts one particular example of a follower of Marx who greatly admired and constantly quoted the Master. As a result of his conversion to marxism, this young man decided that the actions of individuals were totally immaterial in relation to the forces of history which would bring about the eventual overthrow of society, and that nothing could be done either to accelerate or to postpone the historically predetermined event. And so he turned away from his former populist revolutionary convictions and sat quietly chatting to his friends and playing chess, waiting for the moment when the time would be ripe.[26]

The main debate over *Das Kapital* thus took place in the seventies. It had the effect of familiarizing the Russian intellectuals with the principal ideas of Marx, but it did not suggest to them as yet that these ideas and the idea of revolution, let along organization for the purposes of revolution, were in any way connected. The situation in Russia was greatly affected by the breakaway from the bosom of populism of a group of populists which comprised G. V. Plekhanov, Lev Deich, Vera Zasulich, and P. B. Akselrod. These four had in 1879 broken with the part of the revolutionary populist organization Land and Liberty which, under the name of the People's Will, proceeded to organize the assassination of Emperor Alexander II which took place on 1 March 1881. Under the name of Repartition of the Land the dissident group preached for a short time a doctrine of evolutionary social development in which terrorism, and indeed any kind of political activity, was to have no part. However, by 1880 the members of the group were living abroad, much to Marx's indignation, as will be recalled, and by 1881 were beginning to show certain signs of conversion to marxism. On 25 September 1883, Plekhanov and his supporters announced the publication in Geneva of a series of popular political pamphlets for workers which was to be called the Library of Contemporary Socialism. Thus came into existence the first Russian theoretical group devoted to the exposition of the doctrines of Marx, which became known as the Group for the Liberation of Labour.

This first real marxist theoretical group was thus the product of revulsion against terrorist action and against conspiratorial theories of revolution. It was inspired both by a deep conviction that conspiracies for the purpose of seizing power were useless – a point of view which the entirely futile assassination of Alexander II would seem to prove conclusively – and by the conviction that the commune was fast disintegrating, thus removing the linchpin of the whole social foundation on which the doctrine of populism was built. Moreover, the rapid growth, or relatively rapid growth, of the Russian working class, as a consequence of the emancipation of the serfs of 1861, increasingly suggested that Russia was irrevocably launched in the direction of industrialization. However, the Liberation of Labour Group remained pretty remote from Russia, as indeed Marx had feared, and this became especially evident after the arrest of Deich in 1884. Deich had been in charge of organizing contact with Russia and as a result of his arrest, regular contact could not be resumed until 1895. One of the consequences of this was that marxist groups which began to spring up in Russia in the eighties, and especially in the nineties, developed to a large extent quite independently of the theorists in Geneva, and this fact was to lead to serious factional difficulties in the young Russian movement around the turn of the century. With these, however, we are not here concerned. The main doctrines of the group were expounded by Plekhanov both in his vigorous polemics with Tkachev and in two pamphlets, published in 1883 and 1884, and in two programmes, published in 1884 and 1887.[27] Essentially what Plekhanov was advocating was a very long-term, two-stage view of development in Russia. In the first place, the full development of capitalism would take place, and of this the disintegration of the commune and the development of a proletariat were the first beginnings. The advent of capitalism would inexorably be followed by the emergence of bourgeois political parties and of the bourgeois revolution, and this, in the fullness of time, would be followed by a socialist revolution led by the proletariat and its party. It was essential, however, for the proletariat to create its own party as soon as possible. The proletariat would have to co-operate with the liberals in the first phase in order to bring down the autocracy, but, having achieved that, would have separate tasks to pursue and would pursue them in opposition to the liberals. It is fairly clear that this particular adaptation of Marx's analysis to Russia could not be very comforting to revolutionaries who are in general not endowed with very much patience, but in any case were smarting under the catastrophic failure of 1 March 1881. Plainly, in Plekhanov's view, the ultimate socialist revolution was a very long way off.

The association of ultimate revolution with the works of Marx was already a considerable innovation on the Russian scene. There were also certain modifications of doctrine made in the course of years by Plekhanov and his associates, particularly Akselrod, which were designed to make the delay seem less irksome. One of them was the doctrine of "hegemony", which meant that the working-class party, or the social democratic party, would in fact take over the leadership of the liberal parties and exert hegemony over them. This particular piece of nonsense was very soon disproved in practice, and was dropped quietly. The second argument, which had rather more force, was that Russia would benefit from experience of the Western social democratic parties and would therefore be able considerably to speed up the process of advancing the workers' revolution in Russia. It was perhaps a significant and a symbolic fact that the founding congress of the Russian Social Democratic Labour Party in 1898, which could be regarded as one indirect result of Plekhanov's influence, played no role whatever in the future of the Russian party, and that the real history, both of the Bolsheviks and of the Mensheviks, dates from the Second Congress of the Party of 1903 which was dominated by Lenin.

While it is true that there were discernible groups of workers in the eighties which could be described as marxist, the great majority of revolutionary groups, in the very broad sense, should more properly be described as "preparatory". This term owes its origin to the shock of the failure of the assassination of 1 March 1881 to result in any kind of national uprising, as was apparently fervently hoped. The disastrous failure persuaded the revolutionaries who remained at liberty that uprisings were very unlikely to occur unless they had been carefully prepared – a fact which they might have learned before 1881 if the works of Tkachev had been studied more attentively. Like Lenin, and unlike any other Russian revolutionary theorist before him, Tkachev realized the importance of preparing the revolutionary situation before attempting the dramatic *coup d'état*. It was a significant fact that the terrorist group headed by Alexander Ulianov, Lenin's elder brother (the only, or perhaps one of two, active terrorist groups), did not regard the social democrats as a separate category of revolutionaries in the broad sense, or consider that their views were indeed very relevant to revolutionary activity. Ulianov's conspiratorial group worked out a plan to assassinate Emperor Alexander III on 1 March 1887, but the plan was foiled owing to a gross breach in security by one of the conspirators, and those conspirators who did not succeed in escaping were hanged. While in prison, Alexander Ulianov reconstructed from memory the programme of his group. It is a curious amalgam of marxism and traditional Russian revolutionary populist theory. Declaring itself socialist, the group asserts that socialism is an inevitable result of capitalism and of the classes which emerge as a result of capitalism, although it denies that this is necessarily the only path to socialism. It then proceeds to analyse the social classes in Russia and to proclaim that the organization of the working class is the most important task for the future. This, however, is regarded as impossible until some kind of freedom of speech and other civil freedoms are attained. There is therefore nothing left for the group to do but to struggle for a minimum of civil freedoms. This could only be achieved by systematic terror, by which Ulianov meant a continuous sacrifice of the flower of young Russian intelligentsia in the hope that this self-sacrifice would eventually force the authorities to realize that they must make some political concessions to society. The interesting paragraph in the present context is the reference to other parties. The programme explains that the group is prepared to make common cause with the liberals. "As regards the social democrats our disagreement with them seem to us to be very insubstantial and merely theoretical."[28] Ten years later, if not earlier, when social democrats and populists were forming themselves into antagonistic groups and engaging in violent debates, this kind of assertion would have been inconceivable: the rival positions were by that time too clearly pegged out.

Lenin's well-known adaptation of marxism, which in effect replaces social process by the human will, at any rate to a large extent, was plainly of a much more radical nature than Plekhanov's. If one follows Lenin's early revolutionary career, it is significant to note that Lenin (Vladimir Ulianov) began his career at the age of seventeen, in 1887, as a revolutionary without any theoretical label attached to him, very much influenced by the shock of discovering that his brother had been a revolutionary and, of course, the even greater shock of the execution and all the consequences of social ostracism that this entailed for the young Lenin's family. Some years pass before Lenin can be identifiably described as a convert to marxism, although his study of it may very well have begun quite early. It is certainly the case that his general apprenticeship in conspiratorial revolutionary organizations included some active participation in a marxist circle organized by N. E. Fedoseev in Kazan. Fedoseev, an early convert to marxism who, to judge from his writings, was a very remarkable young man, died too early (tragically and by his own hand) to exercise much influence on the development of marxism in Russia. The few writings that he left suggest that in the main his views were not along the lines that were later to become identified with Lenin. However, in one respect

Lenin may have been influenced by Fedoseev, whom he never met, but with whom he corresponded for a long time after the latter's exile.[29] It seems most probable that Fedoseev influenced the young Lenin in implanting in his mind an idea which Lenin expounded as early as 1893, to the effect that capitalism *already* existed in Russia. This was a considerable divergence from the view hitherto held by Plekhanov and other marxists that capitalism would be a necessary stage in Russia's development, but that it was still some way off. In a series of letters (recently published) dating from 1893, Lenin argued that capitalism did not belong to the future but was actually to be found in the Russian village, in the relationship between the rich peasants and the exploited poor peasants; and that although of a more rustic kind, it was in no respect different from the capitalism described by Marx.[30] It was indeed in 1893 that Lenin's extensive correspondence with Fedoseev began. It is evident that Lenin's assertion, if accepted, would advance the development of socialism in Russia very considerably, indeed advance it by a whole historical phase as compared with the view of Plekhanov. This, therefore, was the first adaptation of marxism to Russian conditions which was due to Lenin, who from 1893 onwards became one of the most accomplished experts on Marx in Russia, and one of the most forceful advocates of his views.

But it is not until some time after his arrest in 1895 that the doctrines particularly associated with Lenin become apparent in his writings. These views, which became the foundation of *What Is To Be Done?* published in March of 1902, only became apparent in Lenin's writings toward the autumn of 1899 and appear to have emerged under the influence of reading the works of Eduard Bernstein, and of the fear that revisionism as advocated by Bernstein was widespread in the Russian social democratic movement. The first apprehensions appear in Lenin's writings in 1899, and the organizational prescriptions which are contained in articles published around that time and between then and 1902 culminated in the essential doctrine of Leninism. This expounds the need for organized professional, disciplined, centralized revolutionary activity, and propounds the doctrine that the workers by themselves will never achieve revolutionary consciousness, which has to be brought to them from the outside by their leaders. It is an open question, which it is neither possible nor necessary to discuss here, whether this view must be regarded as a departure from the views of Marx. Certain passages can be found in Marx's works which would substantiate Lenin's interpretation. For example, the last paragraph but one of Marx's *Critique of Hegel's Philosophy of Right* which was much discussed in the Ulianov group and had, in fact, been translated into Russian by one of the members of the group, reads as follows: "Just as philosophy finds in the proletariat its material weapon so the proletariat finds in philosophy its spiritual weapon, and as soon as the lightning of thought has struck deeply into this native popular soil then the emancipation of the Germans to the status of human beings will be complete."[31] Fortunately it is not necessary in this context to consider whether or not Lenin's version of Marx is a perversion, or an adaptation, or an implementation, or indeed a correct interpretation. It is beyond doubt, and suffices for present purposes, that it was an entirely new departure in the Russian reception of Marx. In Russia the doctrine of Karl Marx had hitherto been received as an anlysis of society and an interpretation of history quite unrelated to any revolutionary organizational activity except in the remote and almost academic sense of Plekhanov. Lenin's interpretation transformed this into a revolutionary technique of which the consequences are beyond the scope of this study.

A question of great interest, however, is how it is that a doctrine that was so novel was so readily accepted and so little criticized or objected to at the time when it was first propounded. There was, of course, a great deal of controversy between the rival factions of the party, the Bolsheviks and the Mensheviks, after the split in 1903. But this belongs much more to the realm of party polemics than to the realm of doctrine. As far as doctrine is concerned, no one seriously objected to *What Is To Be Done?* when it was published, and at the Second Party Congress in 1903 only one speaker pointed out that Lenin's doctrine of bringing consciousness from the outside was, in fact, inconsistent with Marx's doctrine of the class struggle. The ease with which Lenin's interpretation of Marx was accepted is perhaps not difficult to understand. In the first place it was a very welcome relief to revolutionaries, fed hitherto on the diet of Plekhanov's long-term doctrine of a revolution which was possibly generations away. Here was something which provided for action here and now and which very considerably shortened the period of waiting.

It must also be recalled that the doctrine of elitist leadership of the masses was by no means new to the Russian revolutionary tradition. It is of course essential to the doctrines of Tkachev, and this revolutionary thinker expressed views on the nature of the proletariat in relation to revolution which were not very different from those expressed by Lenin a generation later.[32] Probably, few Russians were aware of Marx's diatribe against the doctrine of bringing consciousness into the workers' organization from the outside and of treating the working class as material to be worked on, "A chaos which requires the breath of the Holy Spirit of Bakunin's *Allianz* in order to take on form."[33] On the other hand, even if they did know of this remark by Marx they could have been forgiven for wondering why they should prefer this particular diatribe against Bakunin to the very different opinions which had been expressed by Marx in the passage quoted above of some thirty years earlier. Lenin's main proposition was in fact incorporated in a quotation from Kautsky which forms part of the text of *What Is To Be Done?* and indeed, this same view of Kautsky may be cited almost in the same words as those used by Lenin from other works by Kautsky.[34]

If it is true, as has been argued, that after 1903 marxism as far as Russia was concerned became an organizational technique to which doctrine was subordinate, then it follows that the debates which were to revolve for years around the interpretation of Marx became not so much discussions of Marx and his doctrines as discussions of policies which were made desirable or undesirable as the result of their adoption by Russian revolutionaries of a particular kind of Russian adaptation, or perversion, of the doctrines of Marx. These discussions can therefore no longer be subsumed under the title of "Marxism in Russia" – except of course in the very broad sense in which the term marxism could be used to cover the whole history of Soviet Russia since 1917 and the whole history of the rise of Bolshevism after 1903, which is clearly beyond the scope of this paper.

The story could be concluded at this point. However, there is one postscript which is perhaps of interest because it represents another attempt to apply the doctrines of Marx to Russia, which ended in a diametrically opposite result from Lenin's. This concerns the intellectual course of Petr Struve. Struve belonged to a group, which included Berdiaev, Bulgakov, and S. L. Frank, that became known as the 'legal marxists'. Struve's influential book, published in 1894, was basically a plea for the need for Russia to evolve into a fully capitalist society on the grounds that the necessary consequence of capitalism was the development of freedom, and that therefore the sooner Russia went through the unpleasant stage of capitalism the better because at any rate this would be the means of her achieving the kind of freedoms to the defence of which Struve was to devote his life.[35] Incidentally, Struve expressly throws doubt on the question as to whether Marx can in any way be regarded as a revolutionary. By 1901, if not earlier, Struve had come to the conclusion that the principles of liberalism need not depend either on the existence of a middle class or on an economic substructure of the type that exists in Western Europe. His historical researches had convinced him, he wrote in 1901, that the doctrine currently accepted in Russia that liberalism had emerged as the political system of the bourgeoisie and in the material interests of the bourgeoisie was false. On the contrary, the origin of liberalism, he wrote, must be sought in the striving for freedom of conscience, and this was neither the prerogative of any particular class nor dependent on any particular system of economic relations.[36] Consistently with this view, Struve in the following year became the ideological leader of a group formed around a newspaper entitled *Liberation*. His fellow legal marxists likewise had by then also deserted marxism in favour of various degrees of idealism and religious doctrine. Here then is one aspect of the failure of the adaptation of marxist doctrines to Russia to achieve what Marx himself could conceivably have wished them to achieve. If it also be the case, as can be convincingly argued, that Lenin's adaptation of Marx led on directly to Stalin, with all the consequences of that regime, then likewise Marx could have derived little satisfaction from the direct or indirect consequences of the adaptation of his theories to Russia. Perhaps Marx's scepticism in 1880, when he heard of the emergence of a theoretical group of propagandists leaving Russia for Geneva, was a healthy premonition of what the future held.

1. See Helmut Krause, *Marx und Engels und das zeitgenoessiche Russland* (Giessen 1958), pp. 85–6, footnote.
2. *ibid.*, p. 84, footnote.
3. Gustav Mayer, *Friedrich Engels, Eine Biographie*, vol. 2 (The Hague 1934), p. 57.
4. Letter of 12 February 1870. Karl Marx

and Friedrich Engels, *Werke*, vol. 32 (Berlin 1965), pp. 443–4.

5. For the original French text of the letter and the drafts which are much more detailed and exhaustive, see *Arkhiv K. Marksa i F. Engel'sa*, ed. D. Riazanova, Part I (Moscow 1924), pp. 265–86.
6. *Werke*, vol. 2 (Berlin 1957), p. 576.
7. *Perepiska K. Marksa i F. Engel'sa s russkimi politicheskimi deiateliami*, 2nd edn. (Moscow 1951), pp. 285–97.
8. *Werke*, vol. 34 (Berlin 1966), p. 477.
9. *Perepiska* . . . , pp. 309–10.
10. Quoted in J. L. H. Keep, *The Rise of Social Democracy in Russia* (Oxford 1963), p. 19.
11. A. L. Reuel', *Russkaia ekonomicheskaia mysl' 60–70 kh godov XIX veka i marksizm* (Moscow 1956), p. 182.
12. *Werke*, vol. 4 (Moscow 1959), p. 143.
13. P. V. Annenkov, *Literaturnye vospominaniia* (Moscow 1960), pp. 301–7.
14. David McLellan, *Karl Marx. His Life and Thought* (London 1973), p. 419; see also Reuel', *op. cit.*, pp. 226–7.
15. *Perepiska* . . . , p. 39.
16. Quoted in Reuel', *op. cit.*, p. 196; and see *ibid.*, pp. 192–5.
17. B. P. Koz'min, *Iz istorii revoliutsionnoi mysli v rossii.* (Moscow 1961), p. 314.
18. I have discussed this question in my *Rationalism and Nationalism in Russian Nineteenth-Century Political Thought* (New Haven and London, 1967), pp. 139–42.
19. "Ocherki iz istorii ratsionalizma", probably written in 1865, and published in *Literaturnoe nasledstvo*, 7–8, 1933, pp. 124–62, Moscow.
20. This debate is summarized in an unpublished doctoral dissertation (1964) at the University of Indiana by Rolf A. W. Theen, entitled "Petr Nikitich Tkachev. A study in Revolutionary Theory", pp. 89–99.
21. Philip Pomper, *Peter Lavrov and the Russian Revolutionary Movement* (Chicago and London, 1972), p. 125–8.
22. Albert Resis, "*Das Kapital* Comes to Russia", *Slavic Review*, 29 (2), June 1970, pp. 219–37, especially pp. 219–24.
23. *Werke*, vol. 32 (Berlin 1965), p. 567.
24. Mikhailovsky's article is summarized in Resis, *op. cit.*, pp. 232–4; for Marx's rejoinder see *Perepiska* . . . pp. 320–3.
25. In general, for the debates provoked by the appearance of the Russian translation of *Das Kapital* see Resis, *op. cit.*, *passim*, and Reuel, *op. cit.*, ch. 5.
26. Kozmin, *op. cit.*, pp. 381–2.
27. The two pamphlets were "Sotsialism i politicheskaia bor'ba" and "Nashi raznoglasiia". The programmes are printed in volume 2 of the collected edition of Plekhanov's works at pp. 357–62 and 400–4.
28. On Alexander Ulianov see *Aleksandr Ilyich Ulianov i Dello i Marta 1887 g.*, ed. A. L. Ulianova-Elizarova (Moscow-Leningrad 1927). The programme appears on pp. 375–80.
29. On Lenin's relations with Fedoseev see the introduction to a collection of his writings published in Moscow in 1958, *N. Fedoseev. Stat'i i pis'ma.* On the intellectual formation of Lenin see the article by R. Pipes, in *Revolutionary Russia*, ed. R. Pipes (Cambridge, Mass. 1968).
30. For these letters to Maslov see volume 46 of the most recent, ostensibly complete, edition of Lenin's works in Russian, pp. 1–5.
31. *Werke*, vol. 1 (Berlin 1957), p. 391.
32. Theen, *op. cit.*, p. 91.
33. Karl Marx, *Politische Schriften*, edited by H. J. Lieber, vol. 2 (Stuttgart 1960), pp. 999–1000.
34. There are several quite striking parallels in Kautsky's writings with Lenin's doctrine of "bringing consciousness from the outside". The late George Lichtheim maintained in a conversation with me that the parallels were more apparent than real. The real point is, perhaps, that Lenin was skilful enough to make use of Kautsky's authority to bolster a novel view.

35. P. Struve, *Kriticheskiia zametki k voprosu ob ekonomicheskom razvitii Rossii* (St Petersburg 1894).

36. See P. Struve, "V chem zhe istinnyi natsionalizm?" in P. Struve, *Na raznyia temy (1893–1901)*, Sbornik statei (St Petersburg 1902), pp. 526–55.

The Concept of Ideology as Evolved by Marx and Adapted by Lenin

This article originally appeared in *Ideology and Politics*, ed. Maurice Cranston and Peter Mair, Martinus Nijhoff (The Hague 1980).

There is no systematic exposition in the works of Marx of the nature and function of ideology, and his views have therefore to be gleaned from scattered references. Many years after Marx's death, Engels did attempt a definition of ideology, in a letter to Mehring of 14 July 1893:

> Ideology is a process accomplished by the so-called thinker consciously, it is true, but with a false consciousness. The real motive forces impelling him remain unknown to him: otherwise it simply would not be an ideological process. Hence he imagines false or seeming motive forces ... He works with mere thought material, which he accepts without examination as the product of thought, and does not investigate further for a more remote source independent of thought.[1]

The "more remote" causes are, of course, the economic relations which determine the thought – it is evident from the references to "false" consciousness that Engels restricts the term ideology to the "political, juridical and other ideological notions' (to quote the same letter) of the bourgeoisie. In this letter Engels also stresses what he had already emphasized earlier in his correspondence (e.g. in his letter to J. Bloch of 21–2 September 1890) that both Marx and he had tended to over-emphasize the economic side of the derivation of ideological notions, and in a letter of 25 January of the following year to H. Starkenburg, he recognizes that ideological factors can exist separately from the economic condition which does not, he writes, produce an "automatic effect": "Men make their history themselves, only they do so in a given environment which conditions it and on the basis of actual relations already existing, among which the economic relations, however much they may be influenced by the other – political and ideological – ones, are still ultimately the decisive ones . . ."[2]

Although Marx does not seem ever to have used the phrase "false consciousness",[3] the general notion that the bourgeoisie, consciously or unconsciously, uses political, moral or juridical ideas to bolster its own economic hegemony occurs in his writings in a variety of forms. In a sense, *Capital* is an attack on bourgeois ideology, on economic theories which are designed or used to camouflage the nature of bourgeois exploitation. As a sympathetic analyst of the philosophy of Marx has expressed it, Marx "demystified" the ideology "of which capitalism made use in order to draw a veil over the real process by means of which it secreted alienated labour. This is in substance the whole meaning of *Capital*, a work of criticism, as indeed are all the works of Marx which preceded it. He tears away the veils of justification and specious explanation, lays bare the fundamental alienation which expresses itself in the exploitation of the labour of the proletariat, and denounces all the subterfuges of classical economic theory."[4]

The treatment of ideology in *Capital* is, however, more developed and rather subtler than that which is to be found in earlier works. In *Capital* Marx is not concerned to argue that bourgeois ideology is consciously designed to deceive – though, of course, he would not have denied that deliberate deception by the manipulation of others into believing something that is false for advancement of self-interest can and does occur. But, as a recent analyst of the theory of ideology in *Capital* argues:

> It is not necessary to postulate that any basic role in the generation of ideological discourse is played by . . . the desire to deceive, or the deliberate intention to manipulate the beliefs of others in such a way as to protect one's own interests. Nor is it necessary to postulate that ideology need be believed only by the aid of some process of self-deception, or refusal or bad faith . . . Ideology arises from the fact that the situation might be such as to provide a person with reasons for thinking in terms of categories which necessarily generate falsehood and illusion . . . It is the forms of social relations with which we are

> apparently directly acquainted in experience (value, wages, money, commodities etc.) that are deceptive.[5]

In other words, because the relations are accepted as the reality in bourgeois society, whereas they are in fact false, the language which is used to describe them necessarily generates a false ideology – and this can only be put right by changing the actual social and economic relations.

This view of ideology as inherently false because the language in which it is expressed is *necessarily* false was a considerable development when compared to the rather rougher views of ideology which are to be found in the earlier works, and especially in the *German Ideology*, written by Marx and Engels in 1845–6. In this work Marx was primarily concerned to establish the thesis that ideological convictions are determined by material circumstances, but there is no suggestion, as there would be in the later *Capital*, of the way in which ideology is actually conditioned by the false *language* which is a reflection of the deceptive forms of social relations which are accepted as real. "Morals, religion, metaphysics and suchlike ideology, and the forms of consciousness which correspond to them", he wrote in the *German Ideology*, "no longer . . . retain the semblance of independence. They have no history, and no development. Men, as they develop their material production, also change, as the reality changes, their thinking, and the products of their thought. It is not consciousness which determines life, but life which determines consciousness."[6] In this key passage there is no suggestion of fraud or deception. The ideology is a reflection of the material relations, distorted, of course, but not as the result of any deliberate act. This becomes clear if one looks at the following, much quoted, image used by Marx in the same work: "If in all ideology men and their circumstances appear upside down as in a *camera obscura*, this phenomenon arises just as much from their historical life process as the inversion of objects on the retina does from their physical life process . . . we set out from real, active men, and on the basis of their real life process we demonstrate this development of the ideological reflexes and echoes of this life progress."[7] "Reflexes and echoes" clearly do not imply any suggestion of deception or opprobrium. However, there are numerous passages in the *German Ideology* which suggest just this, and it is doubtless on the basis of these passages that the widely accepted picture of Marx's view of ideology as a fraudulent weapon of the bourgeoisie is based. To quote one of the many examples, he refers to "the perverted form in which the pseudo-sacrosanct and hypocritical ideology of the bourgeoisie portrays its own separate interests as universal'.[8]

It would seem that Marx, at all events in his mature writings, generally reserved the term 'ideology' for the moral and juridical principles proclaimed by the bourgeoisie. As will be seen later, this usage was abandoned or, more correctly, never adopted by Lenin, who uses "ideas", "theory" and "ideology" virtually interchangeably. It is of interest to note, therefore, that in his earliest writings Marx uses "idea", or "ideas" in the more generally accepted sense of a political theory underlying a society or a movement. In *The Holy Family*, for example, written in 1845, we find such an assessment as the following: "The revolutionary movement . . . had driven forward the communist idea . . . This idea, worked out to its conclusion, is the idea of the new world order."[9] Again, in *Misère de la Philosophie* (written in 1847) he uses words about "ideas" which suggest that ideas can be the product of every kind of society, though always determined by the mode of production – a view which is repeatedly found in Lenin: "The same men who establish the social relations which correspond to their material production, also produce the principles, the ideas, the categories which correspond to their social relations. Thus, these ideas, these categories are as little eternal as the relations which they express. *They are historical and transitory products.*"[10]

In this context, once again with Lenin in mind, it is of interest to trace in Marx's early writings, so far as it can be discerned, his view of the relationship of the "idea" to political action. Can it be argued that Marx was at any period concerned with this problem? Before looking at the *Communist Manifesto*, which as distinct from other writings was written specifically as a call to action, and much less as a work of analysis, it is of interest to look at the most forcible expression of the notion that the revolutionary idea is a necessary element for revolutionary action. This is to be found in *Critique of Hegel's Philosophy of Right: Introduction*, which dates from the end of 1843 and beginning of 1844, and therefore arguably belongs to the period before Marx had fully formulated his materialist interpretation of history. Stripped of the verbal fireworks in which this essay abounds, what Marx appears to be saying is that for a revolution to be achieved in Germany, socialist ideas are not enough. Socialist ideas, or philosophy, are merely the head: the heart is formed by the proletariat. The revolution can only be brought about by the union of the "head" and the "heart" – in other words, of theory and action: "Just as philosophy finds its material weapon in the proletariat, so the proletariat finds its spiritual weapon in philosophy. As soon as the lightning of thought has struck deeply into the naive popular soil, the emancipation of Germans into the rank of human beings will take place."[11] Not unnaturally, this passage has occasionally been cited to support the view that Lenin's doctrine that revolutionary consciousness had to be brought to the proletariat from the outside has the authority of Marx. This argument is rendered all the more superficially attractive by the following circumstances. The *Introduction* was translated into Russian by a member of the circle of conspirators to assassinate Alexander III, formed in 1876–7 by Alexander Ulianov, Lenin's brother. When Alexander Ulianov was sentenced to death, after the discovery of the conspiracy, his younger brother devoted intense study to all that he could find of the revolutionary literature that had inspired Ulianov, and he made every effort to study all the circumstances which had induced him to become a revolutionary. It is a fair assumption, therefore, that he read the translation of the *Introduction* at the critically formative period of his intellectual development. There is no doubt that Lenin did read the *Introduction* at some stage, since he quotes it a number of times – though not the passage set out above.

However, whatever effect Marx's youthful argument may have had on Lenin (and it will be argued later that Lenin derived his distinctive doctrine of revolutionary consciousness from quite a different source), there is little substance in the case put forward that Marx believed that the proletariat had to have consciousness brought to it from the outside. But even if he believed this in 1843–4 (as phrases like "the naive popular soil" may suggest) this was after all before he had developed, or fully developed, his materialist interpretation of history. Only a year later, at the end of 1844 in *The Holy Family*, when discussing the role of the proletariat in the revolution, he made it clear that the proletariat will be carrying out its historical role quite irrespectively of what it consciously believes to be its objective: "It is not a matter of what this or that proletarian or indeed the proletariat as a whole meanwhile imagines its aim to be. It is a matter of things *as they are*, and of what the proletariat will historically be forced to do by reason of its own *being*. Its aim is . . . inexorably laid down by its conditions of living and by the whole organization of contemporary bourgeois society."[12]

So far as the mature Marx is concerned, both in the works and in the correspondence there are a number of statements which expressly deny the proposition that revolutionary consciousness must be brought to the proletariat "from the outside". The most specific of these denials is contained in a long confidential circular of the General Council of the International, dated 21 July 1873, which was signed by Marx among others (and, unmistakably, drafted by him). The circular was a part of the death-struggle of the International against an attack launched upon it by Bakunin's *Alliance*, and it is mainly concerned with details which are both tedious and, so far as this enquiry is concerned, irrelevant.[13] What is relevant is the vigour with which Marx attacks the theoretical basis of his adversaries. He begins by quoting from one of their resolutions:

> "In order to make the working class into the real representative of the new interests of mankind" its organization must "be guided by the idea which is destined to triumph. The aim must be to develop this idea out of the demands of our epoch, out of the inner strivings of mankind, through constant study of the manifestations of social life. The idea must *thereupon be carried into the midst* of our worker organization, etc." And finally "one must create in the heart of our worker population a really socialist revolutionary *school*". And so the autonomous worker sections are transformed at a stroke into *schools*, whose masters will be these gentlemen from the Alliance. They *develop the idea* through "constant study", which leaves not a trace behind it. They "carry it into the midst of our worker organization". For them the working class is unworked material, a chaos that needs the breath of their Holy Ghost in order to take on form.[14]

Lenin was too good a marxist to claim Marx's authority for what he must have known was a refashioning of the doctrine of the Master, and it was no doubt for this reason that he never adopted Marx's approach to ideology but fashioned a doctrine of his own on the subject. In fact, as will be shown later, it was from a very different source that Lenin derived his doctrine of bringing revolutionary consciousness to the workers from the outside.

Hitherto we have been concerned mainly with analytical writings of Marx (apart from the circular just referred to) in which he is developing his view of the nature of society in general, and the materialist interpretation of history in particular. It is therefore of particular interest to turn to the *Communist Manifesto*, because this was designed as a programme for action, a programme in which the results of past analysis are synthesized in a call to revolution. Although discussion of ideology does not figure as such in the *Manifesto*, there are a number of references to it which enable one to assess Marx's treatment of this question in the context of action. This is, of course, of especial importance to bear in mind when one comes to discuss Lenin's views on ideology, since Lenin was almost exclusively concerned in his writing with the practical task of mobilizing people for action.

The first reference to ideology seems to drive a coach and four through the theoretical structure behind Marx's view of ideology. This theoretical structure can be summed up very roughly in two propositions: (a) ideology, by which he meant bourgeois ideology, is always conditioned by the social relations on which bourgeois society is based; and (at any rate in the mature form, in *Capital*) (b) although what the bourgeois ideologists proclaim is false, the falsity is not due to their deliberate falsification or deception, but is an inevitable result of the false language which corresponds to the false descriptions of social relations to which they are conditioned. In the *Manifesto*, however, where Marx argues that the proletariat is increased by the fact that impoverished members of the ruling class are driven to join the proletariat, he adds that "in particular, a portion of the bourgeois ideologists" goes over to the proletariat and helps to educate it and to supply it with weapons for fighting the bourgeoisie. These are the bourgeois ideologists "who have raised themselves to the level of comprehending theoretically the historic movement as a whole".[15] So far as I am aware, Marx nowhere explains how these ideologists, the falsity of whose views is, as it were, built into their discourse in the very language which they use, come to see the light sufficiently to instruct the proletariat. Nor is it fully consistent with the materialist interpretation of history and the historically predestined role of the proletariat to make a revolution to suppose that the proletariat requires enlightenment from these *déclassé* bourgeois ideologists – though it is the case that this aspect of their enlightenment is only treated as one aspect of the general process of enlightenment. Indeed, a couple of pages further on, Marx stresses that "the theoretical conclusions of the communists are in no way based on ideas or principles that have been invented, or discovered, by this or that would-be universal reformer. They merely express in general terms actual relations springing from an existing class struggle, from an historical movement going on under our very eyes."[16]

The remaining references to ideology in the *Manifesto* are also more consistent with what one can glean of Marx's general view of ideology from his analytical writings. At one point, however, no doubt with an essentially propagandist and inflammatory document in mind, Marx does imply that the falsity of bourgeois ideology is, in fact, rooted in selfish self-interest. In a rhetorical address to the bourgeoisie he says: "The selfish misconception that induces you to transform into the eternal laws of nature and of reason, the social forms springing from your present mode of production and form of property-historical relations that rise and disappear in the process of production – this misconception you share with every ruling class that has preceded you." And the ideology which bolsters these social forms is no more than the expression of the class will: "Your very ideas are but the outgrowth of the conditions of your bourgeois production and bourgeois property, just as your jurisprudence is but the will of your class made into a law for all, a will, whose essential character and direction are determined by the economic conditions of existence of your class."[17]

Indeed, "the ruling ideas of each age have ever been the ideas of its ruling class".[18] The coming revolution will therefore involve a complete rejection of all bourgeois ideology: "Law, morality, religion are to him [i.e. the proletarian] so many bourgeois prejudices, behind which lurk in ambush just as many bourgeois interests . . . The communist revolution . . . involves the most radical rupture with traditional property relations."[19] But nowhere does Marx suggest that the proletariat on coming to power will have an ideology of its own. Indeed, the clear implication of the *Manifesto* is that with the abolition of classes, of class dominance, there will be no room for ideology at all; on what basis the ruling proletariat will develop its law and morality is nowhere discussed. But it is made clear that for communists there is no need for more theory than the abolition of private property. Since the communists' theoretical conclusions are not based "on ideas or principles which have been invented", but merely express "actual relations springing from an existing class struggle . . . in this sense, the theory of the communists may be summed up in the single sentence: Abolition of private property".[20]

The evolution of Lenin's concept of ideology is very different from that of Marx. Imprisoned for a short time in 1895 and then exiled, Lenin's distinctive doctrine of the need to bring revolutionary consciousness to the workers from the outside, since otherwise they would, if left to their spontaneous action, merely pursue "trade unionist" interest rather than revolution, seems in one sense to have emerged quite suddenly and to have been evolved between 1899 and 1902. Indeed, Lenin's thought between 1895 and 1899 has often been described as his "Menshevik period", by which is meant that his view of the function of the Social Democratic Party in its relations to the working-class movement corresponded to what the Mensheviks (with some justification) believed to be Marx's view, namely, that the proletariat develops its revolutionary consciousness in the course of its struggle for its rights against the capitalist employers. Indeed Marx says this quite unequivocally in the passage from the *Communist Manifesto* quoted under the reference in footnote 16. While in prison in 1895 Lenin prepared a draft programme for the social democratic party, on which he wrote a long commentary in exile in the summer of 1896. The main burden of his commentary is the need for the workers to develop revolutionary consciousness through the struggle for their rights: there is no suggestion that this consciousness has to be brought to them "from the outside". On the contrary, he specifically states that "the task of the party does not consist in inventing out of its head some modern means of helping the workers, but to join the workers' struggle – to help them in the struggle which they have started themselves".[21]

Nevertheless, this "Menshevik" phase must not be exaggerated. From the very start of his career as a revolutionary publicist, Lenin's view of ideology was sharply differentiated in several respects from that of Marx. For Marx ideology is, in effect, restricted to the bourgeoisie. It consist of the false moral, juridical and social values which the bourgeoisie – whether innocently and unconsciously or fraudulently – use in order to bolster the order which favours their interests. For Lenin, at the very outset of his long career of revolutionary writing in 1894, ideology in its relation to the class struggle is something quite different: it is the doctrine which enables the working class to conduct their struggle in a scientific manner. He quotes with approval Kautsky's view that social democracy consists of the union of the workers' movement with socialism – a view which recalls the Marx of 1843–4 (in the *Critique of Hegel's Philosophy of Right: Introduction*) but which probably antedated Marx's conversion to historical materialism, and which at any rate does not recur in his later work. Lenin in 1894 refers repeatedly to marxism as the ideology of the working class. Again, this view is widely different from that of Marx who, at any rate in the *Communist Manifesto*, implies that the working class on conquering power requires no ideology and that its conquest of power is in fact signalized by the rejection of ideology, i.e. the ideology of the bourgeoisie. Consistently with his own, seemingly un-marxist view of ideology, Lenin ridicules in these early works those who interpret Marx in such a way as to suggest that his view is that the working class acquires consciousness of its own accord in the course of its struggle against the capitalist employers, and stresses that the duty of socialists is to popularize Marx's theory, to bring it to the workers, to help the workers to assimilate it, and to work out the best conditions for uniting the workers into a political power.[22]

Of course, Lenin's knowledge of the writings of Marx was much too profound for him to have failed to perceive that his use of ideology in the sense of the correct "revolutionary theory" was far removed from the sense in which Marx used the term "ideology". There is, indeed, one instance to be found in Lenin's writings where he does use the term more or less in the sense in which Marx used it – in an essay on Marx, written in 1914. After explaining that, according to Marx, being determines consciousness and not the reverse, he explains how the social revolution comes about when existing production forces come into conflict with existing production relations. In examining such transformations, it is essential to distinguish the material and scientifically determinable transformation in economic relations "from the juridical, political, religious, philosophical – in a word, ideological forms – in which people perceive this conflict and struggle against it".[23] What he seems to be saying here is, indeed, very close to what Marx says – that the bourgeoisie either use "ideology" in order to struggle against the social revolution or, perhaps, are unable to perceive its true nature because they are blinded by essentially false forms of production relations, and therefore confused by the false language to which they are conditioned. Lenin nowhere, so far as I have been able to discover, explains that he used "ideology" in a sense which bears no relationship to the sense in which Marx used the term. But statements abound in Lenin's works to the general effect that the theories of Marx were not to be treated as immutably fixed and rigid, but were to be interpreted creatively in accordance with changing conditions.

Apart from this one essay on Marx which, after all, was intended as an accurate exposition of his views, Lenin does not follow Marx in confining "ideology" to the juridical, moral etc, ideas of the bourgeoisie, but uses the term to express *any* accepted doctrine, whether true or false, whether bourgeois or proletarian. There are to be found in his writing, apart from bourgeois and socialist ideology, such variants as "religious" ideology which is contrasted with "scientific" ideology. There is even an essay on the thought of Tolstoy whose pessimism, non-resistance and appeal to the spirit is the "ideology" which "inevitably" arises in an epoch when the entire old order has been turned upside down, and the masses, which are still dominated by their old habits and traditions, are incapable of seeing what social forces could bring their liberation from the miseries which accompany an epoch of break-up.[24]

In short, "ideology" for Lenin is a neutral term, and his use of it is of little interest or significance in understanding his thought. The really important element in his doctrine is "revolutionary theory", which is the term which he usually employs to designate the ideology of the class struggle of the proletariat. This "revolutionary theory" is a very frequent theme in his writings – there are literally hundreds of references under the heading "revolutionary theory" in the main index to the recently published *Complete Works of Lenin* – including its historical development, its significance in the class struggle of the proletariat, its relation to practical work, its creative character, its importance as a guide to action, revolutionary theory contrasted with revisionism, and many more. It is therefore in the context of the emergence of Lenin's distinctive views on socialism as the ideology of the working class (though, of course, only one ideology among many) that Lenin's original contribution to the theory of ideology becomes of interest. And this brings us back to 1899 since it was between 1899 and 1902 that his views on this question developed and matured.

It has already been suggested that Lenin had recognized in 1894, if not before, the supreme importance of the correct "revolutionary theory" which he from the first designated as an "ideology" for the success of the workers' revolutionary struggle. But it was under the immediate impact of two events which shattered the relative peace of his (far from uncomfortable) exile that the views on this question which particularly distinguish him were formed and developed. The first was the arrival in July of a document sent to him by his sister. This document, to which she had added the derisory title of *Credo*, represented the summary of the views of a private gathering of revisionist-minded social democratic individualists as recorded by one of them, E. D. Kuskova. These views, much influenced by the leader of revisionist marxism, E. Bernstein, in effect rejected the one-class rule of the proletariat as laid down by Marx, and may be summarized as follows: nowhere in Western Europe has the working class won political freedom by its own effort. But, where political freedom has been achieved by the efforts of the bourgeoisies, the workers utilize the opportunities presented by civil and political freedom for the advancement of their own aims. Hence the emphasis laid by Marx on political struggle. But in Russia, where political freedom does not exist, the line of least resistance and the aim which should be followed by the workers is economic struggle. The fight for political freedom should be left to the bourgeoisie, and the task of marxist intellectuals is to support the liberals in their economic struggle. Around the same time Lenin received the Russian translation of Bernstein's famous pamphlet, which is known in its English translation as *Evolutionary Socialism*. It seems to have been the first occasion on which he took the opportunity of seriously studying Bernstein's views, though the explosive pamphlet, published in 1899, had in fact been serialized in 1898 and 1899 in *Die Neue Zeit* of which Lenin was an attentive reader while in exile. He had also both reviewed and translated Kautsky's criticism of the arguments used by Bernstein in the course of 1899. It may be that the impulse to dedicate himself now to attacking the views of Bernstein was sparked off by the remark of Bernstein in the Russian translation of his pamphlet (quite untrue, incidentally) that the great majority of Russian social democrats were converts to his views.

Lenin's immediate reaction to the *Credo* was to organize a meeting of all the social democrats he could muster in exile to condemn the document. The main stress in this protest is on two points. First, on the need for a disciplined organization of Russian social democrats to fight these pernicious views; and secondly, that "the manner of the class movement of the workers can only be the theory of revolutionary marxism, and Russian social democracy must be concerned with its future development and transformation into living action".[25]

There followed later in 1899 a series of articles in which Lenin's specific ideas on the nature of the party and on the role of the revolutionary theory are developed in greater detail. These articles, written in October (though not published until 1925), summarize much of what was to be more fully developed in 1902 in *What Is To Be Done?* They stress the need for a struggle against the ideas of Bernstein, and describe the role of the party as "the organization and direction of the class struggle of the proletariat". Lenin scoffs at accusations which might be levelled against him that he was promoting some kind of "orthodoxy" or aiming at the persecution of "heretics" (which, of course, was exactly what he was doing): "There can be no strong socialist party without a revolutionary theory." Lenin pointed out that the theories of Marx were not fixed once and for all, but had merely laid the foundations which require constant development. Above all, the articles stress that economic struggle without political struggle is useless, and lay heavy emphasis on the need for centralized and disciplined organization and, above all, on the need for a central party newspaper ("organ") to ensure the development of the correct theory.[26]

Although at the end of 1899 Lenin did stress the need to develop a worker intelligentsia which would be capable of explaining revolutionary theory to the more backward workers, there is as yet, at this stage of Lenin's thought, no direct enunciation of the doctrine that "revolutionary consciousness" can only be brought to the workers from the outside. The idea was, however, developing in Lenin's mind, and almost certainly this was under the influence of the works of Kautsky, which he read with great attention and admiration, both in *Neue Zeit* and in book form as forwarded to him by his sister as the works appeared. The idea that workers may require the stimulus from intellectuals to accomplish their historic destiny is not quite foreign to Marx – the famous passage from the *Critique of Hegel's Philosophy of Right: Introduction* has already been referred to; and there is also in the *Communist Manifesto* a reference to "a portion of the bourgeois ideologists, who have raised themselves to the level of comprehending theoretically the historical movement as a whole" who go over to the proletariat, and, presumably, help them to become more revolutionary.[27] But Lenin does not anywhere quote these passages in support of his own theory, presumably since he knew that they were not typical of Marx's real views, and since Lenin was generally honest in his use of sources. In contrast, he frequently quotes Kautsky.

The idea that the workers, whether through lack of time or education, have to learn their revolutionary doctrine from bourgeois intellectuals is one which occurs frequently in the writings of Kautsky. As far back as 1892, he warned that a workers' movement spurred on by utopian, as distinct from scientifically correct, socialist ideas risked ending up "mere trade union stuff" (*nur Gewerkschaftlerei*).[28] His fullest exposition of the ideas now generally associated with Lenin appeared in a long commentary on the new draft programme of the Austrian Social Democratic Party[29] from which Lenin quotes at length in *What Is To Be Done?*:

> Many of our revisionist critics believe that Marx asserted that economic development and the class struggle not only create the conditions for socialist production but directly give birth to the *consciousness* of its necessity . . . The draft states: "The more the proletariat increases as the result of capitalist development . . . the more opportunity it acquires for struggle against capitalism. The proletariat reaches the consciousness" of the possibility and necessity of socialism . . . And this is quite wrong . . . socialism and the class struggle come into being side by side, not one from the other . . . in fact, contemporary economic science is as much a condition of socialist production as, shall we say, contemporary technology and the proletariat

> with the best will in the world can create neither the one nor the other . . . The bearer of science is not the proletariat, but the *bourgeois intelligentsia* . . . In this way socialist consciousness is something brought in from the outside (*von aussen hineingetragenes*) into the class struggle of the proletariat, and not something that has spontaneously arisen in it.[30]

This, in substance, contains the whole of Lenin's theory of the role and nature of revolutionary doctrine in the class struggle, except that he adds (something that Kautsky had also conceded in his earlier writings) that workers also participate in the working-out of the theory – though they participate as theorists of socialism, and not as workers.[31] The whole of Lenin's pamphlet is, of course, an attack on spontaneity of worker action, a plea for organization, discipline and centralized direction within the Social Democratic Party, on the vital importance of the "correct" revolutionary theory and on the harmfulness of debate about what the theory should be when once "the truth" has been established. "There can be no revolutionary movement without a revolutionary theory," he states at the outset. "This can only come from the outside. The history of all countries bears witness that the working class, relying exclusively on its own power, is only capable of evolving a trade unionist consciousness . . . But socialist doctrine has grown out of the philosophical, historical and economic theories which were worked out by the educated representatives of the property-owning classes, the intelligentsia." This was true of Marx and Engels and true of the Russian revolutionary intelligentsia.[32] The rest of the pamphlet follows logically from the all-embracing importance which is attached to the introduction of the correct revolutionary theory of ideology into the struggle of the workers by the intellectuals who form the party: the party leaders must be professional, in other words, liberated from the burden of earning their living, and the party must be centralized and highly disciplined so that orthodoxy can be maintained. And (last but not least, as Lenin was fond of saying) it must be under the direction of a central theoretical "organ", or newpaper, which would be responsible for developing the correct theory.

The contrast between the treatment of "ideology" in the works of Marx and Lenin could hardly be more complete. For Marx, who was primarily concerned with analysis of society, ideology is always the sum total of the moral, juridical and social ideas of the bourgeoisie, false ideas, of course, and therefore fraudulent in their effect so far as the proletariat is concerned – though it is not clear whether Marx always believed that the fraudulence was deliberate. Indeed, there are many passages in his far from systematic treatment of "ideology" which suggest that the falsity of bourgeois ideology was inherent in the falsity of the social relations which the bourgeoisie is conditioned to accept as true, and consequently in the very language used by the bourgeoisie. Lenin was concerned with revolution: analysis for him was subsidiary to this main purpose. He never followed Marx in restricting "ideology" to the ideas of the bourgeoisie but accepted that there may be varieties of ideology – some true, some false, some rational, some irrational – though as an historical materialist he never doubted that the nature of every particular ideology was determined by the material conditions of the society or epoch in which it arose. Lenin, in fact, may be said to have destroyed the classical marxist picture (deriving from Engels, not Marx) of ideology as "false consciousness". As Mannheim has said – though without giving Lenin the credit for the transformation – "it is no longer the exclusive privilege of socialist thinkers to trace bourgeois thought to ideological foundations, and thereby to discredit it. Nowadays, groups of every standpoint use this weapon against all the rest."[33]

Lenin's distinctive contribution, which has no solid foundation in the writings of Marx (if a few casual and untypical passages are disregarded), was to recognize the importance of "revolutionary theory" – used by him interchangeably with such phrases as "scientific socialism", or "ideology of the proletariat", or "socialist ideology" – as a *weapon* for the making of a revolution. Following Kautsky in this respect, he rejected the interpretation of Marx usually accepted among social democrats that socialist consciousness is an inevitable, indeed automatic product of the struggle of the working class for its rights. He argued that this consciousness had to be brought to the workers by bourgeois or worker intellectuals – but intellectuals who had the capacity to understand and interpret economic and socialist theories.

Lenin's interpretation of ideology, developed as and intended to be an instrument of revolution, became, after the seizure of power by the Bolsheviks in 1917, an instrument of rule. This aspect was never discussed by Lenin in his speeches and writings as a question of theory, but became evident in practice, certainly by 1921. From the doctrine of the correct revolutionary theory imposed by central discipline and determined by a central sanhedrin there flowed such familiar features as censorship and other forms of control over information, limitation on debate and criticism and, before long, the notions of "orthodox" and "counter-revolutionary" opinion. It is arguable – though this is not the place to argue it – that the autocratic rigidity of communism can be derived from the theory of "socialist ideology" enunciated by Lenin between 1899 and 1902.

1. Karl Marx and Friedrich Engels, *Selected Works*, vol. II (London, 1950), p. 451.
2. *ibid.*, p. 458.
3. Martin Seliger, *The Marxist Conception of Ideology: A Critical Essay* (Cambridge 1977), p. 30.
4. Jean-Yves Calvez, *La Pensée de Karl Marx* (Paris 1956), p. 244.
5. John Mepham, 'The Theory of Ideology in Capital', *Radical Philosophy* 2, summer 1972, pp. 12–19, at p. 19.
6. *Marx-Engels Gesamtausgabe, Erste Abteilung*, vol. V (Moscow-Leningrad 1933), p. 16. Cited hereafter as *Mega*.
7. Karl Marx and Friedrich Engels, *Basic Writings on Politics and Philosophy*, ed. Lewis Feuer (London 1969), p. 247.
8. *Mega*, V (Moscow-Leningrad 1933), p. 36.
9. *Mega*, III (Berlin 1932), pp. 294–5.
10. *Mega*, VI (Moscow-Leningrad 1933), pp. 179–80.
11. Karl Marx and Friedrich Engels, *Werke*, vol. I (Berlin 1957), p. 391.
12. *Werke*, vol. II (Berlin 1957), p. 38. For further discussion of this aspect of Marx's view of the interrelations between ideas and reality, and of his belief that theory (by which he meant left Hegelian theory) must be subjected to criticism by being made practical through being passed to the masses; and conversely that theory must become no more than an expression of the practical, of the real life of man, in order to be fully realized, see Calvez, *op cit.*, p. 107.
13. See Franz Mehring, *Karl Marx* (3rd edn, London 1951), pp. 472–84; Julius Braunthal, *Geschichte der Internationale*, vol. I (Hanover 1961), pp. 184–94.
14. Karl Marx, *Politische Schriften*, ed. Hans-Joachim Lieber, vol. II (Stuttgart 1960), pp. 999–1000.
15. Marx and Engels, *Selected Works*, vol. I (London 1950), pp. 41–2.
16. *ibid.*, p. 44.
17. *ibid.*, p. 49.
18. *ibid.*, p. 49.
19. *ibid.*, pp. 42, 50.
20. *ibid.*, pp. 44–5.
21. V. I. Lenin, *Polnoe sobranie sochinenii*, vol. II (5th edn, Moscow 1958), pp. 101–2. Cited hereafter as *Lenin*.
22. *Lenin*, I. pp. 332–3, 411.
23. *Lenin*, XXVI, pp. 56–7.
24. *Lenin*, XX, pp. 101–3.
25. *Lenin*, IV, 1959, pp. 165–76, where the *Credo* is reprinted.
26. *Lenin*, IV, pp. 177–98.
27. Marx and Engels, *Selected Works*, vol. I (London 1950), pp. 41–2.
28. K. Kautsky, *Das Erfurter Programm*, (3rd edn, Stuttgart 1892), pp. 239–40.

29. *Neue Zeit, 1901–1902*, vol. XX (i), no. 3.
30. Italics in the original.
31. *Lenin*, VI, 1959, p. 49, footnote.
32. *ibid.*, pp. 24, 30–1.
33. *Ideology and Utopia*, (paperback edn, London 1960), pp. 66–7.

Plekhanov

This recent study of Plekhanov has not been previously published.

Georgy Valentinovich Plekhanov was born on 29 November 1856 in the central Russian province of Tambov. He was thus about twelve and a half years older than Lenin. He came of a military family of minor landed gentry and of Tartar extraction. All three of his brothers spent their careers in military service, one of them, who presumably was a half-brother since Georgy only had two full brothers, as a police commissioner. There is little reason for the psychologists to look for the source of his revolutionary passion in his family origins. He inherited his father's austere, disciplined and unapproachable character. But there is no suggestion whatever that his relations with his rather stern father had any lasting effect on his character. His relations with his mother were warm and affectionate. There is no question whatever of any revolutionary ideas having been propagated in his home – indeed there is even less substance to this suggestion in Plekhanov's case than there is in the case of Lenin.

It would appear that his "free thinking" developed at the Military Academy at Voronezh, where he remained until 1873 when he was seventeen. That this was at all possible was the result of the liberalization of the military schools under the influence of D. A. Miliutin in the sixties. At all events it was here that Plekhanov read Belinsky, Pisarev, Chernyshevsky and Dobroliubov – Chernyshevsky especially made an impression on him for life, as he would fifteen years later on Lenin. The poetry of Nekrasov was also an important intellectual influence, though the burning down of the Plekhanov manor house by their peasants for no apparent reason may have been one of the factors which led to Plekhanov's later firm belief in the idiocy of rural life, as Marx called it. It was possibly under the influence of the current vogue for science which was characteristic of the period that Plekhanov abandoned plans for a military career in favour of the Mining Institute in St Petersburg. He immediately became involved in revolutionary activities and after two years, in 1875, left the Institute as a fully-fledged and already very well-known revolutionary, aged nineteen or twenty. He became a founder member of *Zemlia i Volia* in 1876. I shall deal later with his transition from populism, after the split in 1879 of that organization into *Narodnaia Volia* and *Cherny Peredel*. In 1880 he emigrated with a group of people who were to become his main supporters – Lev Deich, Stefanovich (who soon died), Vera Zasulich, and Akselrod, and in 1883 the now converted marxists founded their group in Geneva. It is amusing to recall that in November 1880 when Marx heard of the emigration of these well-known revolutionaries he wrote scornfully to Sorge about "These gentlemen who are opposed to any revolutionary activity, and are preparing for the leap all in one into the anarchist-communist-atheist millennium . . . by means of the dullest of dull doctrinaire views".[1] Plekhanov was not to return to Russia again until 1917. His periods of political activity can roughly be divided as follows:

(a) From 1883 until the late nineties when he was fighting a pretty lonely battle in trying to "sell" the idea of marxism inside Russia.

(b) The period of partnership with Lenin on *Iskra* which ends in 1903 soon after the Second Party Congress.

(c) A somewhat surprising return to qualified support for Lenin in 1909, which did not, however, last very long.

(d) Isolation and divorce from the great body of the party, especially after 1914, until his death in bitter disappointment, doubt and disillusionment on 30 May 1918.

Plekhanov's important contribution as a theorist and as a scholar is evident. On the other hand he was a total failure as a politician. Why should this have been so? According to the very charitable Potresov this was due to the fact that political activity did not provide a sufficiently broad canvas for his genius. It seems more probable that he was in fact a victim of his own character. He was arrogant, vain, cold and contemptuous of many of those with whom he had to deal. He did not suffer fools gladly and he showed all the marks of a real Russian *barin*, even including anti-semitism which was a most unusual characteristic for a social democrat at that period. Some remarks which he made on the subject of Jews and the Bund during conversations with Lenin in 1900 on the future of *Iskra* were considered by the Soviet authorities to be so offensive that they were left out of all editions of Lenin's account of these conversations until the current fifth edition was published.[2] There is also an interesting remark recorded in 1905 in conversation with Zhabotinsky, the Zionist, that social democrats did not object to Jewish cultural autonomy, though "of course, we may have our own views about this [Jewish] culture and its value from an objective point of view".[3] His correspondence and that of his close associates is a record of frustrated rage, injured egoism and tantrums with which Vera Zasulich alone seems to have known how to deal. It is a curious fact that while intellectually there is a great consistency about Plekhanov with some minor exceptions, when once he was involved in practical politics his intellectual integrity and scholarly standards which characterized his work seemed completely to have deserted him. I will mention three instances though there are many more. One example, that according to Riazanov (as confirmed to me by Valentinov, who discussed the matter with Plekhanov's widow) in 1881 Marx's formal reply to Vera Zasulich (which only surfaced in 1923) was deliberately suppressed by Plekhanov so as not to give aid and comfort to the *narodniki*.[4] The second instance was the conflict with the so-called "economists" in 1899–1901, in which Plekhanov's polemics appalled even his friends. At bottom this was an operation designed to secure the supremacy of the Liberation of Labour and the *Iskra* groups over *Rabochee Delo* which was the organ of the younger men who had been active in the growing labour movement in Russia. Insofar as economism means the view that the workers should not engage in any kind of revolutionary activity but leave this entirely to the bourgeoisie there is not one line in the whole of *Rabochee Delo*, throughout its publication, which supports the charge of economism. Indeed, so far as I have been able to discover the only advocates of economism in the strict sense were three individuals who occupied a somewhat eccentric position in the Russian social democratic movement, namely Kuskova, Prokopovich and Timofei (Kopelzon). Plekhanov's evidence, for what it was worth, of the economism of *Rabochee Delo* was in fact based on extracts which were alleged to have come from their private correspondence and which were quoted out of context. I suppose the whole of this somewhat disreputable incident is to be explained by Plekhanov's zeal, like Lenin, to combat the danger of revisionism which had appeared in the writings of Bernstein around this time. However, there is an interesting difference in my view between Lenin and Plekhanov's attitude to revisionism. Lenin's attitude is quite plain. He regarded it as his duty to save the revolution at all costs and since Bernstein provided reason for supposing that revolution was neither inevitable nor necessary, he had to be attacked. Plekhanov's position, though similar, was more involved and it seems to me that this was another of those cases where he was more concerned with the good of the cause than with intellectual truth. In a letter to Akselrod on the subject of Bernstein, for example, around this time, he seems to reproach Bernstein not so much with being wrong (he admits that Bernstein is right in some respects) 'but truth can be used for a number of ends. Bernstein uses it in order to embellish himself with the philistine's cap."[5] And in a later letter he praises Hegel for his "passion for truth" which is so lacking in Bernstein, and in place of which there is only a mass of "self-satisfied vulgarity". There is incidentally not a single word in this or in the former letter of any argument against Bernstein on the very massive facts with which he supported his case.[6] One could compare with this a letter to Kautsky, which was first published in German in 1898, which reproaches Kautsky for having said that social democrats ought to be grateful to Bernstein for having made them think about his arguments.[7] These are instances which seem to me to underline the difference between Plekhanov as scholar or marxist thinker and Plekhanov the moment he was involved in politics. In this context one may recall the very unfavourable impression which Plekhanov's refusal even to consider what he regarded as politically undesirable philosophy, made on the young Valentinov in Geneva in 1904, as he recalls in his memoirs. I think that this difference between Plekhanov the scholar, who appears to follow the normal standards of scholarship, and Plekhanov the politician is a very striking feature of his character. Indeed, it was Plekanov's conviction that Lenin was doing a useful job against the economists on behalf of *Iskra* that in 1901–2 led to Plekhanov leaving all the work of intrigue inside Russia to Lenin, concerning himself with it so little that he appears to have known nothing at all about it, and to have been extraordinarily surprised when on the eve of the Congress he first heard about it. It was this zeal, I think, for beating the economists that led Plekhanov to accept Lenin's *What Is To Be Done?* which from his point of view must have appeared as inconsistent with marxism and which, indeed, he began to attack very bitterly when he had broken with Lenin shortly after the Second Congress.[8] The third incident, which happened in 1909, seems to me to be even more intellectually dishonest, even more surprising than the other cases, in spite, I may say, of the efforts of his biographer S. H. Baron to offer an explanation which is no explanation at all. (In general, Plekhanov has not been fortunate in his biographers, either in Russian or in English.) Plekhanov remained aloof from both factions of the party after 1905, criticizing both equally. By 1908 Lenin was conducting a campaign which was designed to split the Mensheviks by attracting the "healthy, party-minded" elements away from the "liquidators". The latter included so far as Lenin was concerned anyone who disagreed with him and in fact embraced all the Menshevik intellectuals. The charge of liquidationism was to a large extent a complete invention, though of course it was true that the Mensheviks repudiated, along with Plekhanov, Lenin's methods of running the underground party, his methods of raising money and the like. At the end of 1908, Plekhanov suddenly quarrelled with his colleagues on *Golos Sotsial-demokrata*, who included Martov, Potresov and Maslov. The quarrel was over an article which Potresov wrote for a collective work of which he was joint editor. The article was about social democracy and it is clear on the evidence that the reason for the quarrel was that Plekhanov's role had not been sufficiently stressed for his liking. This is borne out by a letter at the time written by his wife. Ostensibly, the reason given by Plekhanov was that the article did not lay enough stress on the importance of "hegemony". Now hegemony was a theory, originally developed in 1898 by Akselrod, and subsequently adopted by Plekhanov to the effect that the working class would, in Russian conditions, be able to exercise hegemony over the liberal parties when they emerged – a view of which the absurdity was already recognized by Plekhanov in November 1905 when he wrote that only someone who "had not the faintest idea about scientific socialism" could seriously suggest either that the bourgeoisie would follow the proletariat, or *vice versa*.[9]

From 1909 onwards, to the astonishment of his friends, Plekhanov began for the next few years in the pages of the little periodical which he edited to attack his colleagues as liquidators in very much the same terms as those used by Lenin. He formed a group called the Party Mensheviks who tended to support the Bolsheviks, and all this activity was of course very useful and helpful to Lenin in his work to break up the Social Democratic Party, and to advance the cause of the Bolsheviks. This was particularly helpful to him because of the great reputation which Plekhanov enjoyed among German social democrats. This seems to me to be an example of the way in which vanity could drive Plekhanov in his political activity completely off the rails. His association with Lenin, if such it can be called, did not last very long and certainly by 1912 he was once again alienated from him and after 1914 alienated from the whole social democratic movement, because Plekhanov supported the war against the Germans without any qualifications whatever. He regarded the question of victory over Germany as one of primary importance and one to which all socialist aims should be postponed until after victory. His last year of life in Russia was a time of sadness, disillusionment, disappointment and suffering. He felt remote and estranged from the Bolshevik regime: the incident when his house was searched by a party of soldiers and sailors who had never heard his name, followed by Lenin's order that "Citizen Plekhanov" should not be molested (Lenin was never particularly generous to political opponents until they were dead) are well known. Plekhanov died on 30 May 1918 in Finland. He was buried in the Volkhov cemetery in Petrograd. The seven-kilometre-long crowd included many workers (in spite of party advice that they should stay away) who had ignored him in his lifetime.

I will return to the last year of Plekhanov's life below. But it is first necessary to explore the consistency of his thought, which I suggest contrasts noticeably with the inconsistency of his political conduct. There were two main intellectual convictions which dominated and determined Plekhanov's thought all through his life: (a) that the basic principle of human history and human life is materialism, that material factors determine both the course of history and ideas, or in other words that being determines consciousness; and (b) that the history of Russia must be seen as a conflict between the European and the Asiatic trends, between the civilized aspects of a modern society in the Western world and the backward despotic elements of Russia's Asiatic past; and that with the development of capitalism Russia was travelling on the road to the ultimate triumph of the European element.

The fanatical defence of materialism against any and every kind of idealism characterizes Plekhanov throughout his active life. There is no need to stress this after his conversion to marxism in the early eighties: *The Monist Interpretation of History*, published legally in 1894, is the most eloquent proof of this passion, comparable only to the passion of some fundamentalist Christians. This book, incidentally, exercised an enormous intellectual influence in converting revolutionaries to what is quaintly called "scientific" socialism. The materialist interpretation dominates his work on literature and on social thought, on the role of the individual in history and the like. The following passage, which dates from the end of the century, is typical of his general outlook: "Historical factors turn out to be pure abstractions . . . Men do not make several 'histories', separate from one another, such as the history of law, the history of morals or philosophy, and so on, but only one history – the history of their own social relations, which are determined by the state of the forces of production at any given time. The so-called ideologies represent nothing but the varied forms of reflection in the minds of human beings of this one and indivisible history."

So far so good. When faced with imminent death Plekhanov reiterated his passionate, materialist faith. As his wife relates, he reproached her for weeping: "What is the matter with you, Rosa? Are you not ashamed? You and I are old revolutionaries, and we must be firm." And then he added: "And, after all, what is death? A transformation of matter." And glancing at the window, "Do you see that birch tree leaning so gently against the pine? I, too, perhaps will one day be transformed into a similar birch. What is so bad about that?" And on his gravestone, at his own request, are engraved the words from Shelley's *Adonais*: "He is made one with nature."

All this seems determined enough – and yet! When it really came to making his last peace with his conscience, or his Maker whom he would of course have denied, the position did not prove quite so simple. Lev Deich tells us that during his last weeks Plekhanov kept on and on about the thought which deeply tormented him: "Did we not begin the propaganda of marxism too early in backward, semi-Asiatic Russia?"[10] Now, if one really believes, as Plekhanov ostensibly did, that the role of the individual in history is limited to advancing those trends that are already inherent in the material factors of the time, then how could Plekhanov have been premature in creating Russian social democracy? The individual, he wrote in his renowned *Role of the Individual in History*, can only have a very limited effect on events. "Influential individuals, thanks to the distinctive nature of their ability and their character, can change the particular physiognomy of events and some details of their consequences. But they cannot change their general direction which is determined by different forces."[11] Yet surely the beginning of organized social democracy in Russia must be regarded as at the very least such a "general direction" which was determined (as Plekhanov had himself repeatedly pointed out) by such "other forces" as the rise of industry and a proletariat and the decay of the village commune? Indeed, in an essay on Belinsky, written in 1911, Plekhanov in effect dismisses the possibility of social development ever being premature. "It is, of course, not true," he wrote, "that fundamental social situations can appear, as it were, prematurely. Only a partisan of absolute idealism could make such an assertion, a man in whose judgement the logical forms of life precede life itself."[12] His biographer, S. H. Baron, has drawn attention to the two major inconsistencies in Plekhanov's intellectual outlook. These are as between free will and determinism; and as between revolution and evolution.[13] I suppose by selecting passages here and there from twenty-four volumes of collected works one can find contradictions and inconsistencies in any man. I find a man's preoccupations when he is faced with death more significant than short quotations extracted from his writings. Evidently, the instinct of free will dies hard, even in so intellectually convinced a material determinist as was Plekhanov.

Perhaps it is unfair to criticize for inconsistency a man like Plekhanov who in 1918 was absolutely shattered by the events of the past months and was imminently facing death. But, on the other hand, I find no inconsistency in the evolution of the young Plekhanov – from a violent revolutionary prepared to foment revolts in the Bakunin manner, to an opponent of terrorism in 1879 at Lipetsk so violent that (according to Vera Figner) he aroused apprehensions among the revolutionaries that he might be about to denounce them all to the police. On the contrary, I think the distinction is clear if one bears in mind that even before he became converted to Marx's doctrine of revolution, he profoundly believed that a revolution is a social process in which the people as a whole must participate, and not a conspiracy to assassinate an Emperor, which is what was being discussed by *Zemlia i Volia* in 1879. Terror perpetrated by the people is one thing: terror perpetrated by a group of conspirators is clearly another. Given Plekhanov's uncompromising character, his intellectual determination and his readiness to stand alone in the face of any amount of unpopularity I find his conduct in 1879 presents no problem at all. The evolution of his thought to marxism after 1880 followed logically when once he was persuaded that the commune was already in a state of disintegration; and that the advent of capitalism in Russia, though slow, was certain. The result of this evolution was the famous two pamphlets – *Socialism and the Political Struggle* and *Our Disagreements*, which argued the case against conspiracy and Jacobinism and in favour of a workers' social democratic movement to complement the liberal movement which was now, in Russian conditions, inevitable; and to support and encourage the bourgeois, democratic revolution which the liberals would now also quite inevitably have to bring about. To a greater extent than any of the Russian social democrats Plekhanov believed that revolution in Russia must take place in two stages, if conspiratorial *coups d'état* and dictatorship were to be avoided: the imminent bourgeois stage; and then, in the fullness of time when social conditions were ripe for it, but not before, the socialist revolution. Although all social democrats paid lip-service to this doctrine, so far as Lenin was concerned it was conscious, or unconscious hypocrisy; so far as his followers were concerned it was a dogma which under his energetic lead they readily jettisoned in 1917. Even the Mensheviks, who should have known better, after initial resistance to the Bolshevik coup, acknowledged it as "an historical necessity". Plekhanov never wavered in his opposition, or in his fears of the consequences of what he regarded as a violation of historical order in October 1917.

I suppose the general view would be, and I think Plekhanov would have shared it, that his real intellectual contribution was the adaptation which he made or purported to make of Marx's analysis to the circumstances of Russia. How far the adaptation made any sense, except as an intellectual exercise, is another matter. But closely linked to this adaptation was his analysis of the conflict in Russian social history of the Asiatic and European elements – indeed, his decision in the eighties that the time was ripe for a marxist development in Russia was linked to his belief that the Asiatic element in Russian history was beginning to yield to the European element, in other words, capitalism with its concomitant promise of the legal and political order which is a part of it. It is the case that Marx took a very similar view of India in his correspondence with Engels in June 1853, and in an article in the *New York Daily Tribune*, where the break-up by the British of the traditional static pattern of oriental despotism is welcomed by Marx as the first step towards "Europeanization" and therefore the development of capitalism.[14] But there is no indication that Plekhanov knew these views of Marx, so far as I am aware. (The letters, of course, were only first published in 1913.) Plekhanov's fullest exposition of his analysis of Russian history on these lines was contained in the unfinished *History of Russian Social Thought*, of which only the Introduction (127 pages) and the First Part, which takes the story as far as the end of the seventeenth century, were written.[15] In many ways, this is his most original and stimulating work, which still repays study. Its main theme is that different social conditions from Western Europe produced a different social and political outlook in Russia; but that the conditions which would lead Russia towards a development parallel to that of Europe were now in the ascendant, and that the process of Europeanization could no longer be halted. The last sentences of the Introduction seem to me to illustrate Plekhanov's thought and outlook most clearly:

> Whether or not Peter said that Russia will in time have to "turn her back" on Europe, it is quite clear that at the present time she has no possibility whatever of doing so. This is made all the clearer by the fact that even the most typical of the countries of the East are now moving towards the West. There are some among them which even seem to threaten to overtake Russia in the process. China has become a republic, whereas in Russia the parliamentary regime has not yet been consolidated. This is to be explained by one of the most unfavourable peculiarities

> of our historical process: the Russian police state was sufficiently Europeanized to use all the achievements of European technology in its struggle against the innovators, while our innovators have only quite recently begun to lean on the popular masses, which as we have seen, are only Europeanized in respect of one of their parts – the proletariat . . . We can now proceed to the detailed examination of the way in which the *relative* peculiarities of Russian *being* were reflected in the course of development of Russian social consciousness.[16]

Plekhanov retained this optimism when the monarchy fell in 1917: his first interview on return to Russia with an Italian paper began with the words: "Asiatic Russia is defeated and my country triumphantly enters the great family of the free peoples of Europe."[17] That capitalism and hence bourgeois democracy spelt freedom was for Plekhanov, as for Marx, axiomatic, and like Marx he believed that the workers should and could use this freedom in order to attain, in addition, the social justice which capitalism denied them. Neither Marx nor Plekhanov, so far as I am aware, ever supposed that the social justice which they advocated would be achieved, or ostensibly achieved, by the sacrifice of all the freedoms which capitalism offered. There is, of course, the oft-quoted remark at the Second Congress on "*Salus revolutiae suprema lex*". But this did not represent Plekhanov's considered view, and he expressly repudiated and regretted the remark in later life, in fact in the last two articles which he published, in the wake of the rout of the Constituent Assembly. The articles included the following remark: "Victor Adler used to say to me half-jokingly, half-seriously, "Lenin is your son." I used to reply, "If he is my son, then evidently he is my illegitimate son." I still think that the tactics of the Bolsheviks represent a completely illegitimate deduction from the tactical propositions which I put forward, basing myself on the theory of Marx and Engels."[18] How central to Plekhanov's thought was this notion of Europeanization of Russia and its close connection with the question of the relevance of Marx's analysis to Russian conditions is shown by his anxious questioning on his death-bed of Lev Deich to which I have already made reference. Even more indicative of the place which the Europeanization of Russia held for him was his change from the internationalism and pacifism which he had championed in the Second International to militant defence of Russia in the war after 1914, and especially after 1917. He believed that defeat of Germany and her allies was essential in order to remove the backing which Russian reaction could look for from a victorious Germany; and after 1917, that the revolution had no chance of survival unless Germany was defeated, and that therefore struggle for socialist measures had to be postponed until after military victory. Plekhanov and his small band of followers grouped around the paper *Yedinstvo* were a small and despised, if sane, minority in the welter of variety of Bolshevik and Menshevik theory and practice in Russia in 1917. It can with truth be said that Plekhanov and Lenin were the only two social democrats who knew what they wanted: victory and the survival of the Provisional Government on the one hand; and defeat and Bolshevik power on the other. The welter of Menshevik inconsistency, vacillation and self-contradiction on the subject of the war only played into the hands of the Bolsheviks whose victory they did not desire. Baron regards Plekhanov's attitude to the war in 1914 as a complete change of outlook. I am not so sure that Plekhanov's attitude on war before 1914 had been so clear-cut as Baron suggests. As far back as 1893, for example, he had opposed the proposal of the anarcho-syndicalist Domela Nieuwenhuis that the socialists should, in the event of war, declare a general strike and practise fraternization. He argued that fraternization at the front and demoralization of the army by the advocacy of steps purporting to lead to an immediate peace merely played into the hands of less scrupulous aggressors. Besides, why should a revolutionary be consistent on a question of tactics in the event of a war? Marx and Engels certainly were not consistent in this respect.

Plekhanov was a complex character whom it is not easy to sum up. He was arrogant, intellectually not always very scrupulous, and vain beyond all limits; he could be petty, mean and vindictive to friends and foes alike. On the other hand, his intellectual powers were outstanding. But the quality which stands out above all throughout his life, and may be said to redeem his many faults, was his courage. He stood and fought, alone if need be, and he was often alone, for what his intellect told him was right. This happened in 1879 when he did not hesitate to break up the incipient revolutionary party; in 1905 when he broke with both the Mensheviks and the

Bolsheviks; and in 1914. Like Lenin, his main contribution to the Russian revolutionary movement was to adapt the doctrine of Marx to the conditions in Russia for which it was never designed – but with what different results! For Lenin, marxism, and the curious doctrine which he made of it, was merely a stepping stone to the Jacobin revolution which he intended to lead. For Plekhanov, Marx's analysis offered the hope of the complete Europeanization of Russia which he, Plekhanov, believed was already begun. If it was true that it was already begun, then Lenin certainly successfully stifled the process – no doubt the dark hinterland of *Aziatshchina* (Plekhanov's favourite phrase) struck deeper chords in the hearts of the Russian masses than the logical propositions of Marx. "My illegitimate son" was Plekhanov's description of Lenin. As for the "son", he seems to have recognized as far back as 1904 that the future lay with him and not with Plekhanov. "Plekhanov," he is reported to have said, "is a man of enormous stature . . . This is a man in the face of whom we are all pigmies . . . and yet it seems to me that he is already a dead man, and that I am a living man."[19]

And what of Plekhanov's contribution to Russian history? One's estimate must in the last resort depend on one's view of the relevance of marxism to modern society. For Potresov, a learned and convinced marxist, whose generous obituary still remains the most illuminating portrait of Plekhanov that I know, Plekhanov's attempt to lead Russia along social democratic lines was premature and was therefore engulfed by the dark elements which he so much feared; yet, Potresov wrote in 1918, "The Asiatic tide which swept Plekhanov away has not swept Russia away . . . The work of Plekhanov now in ruins will yet come into its own."[20] He may be right. But, as against his view, for those of us who are not so ready to accept Marx's analysis of history and society as valid, the real tragedy of Plekhanov may have been to have failed in a task which should never have begun.

1. *Werke*, vol. 34 (Berlin 1966), p. 477.
2. *Polnoe sobranie sochinenii*, vol. IV (Moscow 1958–66), pp. 338–9.
3. *Khronika evreiskoi zhizni*, no. 41–2, p. 29.
4. Riazanov found a rough draft in 1911 in Lafargue's papers. He asked Plekhanov and Zasulich who both denied all knowledge of any such reply from Marx and it was only later found in Axelrod's archive in 1923 – see

Arkhiv K. Marksa i F. Engel'sa, ed. D. Riazanova, Part 1 (Moscow 1924), pp. 341. Marx, however, does say in this reply that "I regret that I cannot give you a definite reply to your question which is suitable for publication" – *Werke*, vol. 19, p. 242.

5. The letter was dated 12 February 1898. See *Perepiska G. V. Plekhanova i P. B. Akselroda*, vol. I (Moscow 1925), p. 189.
6. *ibid.*, p. 201.
7. *Sochinenie*, vol. XI (Moscow 1923–7), pp. 23–35.
8. *ibid.*, vol. XIII, pp. 1–22.
9. *ibid.*, vol. XIII, p. 346. Hegemony was of course enunciated in 1898 in the Manifesto drafted by Struve for the First Congress of the *RSDLP*.
10. Quoted by Kuskova in *Novy zhurnal*, vol. LIV (New York 1958), p. 139.
11. *Sochinenie*, vol. VIII, p. 299.
12. *ibid.*, vol. XXIII, p. 135
13. Baron, Samuel Haskell, *Plekhanov, the Father of Russian Marxism* (London 1963), pp. 292–3.
14. The article was published in the *New York Daily Tribune* of 25 June 1853. See *Werke*, vol. 9, pp. 127–33.
15. *Sochinenie*, vol. XX, which contains 362 pages.
16. *ibid.*, vol. XX, p. 131 (italics in original).
17. Quoted by Marc Ferro in *The Russian Revolution of February 1917* (London 1972), p. 202.
18. *God na rodine*, vol. II (Paris 1924), pp. 257–68.
19. Lenin to Valentinov in 1904. See M. Valentinov, "Tragediia G. V. Plekhanova", *Novy zhurnal*, no. 12 (New York 1948), pp. 270–93.
20. In *Byloe*, no. 12 (Petrograd June 1918).

Lenin's Intellectual Formation and the Russian Revolutionary Background

This essay was originally intended to be part of a longer study and was completed in 1969.

Vladimir Ilyich Ulianov, who was later to assume the name Lenin, was born on 10 (22) April 1870 in Simbirsk on the Volga and baptized in the Orthodox faith on 16 April.[1] He was the third child of Ilya Nikolaevich Ulianov and of his wife, Maria Aleksandrovna, whose maiden name was Blank. The eldest son, Alexander, had been born in 1866 and a daughter, Anna, in 1864. A third brother, Dmitry, was born in 1874, and two younger sisters, Olga and Maria, in 1871 and 1878. Alexander was hanged in May 1887 for his part in a conspiracy to assassinate the Emperor, Alexander III. Olga, Lenin's favourite sister and a girl of great gifts and charm, died in 1891. Anna, Maria and Dmitry, who died in 1935, 1937 and 1943 respectively, all took active parts in the social democratic movement and in the Bolshevik party when it came into existence.

Ilya Nikolaevich, who was thirty-nine when Vladimir was born, was the son of a small tradesman in Astrakhan. With the help of his elder brother he had struggled through to the University of Kazan, and had gone on to a successful career in education, which raised him to the status of hereditary nobility. In 1874 he was appointed Director of Primary Schools for the whole province. There are many accounts in existence of this upright and admirable man, and all are in substantial agreement. He was outstandingly able and zealous in his duties, even-tempered and tolerant, without a trace of vanity, liberal in outlook, devoted to his family, and much loved by all with whom he came into contact in the course of his work in the schools. He was a religious man, and a church-goer, but does not seem ever to have imposed religious practice on his children – at any rate no evidence has been published which throws any light on the religious life of the Ulianov children, except Lenin's own assertion in subsequent years that he finally rejected religious belief at the age of sixteen.[2] He had never been a revolutionary, and the assassination in 1881 of Alexander II, whose reign remained in his memory as a "luminous interlude" between the grim reigns of Nicholas I and Alexander III, shocked him profoundly. He never spoke of political or social matters within the family – apparently from anxiety to "protect us youngsters".[3]

Vladimir's mother, Maria Aleksandrovna, came from a family of Germans, long settled in Russia. She was a calm and dignified woman, of great courage and character, entirely dedicated to her husband and children. Unlike her husband, she seldom visited church – either the Lutheran, into which she was born, or the Orthodox into which she was received on marriage.[4] All accounts agree that Vladimir was a devoted and dutiful son, and indeed remained such for the rest of Maria Aleksandrovna's life. Everything that we know of the childhood and early youth of Vladimir points to a happy and harmonious family, devoted parents and normal, loving children, kindly and tolerant discipline, and a full and happy life in which parents and children shared alike.[5] The first blow which shattered this united family was the death of Ilya Nikolaevich on 12 January 1886. But the following year was to bring the grimmer tragedy of the arrest and execution of Alexander.

Vladimir entered the Simbirsk Gymnasium in 1879 at the age of nine and a half. He was to remain there until the summer of 1889. He was an exemplary pupil, who excelled throughout his school career, and won a succession of laudatory reports. He was awarded a gold medal and finished first of his year which totalled twenty-seven. His enormous capacity for work and concentration were evident from the earliest years at school. His final matriculation included composition, Latin, Greek, Russian and general history, geography, logic, divinity, arithmetic, algebra, geometry and trigonometry. He obtained the highest mark (5) in every subject except logic – but the lower mark in logic (4) seems to have been the result of an incautious criticism of the officially approved textbook. Although equally proficient in all his subjects, Vladimir appears to have shown a preference for ancient languages. At the end of his school career, with the support of the Director of the Simbirsk

Gymnasium, F. Kerensky (the father of the future Prime Minister of the Provisional Government in 1917), he was admitted to the Faculty of Law of Kazan University for the following session. (This support was very necessary in view of the suspicion which surrounded the brother of an executed revolutionary in the eyes of the authorities.)[6] The choice of the Law Faculty was explained by Vladimir to his cousin N. I. Veretennikov: "In times like these one has to study legal science and political economy. Perhaps at some other time I should have chosen to study something else."[7]

This remark was, of course, a reflection of the shadow which had been cast on Vladimir and the whole family by the arrest of Alexander, followed by his trial and execution in May of that year, 1887. All accounts agree on the profound effect which the tragic end of his elder brother had upon Vladimir. Alexander's involvement in the conspiracy, indeed the very fact that while living in St Petersburg he had been politically active at all, came as a surprise and a shock to the whole family – not excepting Anna, who was aware of Alexander's membership of a revolutionary circle (was indeed a member of it herself) but knew nothing of the conspiracy. It was characteristic of Alexander to take every possible precaution against involving his family or friends in any way in the dangerous enterprise on which he was engaged. Some of the accounts of the effect of Alexander's end on Vladimir can certainly be discounted as pious hagiography – including the often quoted remark, "No, we will not follow this path. That is not the path to follow." The origin of this legend is the recollection of Maria Ulianova, as related in a speech of 7 February 1924.[8] However, since Maria was aged only nine at the time the accuracy of her recollection may be doubted. Indeed there is little, if anything, to suggest that Vladimir had before 1887 shown any interest whatever in political questions, let alone given any thought to revolutionary tactics. As a small boy he had regarded his elder brother as a hero – as small boys tend to do. But in later years, as we know from the testimony of Anna (who was closest in years and in confidence to Alexander), relations between the two brothers were not very intimate. The gentle and warm-hearted Alexander found that he had little in common with Vladimir. He respected his abilities, but found him too "cutting", too ironical and mocking to be able to feel much affection for him. Anna is quite positive that there was no political relationship or community between them. Indeed she stresses that Vladimir showed no interest in politics before 1887 and certainly read no political literature.[9] It is quite certain that while at school Vladimir was involved in no revolutionary or oppositional activities of any kind – and indeed there seems to have been no revolutionary activity going on in Simbirsk at the relevant date.[10]

What then did he read, apart from his school subjects? The Russian classics, certainly – Pushkin, Gogol, Nekrasov (his father's favourite poet) and, above all, Turgenev, whom he read and re-read, and knew intimately, and much better than any other classic.[11] Enthusiasm for Turgenev, whom many consider the finest prose writer in the Russian language, calls for little explanation in an intelligent adolescent who, for all his preoccupation with revolution, which after 1887 became Vladimir's main activity, never entirely lost a taste for fine prose and poetry. Certainly one cannot visualize the liberal, moderate Turgenev, the admirer of order and restraint in all things and the sceptical critic of all political extremism, as the source of inspiration for any kind of revolutionary doctrine. Despised by the radicals for his moderation and deeply suspected by the conservatives for his open admiration of Western European civilization, and for his lack of Russian chauvinism, most of Turgenev's novels were severely criticized at the time of publication. And yet, perhaps because of his lack of all-out commitment, it was Turgenev who more than any other writer produced a faithful social picture of Russia in the decades when revolution was in the air – the sixties and the seventies.

On the Eve, *Fathers and Sons*, *Smoke* and *Virgin Soil* – from these four novels an intelligent and perceptive reader like Vladimir could form his first picture of a world which he did not yet know, and from which both his parents and his school had carefully shielded him. Rudin, Bazarov and the naive revolutionaries of *Virgin Soil* introduced the future Lenin to the "new men", those who rejected the philistine world around them and sought for new ideals. Perhaps they also gave him an inkling of the extent to which these "new men" had failed to make themselves effective, of the fact that they had only glimpsed the promised land without much notion of how to enter it. Turgenev's educative qualities, in this respect, as a social historian were recognized by the revolutionaries of *Narodnaia Volia* (the People's Will) in the obituary which they published on him in their paper in 1883. After stressing that, for all his gradualism, he was really at heart "one of us", the notice went on to state that he was "an honest propagator of the ideals of several young generations"; and "that a whole generation of so-called nihilists had been brought up on the model of Bazarov".[12] Before long Vladimir was to be confronted with a cruder, but even more impressive portrait of the "new men" than the one which he had gleaned from Turgenev.

In 1887 the family of an executed revolutionary was an object of official suspicion, and was likely for that reason alone to be shunned by former friends. It was not surprising therefore that the Ulianov family should have decided to leave Simbirsk and settle in Kazan, where Vladimir was to begin his university studies in the autumn. The summer months before moving to Kazan were spent in Kokushkino, a village some twenty-five miles away from Kazan. In Kokushkino, where the family stayed in the house of Vladimir's maternal grandfather, there was a cupboard full of books which had belonged to an uncle who had been a voracious reader, and these included "old periodicals which contained valuable articles".[13] We know very little of what Vladimir read that summer. Everything suggests that the shock of his brother's death had awakened a new interest in the world in which he lived. He acquired a new seriousness and preoccupation: to a close family friend he kept on repeating, "Evidently he [Alexander] had to act like that – could not act otherwise."[14] if, as seems likely, Vladimir embarked on the study of the political writings of the radicals of the sixties during this summer (the "valuable articles" in the old cupboard) we know nothing of it. But there exists a very circumstantial account of the impact made on him by one book which he did read, Chernyshevsky's novel *What Is To Be Done?* It had been a favourite of Alexander's. Vladimir may have read it before, but it had made little impression on him: he now read it with great attention. Its effect on him was electric. In his own words, as described some seven years later, "It churned me inside out . . . it is a work which charges one up for the rest of one's life."[15]

It will be necessary to return to the question of Chernyshevsky's influence on the future Lenin, which belongs more especially to the following year, 1888. A prolific writer on social, economic and political issues, Nikolai Gavrilovich Chernyshevsky (1828–89) probably made more converts to the cause of revolution by his novel *What Is To Be Done?* than by any other work. Subtitled "Stories about the new men and women", it was written after his arrest, in prison, and published serially in the journal *Sovremennik* (The Contemporary) in the spring of 1863. "The new men and women" was a familiar euphemism in the sixties for "revolutionaries", or those who were to become such – censorship prevented any more direct reference. In *What Is To Be Done?* we are, as it were, given an analysis of their character in both its lower and higher phases of perfection. Vera Pavlovna, the heroine, is rescued from her bourgeois family and a forced marriage by Lopukhov, a medical student and one of the "new men". Their marriage, in which sexual relations play no part, is founded on the principle of complete equality and independence of each partner. A picture of the aged Robert Owen decorates Lopukhov's wall; and much of the novel is devoted to the description of the very successful dressmaking partnership which Vera Pavlovna institutes on strictly co-operative lines. Many of the simpler economic principles of socialism and in particular of Fourier's phalanstery are analysed in the guise of a fictional narrative.

After some years Vera Pavlovna falls in love with Lopukhov's friend Kirsanov, and tells her husband about it. He disappears very quietly and shoots himself. At this point the author introduces the real hero of the novel, the ideal "new man", Rakhmetov, who has hitherto only flitted across the pages as a semi-legendary character. Rakhmetov is a man of iron will: we are clearly given to understand that he is the true revolutionary, the soaring eagle, where the others have scarcely taken wing. Rakhmetov is body and soul devoted to the cause (censorship prevents clearer identification of his activity), he can be deflected from it neither by physical needs, nor by love, friendship or consideration of conventional morality. His time is strictly parcelled out so that none is wasted; he is physically hardened by acts of asceticism and self-torture to the point of almost superhuman endurance. (There is, indeed, something of Superman about him – with a sole weakness, a craving for cigars.) The Rakhmetovs, the author tells us, are "the flower of the best of men, the movers of the movers, the salt of the salt of the earth". Now, bearing a letter from the late Lopukhov, Rakhmetov calls on Vera Pavlovna and lectures her on the inadequacy of her own and her late husband's conduct: they should have accepted the situation which arose when Vera Pavlovna and Kirsanov fell in love, lived all three together, ignored jealousy as unworthy of rational human beings, and continued to work for the cause. As it is, their lack of a fully developed social sense which "new men and women" should possess to the full had endangered Vera Pavlovna's co-operative enterprise, and cost Lopukhov his life. Rakhmetov disappears again. Vera Pavlovna marries Kirsanov (sharing her husband's bed this time) and the story peters out rather inconclusively.

Clearly it was not by its artistic merit or psychological subtlety that *What Is To Be Done?* so impressed the young Lenin. It was the rediscovery by him of the "new man", of the archetypal hero of the generation which grew to manhood in the sixties, and which perhaps sought in the Rakhmetovs and Bazarovs some escape from the bitter sense of failure and impotence from which Russian intellectual reformers all suffered. Other preoccupations of the seventies and eighties were to drive the "new men" out of the imagination of those who grew to manhood in those later decades. But since Lenin was eventually to revive some of the qualities of the "new men" in Boshevism, it is worth looking at the main features of this idol of the sixties.

He had first been adumbrated by Turgenev in the 'nihilist" medical student Bazarov, the hero of *Fathers and Sons*, published in 1861. D. Pisarev's "Realists", written in 1864, is a variation on the same theme. P. N. Tkachev, whose possible influence on Lenin will be considered later, took as his theme for an article, published in *Delo* (Affairs) in 1868 ("Men of the Future and the Heroes of the Bourgeoisie") the protagonists of a novel by Friedrich Spielhagen which had been published in Russian translation in *Delo* in 1866.[16] The men of the future, he wrote, have one idea only: to make the majority of mankind happy. Life has no meaning for them unless they can fulfil this idea. To this end they are prepared to sacrifice friend, wife or mistress – there is no harm in the love of women if it does not interfere with the cause, but the idea that it is necessary in life is an invention "by medieval inspirers of the Maid of Heaven – those same dissolute knights who treated women like stud animals". The morality of the philistines is despicable hypocrisy: the cause will justify any means, including sacrifice of the innocent, of friend or lover, and the use of any stratagem or ploy which, in terms of bourgeois morality, would be (hypocritically) regarded as dishonest.[17]

But for the most complete and radical portrait of the "new men" we have to look to another, secret, document. This document has the advantage that since, unlike the novels and articles referred to, it was not written for publication, it reveals in clear language what Chernyshevsky, Pisarev and Tkachev had perforce to wrap up in circumlocutions. In 1871 the *Revolutionary Catechism* was made public in connection with the trial which arose out of the uncovering of the revolutionary organization of Nechaev, with which Tkachev was associated. The *Catechism* was a kind of book of rules for members of this secret Jacobin organization of revolutionaries dedicated to the destruction of society in its present form.[18] It has hitherto been usually ascribed to Bakunin[19] and it is certainly the case that some of his views are echoed in the *Catechism*. But the recent discovery of a hitherto unknown letter from Bakunin to Nechaev strongly suggests that Bakunin could not have been the author of the *Catechism*.[20] Some influence of Tkachev cannot be excluded, in view of the parallelism of views between the *Catechism* and the article quoted above; but there are also a number of assertions in the document which are quite inconsistent with Tkachev's views,[21] and which therefore suggest that Nechaev, or whoever else was the author, may have plagiarized or echoed Tkachev in the same way as he had Bakunin. The following passages give the main points of the "moral code" of the true revolutionary:

> 1. The revolutionary is a doomed man. He has no interests of his own, no affairs, no feelings, no attachments, no property, not even a name. Everything within him is absorbed by one single all-excluding interest, one single thought, one single passion – revolution.
>
> 2. In the depths of his being, and not only in words but in deeds, he has broken all his links with the civil order and with the entire educated world, with all laws, with all the decencies, with the social conditions and the morality of this world. This world is for him a merciless enemy, and if he should continue to live in it, it would be for the sole purpose of all the better to destroy it . . .
>
> 4. [The revolutionary] despises public opinion. He de-

spises and hates present public morality in all its incentives and all its manifestations. For him everything that helps the triumph of the revolution is moral. Everything that can hinder this triumph is immoral and criminal.

5. The revolutionary is a doomed man, merciless towards the state and towards the whole of society and its existing social structure. He can expect no mercy from them. Between them and him there subsists a war to the death, be it secret or open. This war is ceaseless and without prospect of armistice. The revolutionary must train himself to suffer torture . . .

7. The nature of the real revolutionary excludes every kind of romanticism, every sentiment, every enthusiasm and every elation. It even excludes personal hatred or revenge . . .[22]

This, then, was the intellectual climate of the revolutionary fanaticism of the sixties which, twenty years later, was to "charge" Lenin "for life" through the views expressed in Chernyshevsky's novel. The "democrats" of the sixties were to remain heroes for Lenin even after he began, a few years later, to launch his attack on populism. Echoes of this language of revolution will be heard in Bolshevism as the later story of Lenin's party unfolds in the following pages. And was it not, perhaps, Rakhmetov or the *Catechism* that Lenin had in mind when he wrote, at the end of 1897, that the life of the revolutionary "demands the highest degree of endurance and self-denial; it demands of him that he should dedicate all his powers to work which is monotonous, which provides no visible results, which cuts a man off from all companionship with his friends; it is the kind of work that subjects the whole life of the revolutionary to dry, strict *réglementation*."[23] It is more difficult to discern the features of Rakhmetov or Nechaev in the gentle and kindly Alexander Ulianov. And yet, Alexander had dedicated himself to revolution, and to revolution alone. He had deliberately gone to his death in an act of self-immolation, not as an act of despair, and not in any unrealistic hope of raising a popular revolt, but because he believed (as the discussion of his views below will show) that cumulative acts of terrorism would some day force the Emperor to make concessions to enlightened demands for representative government. He refused to ask for mercy because that would have involved the hypocritical plea that he regretted his action. It was a measure of the quiet heroism and nobility of his mother that she respected his reasons for not trying to save his life and did not attempt to dissuade him.

Meanwhile Vladimir was soon to receive his own baptism as a revolutionary. When, in the autumn of 1887, the family (with the exception of Anna, who remained "under police surveillance" in Kokushkino) moved to Kazan, the seventeen-year-old Ulianov joined a revolutionary circle. Like most revolutionary circles of the time it derived its inspiration from the already defunct People's Will. But in order to understand the revolutionary atmosphere which first greeted the future Lenin at this impressionable age, it is necessary to retrace the development of revolutionary thought in the decades preceding 1887.

"What does the people need? Very simple, the people needs land and liberty." In these historic words N. P. Ogarev on 1 July 1861 summed up the programme of what was to become revolutionary populism.[24] And indeed, in the springtime of the Russian revolutionary movement, in the sixties, the basic problem seemed simple enough: if the Emperor would not yield to the demands of the people, then bloody insurrection must inevitably follow. It was in this form that the revolutionary proclamations which followed almost immediately on the emancipation of the serfs defined their position.[25] The programme of the first short-lived revolutionary organization *Zemlia i Volia* (Land and Liberty) was summed up as the destruction of the autocracy and the summoning of a popular convention of elected representatives of the free people.[26] Some thought was devoted to the problem of the practical organization of a revolutionary conspiracy. Nechaev's *Revolutionary Catechism*, already referred to, contained a plan (which remained very largely on paper) for a strictly conspiratorial, centralized and disciplined organization of revolutionaries. The aim was to create a revolutionary network, under the strict orders of a secret, central "circle", which operates through subordinate "circles of the second category", which are not initiated into the plans of the central "circle". The purpose is to conduct widespread agitation for the propagation of nation-wide insurrection.[27] An elaborate scheme of organization of a "secret society" was worked out by Ogarev in 1860, but it remained unpublished (though no doubt was known through verbal contacts) until 1870, when the gist of it was printed in the form of an article in Nechaev's *Kolokol*.[28] The basis of Ogarev's scheme is a secret centre, with an illegal newspaper, operating both through members of the society as conscious but not fully initiated agents, and unconscious agents, working under the influence of the conscious agents.

The embryonic organizations of the sixties achieved no practical results, and the high hopes of an imminent national uprising were disappointed. The populist revolutionary movement as it developed in the next decade was both more sophisticated theoretically, and longer term in its outlook. Herzen's influence had long ended, and had indeed been short-lived, though indelible traces of his messianic faith in the peculiar destiny of the Russian people, in the need for Russia to avoid the capitalist mode of development, and in the instinctive socialism of the Russian peasant as evidenced in the commune, had evoked deep chords in Russian tradition, and were to remain with populism as long as it survived. But the prophets of the seventies were P. L. Lavrov and M. A. Bakunin, and their main message – though it differed in each case – was that the liberation of Russia must come from the people itself, and that the revolutionaries should not seek to achieve "political" aims by conspiracies to overthrow the autocracy. "The social question is for us the question of first importance," asserted the first issue of *Vpered* (Forward) – the periodical which Lavrov edited, in Zurich and then in London, between 1873 and 1877. The political question is "for us subordinate to the social question, since in the distant future all government is destined to give way to a new, communal social order, of which the basis will be the peasant commune". The transformation of the social order must take place not only "with the aim of benefiting the people, but by means of the people". But revolutions cannot be "evoked artificially": they are the result not of individuals or groups, but of "complicated historical processes". The intelligentsia, the "civilized class", can however help by "going to the people", to live among them and explain to them what they should strive for. A national convention could be acceptable if its overwhelming majority consisted of peasants; but in general the movement is hostile both to programmes of liberal reform and to constitutional parties on the European model. Revolution is "most probably" inevitable: prepare yourselves and the Russian people for it.[29]

Bakunin's views were in several respects close to Lavrov's: he likewise rejected "political" action and rejected every form of central government. No intellectual can determine in advance "how the people will and must live on the day after the social revolution", he wrote in Addendum "A" to his *State and Anarchy*, following it up with an attack on the various categories of "doctrinaires" and "charlatans" who lived as a privileged minority, but nevertheless wished to preserve the reputation of being devoted to national liberation – so long as it was "not bound up with too many discomforts". The latest name these people gave themselves was "marxists". The only true revolutionary faith was to go to the people, indeed, but not for the purpose of peaceful, preparatory, educative work, which was useless, but in order to raise immediate insurrection.[30] Unlike Lavrov, Bakunin believed or persuaded himself that the Russian people was ripe for revolution and only needed a spark to set it off. That he may, at this date at all events, have thought that a certain amount of organizational activity would be needed to induce the peasants to rise is supported by a letter written to Nechaev three years earlier. There is a great force for revolt within the people only waiting to burst into flames, he writes, but it needs helpers. These helpers must come from the young educated men, for three-quarters of whom at least there is no future: here is "the material, most precious for a secret organization". He then lays down twenty-one points for a secret revolutionary society which he recommends Nechaev to adopt. It is to be based on the complete equality and fraternity of all members, without the "jesuitry" and deceit which Nechaev practised and preached. This society of organizers must take control of the chaos and disorder which national revolt will entail. It must act as a "collective dictatorship" in order to lead and guide the insurrection and lead it towards "the fullest possible realization of the social-economic ideal and to the organization of the fullest popular freedom". The high character and self-dedication of the individuals who compose the organization will be a guarantee that the "collective dictatorship" does not become a tyrannous dictatorship, or a government in disguise.[31]

It was in line with this kind of doctrine that the famous "Going to the People" took place in 1874 – with the consequent shattering disillusionment both in the revolutionary potential of the people and in the capacity of the revolutionary intellectuals to find a common language with them.[32] Some of this disillusionment was reflected in the new revolutionary organization, later to be named (like its short-lived predecessor) *Zemlia i Volia* (Land and Liberty), when it first came into existence in 1876. *Zemlia i Volia*'s policy was closer to Bakunin than to Lavrov; but faithful to both and to the populist tradition in looking for a "social" and not a "political" solution. There was no question now of any revolutionary aim in terms of the sixties – the overthrow of the autocracy by an organized conspiracy. Its "political ideal" remained communal self-government, with peasant ownership of the land. But the concrete form of action which the revolutionaries now set themselves as a target was more clearly defined, and much extended. The intentions of *Zemlia i Volia* were divided into "organizational" and "disorganizational": in terms of practice, if not of theory, they were to form the basis of most revolutionary activity for twenty years or more – long after the main object of all the revolutionaries had become the capture of political power.

Organizational:

1 A close-knit organization of formed revolutionaries, both intellectuals and workers.
2 Close contacts with sects hostile to the government of a religious-revolutionary nature.
3 Formation of durable contacts with areas where peasant unrest is at its highest.
4 Attracting robber bands to the cause.
5 Formation of contacts in centres where there are concentrations of industrial workers.
6 Propaganda in university circles.
7 Making contacts with liberals "in order to exploit them for our ends".
8 The maximum propaganda through the publication of literature and through a journal.

Disorganizational: 1 Establishing contacts in the armed forces, especially among officers.
2 Recruiting to the cause civil servants in government institutions.
3 The systematic destruction of the most harmful or prominent individuals who help to support the existing order.[33]

The members of *Zemlia i Volia* were subject to strict centralized discipline and rules of secrecy and conspiracy.[34]

Populists by tradition, and thus orientated towards the village and imbued with faith both in the virtues of the people and in the peculiar differences which were supposed to characterize Russia, and intolerant of "political" acts, the members of *Zemlia i Volia* soon discovered in practice that the most promising area for the revolutionary was not the apathetic village, but the university students and the industrial workers of the towns. After the assassination attempt on Trepov by Vera Zasulich in 1878 and her acquittal by a jury, there followed a spontaneous series of assassinations and other terrorist acts. The severity of government repressions against the terrorists made the members of *Zemlia i Volia* increasingly aware that the immediate, direct enemy was the autocracy, and that its overthrow was the first priority. Demands for a programme of "political" action, which had always existed within *Zemlia i Volia*, and which harked back to the less sophisticated Jacobinism of the sixties, resulted in the split in August 1879 of *Zemlia i Volia* into two: the majority, the adherents of political terrorism, took the name of *Narodnaia Volia* (the People's Will); the conservative minority, faithful to the populist tradition of social revolution, based on agitation in the villages and among the peasants in the factories, took the name of *Cherny Peredel* (Black, or All-Round, Repartition).[35]

Among the most powerful advocates of "political" action in the seventies was Petr Nikitich Tkachev, whose views on the "new men" have already been discussed. Imprisoned for sixteen months in July 1871 for his connection with the Nechaev organization, he escaped abroad at the end of 1873. At the end of 1875 he succeeded in founding a journal, *Nabat* (the Tocsin), in order to propagate his views. *Nabat* appeared, with gaps, until 1881. As he explained himself, Tkachev did not hope to make many converts, but would by quite satisfied if a small number of revolutionaries were influenced by his ideas.[36] In later years Lenin became a great admirer of the revolutionary ideas expounded in *Nabat*, and of Tkachev's works generally. Writing of the years 1902–3 in Geneva, V. D. Bonch-Bruevich, who was responsible for organizing the social democratic reading rooms, recounts his good fortune in securing Nechaev's writings "in whom Vladimir Ilyich was extremely interested, as, incidentally, he was in Tkachev". He used to say that Tkachev "was undoubtedly closer than any other to our point of view". Newly arrived young social democrats were strongly advised by Lenin to "become acquainted with the profound works of this original writer".[37] Tkachev died in 1886.

Since Tkachev was one of the most incisive and original thinkers of the revolutionary movement, very much influenced by the study of Marx, it will be necessary to return to some of his ideas. For the moment we are concerned with his advocacy of "political" revolutionary action at a time when *Zemlia i Volia* rejected it. Completely free from the somewhat sentimental attitude to the peasants and to the commune which usually characterized the populists, Tkachev provided an analysis of the art of the revolutionary *coup d'état* which in its realism far excelled anything that was ever produced by *Narodnaia Volia*. The first aim of the revolution must be to seize power. For this purpose it is necessary to have a strictly disciplined organization of revolutionaries, who should be drawn not only from among the nobility, but from the intelligentsia issuing from the "exploited, ruined and oppressed classes" as well. "The success of the revolution," he wrote, "is possible only with the creation of an organization which can fuse all the revolutionary elements into one living body, acting according to one common plan, subordinated to one overall direction – an organization, above all, founded on the centralization of power, and the decentralization of functions." The aim of this organization must be to seize state power, but not to destroy it in the early stages: before the ultimate stage of anarchy, or communal power, can be attained (and Tkachev remained, theoretically, to this extent an adherent of anarchism) the apparatus of the state must be used by the revolutionaries in the interests of the social revolution. (A very similar argument would one day be used by Lenin in *State and Revolution*.)[38]

What of the people? Tkachev never accepted the view of Bakunin, and of many of his followers, that Russia was on the verge of revolution in the seventies. He argued that there was much potential revolutionary material in popular discontent; but he contended that this potential violence had first to be released by the *coup d'état*, and then guided into the right channels by the "revolutionary minority". This minority begins by freeing the people from the oppression of its government, and thus releases its potential revolutionary energies. It is only then that a National Duma can be convened in order that the revolutionary minority can, with its aid, effect the social revolution. This social revolution includes the building of a new society around improved and strenghened communes; the expropriation and nationalization of the means of production; the gradual abolition of the need for a money exchange system; the gradual elimination of "physical, mental and moral" inequality by means of a new, compulsory system of public education which will teach the principles of love, equality and fraternity; the gradual abolition of the family, which is founded on the subjection of women; and the progressive weakening and abolition of the central functions of government.

We are, however, concerned less with the totalitarian utopia which Tkachev envisaged after seizure of power than with the technique of the *coup d'état*. It is in this sphere that Tkachev made the most significant contribution of any Russian revolutionary thinker – until the advent of Lenin. Tkachev is often described as a "Blanquist" – and he was indeed a follower and admirer of Blanqui. But, unlike Blanqui, he saw a definite and necessary correlation between the seizure of the central power and a popular revolt. "An attack on the centre of power and its capture by the revolutionaries which is not accompanied by a popular revolt (if only on a local scale) can only lead to positive and soundly based results in exceptionally favourable circumstances." It is evident that he visualized the *coup d'état* not as a single act, but as a prolonged series of revolutionary assaults, culminating in seizure of power, which could only succeed when the situation is ripe – or to use a phrase that would later be often used by Lenin, when there is a "revolutionary situation". All great popular upheavals, Tkachev argued, have only taken place when "in the highest ruling circles of society chaos and disorder, anarchy or polyarchy reigned". It is therefore essential, in order to carry out the *coup d'état* successfully, to evoke first "a sense of impunity" in the people: when the dreaded power is seen to be "calumniated, disorientated, disorganized and rendered impotent" then the suppressed forces of hatred and resentment will burst out with an "irresistible force".[39]

The influence of Tkachev's views was evident in some respects in the programme of *Narodnaia Volia*, though in others it reflected more the "constitutional" and "political" trends which had been discernible for some years among some sections of the populist revolutionaries. Only the people's will, it declared, can sanction the form of government which obtains in a country, and therefore, as socialists and populists, the Executive Committee regarded it as its first task to "effect a political revolution with the aim of transferring power to the people". The people's will would be expressed through a Constituent Assembly, elected freely and on the basis of universal suffrage. The revolution would have to be effected by the party – the way in which this was to be done was omitted from the programme for reasons of security. Apart from effecting the revolution, the party proclaimed four other functions that it would carry out:

1. The propagation of its policy and programme, which included extensive local self-government, independence of the village commune, nationalization of all land and worker ownership of factories, freedom of speech, conscience and association, universal suffrage and a territorial army.
2. Terroristic activity, designed to eliminate the most harmful persons in the government, and for self-defence.
3. The organization of secret societies linked together by one Centre.
4. The acquiring of an influential position and contacts in the civil service and armed forces.[40]

The secret instruction, on Preparatory Work by the Party, is in effect little more than an expansion of the tasks enunciated in the programme. In some of its points, however, it shows some practical realization of the problems of effecting a *coup d'état* in a police state, which may well have been echoes of Tkachev. In particular, it recognizes the importance of winning over the army since the "significance of the army in a revolution is enormous. One can say that, with the army behind one, one can overthrow a government even without the help of the people; while, if the army is against one, nothing can be achieved even with the support of the people". There is also recognition of the special importance of the workers in the town for supporting the revolution.[41] It was characteristic of the People's Will to recognize increasingly the importance of the town worker – no doubt as a result of the simple experience that he was obviously more responsive to revolutionary propaganda than the peasant. The observation of one writer in the party's journal that it was more likely that the workers in the towns would make the first move for insurrection rather than the peasants[42] was typical of the new mood: to the orthodox disciple of Bakunin in *Zemlia i Volia* it was blatant heresy. This attitude towards the workers was further demonstrated in the parallel programme, primarily designed to appeal to the factory workers, entitled the "Programme of the Worker Members of the Party of the People's Will", prepared by Zheliabov (the organizer of the assassination of 1 March 1881) in November 1880. It is said to have had as wide circulation as the general programme.[43]

Such was the revolutionary programme, as envisaged on paper, in 1879. Two years later all that *Narodnaia Volia* had to show for its efforts was the death of Alexander II. However, if it had done little or nothing to organize a revolution, some experience in revolutionary organization had been gained, which left its imprint on all subsequent organizations. (Vladimir Ulianov would carefully study this experience some years later.) The "Party", as it was called, meant in practice a fairly indefinite category of like-minded people: where the actual, disciplined conspiracy was meant, this was referred to as the "Organization". "The party is solidarity of thought, the organization is solidarity of action."[44] The new organization, after the split, became highly centralized, with the "Centre" in complete authority over the local "groups". These "groups" were organized by "agents" of the "Centre", and their task was to support the aims of the "Centre". Any individual from within a "group" could be called upon by the "Centre" for service, without even consulting the "group". Above all, no terrorist act by a "group" or a member of a "group" was permitted without the leave of the "Centre".

As for activity, the picture was not a very encouraging one. It was recognized that any thought of mass activity among the peasants was for the time being out of the question, and in any case very little attention was in practice devoted to the peasants. More attention was paid to the factory workers. The task of the "groups" among the factory workers was to enlist their support for the rising, when it came about, by strikes and mass demonstrations. The practical meaning of this can be doubted. But it was the case that *Narodnaia Volia* paid much more attention to the town factory workers than had been paid hitherto. Its activity extended beyond propaganda. It attempted to organize the workers for action, and with some success. For example, the Moscow workers' organization in 1881 extended to between 100 and 200 members. The party was also fairly active among students and among the armed forces – especially among the officers. There were some 200 officers enrolled in the *Narodnaia Volia* military organizations by the spring of 1881.

Yet, this picture must not be regarded as evidence of any kind of widespread, far-flung movement. It was recognized on all sides that "the Party" was in a state of chaos – and especially when contrasted with the excellent order and discipline of "the Organization", and especially of its Executive Committee. Of this Executive Committee it has been said that it was "not only the director and organizer of the movement. It was in effect also the executant of all the plans which were formed."[45] What *Narodnaia Volia* had set out to become was an organizer of revolt on a wide scale in order to provide support for a *coup d'état* at the centre: what it in substance became was a duel between the forces of the autocracy and a handful of brave men and women.

The orthodox, populist opponents of *Narodnaia Volia*, headed by their most prominent member, the Bakuninist Plekhanov, had assailed the new, "political" platform on two grounds: that even if the party were successful in forcing a constitution out of the autocracy, this would inevitably be to the benefit of the rich exploiters, and not of the people; and that the proper duty of a populist socialist was to work among the peasants.[46] The former was never put to the test. As for the latter, the march of events demonstrated the futility of pinning one's hopes on the peasants as a revolutionary force *on their own* – even the worker members of *Narodnaia Volia* had stressed that the town workers would always be defeated by the government if they went into action separately from the peasants, who were the main strength in the country. Marx had sidelined this passage on his copy.[47] Before long *Cherny Peredel* had ceased to exist. Plekhanov, reinforced by several major figures of the former *Zemlia i Volia* (Lev Deich, Vera Zasulich, I. Stefanovich and Pavel Akselrod), from his exile would soon found the first fully marxist Russian group, which advocated the formation of a social democratic workers' party.[48] Peasant populism was beginning to change into revolutionary socialism.

However, the central organization of *Narodnaia Volia* hardly survived the repressions which followed the assassination of 1 March 1881. With the arrest of Vera Figner in the spring of 1883 even the remnants of the Executive Committee ceased to function. Some attempts were made to revive it, but arrests in 1884 put an end to them. The last issue of the journal *Narodnaia Volia* appeared in October 1885. The mood of the issues which appeared after 1 March 1881 is one of increasing despondency at the lack of any signs of revolutionary upsurge in the towns or villages. (Even the pogroms of 1881 were welcomed, if their anti-Jewish aspect was deplored, as evidence of the fact that the people had assimilated the combat methods taught by *Narodnaia Volia*.) However, in these, its darkest days, *Narodnaia Volia* retained its faith in the new doctrine of politics: the aim of the party must remain to exact from the autocrat agreement to the convocation of a People's Convention, in the full confidence that such a convention would be overwhelmingly composed of friends of the people. In a letter to Alexander III, dated 10 March 1881, the Executive Committee called on the Emperor to concede two things: an amnesty for political prisoners and a freely elected People's Convention. Otherwise they foretold that the process of revolutionary terror would inevitably increase as the years went on.[49]

The Emperor ignored the appeal of the Executive Committee, but acts of terror did not increase. The Russian revolutionary movement in fact entered on a period of indecision and lack of clear form to which some Soviet historians have given the apt name of "the transitional period". It was in one sense a transition to marxism: the first quasi-marxist workers' organization, the Blagoev Group, dates from 1883, and the Social Democratic Party would eventually be formally founded in 1898. On the other hand the turn of the century was also to witness the emergence of a new form of populism, the Socialist Revolutionary Party. At the date with which we are concerned, the four or five years which preceded Lenin's arrival in Kazan in 1887, there was no question of the differentiation of revolutionary circles into "marxist" and "populist": the first circles to call themselves "marxist" in express terms were only to appear in Kazan in 1888 or 1889. The many groups and circles which existed in the capital and in the provinces, drawn overwhelmingly from among university students, regarded themselves as the heirs of *Narodnaia Volia* and as partakers of its heritage – even if, after 1884, *Narodnaia Volia* could hardly have been said to exist. In any case it is impossible to understand the real nature of these circles unless one rids oneself of the idea which belongs to a later period that marxism and populism were in opposition, and irreconcilable. On the contrary, the ideas of Marx were in many ways a part of the heritage of populism, and, paradoxically, accepted to a large extent even by those who like Chernyshevsky and Tkachev deplored industrial capitalism, and sought to prevent its advent in Russia by strengthening the commune. Thus it was that a circle glorying in its historic links to *Narodnaia Volia* would see nothing incongruous or inconsistent in adopting or advocating many of the ideas of Marx; or in putting the works of Marx on their study programme reading lists. The group in Petersburg, which Alexander Ulianov joined in 1886, may serve as an illustration of this in practice.

This group was formed in 1885 from students. (It included M. T. Elizarov, Lenin's future brother-in-law.) It made some pretensions to be the "leading" group among the many groups and circles which existed in Petersburg at the time, of different shades of theory. The theoretical division, according to one member of the group, V. V. Bartenev, was not on the issue of "marxism", which in effect all accepted as valid. What divided circles was the question whether one should engage in "militancy", or in "preparatory" work. (In fact, the terrorist group of Alexander and his companions was the only one to be formed, so that the issue of "militancy" was largely theoretical.) This division, according to Bartenev, was the only one – in particular, the advocacy of "militancy" was perfectly compatible with intellectual acceptance of the views of Marx. All groups and circles had by now accepted the primacy of the need for the political liberation of Russia – orthodox peasant populism was as dead as the dodo. However, it is clear that such phrases as "acceptance" of the views of Marx must be treated with caution. Anna Ulianova, who was also a member of the Bartenev circle, denies that any of them could be described as "marxists" in the eighties, and, if by "marxist" is meant unquestioning acceptance of every known opinion of Marx, she is no doubt right. Another member of the circle, S. A. Nikonov, who described himself as having been a "marxist" at that time (1886) explains that while he was fully convinced by Marx's economic analysis, he rejected the exclusive role assigned by Marx to the economic base. He also says that he attached greater importance than Marx to the role of the individual in history.

Alexander, though a member of the circle, remained aloof from its general activities, which consisted mainly of study, and of a certain amount of propaganda among workers. His activities, along with four others (Nikonov, Lukashevich, Shevyrev and Govorukhin), in planning the assassination of Alexander III for 1 March 1887 were carefully concealed from other members of the group. The five formed themselves into a militant group in December 1886: this group took the name of "The terrorist fraction of the Party of the People's Will". In fact no "Party" any longer existed, let alone any central organization: the use of the name was designed to suggest that the dreaded People's Will was active once more. The "terrorist fraction" had composed its own programme, of which Alexander was the author. It is of extraordinary interest as an illustration of the way in which marxist analysis could be combined with the traditional policy of *Narodnaia Volia*. While in prison Alexander reconstituted the text of this programme from memory, and it is in this form that it has come down to us.

The fraction declared themselves to be socialists. Every country comes to socialism by "the natural process of its economic development. Socialism is as much a necessary result of capitalist production and the relation of classes which this engenders as is inevitable the development of capitalism itself, when once a country has embarked on the road of a money economy." Socialism can only be achieved at a "certain stage of maturity of society" and can only come about as the result of the "qualitative and quantitative increase in the strength and consciousness of the working class". The peasants can only give "unconscious support through their general discontent" to the workers, who must form the most active element in the movement towards socialism, and to whom the main attention of the party should be devoted. The activity of the party should in the ordinary way be mainly educational: but under the present regime in Russia such educational activity is virtually impossible. Hence the first task is the struggle for free institutions, free speech and free associations. This political struggle is, to be sure, merely temporary, but it is necessary as a preliminary stage towards the achievement of the ultimate economic ends.

In this political struggle "we hope to act together with the liberals", since the aims of both so far as the limitation of autocracy and civil rights are concerned are the same. It is only in the future that the democratic and socialist aims of the fraction will draw it apart from the liberals. "As far as the social democrats are concerned, our disagreements with them seem to us to be very insubstantial and merely theoretical. These differences amount to this, that we place greater hopes on the immediate transition of the national economy to its higher phase and, because we attach great and independent significance to the intelligentsia, consider it necessary and useful to engage in an immediate struggle with the government."

This method of struggle is, of course, terror, but it is significant that this programme attached a new meaning to terror. It is no longer a question of self-defence, or even of the elimination of the leading enemy figures: it is a policy of a systematic series of acts of assault which are intended by their cumulative effect eventually to force the autocracy to concede civil and political freedoms. (As one of Alexander's fellow conspirators recalls, he used to say frequently: "I don't believe in terror: I believe in systematic terror.") As the programme puts it, terror is "the collision between the government and an intelligentsia which has been deprived of the possibility of peaceful, cultural influence on public life". The aim of acts of terror is, by a cumulative process of successive acts, to prove to the government that it cannot suppress the demands of public opinion. As repression increases, so will the acts of terror: the government will progressively become more and more isolated in the struggle, of which the successful issue is beyond doubt. The government will be forced to seek support from society and hence to yield to its demands for freedom of thought and speech, and for popular representation. Terror will end when the government grants the revolutionaries' minimum demands for civil freedom and a complete amnesty.[50] It was thus as a deliberate act of self-immolation, in the belief that his act of struggle would be only the first of many to come, that Alexander Ulianov went to the scaffold on 8 May 1887.

There existed also during this "transitional" period numerous revolutionary circles in the provincial cities. The links between these circles were, where they existed, very tenuous, and the efforts of the Petersburg circles to maintain contact with and to direct or co-ordinate the policy and activities of the provincial circles met with little success. The last attempt to co-ordinate such provincial activity was made, with little success, by the last member of the old Executive Committee to survive arrest inside Russia, Vladimir, or Natan, Bogoraz in Moscow. But he was arrested in 1866.[51] The nearest to an organization of circles was the one associated with the names of Dr M. D. Fokin and Dr D. D. Bekariukov, two close school and university friends. The aim of these two young men, which they largely achieved, was to organize a network of circles in order to prepare future revolutionary leaders. The question of propaganda among the workers was secondary, and subordinated to the question of security. Their network of circles consisted at one time of as many as twenty-five: the principal centres of activity were Kiev, Kazan, Kharkov and Rostov. Contacts between the circles were maintained by visits and by congresses – four such congresses were held between 1883 and 1892, in Kazan and in Nizhny Novgorod. The network was started in Kazan with the arrival in 1883 of a group of students expelled from St Petersburg, which included Fokin. Fokin reorganized the very rudimentary revolutionary activity which had existed in Kazan and in 1885 left for Kiev, and was replaced by Bekariukov, who arrived from Kharkov. Another member of the group, Motovilov, organized the circle in Rostov. Bekariukov remained in Kazan until 1886, when he was replaced by Lazar Bogoraz, a brother of Natan Bogoraz.

The theory underlying the Fokin-Bekariukov plan of action was that *Narodnaia Volia* had failed to produce a revolution on 1 March 1881 because it had lacked a proper base throughout the country. The task now was to recruit and train "a whole army of future participants in the conspiracy". The "army" must extend its net to all large university and administrative centres. The organization by which this aim was to be accomplished was ultimately to take the form of a network of subordinate circles, all grouped around the central circle, and all acting in accordance with an agreed plan. The number of circles was to be constantly enlarged by a process of "hiving off": a member of a circle who had attained a certain degree of proficiency would move off to become the head of a new circle in another area. In practice, Fokin's organization mainly extended to the universities; but the ultimate aim was to build up a network of leaders not only in the universities, but in the army and among the workers as well. It was intended to make contacts among officers so that they in turn could extend their contacts to the soldiers. In the same way, the workers were to be used for extending contacts among the peasants. Only after all the preparatory work of training of leaders had been completed, would a militant organization be created for disorganization of the central power and for the final assault on the autocracy.

The Fokin organization consisted of the secret "Centre", headed by Fokin, to which the best and most active members were co-opted: there was no question of election, and indeed the identity of the members of the "Centre" was concealed from the rank and file. Below the Centre were the peripheral "circles". Their members were not initiated into the secret plans of the Centre, but were aware of its aims and its programme. These "circles" existed for the study of theory and of the ultimate aims, and of the way to achieve them. The authors studied, so far as available information goes, were Marx, Engels, Lassalle, Shchapov, Chernyshevsky, Spencer, Buckle and Draper. Below these peripheral "circles" extended a series of study circles. The purpose of these circles was self-education, which meant regular discussion and study of the social and natural sciences. The most promising members of these relatively innocuous study circles were recruited to membership of the more conspiratorial peripheral circles. In recruiting members, particular attention was paid to qualities which recalled the "new men" of the sixties – "hardness", ruthlessness, readiness to forgo the attractions of the soft life and to face privations, and so forth. The strictest disciplinary rules permeated the whole organization. It was, for example, forbidden to maintain any contacts with *Narodnaia Volia* (while it survived) because that organization, since the betrayal of Vera Figner by Degaev in 1883, was believed to be penetrated. It was strictly forbidden to meet in the lodgings of any member, and premises had to be hired for all meetings, which were camouflaged as social parties. These methods were successful to the extent that the Fokin-Bekariukov organization was never discovered by the police. On the other hand, the strict discipline made it very difficult to conduct propaganda in the factories for fear of compromising security. A notable feature of Fokin's system (which Lenin was later to adopt) was the practice of maintaining the most able members out of the funds of the organization so that they did not have to waste valuable time earning their living. Quite large sums of money were spent on this. It is not clear how the money was obtained, though rumours were rife that the methods used were not over-scrupulous, and included such devices as the seduction of rich heiresses.[52]

On his arrival in Kazan, Vladimir joined the circle of Lazar Bogoraz, who had taken over from Bekariukov the year before, in 1886.[53] It was a circle completely in the *Narodnaia Volia* tradition: before Bogoraz took it over it had been in contact with Alexander Ulianov. According to the police reports, it was a very restricted circle. Membership was open only to close and trusted friends of certain figures with whom Bogoraz had had contacts: these figures included Alexander Ulianov, which presumably explains why Vladimir joined this particular circle. Bogoraz was still in correspondence with Petersburg, with Zelenenko, of *Narodnaia Volia*. The police records quote him as insisting that "for our country a liberal programme is inappropriate and unsuitable . . ." Since there was no hope of a popular revolt, and since there was no influential class behind the intelligentsia, the only hope that remained was "a social revolutionary party which took it upon itself to struggle against the existing order by every means; and that it could well be that the only means of struggle of practical value was terror, which had justified its value by historical experience".[54]

Such then was the tradition in which the young Lenin received his baptism of revolutionary fire. His activities during the two or three months which he spent in the Bogoraz circle were confined to the student disturbances at Kazan University on 4 December 1887 which led to his arrest and expulsion from the university. The university disturbance was organized by three leading members (not including Vladimir) of the Bogoraz circle in response to disturbances in Moscow University. Demands were first presented to the Director of the Veterinary Institute (the four revolutionaries were all students of the Institute) for liberal changes in the very restrictive student code, and were followed by a riotous assault by a student crowd of some 150–200 on the Inspector of Students – an official and unpopular figure. Vladimir was, apparently, active among the crowd. About forty, including Vladimir, were arrested and spent a few days in prison. Expulsion from the university followed.[55] Vladimir was prohibited from living in Kazan and was placed under police surveillance in Kokushkino. His part in the disturbance had not been a very prominent one. But the police were not likely to take any chances with a brother of Alexander Ulianov.

The Ulianov family moved back to Kokushkino in December 1887, and spent the rest of the winter and the summer of 1888 in the country. In the autumn Vladimir was given permission to return to Kazan, but was refused re-admission to the university. It was during these eight or nine months in Kokushkino, according to his own account, that Vladimir embarked on a serious study of Chernyshevsky – reading him in the copies of the periodicals which had belonged to his uncle, to which Anna refers. He recalled later that he read from morning till night during those months, among other things continuing work on his university course in the hope that he would be re-admitted. But what had mainly left its imprint on him was the work of Chernyshevsky (whose *What Is To Be Done?* he had read the previous summer). It was from Chernyshevsky, he recalled, that he first derived his understanding of materialism and of the dialectic. Vladimir also studied Chernyshevsky's writings on the village communes, his translation and annotation of Mill's *Political Economy*, and the regular accounts of political life abroad which Chernyshevsky skilfully utilized as a vehicle for revolutionary propaganda.[56] Lenin retained his veneration for Chernyshevsky, as we know from many sources, all his life: hardly a sentimentalist, he carefully preserved a photograph of Chernyshevsky inscribed with the date of his death.[57]

A materialist, an extreme utilitarian, a socialist and an uncompromising revolutionary – such were the most marked characteristics of Nikolai Gavrilovich Chernyshevsky. He spent nearly half his life in prison and exile, on the basis of a conviction for revolutionary activity for which the evidence was forged: yet no man exercised a greater influence in educating young Russians for revolution than did this man. The impact of *What Is To Be Done?* on the sixties, and later, has already been referred to, including its effect on both Alexander and Vladimir Ulianov. The study of Chernyshevsky's other writings in the course of 1888 provided an education of a more intellectual, less emotional nature. Chernyshevsky introduced Vladimir to Marx and Feuerbach, and to both socialism and materialism. He convinced him of the pointlessness of reform and converted him to the view that the liberals would always betray the cause of the people and of democracy. To a large extent he provided the future architect of Bolshevism with the kind of language which has characterized it ever since.

The importance of language as a cohesive force in revolutionary activity should not be underrated: it serves the multiple function of creating a sense of companionship, of excluding others, of identifying enemies and friends by means of simple words of hatred and praise; by substituting clichés for thought it enables passion to take command over reason. By some irony of history Chernyshevsky, because of his support of the village commune, was to be reckoned among the fathers of populism, though in ideas and temperament he does not belong either with the indigenous Russian social populists of the seventies, or with the anti-capitalist philosophers of the eighties. Lenin later would, rightly, draw a distinction between Chernyshevsky and the other "revolutionary democrats" of the sixties on the one hand, and the populists of the seventies and eighties on the other. Chernyshevsky was a hard radical, in line with the West European radicals of the day. His support for the village commune was not based on any of the romantic illusions about the Russian peasants which characterized Herzen. Chernyshevsky regarded the commune as a primitive survival in Russia of what had once been a universal feature in Europe. However, since it had survived, it could, in his view, after the autocracy had been swept away, provide a basis for the kind of co-operative or phalanstery socialism which he had learnt from Fourier and from the Petrashevsky circle, with which, as a student, he had been in contact. It is this kind of socialist co-operation, leading to a phalanstery, which is expounded in considerable detail under the guise of explaining

Vera Pavlovna's dressmaking enterprise in *What Is To Be Done?*

The influence of Chernyshevsky on Lenin is beyond question, if only because of the frequency with which he quotes him. We are, however, able to trace the main elements which Lenin valued in Chernyshevsky's writings from a recently published document: Lenin's marginal commentaries, underlinings and markings (which were always of a very dramatic and characteristic nature) on a book about Chernyshevsky by Yu. M. Steklov. This book was published in Petersburg in 1909, and Lenin read and annotated it soon after.[58] It was from Chernyshevsky that he had first become acquainted with Marx at second hand. But it was not primarily this aspect of Chernyshevsky which interested Lenin over twenty years later: it was the "revolutionary democrat", the uncompromising enemy of reform and liberalism and advocate of revolution, his temperament, perhaps more than his doctrines. "*Bien dit*," notes Lenin against a quotation from Chernyskevsky: "He who strokes the fur of everyone and of all, loves nothing and no one but himself; he whom everyone is pleased with is a man who does no good, since one can do no good deeds without insulting evil; he whom no one hates has earned no gratitude from anyone for anything." Every passage in which the author stresses the irreconcilable enmity between Chernyshevsky and the "revolutionary democrats" on the one hand and the liberals or reformers on the other, is heavily sidelined, and sometimes marked with an "N.B"; similar approval is expressed for a remark by the author that Chernyshevsky provided all the arguments for the populists "who assimilated the letter but not the spirit of their great master". Steklov was anxious to show that Chernyshevsky had absorbed a good deal of Marx's doctrine, and saw it as applicable to Russia – and some of the passages which the author adduced in support of his argument bear marks of Lenin's approving pencil. However, other passages, in which Steklov appeared to have overstated the case for Chernyshevsky's "marxism" bear marks of disapproval or doubt. But it was perhaps characteristic that Lenin should have placed a question mark against a sentence quoted from Chernyshevsky expressing the view that socialism, if not 1,000 years off in Russia, was certainly 100 or 150 years away – though in truth one may well doubt if this really represented Chernyshevsky's considered view. All in all, what stands out in the heavy scoring of these pages is that for Lenin the merit of Chernyshevsky lay primarily in the fact that he was a radical democrat, an enemy of liberalism and an implacable fighter for a revolution.

It would be of great interest to know what else Lenin read during these months, but we have no information. It is possible that one of the authors he read was Tkachev, whose articles during the sixties were published in the periodical *Delo* (Affairs). He may also have read the various expositions and criticisms of the doctrines of Marx which mainly appeared in the periodicals in the seventies and eighties. By the autumn Vladimir was allowed to return to Kazan, though his application to return to his studies at the university was rejected. Several applications to be allowed to go abroad (ostensibly on grounds of health, but in fact in order to enter a university) were also rejected. Vladimir therefore settled down to a course of serious reading. According to what appears to be the evidence of library requisition slips the main subjects which interested him were the French revolution, Greek history, civilization in England, Russian law and legal history, and statistics.[59] There is no mention of economics, which was certainly to become Lenin's main preoccupation for years to come. According to Anna, Vladimir first applied himself to a serious study of the first volume of *Capital* in the autumn of 1888.[60] According to the recollection of N. V. Volsky of what Lenin himself had to say on the subject in 1904, he first read *Capital* in January 1889.[61] Whichever may have been the correct date for the reading of *Capital*, there is no doubt that it was in Kazan in the autumn of 1888 and the spring of 1889 that Lenin first began to read the works of Marx with serious attention. There is some doubt about which revolutionary circle or circles Vladimir frequented during his second stay in Kazan. (The Bogoraz circle had, of course, ceased to exist after the arrests of December 1887.) Anna mentions two such circles: that of Chetvergova and that of Chirikov.[62] That Vladimir frequented Chetvergova's circle is confirmed from other sources.[63] Chetvergova was an old adherent of *Narodnaia Volia*, and Krupskaia records that Lenin retained a great respect and affection for her in later years.[64] Of Chirikov nothing is known except that he soon abandoned all revolutionary activity, and that he was a member of "one of the Fedoseev circles" to which Lenin belonged, and was arrested in 1889 when the circle was broken up.[65] N. E. Fedoseev, one of the earliest converts to marxist social democracy, was at that date active in Kazan, and influenced in his outlook by the marxist scholar, P. N. Skvortsov, then also living in Kazan.

Fedoseev certainly exercised a direct influence over the young Lenin: but this was at a later date, when the two corresponded, and perhaps even met, and will be dealt with below. As Lenin himself recorded later, he did not meet Fedoseev while he was in Kazan; but, after leaving Kazan, he heard of the arrest of Fedoseev in the summer of 1889, "and of other members of Kazan circles – including, incidentally, the one in which I participated".[66] The explanation seems to lie in the fact that while Fedoseev directed one main circle, in which he himself participated, there were a number of subordinate circles over which he exerted general influence and supervision. His influence was apparently mainly exerted by means of a study list which Fedoseev had compiled in order to replace the study list hitherto in use (the so-called "Cheliabinsk List") and which was considered out of date. It seems clear that Lenin was not a member of the main circle, since otherwise he could hardly have failed to meet Fedoseev. But it may well be that the main subject of study in the circle which he did frequent was marxism, and other sources confirm that while in Kazan in 1888–9 Vladimir frequented a "marxist" circle.[67] However, the question of Vladimir's adherence to any particular "marxist" circle at this date is of less interest to the historian than to the Soviet propagandist, anxious to conceal Lenin's early connections with *Narodnaia Volia*. The precise date at which Lenin seriously began the study of marxism – 1888 or 1889 – is likewise not of vital importance. The boundary between the marxist and the People's Will revolutionary was not strictly drawn in 1888 or 1889, and opinons could legitimately vary (and do among the accounts left by participants) whether the Fedoseev circle or circles were already strictly "marxist" by that date.[68] What is quite certain is that on his return to Kazan in 1888 Lenin began to make the acquaintance of some of the works of Marx:[69] the more prolonged and serious study would begin in Samara, where the family moved in the spring of 1889. What emerges from a study of the first eighteen months of Vladimir Ulianov's adult life is that for some time before he began to devote his attention to Marx, his imagination had been fired and his outlook influenced – probably for life – by the "revolutionary democrats" of the sixties; and by the epigones of *Narodnaia Volia*.

The Ulianov family spent the summer of 1889 in Alakaevka, a village some thirty miles east of Samara. (Mrs Ulianova had bought a house and estate here, some thirty-five acres in extent, apparently in the hope of tempting Vladimir to forsake politics for agriculture.) Mark Elizarov, an active *Narodnaia Volia* revolutionary, who would later become Anna's husband, was living with the Ulianov family, helping to manage the estate. During the summer Vladimir, as was his custom, read seriously and systematically. The authors mentioned in the relevant memoirs include Ricardo, Danielson (the populist economist), and Guizot.[70] For the winter the family moved to Samara. This was to be Vladimir's mode of life until the autumn of 1893, when he moved to Petersburg.

Samara was much less of a revolutionary centre than Kazan, so far as "circles" were concerned. It was, however, much better equipped than Kazan as a place for study. The public library was reasonably well stocked. But, more important, there existed a fair-sized "illegal" library, which had belonged to one V. I. Popov, a "progressive" man who had served a sentence of imprisonment for some bold verses. His illegitimate son, A. Skliarenko, was, at the time of Lenin's arrival in Samara, active as a revolutionary, and he placed the library at the disposal of Samara's revolutionary youth. The library included all the "progressive" periodicals of the sixties, seventies and eighties (including *Delo*, in which Tkachev published in the sixties), the works of Dobroliubov, Pisarev and Chernyshevsky, and many works on the peasants. There were, or so it would appear, none of the works of Marx in this library – though there would have been many articles on Marx (including those of learned marxists like N. I. Ziber), to be found in the rich collection of periodicals. Vladimir, already "converted" to marxism, soon met Skliarenko through Elizarov, who had, by the time the family moved to Samara, married Anna. Under Vladimir's influence, Skliarenko was soon likewise converted to marxism, and the library considerably enriched with the works of Marx and Engels and of Plekhanov, with other publications of the Liberation of Labour Group, and with *Die Neue Zeit*, the theoretical organ of German social democracy to which, among others, Kautsky contributed.[71]

The years spent in Samara were years of intense intellectual activity for the young Lenin. He set to work to sway the Samara leaders of revolutionary youth to the higher truths of Marx. After

Skliarenko came V. A. Ionov, a friend of Elizarov, and also a *Narodnaia Volia* adherent. He had most influence on Samara youth. Like Elizarov, he took longer to shift from his allegiance than Skliarenko.[72] With his characteristic intellectual energy and battering-ram technique, Vladimir mastered the works of Marx and engaged in indefatigable debate until his opponents were vanquished. Evidently the fanatical conviction that there is one complete answer to all questions, past and future, if only it can be found, so characteristic of the Russian *intelligent*, was not confined to Lenin in Samara in those years. And so Marx (or Marx as each saw him) became, by early 1893, the light and the salvation for a group of young men, headed by Lenin: a split in the Samara revolutionary ranks in the autumn of 1892 was followed by the formation of a marxist circle in March 1893.[73] Its undisputed leader and intellectual guide was Vladimir Ulianov. Meanwhile, Vladimir had also found time to pursue the study of law. He was eventually given permission to take his law examinations in the University of Petersburg as an external student. In March 1891 he went to the capital and at various dates between April and November was examined in criminal law, the history of Russian law, jurisprudence and the philosophy of law, Roman law, civil, commercial, ecclesiastical and international law. He was awarded a diploma of the first class. He returned to Samara, and, until September 1893 when he moved to Petersburg (his move had been delayed by the death of Olga in 1891, which made him reluctant to leave his mother) practised law as assistant to a Samara advocate.

The young Lenin's activities in Samara were not confined to the study of law and Marx. In particular, he had by no means lost his interest in *Narodnaia Volia*. As would soon become evident, Lenin rejected the gradualism and anti-capitalism of populist philosophy, but, unlike Plekhanov and many other social democrats, did not repudiate with nearly as much vehemence either the terrorist and Blanquist elements in populism or the "revolutionary democrats" of the sixties. Indeed his somewhat ambivalent attitude towards them continued for some time to make the more "orthodox" social democrats at times suspicious of the true purity of Lenin's marxism.[74] His main informants on revolutionary history while he was in Samara were A. I. Livanov and M. P. Golubeva (Yasneva). Livanov was a much older man (he was born in 1851) and his activities as a populist related to the seventies: he was one of those sentenced in 1878 in the Trial of the 193. Lenin had a great respect for Livanov, and questioned him closely on revolutionary practice and methods, on revolutionary security, on conditions in prison, on the ways of keeping in touch with the outside world as a prisoner, and the like.[75] M. P. Golubeva, born in 1861, was a disciple of the Orel Jacobin revolutionary P. G. Zaichnevsky, and, at that date, herself a convinced Jacobin and adherent of the revolutionary *coup d'état*. (She eventually joined the Bolsheviks.) She has left several accounts of her conversations with Lenin in Samara,[76] which were long and frequent. Lenin was, of course, deeply interested in her experiences and in the practices of the Orel revolutionaries. Apart from that, they mainly discussed her favourite subject – the seizure of power. Vladimir, as she recalls, did not dispute either the possibility or the desirability of seizing power. "But he could not understand what we meant when we said that we would look to "the people" for support, and began to explain at length that the people is not a homogeneous whole, but consists of classes with different interests, etc."[77]

Indeed, a detailed study of the life of the peasants and of the peasant economy, the survival or disintegration of the commune, the relations of the poor and wealthy peasants and the like formed a subject of absorbing interest to Lenin during this period. The earliest written work of Lenin to have reached us is a study of "New economic trends in peasant life", probably written in 1893. It is a detailed statistical study (based on data contained in a book by V. E. Postnikov on the peasants in the south of Russia, published in 1891), designed to show the extent to which economic differentiation was taking place in the villages.[78] Samara also offered Vladimir some opportunities for practical study of the life of the peasants. This was made possible through Elizarov who was of peasant origin, and had retained his contacts in the villages. Lenin also accompanied Skliarenko, who was secretary to the local Justice of the Peace, Samoilov, on his trips into the villages in the course of his professional duties.[79]

There is much confusion in the term "marxist". The truth is that each man who falls under the spell of Marx reinterprets him in his own way. Both Tkachev and Chernyshevsky called themselves marxists – yet it would be very difficult to reconcile much of the emphasis which each of these thinkers laid on the deliberate voluntary acts of individuals as a factor in history with the views of Marx. Until he moved to Petersburg Lenin had had comparatively little contact with industry and with the industrial workers. However much at home intellectually in the social democratic world of capitalism and the factories, so far as his experience went the life of the village was still closer to him. Moreover, in Russia in the last decade of the last century, with industry just in its early "take-off" stages, no practical revolutionary could ignore the peasants. So, marxism for Lenin was, in the early stages of his practical activity, reinterpreted in village terms. Plekhanov and the members of the Liberation of Labour Group had interpreted marxism in its application to Russia as an aspect of the development of industrialization. They argued that the commune was disintegrating, that industry and a proletariat were rapidly growing and that therefore the time had come to form a Russian social democratic worker party. The immediate aim of this party would be to guide the ever-increasing industrial struggle which, in conjunction with the middle-class liberal parties which would emerge, would effect the bourgeois democratic revolution. Thereafter, the party would continue to guide the workers' struggle towards the ultimate socialist, proletarian revolution. They thus saw Russian development as similar to that which they believed applicable to Western Europe, though they certainly foresaw a considerable acceleration of the process in the case of Russia which could profit from Western European experience and support.

Lenin, certainly by 1893, if not before, had come to the conclusion that capitalism in Russia was not something which belonged to the future, however imminent, but something which was already in existence, and present in the villages as well as in industry in the towns. He is reported to have held this view in 1891,[80] but at all events in 1893 he expounded it in a series of letters to P. P. Maslov, a marxist economist, who specialized on the agrarian question. In the first of these letters he referred to the "myth" that peasant economy was somehow different from the rest of the national economy. The "so-called workers" were not a small group "of people in a special position, but only the upper layers of that enormous mass of the peasants which already now lives more by the sale of its work power than by its own household". In short, the peasant form of economy is "the same as the bourgeois form, except for the distinction that it is much more entangled in feudal muddle".[81] It does not appear that Lenin at any time thought that the poor peasants could play an independent revolutionary role as a "proletariat" – a view which even *Narodnaia Volia* abandoned. (Certainly, in the discussions on the party programme in 1902 Lenin, while strongly contending that capitalism was *already* the dominant form of economy in Russia, not just *becoming* the dominant form, insisted that the workers should exercise dictatorship since they could not be sure of the support of the petty bourgeoisie.[82]) The effect of the assertion that capitalism already existed in Russia in 1893 was to advance the advent of the next phase: socialism – if nothing else, psychologically – and thus to cater for the natural impatience of revolutionaries who want to live to see the results. It is probable that in this analysis of Russian capitalism, though not in the conclusions that he would later tend to draw from it, Lenin was influenced by Fedoseev.

Nikolai Yevgrafovich Fedoseev was born on 27 April 1871, and was therefore a year younger than Lenin. His revolutionary activity began already at school, and led to his expulsion in 1887. By 1888 he was active in Kazan, and this ended with his arrest in the summer of 1889. He spent two and a half years in prison. He managed, with the aid of Maria Gopfengauz, who pretended to be his cousin, to correspond with marxists like A. Sanin and P. P. Maslov, and to pursue his study of marxism. At the end of 1891 he was released, and settled in Vladimir, where he continued his researches and writing which he had, with tremendous persistence, pursued while in prison. But he was arrested again in November 1893, and exiled to Vologda for three years. There followed a further arrest in May 1895, when he was imprisoned again, and exiled to eastern Siberia this time – with an intermediate period of imprisonment, once again in Moscow. His conditions of exile to a colony of political prisoners were exceptionally hard – even for Russia. Driven to distraction by a combination of the hardships and a campaign of defamation conducted against him by his fellow exiles, aggravated by the refusal of the authorities to let Maria Gopfengauz join him, he shot himself on 21 June 1898. Maria Gopfengauz, who received permission to join him at the same time as his letter of farewell, also put an end to her life. The influence of Fedoseev on those with whom he came into contact was out of all proportion to his written work, which consists mainly of his correspondence,[83] and some writings which have been lost. Among those who came under his influence was Lenin, who in later years referred to him in terms of high praise.[84] His correspondence with Fedoseev (which has all been lost) extended over many years, beginning in 1893. The subjects discussed included, it would seem, a manuscript on the consequences of the emancipation of the peasants, which Fedoseev sent to him, and Lenin's reactions to criticism of the marxists by Mikhailovsky, to whom Fedoseev sent several letters.[85]

Where Fedoseev is most likely to have influenced Lenin is on the question of the existence of a differentiated class structure among the peasants, which is a recurrent theme in his surviving writings, from as early as 1891.[86] The theme was in fact not a new one – it had already been developed much earlier by populist writers, influenced in this respect by the descriptions of village life in the works of Gleb Uspensky.[87] Fedoseev, like Lenin apparently, did not at any time imply that the leadership of the revolution could fall on anyone other than the workers, who were "by the very conditions of their life more prepared for the reception of the idea of the need for political struggle than the peasant mass".[88] In general, Fedoseev's views are in many ways quite distinct from those of the later Lenin, and it seems improbable that, had he survived, he would have found himself on Lenin's side in 1903. Like Plekhanov, Fedoseev stressed the need for a workers' party, which would conduct a struggle for political freedom and for the interests of the workers, as the first stage on the road to socialism. The function of the party, according to him, was not to devise a programme for the people, but to find out what the people wanted, and help them to formulate their demands.[89] It is of incidental interest, as an illustration of the difference of outlook and temperament between the two men, that Fedoseev ridiculed those marxists who had refused to take part in assistance to the starving peasants during the famine of 1891, on the grounds that this would merely create an obstacle to the process of the formation of capitalism.[90] Lenin, as we know from Golubeva, was in fact one of the marxists who adopted this attitude.[91]

The earliest published works of Lenin were almost certainly the fruits of his extensive researches, debates and expositions while still in Samara. They consist of the review of Postnikov already referred to; two (out of an original three) long essays on populism; and a long attack on P. Struve's *Critical Remarks on the Question of the Economic Development of Russia*, which had appeared in 1894.[92] They may be presumed to reflect the state of development of his outlook at that date – with one possible qualification. According to both Struve and A. N. Potresov, in detailed accounts which they gave to N. Volsky in 1918 and 1933, Lenin had already reached the conclusion by 1894 that the forthcoming revolution would not merely herald the collapse of the autocracy, but would bring about the destruction of the whole bourgeois capitalist order which the autocracy alone kept in being. Passages to this effect were contained in an earlier criticism of Struve, which has been lost, and were also included in the original manuscript of *Chto takoe 'druzia naroda' i kak oni voiuiut protiv sotsial-demokratov*. They were, however, omitted by Lenin on the insistence of Fedoseev, to whom he had sent the manuscript, and whose authority for Lenin was "enormous".[93] It is, of course, difficult to estimate the value of evidence which is based on a recollection of recollections set down many years after the events – and perhaps influenced by the policy which Lenin in the event pursued in 1917. However, that Lenin in fact did send the manuscript of his attack on Mikhailovsky to Fedoseev is very probable.[94] Besides, as the story of Bolshevism unfolds hereafter the issue of Lenin's attitude to the two-stage revolution – the bourgeois and the socialist – which Plekhanov expounded will be seen to be the crux of the conflict between Lenin and his social democrat opponents on a number of occasions: in 1902, in the discussions on the programme, and in 1906 in the discussion on agrarian policy, to name only two. On each occasion Lenin's views – in favour of proclaiming in the programme that capitalism was already established in Russia, and in favour of nationalization of all land – could, in the last resort, only be justified if the forthcoming revolution he had in mind (whether consciously or unconsciously) was a proletarian and not a bourgeois revolution: if capitalism is already established (in 1902) then the next phase must be socialism; if all land is to pass to the government after the revolution, this can only make sense if the government is a proletarian one, since otherwise it would lead to the strengthening of the bourgeois government. Besides, Lenin's policy of outright war against the liberals, on which he was to clash with Plekhanov for many years to come, was also an indication of a conviction (again, unconscious perhaps) that the coming revolution must be the last. For, if the first stage was believed to be the bourgeois stage, then logic demanded – as Plekhanov preached – collaboration with the liberal bourgeoisie until the autocracy was brought down, and only then, in the favourable conditions of political freedom created by the bourgeois revolution, the assault on the bourgeois, liberal structure in order to create socialism.

These first published works of Lenin, even without any passages which may originally have been included in them, show the stage of development which he had reached by the time he left Samara for the capital. In the first place, he argues, the political task of the social democrats consists in helping "the development and organization of the worker movement in Russia" to transform it from sporadic revolts and protests into "the organized struggle of the *entire* Russian working *class* directed against the bourgeois regime and striving for the expropriation of the expropriators, for the destruction of those social conditions which are founded on the oppression of the toilers". Quoting "a certain manuscript" by a marxist, he stresses that the workers are the only representatives in this task of all the toiling Russian population: this is because it is only "heavy machine industry which creates the material conditions and social power which are necessary for this struggle". (It is probable that this passage is a reflection of the views of Fedoseev in his second letter to Mikhailovsky, which was referred to above.) When the working class has achieved class consciousness and absorbed the principles of scientific socialism, "then the Russian *worker*, rising at the head of all democratic elements, will overthrow absolutism, and will lead *the Russian proletariat* (by the side of the proletariat of *all* countries) *by open political struggle to the victorious communist revolution*".[95]

Lenin does not say anywhere that the toppling of absolutism and the victory of communism will be one simultaneous or even continuous battle. At one point he seems, indeed, to be envisaging a two-stage revolution when he talks of "the struggle by the side of radical democracy against absolutism" as the "plain duty of the working class". But in urging this duty upon the workers, the social democrats "must not for a moment omit to urge upon them that the struggle against all these institutions [i.e. of absolutism] is necessary only as a means for facilitating the struggle against the bourgeoisie, that the realization of all-round democratic demands is necessary for the workers only in order to clear the path which leads to victory over the main enemy of the toilers – *capital*, which in our Russian conditions is particularly prone to sacrifice its democratic principles and enter into alliance with the reactionaries in order to keep the workers down, and the better to put a brake on the emergence of a working class movement."[96] But this approval of alliance with the liberals is an isolated instance. Elsewhere he stresses that the days when the aims of socialists and democrats (by which he means the populists of his day, like Mikhailovsky) were one and the same, as they were in the time of Chernyshevsky, are gone for ever. "A whole chasm now lies between the ideas of the democrats and those of the socialists", and "it is high time that Russian socialists understood that it is *inevitable* and *urgently necessary* for them to make *a complete and final break* with the ideas of the democrats".[97] It may be that in 1894, as indeed at many points until 1917, Lenin persisted in the ambiguity of his views on the attitude which his party should adopt towards liberals up till March 1917 when his view on the Provisional Government was plainly formulated: "Our tactics: absolute mistrust, no support of new government. Kerensky particularly suspect: to arm proletariat only guarantee; ... *no rapprochement with other parties*."[98]

It is also possible that in the conditions which obtained in Russia at the time, Plekhanov's "two-stage" scheme of revolution was impossible, and that the only practical effect of trying to work for it would be to lead back to a *Narodnaia Volia* type of *coup d'état*. This was the view expressed by the veteran ideologist of populism, P. L. Lavrov, in 1895: In the West, he wrote, social democratic organization of the workers takes place on the basis of existing legal forms and rights. These do not exist in Russia. Therefore it will be necessary to organize the Russian workers' party in conditions of "all the delights of absolutism". It is doubtful if it will be possible for the social democrats to create a workers' party "without at the same time organizing a conspiracy against absolutism". If they have to do both these things at once "then, whatever they may call themselves, the Russian social democrats will *in actual fact* take over the programme of their opponents, the followers of the People's Will". Prophetic words![99]

The main argument of the articles directed in 1894 against Mikhailovsky and other populists of the day is that their advocacy of reform is illusory. No government drawn from the exploiting class will ever act for the benefit of the toilers whom it is in their interest to keep down. Populism, Lenin argues, has undergone degeneration. "Out of a political programme, calculated to *raise the peasants* in a socialist revolution *against the foundations of contemporary society* has evolved a programme calculated to patch up, to 'improve' the position of the peasants *while at the same time preserving the foundations of contemporary society*." And he adds a footnote to say that all the populists, from the Bakuninists to the revolutionaries of *Narodnaia Volia*, aimed at the destruction of the existing base of society: the latter, in particular, believed that the peasants would delegate an overwhelming number of socialists to the National Assembly.[100]

This was true enough: the distinguishing feature of all the populist revolutionaries was that they believed in a once-for-all revolution, which would replace the autocracy either by socialist self-government, or by a government vowed to establish socialism. If some elements of an indigenous, Russian doctrine of revolution remained implanted in Lenin even after he had been exposed to West European marxist doctrines, this is where they would have been drawn from. By 1894 Lenin's view of the past history of the populist movement had become clear enough. He drew a sharp line between revolutionaries and reformists – placing his contemporaries among the populists, headed by Mikhailovsky, squarely in the latter category.[101] They failed to see, he argued, the significance of the fact that the peasants were not a homogeneous class, but were differentiated into exploiter bourgeois and exploited proletariat, and thus failed to see that a policy of peasant reform, based on the existing communal structure, would only strengthen the bourgeois, exploiter elements at the expense of the toilers. To be sure, the old populists had also failed to see this differentiation, but at any rate they had seen the necessity for a revolution. The modern populists, "having lost the good sides of the old Russian social-revolutionary populism have firmly seized upon one of its big errors – the failure to understand the class antagonism among the peasants".[102] Not peasants against the rest, but class against class – this is the sum total of the moral which Lenin repeatedly drew from the analysis which he had, possibly under Fedoseev's influence, made during his years in Samara.

The populists accused the marxists, he says, of wishing to impoverish the peasants, to turn them into proletarians, but this is nonsense. In fact, the drawing of an increasing number of peasants under the yoke of capitalism is progressive since it will accelerate the class consciousness of all the toilers, and will ensure their more rapid liberation.[103] And he invokes Chernyshevsky, who had seen no reason "to get hot under the collar even about the question whether the peasants will or will not be emancipated; and still less about who is going to free them, the liberals or the landlords. It is all one to me. The landlords would really be better." Why? Because this would create fewer illusions. Chernyshevsky had understood that "the Russian serf-owning bureaucratic state was incapable of freeing the peasants, that is to say, overthrow the serf-owners"; it could bring about a wretched compromise between the interests of the liberals and the landlords "which would deceive the peasants with the illusion of security of freedom, but which would in fact ruin them and leave them at the mercy of the landlords".[104] It need hardly be said that Lenin's strictures on Mikhailovsky should not be taken as a fair exposition of his views at this date, which were in fact a good deal more complicated than Lenin's simple abuse would suggest.[105]

There is one more aspect worth noting in these early articles, which as yet played little part in Lenin's outlook, but which would before long figure very prominently in his polemics. In his review of Struve's book there occurs a mild attack on revisionism, of which Struve was to be one of the earliest Russian exponents. He takes Struve to task for saying that Marx's successors have "introduced an important correction" into the views which he held in the forties that the "downfall of capitalism" was necessary before society could pass to a new order of things; that capitalism was not separated from the new order by a "chasm", but by "a whole series of transitions". On the contrary, says Lenin, Marx expressed the view on the necessary downfall of capitalism in all his work, nor has his doctrine been "corrected" in any way by his successors: the struggle for reforms in no way does away with the "chasm", since this struggle is conducted with the open and avowed object of bringing about the "downfall" of capitalism.[106]

Lenin's move to Petersburg in September 1893 brought him into contact with a group of experienced social democrats like S. I. Radchenko, Iu. O. Martov and G. M. Krzhizhanovsky, whose revolutionary work had been entirely among urban factory workers. For Lenin this contact with practical social democracy was virtually new – it is possible, but not certain, that he may have conducted some propaganda among factory workers in Kazan, but in any case this had been a long time before Lenin's practical activity in Petersburg, before his arrest on 8–9 (20–1) December 1895. But in the course of 1895 he went on an extensive tour abroad with the object of meeting the leading lights of the social democratic movement, which lasted from early May until early September. He visited Switzerland, Berlin and Paris. He met the leaders of the Liberation of Labour Group, Plekhanov, Vera Zasulich, and P. B. Akselrod, and also Kautsky and Lafargue. He had long, extensive talks with them, above all with Plekhanov for whom at that date he felt a great veneration. He listened respectfully to Akselrod, who lectured him on his intransigent attitude to the liberals, as indeed Plekhanov had done some days before. But both the veterans were deeply impressed with this serious, modest and above all determined social democrat who seemed quite ready to accept the pre-eminence of the Geneva prophets in questions of theory.[107] In Paris and in Berlin he saw a good deal of the day to day work of social democracy. He made practical arrangements for establishing proper links, on a sound conspiratorial footing, with the Liberation of Labour Group.[108] It was perhaps as the result of this experience that for the few years to come, which Lenin spent in prison and in quite comfortable exile, tones of moderation, statements of the kind of marxist "orthodoxy" which would later be associated with Menshevism, appeared in his writings.

It was a period of intense intellectual activity. Three years, from 1896 to 1898, were spent on what is undoubtedly Lenin's major economic work, *The Development of Capitalism in Russia*. In it, according to his own statement some ten years later, he established that the development of agrarian relations was taking place in the capitalist manner in the landlords' part of the economy as well as in the peasants', both within and outside the commune. And secondly, that the developments to date had determined that only capitalist development and a capitalist class structure were possible in Russia, and that there could be no going back on this.[109] He read voraciously everything that he could get hold of which appeared in the Russian and foreign periodicals, commenting on it extensively to his friends. He also embarked on philosophy, which he had not hitherto tackled, reading especially Kant and Hegel, and the French materialists,[110] and produced a number of long articles.

We are, however, primarily concerned with the evolution of Lenin's views on the political problem. While in prison, in 1896, he produced a draft of a programme for the, as yet, unborn Social Democratic Party, with a long "explanation" appended to it. This document, which can be taken to represent Lenin's considered view at that date on the role and tactics of the party, won the warm approval of Akselrod,[111] and there is indeed nothing in it of which one can imagine any future Russian Menshevik or "orthodox" social democrat disapproving. The short programme recites the evolution of the workers' struggle in Russia, and states the first task of the party as that of helping the workers to achieve their main aim – political freedom. The first demand which it makes is for the summoning of a National Assembly (*Zemskii sobor*); and for the basic civil freedoms. In order to achieve this demand, it will support "every movement within society directed against the unrestricted power of the autocratic government" and against the privileged class of exploiters.[112] The explanatory section adds the rider that the workers must remember that "the propertied classes can only be their allies temporarily, that the interests of the workers and the capitalists are irreconcilable, and that the abolition of autocracy is only needed by the workers in order to be able openly to conduct their fight against capitalism on a broad front".[113] This is the classical "two-stage" pattern of revolution – first, jointly with the liberals, make the bourgeois revolution; then, turn against the liberals and destroy capitalism in the socialist revolution.

Of equal interest in this explanatory section is Lenin's view on the relations between the party and the workers. The function of the party is to help the workers to develop their class consciousness. Its task does not consist "in thinking up out of our heads some modern methods", but in helping the workers in their struggle. This view of the party's function is, of course, very close to the German Social Democratic Party's view of its function at the time. But it was also not far off the tradition of both *Zemlia i Volia* and *Narodnaia Volia* that ultimately the people must decide for itself what its programme is to be: the role of the party is merely to help the people to achieve the power to put the programme into effect. But the workers' struggle will only be effective if it is a struggle for political power. However, the consciousness of the need to struggle for political power grows up of its own accord among the workers in the course of their struggle for their daily needs against the factory owners, which "of its own accord and inevitably brings the workers up against questions of government and of politics", and to the realization that economic and political demands are indissolubly linked.[114] Three or four years later Lenin was to argue the exact opposite: that the function of the party is, precisely, to provide the workers' movement with the right theory which it is quite incapable of working out for itself; and that class consciousness cannot develop among the workers of its own accord in the course of their struggle for economic needs, but must be brought in from outside. What happened to make him change his mind?

All the evidence points to the conclusion that Lenin's views on the role of the party which he had evolved, in part at all events, under the influence of Plekhanov and Akselrod, suffered a drastic and fairly sudden change at the end of August 1899 when he first became fully aware of the revision of marxism in Germany by Eduard Bernstein; and of the existence of similar views among marxists in Russia. The evolution can be traced quite clearly in his correspondence during his years of exile.[115] His relations with Akselrod (who was to become a bitter opponent after 1903) during his exile remained warm and friendly, and outwardly there was complete identity of views between them. Lenin had evidently taken note of Akselrod's fears that the old tradition of conspiracy and *coup d'état*, against which Plekhanov had directed his main attacks fourteen years before,[116] might still manifest themselves in the young Russian social democratic movement. A pamphlet written by Lenin at the end of 1897 intended to rebut any fears that might still remain on this score was published the following year, with a Preface by Akselrod. "And let no simple-minded reader have any fear that he [i.e. the author] is proposing to summon the workers to the barricades, or to engage in conspiracies. Nothing of the sort."[117] A year later, in a letter to A. N. Potresov (a future co-editor of *Iskra*), he expressed "complete acceptance" of the view which

Akselrod had expressed in an article. In this article Akselrod had argued that there were two main dangers facing the Russian labour movement. The first (from which he was quite confident the imperial government's brutality would itself preserve it), that it would fail to develop beyond the stage of isolated conflicts in the factories. The second danger was a revival of "Bakuninist and Blanquist tendencies", which would dissipate the strength of the movement in pointless acts of violence.[118]

It took quite a long time for Lenin to reach the conclusion that revisionism was a dangerous trend which could undermine, as he saw it, the whole revolutionary effort of Russian social democracy. He had brushed aside in 1895 Struve's suggestion that the old marxism was now out of date. However, in the following years, as he read the political literature of the day, he became aware of the existence of a new trend in marxism which was more serious than he had supposed. His first reactions were very calm: the Stuttgart Congress in October 1898 where revisionism was first raised as a practical issue was "very interesting".[119] He was somewhat more moved when S. Bulgakov published an article in *Nachalo* in which he questioned the theory of the *Zusammenbruch*, in other words, the need for violent revolution. The article, Lenin wrote, was "disgusting", with its "echo of Bernstein's so-called criticism". Of course, he goes on, polemics "between our own people" are "unpleasant", and he, Lenin, had therefore toned down his reply to Bulgakov. But the "fundamental" disagreements between the "orthodox" and "the critics" cannot "be kept quiet".[120] Bernstein's pamphlet,[121] which had already been out a few months when this letter was written, had not yet reached Lenin in Shushenskoe. In the following month he writes to his brother: "I am becoming more and more a decisive opponent of the latest 'critical stream' in marxism".[122] Two months before he had written to Potresov to say that he found the "new critical stream" extremely "suspect". He is now convinced, he says, that the fragments of Bernstein which he had read had given him a false impression, and that it was dangerous, in particular, for Russia. "Do you know," he continues, "that it [i.e. Bernstein's theory] is already being exploited by our 'young men', the ultra-economists who are claiming Bernstein's support for their view that workers' activity should be confined to economic matters, and should avoid politics?"[123] However, on 27 June, he still found Potresov's assertion that "a reaction against marxism had started in Petersburg" quite incomprehensible and impatiently demanded further details.[124]

The growing suspicions and apprehensions burst into flame at the end of August or the beginning of September. On 1 September Bernstein's explosive pamphlet arrived, with its argument in favour of reforms and against revolution, and with its criticism of Marx's analysis in the light of more recent experience. Lenin and his wife immediately sat down with the book. They found it "unbelievably weak" on the theoretical side: it was all opportunism and Fabianism. Most of it was in the Webbs' books, anyway. They (Lenin and his wife) had been "particularly disgusted" by Bernstein's contention that many Russians supported his views. A more detailed comment was promised in a few days' time. But it was written in secret ink, and is unfortunately lost.[125] Whatever Lenin may have believed, Bernstein's claim that he had wide support inside Russia was wildly exaggerated. Revisionism, in its Russian form of "economism" – that is to say the view that workers should confine their activity to "economic" claims for better wages and working conditions, and leave "political" claims for civil and political freedom to the bourgeoisie – was at most the view of a handful of intellectuals.[126] The threat of "economism" was shortly to be exploited by Lenin and Plekhanov as a device to build up the *Iskra* group against its opponents. To return to the Shushenskoe exiles in August and September 1899, something else happened which, together with Bernstein's book, was to effect a complete transformation in Lenin's outlook, and thus to lay the foundations of Bolshevism.

This was the arrival at the end of July or at the beginning of August enclosed in a letter from Anna of a document with the heading *Credo*. The heading had in fact been added by Anna, and the document, which had all the appearance of being the profession of faith or programme of a new group of Russian marxists, was in fact an expression of the views of one individual, Kuskova, jotted down on a piece of paper.[127] Its argument was that nowhere in Western Europe has the working class won political freedom by its own efforts: but where political freedom has been won by the bourgeoisie, the workers utilize the opportunities presented by political freedom to advance their own aims. In Russia where political freedom does not exist, the fight for it should be left to the bourgeoisie, and the marxist intellectuals should support the bourgeoisie in this effort. The workers should confine themselves to economic struggle. Lenin was incensed by the *Credo*.[128] He organized a joint meeting of the exiled social democrats in his (relative) vicinity and produced a protest against the *Credo* signed by seventeen of them, including several prominent future Bolsheviks. Other social democrats, including Martov and Potresov, adhered to the protest later.[129]

More important than this protest was the complete change in Lenin's views which soon after began to become apparent in his writings. According to Krupskaia, the organizational plan, subsequently to be developed in *Iskra*, in *What Is To Be Done?* and in the *Letter to a Comrade*, took shape in this last year of exile. "Vladimir Ilyich could not sleep, and lost a great deal of weight. During the sleepless nights he thought out his plan in all its details, and discussed it at length with Krzhizhanovsky . . ."[130] It was in an article, written in 1899, and probably in the latter part of the year, that there appeared for the first time, in embryonic form, the basic ideas which were to become the characteristic features of what would later be called "Bolshevism" or "Leninism". This article, entitled "Our Immediate Task", was one of a series of articles destined for No. 3 of *Rabochaia Gazeta*, which had been declared the party organ at the First Congress of the Social Democratic Party, which had met in March 1898. (Arrests and other difficulties prevented the issue from ever appearing.) Social democracy, Lenin argued, "cannot be reduced to simple servicing of the workers' movement: it is 'the union of socialism with the worker movement' (to use the description of K. Kautsky, which reproduces the basic ideas of the *Communist Manifesto*); its task is to bring into the spontaneous worker movement certain specific socialist ideals . . ." There are no models available for the Russian movement: the conditions of the Russian working-class movement are "quite different from those of the Western European labour movements". On the other hand, Russian social democracy is very different indeed from the former revolutionary parties in Russia. Thus, the "need to learn revolutionary and conspiratorial technique from the old revolutionary leaders (and we acknowledge this need without the slightest hesitation) in no way relieves us of the duty to take up a critical attitude to the old revolutionaries, and to work out our organization for ourselves". The two problems, in this respect, which arise are: "(1) How to reconcile the necessity for complete freedom of local social democratic activity with the necessity of forming a united – and therefore centralized – party? . . . (2) How to reconcile the striving of social democracy to become a revolutionary party, which has as its main aim the struggle for political power with the fact that social democracy decisively refuses to engage in political conspiracies or to 'summon the workers to the barricades'." The party has every right to say that these two problems have already been solved theoretically, adds Lenin – in a characteristic phrase about the two "problems" which were to bedevil Russian social democracy so long as there was a Menshevik or Bolshevik oppositionist left alive and out of gaol. The only practical solution of these problems is "*the setting up of a press organ of the party, published regularly, and closely linked to all the local groups of the party*". But this is only a solution for the two problems until such time as political freedom has been achieved in Russia.[131] Here, in the immediate aftermath of the effects on Lenin of the *Credo* and of Bernstein's revision of marxism, were all the main features which Lenin would develop during the following years, and notably in *What Is To Be Done?* and in the *Letter to a Comrade on our Organizational Tasks*, both written in 1902. Both were part of the campaign by Lenin, on behalf of the *Iskra* group, to secure ascendancy over all the local committees inside Russia.

What Is To Be Done? (so named in conscious deference to Chernyshevsky) was published in Stuttgart in March 1902: it was written between the autumn of 1901 and the following February. The basic idea of the central newspaper, conceived at the end of 1899, had been the main theme of an article published in *Iskra* in May 1901. "The technical problem alone," Lenin had then written, of ensuring supplies for and distribution of the paper, "forces one to create a network of local agents of a single party" all in close contact and well informed, "and acquiring the habit of each regularly carrying out on a local scale a minute part of the all-Russian work".[132] Even at the time when these words were written *Iskra*'s agents were doing just that, and building up a hard core of future Bolsheviks in the process. Not all would survive on Lenin's side in the end: but as the Epigraph (from a letter of Lassalle to Marx) of

What Is To Be Done? proclaimed, "Struggle within the party gives the party strength and vitality . . . the party grows stronger by purging." *What Is To Be Done?* was intended to supply the theoretical justification for the organizational practice which *Iskra*, or at all events Lenin on its behalf, was already putting into practice. But, while it contains in essence the whole theory of Bolshevism, *What Is To Be Done?* was primarily a polemical pamphlet (not always scrupulously honest in its methods) against "economists", whether real or – more often – invented, and therefore an instrument in *Iskra*'s fight for ascendancy over the entire movement.

What Is To Be Done? opens with a lengthy attack on freedom of criticism – a slogan often invoked by *Iskra*'s opponents. In fact, says Lenin, freedom of criticism has in practice meant the freedom to preach "economist" and "revisionist" ideas. In a country like Russia, where the revolutionary consciousness of the working class is particularly weak, the spreading of such ideas is especially damaging. "Without a revolutionary theory there cannot be a revolutionary movement", and a party which is only just beginning to emerge is unusually vulnerable to the wrong theories, or to the absence of all theory: "Those who were really convinced that they had succeeded in advancing scientific knowledge [of society] would not be demanding freedom for the new views alongside of the old, but the replacement of the latter by the former."[133] The real vice of "economism" is its worship of spontaneity in the workers' movement, without realizing that spontaneously and of its own accord the labour movement leads only to the triumph of bourgeois interests and bourgeois ideology. For the workers have no social democratic consciousness. This can only be brought to them from the outside. "The history of all countries bears witness that by its own efforts alone the working class is capable of developing a trade union consciousness only, that is to say, a conviction that it is necessary to unite in trade unions, to conduct a struggle against the factory owners, to exact from the government the passing of this or that piece of legislation which is needed by the workers, and so on. But the science of socialism grew up out of those philosophical, historical and economic theories which were worked out by the educated representatives of the propertied classes, by the intelligentsia. This was true of Marx and Engels and it was true of Russia where theoretical social democracy arose quite independently of the spontaneous growth of the labour movement as a natural and inevitable result of the evolution of thought among the revolutionary socialist intelligentsia."[134]

Much space was devoted by Lenin to demonstrating the fallacy of the view that economic struggle of its own accord leads the workers into political struggle. Actually, everyone in the labour movement in Russia could see this process happening before his eyes: Lenin himself had repeatedly stressed the fact before 1899.[135] But if Lenin's polemics on this theme were not very convincing, the argument was essential to him in order to lead on to the main theme of *What Is To Be Done?* – the need for a centralized, professional revolutionary organization. "Economic struggle only 'brings the workers up' against questions of the relations of the government to the working class, and therefore, *however much we exert ourselves* 'to give the economic struggle a political character' we can *never* develop the political consciousness of the workers" within this framework. "Class political consciousness can be brought to the worker *only from the outside*, that is to say from outside the economic struggle, outside the sphere of relations between workers and factory owners. The only sphere from which this knowledge can be derived is the sphere of the relationship of *all* classes and sections to the state and to the government, the sphere of relationship between *all* classes . . . In order to bring political knowledge to *workers*, social democrats must *direct themselves to all classes of the population*, must send out *in all directions* detachments of their army."[136] To critics who might question what would then be left of the class character of the movement, Lenin replied that the illumination shed on all problems would be social democratic illumination, with no concessions to perversions of marxism; and that this all-round political agitation would be conducted by the party which would exercise pressure on the government, combining it with education of the proletariat and direction of its economic struggle "in the name of the whole people".[137] Lenin's critics might perhaps have been forgiven if they remained puzzled on the connection between all this and the theories of Marx. For such critics he ended with a warning: "He who sees these tactics as something which dims the class consciousness of the proletariat and as a *compromise with liberalism* reveals by this very fact that he completely fails to understand the true significance of the programme of the *Credo* and is de facto *putting this very programme into practice*, however much he may repudiate it."[138]

It is because the task of the party is much wider than the mere direction of the labour struggle that an entirely different kind of organization is required for it. A labour party consists of full-time workers, is as widely based as possible, and should be as little conspiratorial as possible. In contrast, an organization of revolutionaries should "first and foremost comprise people whose profession consists of revolutionary activity". The common character of the members of such an organization "*must completely obliterate all distinction between workers and intellectuals* . . ." Such an organization should not be very widely based; and it should be as conspiratorial as possible.[139] The remainder of the pamphlet is devoted to further discussion of the kind of organization that is needed and of the role and function of the central party newspaper, or "organ"; and also to arguments designed to meet the objections of those who held that Lenin's plan would replace social democracy by a revolutionary conspiracy, and moreover would destroy democracy within the party.

Lenin's views on the organization of the party around this time are dealt with in most detail in a document known as *Letter to a Comrade on our Organizational Tasks*. It was originally designed for the enlightenment of a Petersburg *Iskra* supporter, A. A. Shneerson (who later became a Menshevik); but it was in fact widely circulated among the *Iskra* committees as a general directive.[140]

At the head of the whole organization, says the *Letter*, there must first be a newspaper, or central organ, for theoretical guidance and in order to formulate general tasks. But a newspaper cannot direct practical activity: for this there must be a central group, to be called, perhaps, a Central Committee. "Unity of action and the necessary solidarity between the two bodies will be achieved not only by a single party programme, but by *the composition of both the bodies* (it is essential that the Central Organ and the Central Committee should consist of people who work in complete harmony)."[141] The Central Committee must consist of professional revolutionaries, and principally worker revolutionaries who have the best repute within the working class. It must not be too big; and it must be composed by co-optation. If it should seem too dangerous for all the members of the Central Committee to gather together at any one time, then "it may become necessary to separate off from out of the Committee a special, very small (say five, or even fewer) *Directive Group*, which absolutely must include in its members the Secretary, and the persons most capable of being the practical directors of the party work as a whole".[142]

The *Letter* then deals in great detail with the various subordinate committees, which are both territorial, i.e. set up in areas which are subdivisions of the local committee's area, and functional, i.e. set up in the individual shops and factories. The subordinate committees are appointed, not elected; their activity is at all times subject to control by the committee of the area, which must always "have the right to send its delegate into each group, subgroup or circle, which has any relationships to the movement at all".[143] All local groups and the like should have the right to communicate with the Central Organ and Central Committee – but only through their own area committee. This is much more secure a system of ensuring full consultation with all members of the party than any kind of general gathering of the party which exposes the party to risk at the hands of the police.[144] The *Letter* then deals with a possible objection that such strict centralization may endanger democracy. In particular, some might fear that "by some *chance* there might appear at the centre an individual endowed with enormous power and *lacking in capacity*". This is, concedes Lenin, possible, "but neither elections nor decentralization will provide a safeguard against the risk, nor can one frame rules about it". Elections and decentralization are in any case very dangerous for security. The only means available are those of "comradely influence", beginning with resolutions at the local level and appeals to the Central Organ and Central Committee, and "ending (in the worst case) with the *overthrow* of an office holder shown to be incapable".[145]

Finally, the *Letter* deals with the "most important principle of the entire party organization and party activity". While ideological and practical direction of the revolutionary struggle requires the maximum degree of centralization possible, so far as responsibility to the party is concerned the highest degree of decentralization is required. This decentralization of responsibility is no more than the obverse of that division of functions which is recognized as one of the most urgent needs of the movement. It is no good carrying on as at present with committees in which every function is carried out by each member, and "time and energy are spent on radical hurly-burly" in which nothing gets done on the one hand, and on the other, all kinds of student and worker circles, half of them quite unknown to the Committee, engaged in endless conferences about everything under the sun, without special tasks, and without any experience. The principle should be: each to his own task at his own level, with the Centre directing everyone, as a conductor directs an orchestra. "In order that the Centre should be able not only to advise, persuade and argue (as has happened up till now) but really conduct the orchestra, it is essential that it should be known precisely who is playing what fiddle, and where, where each player learnt to play and what particular instrument he studied and is studying, who is playing the wrong notes and where, and for what reason (when the music begins to grate on one's ear) and whom it is necessary to transfer and in what manner and to what place, in order to put an end to discord, and so forth."[146]

It is easy to jump to conclusions about this organization – for example, that it derives wholly from Lenin's inordinate lust for power, and that this explains all subsequent evolution of Bolshevism; or that it derives entirely from the traditions of *Narodnaia Volia*, and is alien to the traditions of social democracy. The problem does not admit of quite so straightforward an analysis. It could scarcely be disputed that the organization of the party which Lenin envisaged in 1902 derived in many ways from his temperament – impatient, intolerant of those less intelligent than himself, and seldom capable of believing that an opponent might perhaps be right. The heritage of Chernyshevsky was well implanted in him in this respect. But it was also true that many of the provisions for the future organization which he envisaged were dictated by genuine needs of security. The party was illegal, as was indeed all industrial action such as strikes. The police were active in penetrating all suspect political movements with their agents. A growing political party could ill afford to lose its best members through arrests. Many of the provisions which Lenin envisaged must therefore be seen as genuinely inspired by considerations of security. The lack of democracy could also be explained, in part, as dictated by the conspiratorial conditions in which the party could expect to have to work.

It is, of course, beyond dispute that many of the features of

Lenin's proposed organization derived from the traditions of *Narodnaia Volia*, and indeed Lenin said so himself. Many, but not all: aside from one reference to the need for a party newspaper as one feature of the directive mechanism in Ogarev's article on secret societies this aspect of Lenin's plan was completely original. More important was the fact that Lenin's plan of action went a long way towards an attempt to avoid what had been *Narodnaia Volia*'s failure: the fact that it remained in the end a centre without a base. Its plans for seizure of power remained in the air: what it became was, in effect, no more than an assassination conspiracy. Tkachev had pointed out with force that a seizure of power at the centre was not, by itself, enough: it had to be accompanied by a carefully controlled national rising, in itself the result of a cumulative period of disturbance; and, above all, it had to be planned to take place at the right moment, when the people, driven to exasperation by its hardships, has also lost its fear, and moreover has acquired a sense of impunity, inspired by the repeated discomfitures of the government. This, and not the mere conspiracy, is the essence of the successful revolution. *Narodnaia Volia* had failed to understand, or at any rate to create, the machinery necessary for the carrying out of such a revolution. Those who, since 1903, have been repeatedly asserting that Lenin borrowed the conspiratorial mechanism of Bolshevism from *Narodnaia Volia* might have done well to remember that he considerably improved on what he had borrowed – as indeed he had claimed he would do in 1899.

It was also true that the tradition of the importance of the elite, and the lack of influence that could be effected by the mass of the people, was central to Russian radical and populist thinking. D. I. Pisarev, the radical of the sixties, who inherited the mantle of Chernyshevsky and Dobroliubov, put all his hopes on an elite, believing that a properly trained and educated elite would, out of rational self-interest, at the same time benefit the people. "The fate of the people is decided not in the primary schools, but in the universities."[147] For Pisarev, the "nihilist" and utilitarian, the moral or ethical factor did not enter into it. Lavrov, the main ideologist of the populists, based his elitism on the moral duty which those who enjoyed the privilege of leisure and education owed to repay their debt to the amorphous people who lacked the power to alter their own destiny by themselves. The "critically thinking individuals", on whom the duty would fall of organizing the party which would fight for truth and justice for the people, must be united, disciplined, and determined. It must not be deflected or discouraged by the fact that it will find little support from the people. "It is quite possible that the suffering masses will not at once recognize their allies, will distrust them, and will be unable to see that the struggle now beginning . . . is the same struggle which they themselves instinctively demand on the basis of unenlightened inclination and belief. This means nothing. The party must nonetheless be organized with a view to union with these social forces – a union which is inevitable, if not today, then tomorrow."[148] Or, to put it in Lenin's language: consciousness must be brought to them from the outside. Bakunin, it will be recalled, for all his faith in the beneficent nature of a wild, all-destroying revolt, and his condemnation of any attempts to make up the people's minds for them, nevertheless, in the privacy of his correspondence, argued in favour of a secret revolutionary network to act as a dictatorship to guide the cleansing fury of the people along the right lines. Many more instances could be cited to show that in the populist tradition a firm belief in the special destiny, and duty, of an elite was in no way incompatible with a faith that ultimately the people knew best what they wanted, and displayed an inherent wisdom which leadership should seek to benefit from, but not to displace.

Perhaps the Russian intellectuals' frustrating experience of trying to guide the peasants to a better life led on naturally to elitism of this kind. Be that as it may, somewhat comparable ideas on the special, indeed indispensable, role of the elite arose within the much more mature German labour movement. When Lenin, in 1902, cast around for some authority among the marxist theorists for his proposition that revolutionary consciousness had to be brought to the workers from the outside (which he could scarcely hope to find in the writings of Marx), he invoked Karl Kautsky. It is not, of course, possible to say to what extent, if any, Lenin was influenced by Kautsky. But Lenin quotes a long passage from Kautsky in *What Is To Be Done?*[149] in which the German social democratic leader criticizes a statement in the draft revision of the Austrian social democratic programme to the effect that as the development of capitalism swells the ranks of the proletariat, so the proletariat is forced to take up the struggle against capitalism. It thus arrives at the consciousness of the possibility and necessity of socialism. "In this context," says Kautsky, "the socialist consciousness of the proletariat is made to appear as the inevitable and direct result of the class struggle. But that is false . . . Modern socialist consciousness can only arise on the basis of profound scientific insight. But the bearers of this scientific insight are the *bourgeois intelligentsia*, not the proletariat . . . Socialist consciousness is therefore something which is introduced [*hineingetragen*] into the proletarian class struggle from the outside, and not something which arises within it spontaneously [*urwüchsig*]."[150] Nor was this an isolated view of Kautsky. A very similar argument was used by him in his commentary on the Erfurt Programme, published in 1893, and translated into Russian in 1894, with which Lenin was certainly familiar.[151] The proletariat, he argued, can at best, so long as it remains proletariat, assimilate only a part of the knowledge which bourgeois scholars have brought to light. Without the aid of these bourgeois intellectuals working-class activity was likely to remain in the sphere of "mere trade union stuff" (*nur Gewerkschaftlerei*).[152] The German phrase, *nur Gewerkschaftlerei* occurs twice in *What Is To Be Done?*[153]

However, it was not in the end, perhaps, primarily a matter of theory. In a mature labour movement like the German it was, it may be, only a matter of common sense that the intellectuals should provide the theoretical basis for the practical working-class leaders to use as the basis for their socialist capitalism. The German movement had its Bebels as well as its Kautskys: there was less risk than in Russia that the theorists would in the end bend the movement entirely to its will. In Russia, at the dawn of social democracy, with no developed trade union movement, in conditions of police repression, the threat to independence and to practical common sense presented by dogmatic theorists was bound to be considerably greater. What Lenin proposed in *What Is To Be Done?* was to apply to the Russian labour movement something of the elitist practices which sheer necessity and the shattering experience of trying in vain to make any kind of contact with the peasants had forced upon an earlier generation of revolutionaries. Yet, the Russian labour movement, even in its infancy, was scarcely comparable to the nineteenth-century peasantry. But even in 1902 revolution in Russia still seemed a very long age away, and Lenin was a man in a hurry

– perhaps in the end this was the dominant element in his character as a revolutionary.

> Today our state is a fiction, a tradition, it has no roots in national life. It is hated by everyone; it evokes among everyone, even among its own servants, a feeling of dull bitter resentfulness and servile fear, mingled with the contempt of the lackey. The state is feared because it has the physical power, but when it once loses this power, not a hand will be lifted to defend it. But tomorrow those who are today its enemies will arise in its defence: tomorrow it will express their interests, the interests of the village capitalist and usurer, the interests of private property, the interests of trade . . . the interests of the emergent world of the bourgeoisie. Today this state is idiotically absolute and absolutely idiotic: tomorrow it will become moderate and constitutional, and show calculating reasonableness . . . Today our enemies are weak and divided: against us are only the government, with all its officials and soldiers, but these officials and soldiers are . . . only the blind and often unconscious instrument in the hands of a few autocrats . . . But what about tomorrow? Do not put too much faith in the stupidity of our enemies. Use the moment of opportunity. Such moments are not frequent in history. To let them slip means wilfully to postpone the possibility of the social revolution for a long time, perhaps for ever.[154]

So wrote Tkachev in 1875. It was above all this sense of pressing urgency, of the moment not to be lost, that was to characterize Lenin throughout his revolutionary career.

1. Lenin's birth certificate is in the Central Lenin Museum, and is reprinted in *Molodye gody V. I. Lenina*. Po vospominaniiam sovremennikov i dokumentam, ed. A. I. Ivanskii (Moscow 1957), p. 46. Cited hereafter as *Molodye gody*.
2. See *Lenin* (5th edn.), vol. 44, p. 509.
3. Quoted from the memoirs of Anna, first published in 1927; see *Aleksandr Ilyich Ulianov i delo l Marta 1887g*, ed. A. I. Ulianova-Elizarova (Moscow-Leningrad 1927), p. 55. Cited hereafter as *Anna*.
4. *Anna*, p. 43.
5. See the extracts reprinted in *Molodye gody*, pp. 46–157. A delightful picture of the life of the Ulianov family in Simbirsk is given by Marietta Shaginian, *Semia Ulianovykh. Ocherki. Stati. Vospominania.* (Moscow 1959).
6. For sources and documents see *Molodye gody*, pp. 78–196.
7. *ibid.*, p. 198.
8. *ibid.*, 185
9. A. Elizarova, "Vospominaniia ob

Aleksandre Ilyiche Ulianove", *Proletarskaiia revoliutsiia* No. 2–3 (61–2), 1927, pp. 278–316, at pp. 284–7. The belated disclosure, in 1941, by a former school friend, D. M. Andreev, that while at school Vladimir had been a voracious reader of Chernyshevsky, Herzen, Pisarev, Belinsky and Dobroliubov, and the radical journals of the sixties like *Delo* and *Sovremennik*, obtained illegally, must be treated with scepticism – see *Molodye gody*, pp. 146–7.

10. See V. Alekseev and A. Shver, *Semia Ulianovykh v Simbirske (1869–1887)*, edited and annotated by A. I. Ulianova (Elizarova) (Moscow-Leningrad 1925), pp. 50–1 and footnote by Anna Ulianova on p. 51.

11. That Turgenev was the favourite author of the young Vladimir is not only related by Anna, but is borne out by what Vladimir later (in 1904) told N. V. Volsky. See Nikolai Valentinov (Volsky), *Encounters with Lenin* (London, 1968), pp. 54–58.

12. *Literatura partii "Narodnoi Voli"* (Moscow 1907), pp. 476–7.

13. From the recollections of Anna in *Vospominaniia rodnykh o V. I. Lenine* (Moscow 1955), p. 22.

14. V. V. Kashkadamova, a schoolteacher in Simbirsk and lifelong friend of the Ulianov family; see *Anna*, p. 274.

15. See N. Valentinov, "Chernyshevsky i Lenin", *Novy zhurnal*, No. XXVI (New York 1951), pp. 193–216. It is of interest to observe that P. N. Tkachev had, in 1880, expressed views very similar to those of Lenin on the subject of *What Is To Be Done?* in his preface to the version of the novel which appeared in *Ni Dieu ni Maitre*; see P. N. Tkachev, *Izbrannye sochineniia na sotsial'no – politischeskie temy*, vol. IV (Moscow 1932–36), pp. 413–14.

16. Tkachev's review also dealt with George Eliot's *Felix Holt* and George Sand's *Mademoiselle Merquem*. On the popularity of Spielhagen's and other novels of this character in the sixties see V. Korolenko, *Istoriia moego sovremennika*, vol. I (Moscow-Leningrad 1933), p. 499.

17. "Liudi budushchego i geroi meshchanstva", P. N. Tkachev, *Izbrannye sochineniia*, vol. I, 1865–1869 (Moscow 1932), pp. 173–233.

18. On Nechaev see F. Venturi, *The Roots of Revolution* (London 1952), ch. 15; and B. P. Koz'min, *P. N. Tkachev i revoliutsionnoe dvizhenie 1860-kh godov* (Moscow, n.d. [1922]), ch. VIII.

19. By the lawyers concerned at the trial, by N. Utin, by Iu. Steklov, F. Mehring, E. H. Carr, B. P. Koz'min and F. Venturi.

20. See Michael Confino, "Bakunin et Nechaev. Les débuts de la rupture. Introduction à deux lettres inédites de Michel Bakunin – 2 et 9 Juin 1870", *Cahiers du Monde Russe et Sovietique*, vol. VII, 1966, pp. 581–699. This letter, in which Bakunin finally broke relations with Nechaev because of his dishonest practices as applied to his friends, contains the following phrase: "Do you remember how angry you were with me when I called you an *abrek*, and your 'Catechism' an *abreks'* catechism?" (p. 632). *Abrek* is a Caucasian mountaineer banished from his clan, on having vowed an oath of bloody vengeance. In the broad sense, it means a fighter impelled by the courage of desperation.

21. For the inconsistencies with Tkachev's views see B. P. Koz'min, *op. cit., loc. cit.*

22. The text of the "Catechism" was published after the trial in the official government gazette, *Pravitel'stvenny vestnik*, for 1871. It is reprinted in *Pis'ma M. A. Bakunina k A. I. Gertsenu i N. P. Ogarevu*, ed. M. P. Dragomanov (Geneva 1896), pp. 490–8.

23. *Lenin*, vol. II, p. 190. Quotations from Lenin are normally from the 2nd–3rd edition; quotations from the 4th or 5th editions are so indicated.

24. The article "What does the people need?" was published anonymously in *Kolokol* (The Bell), but the evidence of Herzen's papers establishes Ogarev as author – though others, including N. A. Serno-Solovievich, N. N. Obruchev and A. A. Sleptsov participated in the composition of the article. See N. P. Ogarev, *Izbrannye sotsial'no-politicheskie i filosofskie proizvedeniia*, vol. I (Moscow 1952), pp. 527–36, 843.
25. "K molodomu pokoleniiu", 1861; "Velikoruss", 1861; "Molodaiia Rossiia", 1862. See V. I. Burtsev, *Za sto let.* Sbornik po istorii politicheskikh i obshchestvennykh dvizhenii v Rossii (London 1897), pp. 35–46.
26. *ibid.*, pp. 67–9.
27. M. P. Dragomanov, *op. cit.*, pp. 490–3.
28. N. P. Ogarev, *op. cit.*, vol. II, pp. 68–80, 559–60; vol. I, pp. 800–3, 861. The published article included a mendacious claim, inserted in all probability by Nechaev or at his insistence, that such an organization "already exists in Russia". *Kolokol*, published in Geneva in the course of 1870, after Herzen's death, was edited by Nechaev.
29. "Vpered! Nasha programma", *Vpered*, Zurich, August 1873, reprinted in B. S. Itenberg, *Revoliutsionnoe narodnichestvo 70-kh godov XIX veka*, vol. I, 1870–5 (Moscow 1964), pp. 20–38.
30. Reprinted *ibid.*, pp. 38–55. It was written in the autumn of 1873.
31. See Michael Confino, *op. cit.*, pp. 666–72 and 658–62. This long letter was in the form of an ultimatum to Nechaev, demanding that he should mend his ways in his relations with his fellow revolutionaries on the threat of breaking off relations.
32. Turgenev's *Virgin Soil*, though the date of its action is a little earlier than 1874, gives an accurate picture of "going to the people". In spite of the storm of protests from radical critics at the time, the ineffectiveness and lack of contact of the revolutionaries is aptly borne out by the collection of letters from revolutionaries seized by the police at the time and now published in B. S. Itenberg, *op. cit.*, pp. 202–345.
33. The text of both the earlier (1876) and later (1878) versions of the Programme are reprinted in *Revoliutsionnoe narodnichestvo 70-kh godov XIX veka*, ed. S. S. Volk, vol. II (Moscow 1965), pp. 27–33.
34. *ibid.*, pp. 34–42.
35. For the story of the split see F. Venturi, *op. cit.*, ch. 21. The latent "political" trends within *Zemlia i Volia* have recently been admirably analysed by V. A. Tvardovskaiia in her *Sotsialisticheskaiia mysl', Rossii na rubezhe 1870–1880-kh godov* (Moscow 1969), pp. 9–54.
36. See B. P. Koz'min, *Iz istorii revoliutsionnoi mysli v Rossii* Izbrannye trudy (Moscow 1961), pp. 359–67.
37. V. D. Bonch-Bruevich, *Izbrannye sochineniia*, vol. II (Moscow 1961), pp. 246 and 314–15.
38. The view also had the support of Engels, and, according to Engels, of Marx. See a letter from Engels to Philip van Patten of 18 April 1883, Karl Marx, Friedrich Engels, *Werke*, vol. 36 (Berlin 1967), p. 11.
39. This summary is based on Koz'min, *op. cit.*, pp. 392–403; and on Tkachev's published work, *Izbrannye sochineniia* (Moscow 1932–7), of which six volumes have been published.
40. S. S. Volk, *op. cit.*, pp. 170–4.
41. *ibid.*, pp. 175–83, 379–80.
42. See A. Doroshenko in *Narodnaia Volia* No. 5, 5 February 1881, reprinted in *Literatura partii "Narodnoi Voli"* (Moscow 1907), p. 173.
43. The text is printed in S. S. Volk, *op. cit.*, pp. 184–191, and see p. 380 for its history. See *ibid.* for the photograph of the copy which was owned and marked by Marx.

44. A. D. Mikhailov, in 1882: see *Byloe*, 1906, No. 1, p. 304. Was Lenin to recall this distinction in the debates in 1903 over Paragraph 1 of the Party Rules? It is strange that no speaker seems to have remembered this point.

45. V. A. Tvardovskaiia, "Organizatsionnye osnovy 'Narodnoi Voli' ", *Istoricheskie zapiski*, vol. 67 (Moscow 1960), pp. 103–44, at p. 143. This is the best study available of the organization of *Narodnaia Volia* between 1879 and 1881.

46. The principal documents setting out the views of *Cherny Peredel* are reprinted in Burtsev, *op. cit.*, pp. 195–208.

47. S. S. Volk, *op. cit.*, *loc. cit.*

48. [See pp. 131–155 above. (ed.)]

49. For the text see Burtsev, *op. cit.*, pp. 173–9.

50. The programme is reprinted in *Aleksandr Ilyich Ulianov i delo l Marta 1887g*, ed. A. I. Ulianova-Elizarova (Moscow-Leningrad 1927), pp. 375–80. This volume also contains memoirs of a number of the participants in the conspiracy who escaped or whose sentences were commuted.

51. For his memoirs of his activity see V. Tan (pseudonym of Bogoraz), "Povesti proshloi zhizni", *Russkoe bogatstvo* (St. Petersburg 1907), No. 9, pp. 107 *et seq.*; No. 10, pp. 158 *et seq.*

52. There is a considerable primary literature on the Fokin circles. See especially N. Moshinsky, "Deviannostye gody v kievskom podpolye", *Katorga i ssylka*, vol. 34, 1927, pp. 7–24 (based *inter alia* on the recollections of Dr Fokin, who was still alive and in practice in 1927); "Istoricheskaiia zapiska o tainom obshchestve 'zagovor-shchikov' ", signed by Fokin, Bekariukov and L. D. Sinitskii, *Katorga i ssylka*, vol. 49, 1928, p. 52; M. Berezin, E. Pechorkin, E. Gauenstein, M. Gauenstein, "Vospominaniia iz zhizni narodovol'cheskikh kruzhkov v Kazani", *Katorga i ssylka*, No. 10(71), 1930, pp. 111–36; I. Freifeld, "Zapozdalaia popravka". *Katorga i ssylka*, vol. 4(113), 1934, pp. 122–8.

53. For a list of the leading members of this circle see the extract from the police archives reprinted in *Molodye gody*, p. 211.

54. The police documents are quoted in "V Kazanskom kruzhke", edited by G. E. Khait, *Novy mir*, No. 4, 1958, pp. 189–93. See also, by the same editor, "Iz zhizni semyi Ulianovykh v Kazani i Samare", *Novy mir*, No. 4, 1957, pp. 145–52. See also on the Bogoraz circle M. K. Korbut, "Kazanskoe revoliutsionnoe podpolye kontsa 80-kh godov i Lenin", *Katorga i ssylka*, No. 8–9 (81–82), Moscow 1931, pp. 7–27.

55. There are numerous accounts of this incident which, but for its connection with Lenin, was quite unimportant. Adequate extracts from both police and other accounts will be found reprinted in *Molodye gody*, pp. 207–29.

56. See the extracts from a conversation which took place in 1904 among Lenin, Vorovsky and Volsky (Valentinov) printed in N. Valentinov "Chernyshevsky i Lenin", *Novy zhurnal*, No. XXVI (New York 1951), pp. 193–5.

57. The photograph and inscription are reproduced in *Literaturnoe nasledstvo*, No. 3 (Moscow 1932), p. 77.

58. See "Pometki V. I. Lenina na knige Yu. M. Steklova 'N. G. Chernyshevskii, ego zhizn' i deiatel'nost' (1909)' ", *Literaturnoe nasledstvo*, vol. 67 (Moscow 1959), pp. 9–78.

59. "Iz zhizni semyi Ulianovykh v Kazani i Samare", edited by G. E. Khait, *Novy mir*, No. 4, 1957, pp. 145–52, at p. 149.

60. *Vospominaniia rodnykh o Lenine* (Moscow 1955), p. 22. Anna's account is detailed and circumstantial. There are numerous accounts in the Soviet hagiography which date the study of *Capital* from

Lenin's school days, but they can be safely discounted.

61. N. Valentinov (N. V. Volsky), *Vstrechi s Leninym* (New York 1953), p. 281.

62. A. I. Ulianova-Elizarova, *Vospominaniia ob Ilyiche* (Moscow 1926), pp. 18–20.

63. See "Iz zhizni semyi Ulianovykh v Kazani i Samare", edited by G. E. Khait, *Novy mir*, 1957, p. 145–52.

64. See N. K. Krupskaia, *Vospominaniia o Lenine* (Moscow 1957), p. 37.

65. A. I. Ulianova-Elizarova, *op. cit.*, *loc. cit.*

66. *Lenin*, vol. XXVII, p. 376.

67. See M. L. Mandel'shtam, in *Moskva*, No. 4, 1958, p. 55; and M. K. Korbut, *op. cit.*, p. 24.

68. On the Fedoseev circles see: N. L. Sergievskii, "O Fedoseevskom kruzhke 1888–1889 gg", *Krasnaiia letopis'*, 1923, No. 7; "O Fedoseevskom kruzhke 1888–1889 gg", *Krasnaiia letopis'*, 1922, No. 5; "Tak chto-zhe takoe Fedoseevskii kruzhok 1888–89 gg", *Istoriko-revoliutsionny sbornik*, vol. I (Leningrad 1924), pp. 67–96; M. K. Korbut, *op. cit.*, *loc. cit.*; I. Lalaiants, "O moikh vstrechakh s V. I. Leninym za vremia 1893–1900 gg", *Proletarskaiia revoliutsiia*, No. 1 (84), 1929, pp. 38–70; A. K. Petrov, "K 35-letnemu iubeleiu pervykh s-d rabochikh kruzhkov v Kazani (1889–1924 gg)", *Proletarskaiia revoliutsiia* No. 2 (37), 1925, pp. 186–91; *Nikolai Evgrafovich Fedoseev*. Sbornik istparta. (Moscow 1923); M. G. Grigoriev, "Vospominaniia o Fedoseevskom kruzhke v Kazani (1888–1889 gg)", *Proletarskaiia revoliutsiia*, vol. 8 (20), 1923, pp. 55–66.

69. *Capital* was in fact a great rarity in Kazan – see I. Lalaiants, *loc. cit.* p. 39. But it was available to the Fedoseev circle, along with the *Manifesto*, the *Critique of Political Economy*, Engels's *Anti-Dühring* and *Origin of the Family*, Plekhanov's two fighting pamphlets and Kautsky's *Economic doctrine of K. Marx* – see Yu. Z. Polevoi, *Zarozhdenie marksizma v Rossii* (Moscow 1959), p. 354 (information based in part on police archives). For further details on the books available in the Fedoseev circle see L. K. Fedorov, "Nelegal'nye biblioteki s nachala 70-kh godov do vtoroi poloviny 90-kh godov proshlogo stoletiia", in *Iz istorii nelegal'nykh bibliotek revoliutsionnykh organizatsii v tsarskoi Rossii*. Sbornik materialov, ed. E. D. Stasova (Moscow 1956), pp. 23–61, at pp. 39–41.

70. See extracts reprinted in *Molodye gody*, pp. 254–66.

71. See L. K. Fedorov, *op. cit.*, at pp. 43–6.

72. See A. I. Ulianova-Elizarova, *Vospominaniia ob Ilyiche* (Moscow 1926), pp. 24–7.

73. L. K. Fedorov, *op. cit.*, p. 46.

74. According to G. M. Krzhizhanovski, *O Vladimire Ilyiche* (Moscow 1924), pp. 13–14, when Lenin sought admission to a circle of Petersburg "propagandists" in the autumn of 1893, he was closely examined on his attitude to terror, and was found to be temperamentally "too red" – quoted in *Revolutionary Russia*, ed. Richard Pipes (Cambridge, Mass. 1968), p. 40, note 48.

75. A. I. Ulianova-Elizarova, *Vospominaniia ob Ilyiche* (Moscow 1928), pp. 24–5.

76. M. P. Golubeva, "Poslednii karaul", *Molodaia gvardiia*, 1924, No. 2–3; "Iunosha Ulianov (V. I. Lenin)", *Stary bol'shevik*, 1923, No. 5; *Moia pervaia vstrecha s Vladimirom Ilyichom*. Vospominaniia o Vladimire Ilyiche Lenine (Moscow 1956).

77. See *Molodye gody*, pp. 332–3, where Golubeva is quoted.

78. *Lenin*, vol. I, pp. 3–49.

79. A. I. Ulianov-Elizarova, *Vospominaniia ob Ilyiche* (Moscow 1926), pp. 26–7.

80. From the unpublished reminiscences of A. A. Beliakov, of which an extract is printed in *Molodye gody*, pp.

308–10. Beliakov was a member of Lenin's circle in Samara. His memoirs, first published in 1957, contain many assertions which are otherwise uncorroborated, and of very doubtful validity – for example, a supposed public debate between Lenin and Mikhailovsky in Samara in 1892, which no other source has ever referred to. See *Molodye gody*, pp. 335–63.

81. For these letters (first published in 1940) see *Lenin* (5th edn), vol. 46, pp. 1–6.

82. See *Leninsky sbornik*, vol. II (Moscow-Leningrad 1924), pp. 65–160, especially at pp. 80–1.

83. His literary remains were published in collected form in 1958 – see N. Fedoseev, *Stat'i i pis'ma* (Moscow 1958).

84. See "Neskol'ko slov o N. E. Fedoseeve", written in December 1922, *Lenin*, vol. XXVII, pp. 376–7.

85. For details of all this, based on meticulous researches on Lenin's lost correspondence in police archives, see. I. S. Zilbershtein, "Nekotorye voprosy biografii Molodogo Lenina" in *Katorga i ssylka*, vol. 62 (Moscow 1930), pp. 7–23. Fedoseev's letters to Mikhailovsky are on pp. 96–107 of his collected works. Lenin (*loc. cit.*) says he never met Fedoseev; according to Martov, *Zapiski sotsial-demokrata* (Berlin 1922), pp. 335–6, the two men met for a short time in Krasnoyarsk, when their paths crossed on their way to their respective exiles. (According to Zilbershtein the untraced correspondence of Lenin, apart from his letters to Fedoseev, includes his letters to Lalaiants and Skliarenko after he had left Samara; correspondence with the Liberation of Labour Group after he had returned from his journey abroad in 1895; and his correspondence with Martov between 1896 and 1899.)

86. Letter to E. A. Sanina, on pp. 54–9 of the collected works.

87. The earliest exponent of this view was, apparently, E. V. Loboiko, in 1878 – see a letter by him published with a commentary by A. Sanin, who was a member of Fedoseev's circle in Kazan, in *Istoriko-revoliutsionny sbornik*, vol. II (Moscow-Leningrad 1926), pp. 118–47.

88. From his second letter to Mikhailovsky, on p. 104 of his collected works. (Dated 10 March 1894.)

89. N. Sergievsky, "Tak chto-zhe takoe Fedoseevsky kruzhok 1888–89 gg?" in *Istoriko-revoliutsionny sbornik*, vol. I (Moscow-Leningrad 1924), pp. 67–96. (Sergievsky was a close friend of Fedoseev, and wrote from personal recollection.)

90. From the first letter to Mikhailovsky, p. 100 of the collected works.

91. She and Lenin were the only exiles in Samara to refuse their help – see M. Golubeva, "Poslednii karaul", *Molodaia gvardiia*, No. 2–3, 1924, p. 30. (Quoted in *Molodye gody*, p. 341.)

92. "Chto takoe 'druz'ia naroda' i kak oni voiuiut protiv sotsial-demokratov? Otvet na stat'i 'Russkovo bogatstva' protiv marksistov"; and "Ekonomicheskoe soderzhanie narodnichestva i kritika ego v knige P. Struve. (Otrazhenie marksizma v burzhuaznoi literature)", *Lenin*, vol. I, pp. 55–222 and 225–362.

93. N. Valentinov (N. V. Volsky), "Iz Proshlogo: P. B. Struve o Lenine", *Sotsialisticheskii vestnik*, No. 8–9, New York, Paris, August–September 1954, pp. 169–72.

94. According to I. S. Zilbershtein, *op. cit.*, *loc. cit.*

95. *Lenin*, vol. I, pp. 193–4. Emphasis Lenin's.

96. *ibid.*, p. 187.

97. *ibid.*, pp. 170–1. Emphasis Lenin's.

98. *Lenin*. vol. XXIX, p. 343. Emphasis Lenin's.

99. From an article published on 9 December 1895, reprinted in part in *Lenin*, vol. II, pp. 605–9. For Lenin's reply see *ibid.*, pp. 179–85.

100. *Lenin*, vol. I, p. 165.

101. "The police populists", as he would later describe them – see *Lenin* (4th edn), vol. VI, p. 180.

102. *ibid.*, p. 157.

103. *ibid.*, pp. 111–13.

104. *ibid.*, pp. 179–80. The first passage quoted is a quotation by Lenin from Chernyshevsky's second novel, *Prolog*, where it is put into the mouth of Volgin, for whom Dobroliubov was the model.

105. For the best recent study of Mikhailovsky's attitude to revolution see V. A. Tvardovskaiia, "N. K. Mikhailovskii i 'Narodnaiia Volia'", *Istoricheskie zapiski*, No. 82, 1968, pp. 163–203, at pp. 189–203.

106. *ibid.*, p. 307.

107. See Akselrod's account of his meeting with Lenin, reprinted in *Lenin*, vol. I, pp. 488–91.

108. As is evident from the only two letters written on his return that have survived – there must have been many more. See *Lenin* (5th edn), vol. 46, pp. 8–11.

109. The work is printed in *Lenin*, vol. III. Lenin's summary of the importance of the work is contained in a letter of 16 December 1909, quoted *ibid.*, p. viii.

110. See his correspondence for this period printed in *Lenin* (5th edn), vol. 46 – though a great deal of it has not yet been discovered – *ibid.*, pp. 462–3. See also his letters to members of his family for this period, and especially to Anna who was his main supplier of reading matter, printed in *Lenin* (4th edn), vol. 37.

111. See *Lenin*, vol. I, p. 508.

112. *ibid.*, pp. 426–7.

113. *ibid.*, p. 444.

114. *ibid.*, pp. 439–41.

115. For the fullest edition of his political correspondence see *Lenin* (5th edn), vol. 46, pp. 12–33, but the best annotation is in *Lenin*, vol. XXVIII, pp. 17–45. The relevant correspondence with his family is of equal importance, and is printed in *Lenin* (4th edn), vol. 37, pp. 25–212.

116. In his *Sotsialism i politicheskaia bor'ba.*

117. *Lenin*, vol. II, pp. 603–5, 171–90.

118. *Lenin*, vol. XXVIII, pp. 23–7.

119. *Lenin* (4th edn), vol. 37, p. 128.

120. *ibid.*, pp. 188–9, 1 May 1899.

121. *Die Voraussetzungen des Sozialismus und die Aufgaben der Sozialdemokratie*, ed. Bernstein (Stuttgart 1899). It was published in March.

122. *ibid.*, p. 195, 20 June 1899.

123. *Lenin*, vol. XXVIII, pp. 31–2.

124. *ibid.*, pp. 40–1.

125. *Lenin* (4th edn), vol. 37, pp. 209, 574.

126. P. B. Struve, E. D. Kuskova, S. N. Prokopovich, and T. Kopel'son were the most prominent, and indeed the only ones known for certain to have held this view.

127. *Lenin* (4th edn), vol. 37, pp. 198, xxxvi–xxxvii. See also E. D. Kuskova's account in *Byloe*, No. 10, 1906, pp. 324–6, note.

128. *Lenin* (4th edn), vol. 37, pp. 198, 207. His letter to his sister commenting on it in detail has been lost.

129. *Lenin*, vol. II, pp. 636–7 and 477–86, where the text of the *Credo* is reprinted.

130. *Krupskaia*, pp. 35–6.

131. *Lenin*, vol. II, pp. 494–9. Emphasis Lenin's.

132. *Lenin*, vol. IV, p. 111.

133. *ibid.*, pp. 366–80.

134. *ibid.*, pp. 384–5.

135. See, e.g., the quotation *supra*, p. 232.

136. *Lenin*, vol. IV, p. 422. Emphasis Lenin's.

137. *ibid.*, p. 430.

138. *ibid.*, p. 434. Emphasis Lenin's.

139. *ibid.*, p. 417. Emphasis Lenin's.

140. *Lenin*, vol. V, pp. 179–92, 411.

141. *ibid.*, p. 180. Emphasis Lenin's.

142. *ibid.*, p. 181. Emphasis Lenin's.

143. *ibid.*, p. 184.

144. *ibid.*, p. 182.

145. *ibid.*, pp. 184–5. Emphasis Lenin's.

146. *ibid.*, p. 190. Centralization of power and decentralization of functions was one of the organizational principles stressed by Tkachev – see above, p. 202.

147. D. I. Pisarev, *Sochineniia*, vol. III (Moscow 1956), p. 126 (from "Realisty" ("The Realists")), written in 1864.

148. Peter Lavrov, *Historical Letters*, translated with an Introduction and Notes by James P. Scanlan (Berkeley and Los Angeles 1967), pp. 178–9; see also Letter Four. The *Historical Letters* were published in 1868.

149. *Lenin*, vol. IV, pp. 390–1.

150. The quotation is from Karl Kautsky, "Die Revision des Programmes der Sozialdemokratie in Oesterreich", *Die Neue Zeit*, vol. XX (Stuttgart 1902), pp. 67–82, at pp. 79–80. Emphasis Kautsky's.

151. Lenin frequently quoted Kautsky in his writings; he met and talked with him in 1895, and he was a regular reader of *Die Neue Zeit*, to which Kautsky frequently contributed, during his exile.

152. Karl Kautsky, *Das Erfurter Programm in seinen grundsätlichen Theil*, 4th edn (Stuttgart 1902), pp. 235–6. The Russian translation was made from the first German edition and published in Geneva. Compare also his "Bernstein und die Dialektik", *Die Neue Zeit*, vol. XVII (Stuttgart 1899), pp. 36–50, at p. 49.

153. *Lenin*, vol. IV, p. 389, note, and p. 392.

154. P. N. Tkachev, *Izbrannye sochineniia*, vol. III, pp. 220–1.

The Mensheviks

This article originally appeared under the title "Russia's 'Minority Men'" in *The Russian Revolution*, CBS Legacy Books, (New York 1967).

In August 1903 at their Second Congress the Russian Social Democrats split into one group composed of Lenin and his followers, and another consisting of those who refused to accept Lenin's leadership. Lenin and his supporters thereafter called themselves the "Bolsheviks", or "Majority Men", and dubbed their opponents the "Mensheviks", or "Minority Men", because at the Congress Lenin had, through an accident, secured a sturdy majority of twenty-four votes against twenty. It was perhaps symptomatic of the lack of tactical cunning on the part of the Mensheviks that they accepted, and indeed applied to themselves, what was in essence a derogatory nickname; and even continued to tolerate this appellation during the many periods after 1903 when they clearly enjoyed the support of the majority of members of the party.[1] At the turn of the nineteenth century, most social democratic leaders saw their function not as preparing revolution, but as guiding and leading the workers in their strikes and other actions in order to ensure that their protest did ultimately culminate in revolution. But some social democrats, notably V. I. Ulianov (1870–1924), better known as Lenin, and Iuly Osipovich Tsederbaum (1873–1923), better known as Martov, were beginning to think on different lines. The two young men, though very dissimilar in character, were close friends, and were soon arrested (in 1895 and 1896 respectively). By 1900 both had emerged from their Siberian exile fired with an idea which had originated in Lenin's mind: to found a social democratic revolutionary newspaper outside Russia, and to make this newspaper both the organizational hub of the whole social democratic movement inside Russia, and the directing centre of its ideological orthodoxy. Lenin and Martov joined up with Plekhanov, Vera Zasulich, Akselrod and A. N. Potresov as editors, and the first issue of the new paper appeared in Leipzig in December 1900. It was called *Iskra*, which means *The Spark*. (Potresov and another benefactress provided the money.) The intention, soon to be very successfully achieved, was that *Iskra* should be introduced by illegal means into Russia.

Although this intellectual revolutionary Sanhedrin of the six exiles was far from unanimous on all questions, it was held together by a firm bond: the resistance and opposition to it of many of the social democratic leaders inside Russia. These leaders did not readily accept the kind of direction over their activities which the editors of *Iskra* now asserted; and, in particular, resisted the attempt, as they saw it, to foist all-out revolutionary action upon the workers, believing as they did that the workers should learn that revolution was unavoidable only from their own experience. Plekhanov, Lenin, Martov and the others in turn branded these social democrats as "economists" and "revisionists" who had renounced revolution altogether.

For over two years *Iskra* struggled to obtain control over the whole social democratic movement inside Russia. By the end of 1902 the time was considered ripe to summon a party Congress at which the supporters of *Iskra* could be sure of an overwhelming majority. The Congress met first in Brussels and then in London in July and August 1903. (It was the Second Congress of the party, because the founding congress, the First, had been held in 1898, inside Russia; but this congress had had little effect on the development of the movement.) As expected, supporters of *Iskra* predominated: of the 51 votes at least 41 could be confidently regarded as "Iskrite". Before long the holders of the mandates which controlled the ten anti-Iskrite votes had been driven from the Congress, or had at all events chosen to walk out. Why then did the victorious majority split into two warring factions which were never again to become reconciled?

There were two causes behind the split: an immediate cause and an underlying general cause, and the latter was of much greater importance than the former. The immediate cause, a disagreement on organizational questions, appears from the course which events took at the congress. The discussion of the proposed party programme during the early sessions of the Congress revealed no division on doctrine among the Iskrites. But at the twenty-second session the draft of the party rules came up for discussion, and

Martov, who had hitherto voted with Lenin on all issues, changed sides. The point in dispute was the first paragraph of the rules, which dealt with membership. Lenin's proposal sought to restrict membership to those who, apart from accepting the programme and paying their dues, *participated* in a party organization; Martov's, which clearly implied a less rigid form of central discipline, extended membership to anyone who (in addition to Lenin's first two points) gave the party his "regular personal co-operation under the direction of one of the party organizations". Martov's formula was adopted by 28 votes to 23. But Martov's support included the votes of the delegates of the Jewish social democratic organization, the Bund, and of several other non-Iskrites. A few sessions later the question of future relations with the Bund came up for discussion. All the Iskrites, including Martov and his supporters, were united in opposing the desire of the Bund to enjoy a measure of autonomy within the party. Outvoted by 41 votes to 5, the Bund delegates walked out. They were shortly followed by several other non-Iskrite delegates. The result was that Martov and his supporters were now outnumbered in the voting by Lenin and his supporters, by 24 votes to 20. The fact that Martov and his supporters had done nothing whatever to save their Bundist allies, indeed had joined with gusto in doing them down, proved that they, at any rate, had had no plan of trying to dominate the Congress.

Lenin, however, proceeded to exploit his, possibly unexpected, advantage in order to ensure predomination of himself and of his supporters in all the organs of the party. He could be sure, in view of his majority at the congress, of voting his own nominees onto the Central Committee of three. But it was also essential for him to secure control of the party Council of five – the Central Committee operated inside Russia, the Council outside. Of the five members of the Council the one who was required to be elected by the Congress was quite certain to be Plekhanov, and he was on Lenin's side. The two members of the Council seconded by the Central Committee were also now certain to be Leninites. The trouble was that two had to be seconded by the editorial board of *Iskra*, and the majority of this board (Martov, Zasulich, Potresov and Akselrod) was now opposed to Lenin. Lenin therefore was determined to curtail this board so that it should include only its most active members – himself, Martov and Plekhanov. This would ensure that the two members of it seconded to the Council would be himself and Martov, and Lenin, together with the two Central Committee nominees and Plekhanov, would be sure of a comfortable majority of four.

Lenin's proposal to truncate the editorial board of *Iskra* evoked general indignation, and especially from Martov, who regarded it both as a slight on old and respected colleagues and as an attempt to implicate him in Lenin's intrigue. Lenin's insistence on this issue produced the final split in the party. Martov's refusal to serve on the board of *Iskra* led to a deadlock. Before very long Plekhanov changed sides, co-opted the old members of the board (except Lenin, who resigned) and *Iskra* was now entirely in Menshevik hands. In the course of 1904 Lenin found himself isolated in the party, since many of his former supporters were also alienated by what they regarded as his intransigent behaviour. Henceforward, so far as Lenin was concerned, it was to be war to the end. He set about rebuilding his own following and his own Bolshevik party – his success is not part of this story. We are concerned with the failure of the Mensheviks to exploit their obvious advantages, as they seemed in 1904 – control over the party funds and the party organ, and a majority (in spite of their nickname) in the party. To understand this we must return to the general underlying cause of the split at the Congress.

The evidence suggests that Lenin had not planned or even expected the split among the Iskrites at the Congress, and was surprised that it had occurred. His organizational ideas were not new. His doctrines of discipline and centralization, of the need for a hard core of professional revolutionaries to lead the party, of the danger of "spontaneity" had been familiar since he began expounding them in 1899. His main statement of his doctrines, in *What is To Be Done?* in 1902, had been approved by all his fellow members on the board of *Iskra* – after all, this pamphlet had been a powerful weapon against the common enemies inside the party, those who rejected *Iskra*'s lead and were dubbed "economists" and "revisionists". Moreover it had been with the full approval of his five colleagues on the board that Lenin had devoted his energies between 1901 and 1903 to securing support for *Iskra* in the great majority of the committees inside Russia. This was a sphere of action in which Lenin excelled – his correspondence during this period, some of it only recently published, illustrates his genius for this kind of political manoeuvre. It also reveals the nature of the methods which he did not scruple to use in order to achieve his aim.

But if Lenin's fellow-Iskrites had accepted, or at all events not disapproved, his theories, they were probably to a large extent unaware of his practice, until the Congress made it plain for all to see. Perhaps if they had thought more deeply about the matter they would have realized that the doctrine of *What is To Be Done?* logically entailed the kind of virtual one-man dictatorship which Lenin envisaged for the party in 1903. Perhaps if they had tried harder to understand Lenin's temperament they would have understood that such a man would never have tolerated any situation in the party in which he was not the undisputed master. When at the Congress (both in the open sessions and at some very crucial behind the scenes meetings which took place before the first clash between Lenin and Martov) they saw Lenin in action for the first time, they were unable to accept a form of leadership which they regarded as inconsistent with what they understood by social democracy. Lenin was genuinely dismayed by this sudden change of attitude on the part of his hitherto fairly docile colleagues. After all, who was there capable of running the party except himself? he asked a confidant some months later. Plekhanov was incapable of running anything. Martov was an excellent journalist, but "an hysterical intellectual who needs watching all the time". As for Akselrod, Potresov, Dan or Trotsky – why the very idea was enough to "make a chicken laugh".

Not all the men cited by Lenin (with characteristic contempt for anyone who disagreed with his views) could be described as Mensheviks at all. Neither Plekhanov nor Trotsky (Lev Davydovich Bronstein, 1879–1940) could ever accommodate himself for long within any faction, and both pursued individual and often aloof political courses for much of their pre-revolutionary careers. Plekhanov, the "Father of Russian marxism", who at a number of periods before the revolution supported Lenin (my "illegitimate son" as he once referred to him) died a bitter and disappointed man in 1918.[2] At the end of his life he was haunted with remorse for fear he might have done his country harm by urging on the development of a social democratic party and movement before the social basis required for them had come into existence. The brilliant Trotsky remained a devastating, and prophetic, critic of Lenin's policy right up to 1917. Thereafter, his alliance with Lenin was probably the most important factor in ensuring both the victory and the subsequent survival of the Bolsheviks. Later, both in his conflict with Stalin and in his tragic exile he remained a Bolshevik according to his lights.

Martov, the most left-wing and internationalist of the Mensheviks, was perhaps also the most representative of the temperament of Menshevism, if not always of the divers doctrines of those who accepted this allegiance; and, as the main opponent of Lenin in the party, was also the one who offered the most complete contrast to the Bolshevik leader. Martov, a Jew by birth, was a revolutionary in every fibre of his being from his youth – perhaps the early awareness of the debased status of the Jew in Russia contributed to make him a revolutionary. However, any special Jewish allegiance he may have once felt was very soon submerged in his internationalist faith. He was a man of complete and shining integrity, which even his enemies were unable to deny. He experienced a profound moral revulsion from the political tactics adopted by Lenin which he never overcame. For Lenin the end was everything, the means irrelevant. Martov, perhaps more realistically, believed that if evil and unworthy means were adopted, then the end, when once achieved, would be tarnished and transformed. A fanatical marxist, Martov, again in contrast to Lenin, was in many ways a slave of his own theories. He never ceased to believe that, since the class interest of the proletariat was one, the two factions which claimed to act in its name must inevitably end in unity. He refused to see, in the face of mounting evidence, that the determined aim of the Bolsheviks was precisely the political destruction of the Mensheviks; and was consequently unwilling, and probably unable, to meet their tactics with any actions which had a chance of success when once battle was joined. In his heart he believed that sooner or later the Bolsheviks must come to their senses. Even after Lenin's victory in 1917, Martov still refused to abandon hope. Under his leadership the Social Democrats (as the Mensheviks now called themselves) expressed their support for a revolution which they had originally condemned as nothing more than a *coup d'état*. While resisting with courage and determination the fraud and violence with which the

Bolsheviks sought to oust them from the political scene, Martov and his followers rejected any means of opposition other than constitutional means. By 1920 when the Communists (as the Bolsheviks were known after 1918) allowed him to emigrate, Martov was a sick and broken man. "They say Martov is dying too", was one of the last remarks that the dying Lenin made to his wife. The two men had been intimate friends in their youth, and Lenin, who could seldom understand why the most violent political intrigues and polemics should affect personal relations, retained an affection and even respect for Martov to the end. Perhaps this was the most telling contrast between the two men. For Martov, though he never ceased to work for unity in the party, the personal break with Lenin in 1903 had been final. Doctrine demanded reunification of the factions, and for this he was prepared to strive, whatever his opinion of the leader of the opposing faction. But the dishonesty, as he saw it, of Lenin's behaviour at the Second Congress and after put an end for Martov to all personal feelings and respect for the man.

For the historian who wends his way through the jungle of party polemics before 1917 it is not easy to see precisely where the dividing line of theory falls between the two factions. So much of the debate – conflict, more accurately – centred around tactics, intrigues, manoeuvres and mutual recrimination that little room remained for theory. It was for this reason that the rank and file party members were at all times bewildered at the antics of their leaders, and anxious for unity in a movement which to them seemed to be at one so far as concerned its main objective – revolution. Moreover, neither faction was ever "monolithic". Even the disciplined Bolsheviks had their left-wing extremist groups, and their right-wing conciliator elements. The Mensheviks ranged from an internationalist revolutionary left wing, to which Martov belonged, to a right wing, which (mainly inside Russia) was primarily preoccupied with the practical task of trying to build up a real labour and trade union movement in the semi-constitutional conditions which prevailed after 1906.

However, two broad divisions can perhaps be discerned in the guiding theories of the two factions – in the attitude to revolution, and in the concept of leadership. Both factions believed in revolution as the ultimate aim: the frequent charge by the Bolsheviks, and by Soviet historians, that the Mensheviks were revisionists and had abandoned the marxist aim of revolution for peaceful reform was and is palpably false, so far as the overwhelming majority of Mensheviks was concerned. Both in 1905 and in 1917 Mensheviks played as important a part as Bolsheviks in revolutionary activity – more important, indeed, in the revolution of February 1917. But, in theory, there was a difference of approach. The Bolsheviks, inspired by Lenin's essentially voluntaristic political philosophy, often seemed prepared to organize and even provoke violent action. The Mensheviks believed that revolutionary action should grow naturally out of the protest activities of the labour movement. Only then, when the protest grew into revolt, should the leaders take their place at the head of the revolt and guide it into more purposeful and organized revolutionary deeds. This, somewhat theoretical, difference had one practical consequence, especially between 1906 and 1914. For the Mensheviks were impelled to concentrate their energies increasingly on activity in the labour movement, and less on the conspiratorial side of party activity, believing that the revolution would in the end grow out of such actions as strikes, mass worker protest meetings and the like (as in a sense it in the end did). The Bolsheviks, whose leader Lenin was already thinking in terms of a victory of his own *party* (which is precisely what he was to achieve in October 1917 when the Bolsheviks overthrew the socialist Provisional Government), were much more intent on forging a disciplined elite of leaders.

One should perhaps add that theoretical divisions between the two factions became much more evident during the years of the First World War. The Bolsheviks in the main (there were exceptions) were the more resolute opponents of the war, believing with Lenin that the defeat of Russia was, from the point of view of advancing the revolution, the "lesser evil". The Mensheviks were less united on the whole question. The Internationalist Mensheviks, led by Martov, opposed the war, but retained their faith in a policy of joint action with their fellow-socialists in the belligerent countries in order to force a speedy and just peace, to be followed by all-round disarmament. But many Mensheviks were "defensists", that is to say they believed that socialists in Russia should support the war effort of their country against the reactionary Central Powers, while at the same time pressing both for peace on equitable terms and for political reforms at home. A small minority, headed by Plekhanov, even believed that demands for reform should be postponed till after victory.

Thus it is probably true to say that what divided the two factions was more temperament than doctrine. Lenin often used the terms "hard" and "soft" to point the difference between his supporters and his opponents. But the Mensheviks were not "soft" in the sense that Lenin meant – though it was probably true that they often shrank from the kind of methods of inter-factional strife that Lenin employed. They were not "soft" in their revolutionary activity; and, for all their criticism of Lenin's theories of leadership, were not usually noticeably more democratic in running their committees than the Bolsheviks. It would approximate more to the truth to say that the Bolshevik temperament was closer to the traditional Russian conspiratorial revolutionary movement; while the Mensheviks looked more to the model of Western Europe, with its free institutions and its developed labour movement. Like Struve and the other early marxists in Russia they still, unconsciously perhaps, embraced the doctrine of social democracy because they saw it as a powerful westernising force for backward Russia. Lenin and the Bolsheviks, closer perhaps to some traditional Russian roots, were more intent on capturing autocratic power and using it for the ends in which they believed. The Mensheviks were more concerned with the popular mass institutions of the future – the Soviets, the trade unions and the like, by which, as they believed, the autocracy would be replaced.

The simple answer, which contains much of the truth, is that they did not try to win. In a letter written in 1907, when the two factions were nominally reunited, but when it was obvious to all that the Bolsheviks were only waiting for a favourable moment to force a split again, Plekhanov remarked: "The Bolsheviks behave as if the split had already taken place, while the Mensheviks act as if they thought that no split will ever take place." The Mensheviks indeed either refused or were unable to recognize the plain fact that after 1903 the simple aim of Lenin and the Bolsheviks, so far as the Mensheviks were concerned, was to destroy them politically. And hence the Mensheviks did not wage war for the victory of their faction: they engaged in a struggle of principle within what they continued to believe was still one movement. They opposed Lenin by debate and argument, and seldom, and ineffectively at that, by intrigue, chicanery and manoeuvre. Today, after more than sixty years' experience of Bolshevism (and its modern guise, communism), it is easy to see the futility of trying to oppose its organizational machine by arguments and appeals. But it required the full rigour of the regime of Lenin's heir and successor, Stalin, for this lesson to be learned – and not all have learnt it yet. Looking back on the period when Lenin was waging his battle for all-out supremacy in the social-democratic movement, it is easy enough to see that in the realm of theoretical debate the Mensheviks might well have enjoyed an overwhelming advantage – there were very few, if any, on the Bolshevik side who could compare in erudition with Plekhanov, Potresov or Akselrod. Lenin knew this well, and much preferred to harass his opponents on the ground on which he excelled. If the Mensheviks can no longer attack us on theoretical grounds, he wrote to Gorky in 1908, with reference to a philosophical issue then in dispute, that will be to our advantage: they will be reduced to politics, "which means death to them".

Thus the Mensheviks were the first of the many socialist victims of the illusion which dies hard among socialists: that genuine cooperation is possible with communists on any terms other than complete surrender. They were on the verge of discovering this – too late – in 1917. They were the dominant socialist party after the February revolution – the Bolsheviks were still a handful, and the Socialist Revolutionaries were without effective leadership. With the benefit of hindsight one can now see how a different course of action by the Mensheviks could have led to a very different trend of events. For, had they recognized in time the Bolshevik danger for what it was (and Lenin, at any rate, made little secret of his intentions) they might have given more effective support to the Provisional Government and to the forces of order, instead of adding fuel by their revolutionary ardour to the forces of anarchy. As it was, the Bolsheviks rapidly outbid them in demagogy and reckless promises and won – if only for a time – much of the popular support which the Mensheviks had, at the outset, enjoyed. It was only in the last stages of the eight-months drama of the reign of the Provisional Government that the Mensheviks discovered what Lenin and the Bolsheviks were aiming at – sole power and ruthless dictatorship; and nothing that the Mensheviks could then have done could have stopped a Bolshevik victory which they undoubtedly had helped to bring about.

Historians, and not only Soviet historians, have usually dealt scantily and contemptuously with the Mensheviks in defeat. Perhaps future historians will be less hypnotized with what, in the perspective of time, may appear a less permanent victory for Lenin. The Mensheviks managed to exist as a political force for several years after the Bolshevik seizure of power. Except for a few months, they were never outlawed or prevented by legislation from exercising political rights. They were destroyed by force, by fraud, and by the abuse of legal process. Yet in spite of arrests, framed-up charges, violence organized against them and a shower of constant abuse from the Bolshevik-monopolized press, the Mensheviks survived as a party until 1922. They then had to accept defeat. Most of their leaders, who had long been in prison, were allowed to emigrate. Those who remained in Russia were later (in 1931) made the victims of one of the first of the many political show trials which have disfigured our generation.

So long as they survived as a political party, the Mensheviks played a twofold role in the new Soviet state. First, as trenchant critics of Bolshevik rule. They supported the victory of the Bolsheviks in the sense that they recognized the October Revolution as "inevitable", and condemned every form of armed opposition to it. But they exercised as best they could, so long as it was physically possible for them, what they regarded as their right as social democrats to criticize the betrayal of socialist ideals. Much of their criticism of Lenin's leadership in practice recalled the debates of the early years, when *Iskra* had broken with Lenin on the issue of dictatorship. Even more significantly, the arguments used by the Mensheviks between 1917 and 1921 foreshadowed much of the criticism which the communists themselves were to advance against their system after the death of Stalin: atrophy of the Soviets, for example, or the growing bureaucracy, threatening to become a state within the state. By 1920 the arguments of the Mensheviks were beginning to find a ready hearing among the weary, disillusioned and disheartened city workers. It was small wonder that Lenin decided that the time had come finally to get rid of them.

But the Mensheviks were not only critics: they were also theorists of revolutionary policy. They did not content themselves with criticizing the Bolshevik *coup d'état* of October 1917 as premature and misguided, which had been their first reaction. Having once accepted the premature leap into socialism as "inevitable", they began to ask themselves how the harm done by the forcing of socialism onto a largely peasant country which was not yet ready for it, could be alleviated. In a manifesto published in the summer of 1919 they advocated a series of measures which were a complete blueprint for the New Economic Policy of March 1921. Like Lenin's policy adopted in 1921, that of the Mensheviks was intended to retain all political power in the hands of the "Party of the proletariat", while at the same time restoring the shattered economy and winning some support from the hostile peasants by permitting some controlled private enterprise. It was again small wonder that Lenin had to ensure that the Mensheviks were safely under lock and key before launching their policy as his own. No dictator can afford to leave at liberty a critic who has been proved right by events.

When in October 1917 most of the Mensheviks stumped out of the Congress of Soviets in protest at the Bolshevik coup, Trotsky contemptuously consigned them to the "dustbin of History". But "History" (whatever that may mean) is not so accommodating as politicians affect to believe. Of course, if we regard the Mensheviks as one of many political parties competing for power, then it is true to say that they lost and the Bolsheviks won. But they never so regarded themselves, and it is doubtful if they ought to be so regarded by historians. They stood for a *trend* inside the Russian social democratic movement – the only true trend, as they of course believed – and they defended their point of view both in defeat, and later in exile. Their contribution in exile to the interpretation of Bolshevism was enormous, and its effect on world opinion and on the course of politics must not be underestimated. For some fifty years the *Socialist Courier*, which Martov founded shortly before his death, remained the most important single source of authentic information on Soviet politics and economics. After the Second World War it was former Menshevik leaders, like the late David Dallin and Boris Nicolaevsky, who laid the foundations of that scholarly study of communist rule which was to break the spell of the illusion about communism which had gripped so many socialist and left-wing intellectuals.

But the matter does not end there. Fifty years after the victory of the Bolsheviks the principles which Lenin put into practice are being questioned not only in the non-communist world, but in the Soviet Union and in some of the communist countries which have modelled their political systems on the Soviet pattern. The old issues on which the Mensheviks challenged the Bolsheviks in 1903 and thereafter have once again revived – the "monolithic" discipline of the party, the indiscriminate and uncontrolled use of state terror, the subjugation of the trade unions, the suppression of all criticism, the iron control over the creative effort of the mind, and a score of other matters are once again being debated. Hesitantly and cautiously communist parties seem to be groping their way towards some form of evolution in the direction of genuine social democracy, which would leave the crude extremism of Lenin behind. How far they will succeed, if at all, only the future can show. Some have seen grounds for cautious optimism in the growth of education, material prosperity and technical advancement in what were relatively backward countries when the communists first seized power. The new educated citizen of a modern state, it is argued, will not forever remain content in the leading strings to which Lenin's primitive paternalism would confine him. He will rather assert his right to take his place in politics as a responsible and mature individual. This is not the place to discuss how far such arguments are valid. But if indeed some evolution from totalitarian dictatorship to genuine social democratic self-government should ever take place in the Soviet Union, the work of the Mensheviks will be seen not to have been in vain. For it will be their arguments, their criticism, their ideals which, no doubt without acknowledgment, will have contributed to the process of change; and which, in turn, may provide some of the bases of any new order which emerges.

1. [I have here deleted a discussion of the circumstances in which the labour movement and marxist thought developed in Russia, in order to avoid repetition. (ed.)]
2. [See pp. 174–87 above. (ed.)]

The Role of the Jews in the Russian Revolutionary Movement

This article first appeared in *The Slavonic and East European Review*, XL, December 1961.

In the late summer of 1903 Theodor Herzl paid a visit to Russia. Among those whom he saw was Count Witte, then Minister of Finance, who had the reputation of being at any rate more liberal than some of the Emperor's ministers. The impression created by the massacres of Jews in Kishenev and Gomel was still fresh, and Witte was aware that the more reactionary ministers, notably the Minister of the Interior, Plehve, whom Herzl had also seen, scarcely concealed their belief that pogroms were a well-merited retribution meted out by a supposedly loyal Russian people for the leading role which Jews were playing in the revolutionary movement. Witte duly pointed out to Herzl that while the Jews formed only 7 million out of a total population of 136 million, about 50 per cent of the membership of the revolutionary parties was Jewish. Herzl then asked him whose fault this was. Witte replied: "I think it is the fault of our government. The Jews are too oppressed."[1] The views of Plehve and his like, who welcomed the pogroms as a diversion which might prevent the Russian population from avenging their grievances on the government, need not detain us. But Witte was honest enough in his belief that the Russian government policy of maintaining a large section of the population of the country in permanent subjection was disastrous, and his analysis of the motives of the Jewish revolutionaries, if somewhat over-simplified, can well serve as the starting point for our enquiry. Was the Jewish revolutionary in Russia primarily, or at all, impelled by a personal sense of grievance due to the oppression of the Jewish people living within the Russian empire?

The story of the Jew in the Russian revolutionary movement really only begins in the 1870s – indeed the Russian movement as a whole only began to take shape during this decade. So far as the Jews were concerned, the reasons were plain. Revolutionary movements are created by intellectuals, and until there existed a Jewish intelligentsia, sufficiently assimilated through knowledge of Russian language and conditions, there could be little question of the participation of Jews alongside Russians in the work of revolution. The emergence of such a Jewish intelligentsia was largely the result of the trend towards liberal reforms which characterized the first decade of the reign of Alexander II from which the Jews also benefited. Although he had no immediate intention of allowing complete Jewish emancipation from the disabilities to which they were subjected, Alexander II was prepared to allow the emergence of a Jewish aristocracy of brain and wealth. By ending the system whereby Jews in Russian schools had hitherto been subjected to official proselytizing pressure, he opened up the road from the ghettoes to the universities, and hence to the professions. Moreover, Jewish university graduates and wealthier merchants were permitted to reside in the larger cities from which Jews had hitherto been excluded. The number of Jewish boys in the secondary schools increased from 1.25 per cent of the total number in 1853, to 13.2 per cent in 1873.[2] Jewish university students increased in proportion. Jewish youth rapidly began to absorb the current radical and revolutionary ideas which were agitating their Russian compatriots. Many of the future Jewish revolutionaries of the 1870s and after were to come from among them. But before dealing with them, two somewhat isolated figures must be mentioned, who belong to an earlier period, and whose outlook seems to throw some light on the main question – the "Jewishness" of the Russian Jewish revolutionary.

One of them was Grigory Abramovich Perets, a baptized Jew, the son of a rich merchant, one of the three whose presence in St Petersburg was tolerated at the beginning of the nineteenth century. Perets, a fairly high government official, was the only Jewish member of the Decembrist movement. His sympathies lay with a minority group within the Decembrist movement, which was strongly influenced by the constitutional ideas of Western Europe. For the most part the Decembrists advocated distinctively Russian socialist ideas, but with a strong Jacobin tinge. Perets seems to have combined some consciousness of his Jewish origins with his admiration for Western constitutionalism: he chose as the secret password for communication with his fellow conspirators the Hebrew word for freedom – *Heruth* – and is reported to have buttressed his arguments in favour of a constitutional regime in Russia with citations from the Old Testament. His participation in the Decembrist movement was unimportant, and short-lived. The other precursor was Nikolai Utin, another baptized Jew, also the son of a rich merchant, settled in St Petersburg. Utin took an active part in revolutionary activity among the students of St Petersburg University, and was a member of the first short-lived revolutionary organization, which was founded in 1862. The following year he had to escape abroad, and the remainder of his revolutionary activity took place in exile, under the wing of Marx, in the First International. He was instrumental in creating a Russian Section in the First International, and is sometimes referred to as the first Russian marxist, somewhat inaccurately perhaps. His most important activity was his struggle inside the International, at the side of Marx, against the anarchist Bakunin, who together with the infamous Nechaev represented at the time the most extreme and violent trend in Russian revolutionary doctrine – incidentally drawing upon himself a good deal of anti-semitic abuse from these two worthies. Utin was perhaps no angel, when it came to political tactics; neither was Marx. But it is probably true to say that, like Marx himself in this period, he genuinely rallied to the defence of social democratic principles against the Jacobin terroristic element which was never far below the surface in the incipient Russian revolutionary movement. These two rather isolated figures cannot, of course, be said to typify any peculiar features of Jewish revolutionaries. But it is of some interest that both these precursors should have looked to Western Europe for their inspiration, and turned their backs on the indigenous Russian form of Jacobinism.[3]

It was, it will be recalled, only during the 1870s that a real revolutionary movement came into being in Russia. It immediately attracted a large, though not disproportionately large, number of Jews. We are as yet dealing with the pre-marxist stage in Russia, the populist or *narodnik* stage. The *narodnik* movement was an essentially indigenous Russian movement, and owed almost nothing directly to Western European influences. Its objective was a peasant uprising which would sweep away the hated tyranny and usher in an era of freedom. This faith of the *narodniki* was in part inspired by the long tradition of revolt which existed among the peasants; and in part by a belief that the Russian peasant was a socialist by instinct. Mingled with this faith was a passionate sense of guilt on the part of the intellectual *narodniki* because their own comparatively privileged position in society had only been inherited at the price of the suffering of the peasants, and the debt had to be repaid. There was an exalted nobility and sense of moral responsibility about the movement which has fired the imagination of the many who have written about it. It did not start as a terrorist movement, but more as a missionary movement. Thousands of young men and women threw up their university or other careers and went to the people, to live and work in the villages, or occasionally in the factories. Bitter disappointment awaited these idealists – both those who, under the influence of Bakunin, were intent on stirring up the peasants to an immediate revolt, and the more moderate among them who made it their aim to train leaders among the peasants in readiness for the revolution of the future. The gulf between intellectuals and peasants proved too great to bridge, and the peasants usually met their champions with indifference, or even hostility. Out of this disillusionment was born the revolutionary party, Land and Liberty, founded in 1876. One of its founders was a Jew, Mark Natanson. The seeds of discord were already inherent in this organization: some of its members believed that the immediate aim should be the overthrow of the monarchy, by acts of terrorism and by conspiracy; others still regarded socialism as the main objective, and this they believed could only be achieved by a popular revolt carried out by the peasants themselves. Before long, in 1879, the party had split into two. One organization, the People's Will (or Freedom – the Russian word is the same) now proceeded to plan the assassination of the Emperor, which was eventually carried out on 1 March 1881; the other, which called itself Black Repartition, soon became the cradle of the marxist movement.

Jewish revolutionaries participated at all stages and in all aspects of this movement. Let us look at this Jewish contribution to the first major phase of the Russian revolutionary movement: what were the measure and importance of this contribution? And secondly, to what extent, if at all, was the contribution specifically Jewish in its nature, and activated by motives of a Jewish nature – as against motives which were common to all members of this distinctively Russian movement?

Statistics are perhaps not a very reliable guide in assessing the importance of the Jewish role. However, for what they are worth, the figures, prepared by the Russian authorities during the 1870s, and published after the revolution of 1917, on the number of Jewish revolutionaries participating in the movement at the time do not suggest that the number of Jews was disproportionate to the total number of Jews in Russia – in fact the percentage of revolutionaries up to 1877 remained roughly proportionate to the percentage of Jewish inhabitants within the Russian empire.[4] (The figure rose sharply after the assassination of the Emperor in 1881, and the pogroms which followed.) Turning to the more reliable evidence on the part which individual Jews actually played in the movement, we find Jews in positions of importance at all points – with one exception: there are no important Jewish ideologists of populism. It would have indeed been strange if there had been, since populism derived essentially from a tradition rooted in the mystique of Slav nationalism, which even the Jew, for all his great capacity for assimilation, would have found difficulty in absorbing. But ideological leadership apart, the Jewish contribution was very significant. The foundation of Land and Liberty owed much to a Jew, Natanson, to whom reference has been made, and another Jew, Aaron Zundelevich, played an important part on its executive committee. There were Jewish propagandists, Jewish organizers, Jewish terrorists – a young Jewish woman, Hesia Helfmann, was among those sentenced to death for the assassination of Alexander, though the sentence was commuted on the grounds of her pregnancy. She died soon after the birth of her child. Several other Jewish terrorists paid with their lives. Most historians of the Jewish revolutionary movement in Russia have suggested that the Jewish part in actually carrying out acts of terrorism was conspicuously small, and have argued that this fact was due to some peculiar character of the Jew, which was ill adapted to bloodshed and the role of an assassin. The argument is unconvincing. Given sufficient emotional stress, the Jew is as capable of bloodshed and terrorism as anyone else. When Jews thronged into the party after 1881 the number of Jewish terrorists was very high. There were important Jewish terrorists, like Gershuni, for example, in the Socialist Revolutionary Party which evolved during the present century as the heir of the People's Will. For a very short period even the Jewish social democratic Bund, about which more will be said below, was prepared to countenance terrorism, under the impact of particularly brutal reprisals against Jewish workers by the Russian authorities. In more recent times one could cite the extensive Jewish participation in the savageries of the Red Terror of the Cheka – or even events in Palestine. The Jewish contribution to the Russian revolutionary movement was in many respects a noble one, so long as Jews tried to seek out the meeting point of what was best in Russian and in Jewish tradition. But nothing is to be gained by false nationalism. If it was true, as it probably was, that during the 1870s the Jewish revolutionary was to be found less often than his Russian comrades actually wielding bomb or revolver, this was due to the policy of the People's Will. The act of terrorism was regarded as a demonstration of the people's wrath against tyranny and injustice. Obviously this demonstration was more likely to achieve its object if the terrorist was a Russian, and not a Jew, whose national motives could be suspected. Moreover the People's Will was a very disciplined organization, which strictly controlled the actions of its members. Again, a number of historians, of whom probably Lev Deich, himself an important Jewish participant in the revolutionary movement, was the first, have tended generally to minimize the importance of Jews in the movement. This tendency may have been due to the absence of Jewish names among the more dramatic figures of the movement; or more likely, to a natural desire to counteract the dishonest exaggeration of the role of the Jews in which the Russian authorities indulged for their own ulterior purposes. But now, since the researches of that great historian, Tscherikower, it is impossible to doubt the importance of the Jewish contribution to the less spectacular business of organization and staff work. It was the Jews, with their long experience of exploiting conditions on Russia's western frontier which adjoined the Pale for smuggling and the like, who organized the illegal transport of literature, planned escapes and illegal crossings, and generally kept the wheels of the whole organization running. A particularly important part was played by Zundelevich, who in 1872 had formed a revolutionary circle mainly among students of the state-sponsored rabbinical school, at Vilna.[5] Vilna was also destined to become one of the main centres of social democracy when this movement swept Russia some fifteen or twenty years later.

And now, what were the motives of the Jewish revolutionaries in the People's Will? It seems impossible to extract any specifically Jewish motives which actuated these revolutionaries, except in the most general and indirect sense: if liberty were achieved for the whole of Russia, the Jews among others would benefit. Indeed, the most striking feature of the Jew in the revolutionary movement at this period is the extent to which his whole mode of action and thought became assimilated to a specifically Russian form and tradition, even in some cases a Christian tradition. It would perhaps have been impossible for him to have acted otherwise, since the whole populist movement was steeped in Slav nationalism and peasant tradition. Even where propaganda activity was conducted among factory workers, the attitude towards them was not that of the social democrats, for whom the workers became a special privileged and progressive class. To the *narodnik* the worker was merely a peasant who happened to be in the factory, and the strike was merely an adjunct to the traditional village revolt. The Jewish populist had to turn his back on his Jewish tradition, and seems to have done so with very great readiness. Very many, especially the women, were baptized. No doubt in many cases baptism was merely a convenience in order to avoid restrictions on residence in the capital and other disabilities. But there were also instances of genuine conversion to the Orthodox Church where the Jewish revolutionary was drawn by his revolutionary faith in the people to embrace the traditional faith of the peasant, and became a devout Christian. However, Christianity played a comparatively small part in the faith of the movement as compared with the rationalist mystique which is usually described as "nihilism", and which exercised such a large influence on the spiritual development of the Russian intelligentsia. The young Jewish intellectual found the wine of nihilism as intoxicating as his Russian counterpart – perhaps, after the somewhat sterile intellectual nourishment of confined Jewish life in Russia, even more so. Lev Deich describes how *yeshivah* students, hitherto almost fanatically absorbed in the minutiae of scriptures and Talmud, would throw over the whole tradition in which they had hitherto lived after only two or three conversations with a nihilist.[6] This may be an exaggeration. But of the fact that becoming a revolutionary involved a complete break with Jewish environment and tradition in the 1870s there is no doubt: the bulk of the Jewish population, including the great majority of the intellectual and commercial aristocracy, felt a loyal and hopeful devotion to Alexander II and it is not to be wondered at that Jewish families used sometimes to hold the ceremonial week of mourning (*Shivah*) when a son or daughter joined the revolutionaries.

Sometimes assimilation involved rather more than a mere break with Jewish tradition, and the Jewish revolutionary was faced with a direct conflict between the policy of the party and the interests of the Jewish people from whom he sprang. This occurred particularly forcibly for the first time in 1881 and immediately after, as a result of the anti-Jewish pogroms which followed after the assassination of Alexander. The attitude of the Russian populists to violent anti-semitism was, to say the least, ambivalent. They were not primarily anti-semitic. But since they identified themselves with all and every kind of peasant revolt, they were reluctant to restrain the anti-Jewish tendencies of the peasants, for fear of alienating their sympathies. They comforted their consciences with the rather specious arguments that all revolt in Russia had to start as anti-Jewish rioting before it could develop into a full-scale revolution; and that in any case the popular fury was directed against Jewish shopkeepers and money-lenders and was therefore a respectable form of class war. This line of reasoning was applied as much by the terrorists as by the opponents of terrorism, who were now grouped together in the Black Repartition. It is known, from documents which were only published years later, that a serious conflict arose in 1881 over the issue of anti-semitism between a leading member of Black Repartition, Pavel Akselrod, who was of course himself a Jew, and his colleagues, including his Jewish colleagues, among them Lev Deich. Akselrod was disturbed by the policy of the populists towards the Jewish pogroms (the People's Will had actually put out leaflets of an openly anti-Jewish nature) and wanted to publish a pamphlet explaining what the duties were of both Jews and revolutionaries on this issue. He was prevented from doing so by his colleagues, who, in the words of Deich, argued that to come out in support of the Jews was to risk alienating the support of the peasants. The Jewish question was, in his view, "insoluble" so far as the revolutionary was concerned. Akselrod's pamphlet remained unpublished, and indeed unfinished.[7] It is perhaps of interest that whereas Akselrod was the son of poor Jewish parents who lived within the Pale, Deich came from a rich assimilated family in Kiev. Indeed, the Jewish question sometimes remained "insoluble" even for the heirs of the *narodniks*, the socialist revolutionaries of the present century. Years later, for example in 1904, there is an echo of the arguments used in 1881 in the socialist revolutionary press, in answer to an appeal by the Jewish social democratic Bund for armed support against those participating in anti-Jewish pogroms. How can we do so? – reply the socialist revolutionaries. "After all, the main mass of the pogrom-makers will consist of those same destitute toilers whose interests socialists are pledged to defend . . . Is it really to be expected that we, the socialists, should go forth and beat up our admittedly blinded brothers, but brothers all the same, hand in hand with the police? Or, at best, hand in hand with the Jewish bourgeoisie armed in the defence of its property?"[8]

It would be unfair to suggest that the socialist revolutionaries were anti-semitic as a general rule. Far from it. Indeed many instances could be quoted, from Jewish sources, which show how frequently the socialist revolutionaries did turn out, especially after 1905, in support of the organizations of self-defence against pogroms which the Bund was active in maintaining. As the tide of revolution mounted, anti-semitism became such an evident weapon of the reactionaries that revolutionaries no longer needed to be reticent in condemning it. But the instances cited show the kind of conflict that could and did arise when the Jewish revolutionary was required as part of his duty to sever completely all links with his Jewish past and tradition by embracing a nationalistic, Russian movement. The revolution of 1917 will show to what extent the Jew failed to assimilate into a nationalist Russian movement – which is what Bolshevism first and foremost was. But first a glance is necessary at the development of social democracy inside Russia so far as it affected the Jewish revolutionary.

The role of the Jew in Russian social democracy was, of course, very much greater than it could ever be in the populist movement. There were certain obvious reasons for this. Marxism was from the outset an internationalist doctrine, and the Russian Jew, although he was capable of entering a purely Russian movement, and of sinking his national interest in what he believed was the more important general aim, nevertheless often retained sufficient sense of contact with his coreligionists outside Russia to feel rather more at home in social democracy. Secondly, the appeal of marxism to many Russians at the outset lay precisely in the fact that it turned its back on the somewhat reactionary traditionalism of the *narodnik* peasant movement, and offered a solution for Russia in line with developments in Western Europe – first capitalism and industrialization, but thereafter also democratic freedom for the emancipated proletariat. It was after all to be some time before the "democracy" of social democracy would be immolated on the altar of "socialism". Thirdly, marxism attached special historical importance to the working class as the destined bearer of liberation. For the Jew, always rather more at home among the town workers than among the more backward, traditional and often anti-semitic Russian peasants, this was an important factor.

It was therefore not surprising that Jews should have figured as pioneers in bringing the light of marxism from Western Europe into Russia. Outside Russia, Akselrod was next in importance to Plekhanov, if not equally important, as a theorist in the émigré marxist group Liberation of Labour, which the heirs of Black Repartition founded in Geneva in 1883. Inside Russia Jewish names abound among the pioneers who were busy creating social democratic groups and circles in the 1880s and 1890s. Jews worked indiscriminately among Jewish or Russian workers inside Russia, without any sense that their duty lay among the former rather than the latter. Indeed, the very internationalism of marxism precluded any sense of nationalism in those early days: the proletariat was one, all were oppressed, and the liberation of all was the only solution for any particularly oppressed section. Jewish social democrats showed particular hostility towards the Zionists, who advocated an entirely different solution for Russian Jewry – if somewhat utopian, at that date.

It was therefore by accident rather than design that a Jewish revolutionary worked among Jewish workers instead of Russian workers. Take the case of the future leader of the Menshevik wing of the party, Martov. It was due to the accident of having been exiled there that Martov made Vilna the centre of his social democratic activity, and in fact he was one of the main influences which led in 1897 to the founding of the General Jewish Workers' Union in Lithuania, Poland and Russia, usually known as the Bund. But before then, in 1895, Martov had returned to St Petersburg where he influenced Lenin to found the important Petersburg Union for the Liberation of Labour. For years after, at Lenin's side, Martov fought all attempts of the Bund to retain a measure of autonomy within the all-Russian party. Yet, ironically, it had been Martov, in his famous May Day speech of 1895, who had formulated the reasons why the Jews needed a separate Jewish social democratic party: the Jews, he then argued, have certain special needs and demands, and there is always a risk that victorious social democracy faced, at any time, with the necessity of jettisoning some of its aims *might* be tempted to sacrifice those of specifically Jewish interest. The decision of the Bund to use Yiddish as the language of propaganda was also due to quite empirical reasons – it was the only language in which a mass Jewish audience could be reached. (It is interesting to recall in this connection that when, in the 1870s, one of the pioneers of the Jewish revolutionary movement in Vilna, Lieberman, insisted on Hebrew as the language of propaganda, it was also for a practical and not nationalistic reason: Hebrew, he thought, was the best literary vehicle for training revolutionaries among Talmudic students. It was Lieberman, incidentally, who in Vienna, in 1877, founded a revolutionary newspaper *Haemeth* – The Truth – a distant ancestor, perhaps, of Trotsky's "Truth", *Pravda*, from which Lenin borrowed the name for his paper in 1912.) Expediency, then, was at any rate the origin of the "nationalism" of the Bund, as it would later be described by its opponents, and probably the main motive underlying the doctrine of national cultural autonomy for the Jews which the Bund ultimately evolved.

The question of nationalism becomes very material in considering the break between the Bund and the Russian party under Lenin's leadership in 1903. But first attention must be drawn to the important influence which the Bund exercised over the Russian party in its formative years. Two instances must suffice. One was perhaps more of symbolic importance: the considerable part played by the Bund and the Jewish social democrats in Vilna in the organization of the First Congress of the All-Russian Social Democratic Labour Party in Minsk in 1898, a year after the foundation Congress of the Bund. The main influence of the Bund went to the root of the whole conception of social democracy. According to the Western European conception, at any rate, marxism pre-supposed the progressive development of social consciousness by the workers so that they could prepare themselves for their ultimate task of taking power from the bourgeoisie, who should historically precede them, the workers, in power. The Bund interpreted this to mean that the party should be broadly based on the active support of the workers in whose name it spoke. They believed that the workers, grouped in trade unions, should by learning to act as one man in defence of their interests in industrial disputes, demonstrations etc., grow into a mass party fit to seize the reins when the time came. It is, of course, common knowledge that Lenin's theory of the party was very different – the party was to be a close-knit caste of intellectual professionals who would bring to the workers from the outside the social consciousness which they were otherwise incapable of developing by themselves. It is not in the present context material to decide who was right. But the fact remains that long before Lenin had succeeded in getting his ideas accepted, around 1901 or 1902, the Bund had succeeded in creating something resembling the mass party which its leaders advocated – within the area of the Pale, of course – which was very different indeed from anything which the Russian committees had so far succeeded in creating. And in so doing the Bund spread its influence and example inside the Russian party. To take a concrete instance. The decision taken after 1895, under Martov's influence (after he left Vilna in 1895) to try to reach a wider audience and to build up a mass party instead of, as hitherto, concentrating only on training up a few future leaders, was the direct result of experience in Vilna. The achievements of the Vilna organization were embodied in a famous manuscript pamphlet of which one of the founders of the Bund, A. Kremer, was the author. This pamphlet remained for some years the bible of most Russian social democrats.

The break between the Russian party and the Bund came in 1903, at the famous Second Congress, which was the origin of the division of the Social Democratic Party into Bolsheviks and Mensheviks. It had to come, if Lenin was to remain master of the Russian party, if only because of the complete incompatibility of views between Lenin and the Bund on what should be the nature of the party. The Bund was easily outvoted because those Russian social democrats, who would within a very short time be loudly opposing Lenin for his dictatorial methods, sided with him at the Congress in condemning the "nationalism" of the Bund. But Lenin did not long remain master of the party, and indeed did not begin to regain anything like mastery until after the revolution of March 1917. Hence, when a large number of those who supported him at the Congress later turned against him and repudiated his doctrine of the party which they had hitherto approved (or more accurately, not publicly disapproved), it was natural enough that they should move closer to the Bund. The general kinship between the Bund and the Mensheviks, and indeed the prevalence of Jews among the Menshevik leaders and their supporters, are both to be explained in this way. Besides, as already pointed out, it was often purely accidental circumstances which decided a Jewish social democrat to work among the Jewish proletariat within the Pale, or among Russian workers in one of the cities.

Were the members of the Bund nationalists in the sense in which their accusers used the word? In other words, were they Jews first and social democrats second? Lenin, and his supporters, many of whom were themselves Jews, argued in 1903 that the Bund's demand for autonomy in propaganda and organization, even if coupled with acceptance of the overall party programme and of party discipline in all matters which did not affect the Jewish proletariat, was nationalism, and was inconsistent with marxist internationalism. The Bund maintained that Lenin's group, *Iskra*, had set its heart on destroying the Bund. From the point of view of *Iskra*, which was determined to create a single disciplined party organization, the existence within the districts inhabited by Jews of a Jewish social democratic organization side by side with a Russian one, exercising the kind of autonomy of action which the Bund demanded, was indeed hardly acceptable. It is true that a similar situation had to be accepted in the Lettish or Polish parts of the empire. But then it could be argued that the Letts and Poles were nations with a distinct territory, and the Jews, who had no territory, were not. It is also fair to say that the Second Congress revealed none of those undertones of anti-semitism which were to become a recurrent feature of Bolshevism in later years. Indeed, no one at the

Congress even quoted Marx's *Judenfrage* in support of the argument against the autonomy of the Bund, no doubt for fear that its outspoken and quite vulgar anti-semitism might prove out of place in a social democratic audience. Thus, the Master remained sacrosanct, so far as Russian social democrats were concerned, and immune from criticism. The Bund later advanced the opinion that the views expressed in *Die Judenfrage* were out of date. But even Lenin himself, around the time of the Kishinev pogroms, might well have hesitated to quote, say, Marx's opinion of the Jews as a kind of recurrent disease which bourgeois society generates from its own entrails, and which is only curable by revolution.

It was, however, true that *Iskra* committees had for some time before the Congress been working to break up and absorb Bund organizations, and Lenin's correspondence shows that he had determined to force the Bund out into the wilderness some time before the decision was taken in 1903. There was thus little room for compromise. So far as nationalism was concerned, the bald charge made by Lenin was false, in the sense that the Bund never put national interests before social democratic interests. Nor did the Bund leaders, at all events, ever put forward any chauvinistic doctrine such as some special Jewish instinct or aptitude for social democracy. Bundists believed that the aims of social democracy were best achieved by a broadly-based party, and such a broadly-based party of Jewish workers could not be run by Lenin's professional revolutionaries. Moreover, such a party could not be maintained in existence unless certain specific adaptations were made to the general pattern which took account of a Yiddish-speaking, Jewish working mass. At this date, 1903, the Bund was still "neutral" in its attitude to Jewish nationalism – concessions to it were regarded as necessary for purely practical, even temporary considerations. Complete assimilation was not excluded. Later, it is true, the Bund was to go rather further, and formulate concrete demands for national cultural autonomy, that is to say autonomy in cultural and communal matters appropriate to a nation which had no definite territory, but which claimed national distinctiveness. All this still lay ahead in 1903. But behind the theoretical debates in 1903 there was already a great deal of clash of temperament. The Bund may not have been nationalistic, but it was very conscious of the superiority of its own over the Russian organization. It claimed, with some justice, that its organization was much more democratic than the Russian. It had a tradition of mass worker action which the squabbling Russian committees could not begin to equal, and it had reckoned its members in thousands at a time when the Russians could only be reckoned in tens. At the beginning of 1905, for example, on the eve of the revolutionary year, the entire Russian party (not, of course, the Poles or the Letts) numbered only 8,400; in the summer of the year before, the Bund, representing the Jewish workers alone, could claim a membership of 23,000.[9] The Bund could also claim that its leading cadres were not invariably intellectuals, but were also drawn from among the workers. This was to a large extent true. For example, of the thirteen delegates who met for the foundation Congress of the Bund in 1897 only five were intellectuals, and the rest artisans or workers. Of the nine delegates who met the following year for the Russian foundation Congress all but one were intellectuals – the delegate of the Bund. The Bund therefore could with some justification claim to be building the kind of party that the Western interpretation of marxism contemplated. It was certainly not the kind of party that Lenin wanted; but it carried a good deal of appeal for many of the more traditionalist marxists who still remained inside the party. The Bund perhaps also indulged occasionally in displaying an understandable but none the less irritating consciousness of its own superiority. And nothing could be more calculated to infuriate not only many Russians, but even those Jews on Lenin's side who had thrown in their lot with the Russian party.

This first, and fatal quarrel, between the Bund and Bolshevism was important because the factors which kept the two apart in 1903 were the same in many respects as those which in the years after the Congress of 1903 kept so many social democrats apart from Lenin, and among them a great many Jewish Mensheviks who could certainly not be accused of any nationalist hankerings. The history of the Bund after 1903 paralleled very closely in many respects the history of the Mensheviks, precisely because each group was trying to assert and uphold the same kind of principles of social democracy which it believed were in danger of being destroyed by Lenin. The preponderance of Jews in the Menshevik faction was certainly very great. For example, of all the delegates to the Party Congress in 1907 (at that date the party was nominally reunited) Jewish delegates numbered nearly 100, or about one-third of all the delegates, if the 57 delegates of the Bund are included. Over one-fifth of the delegates who followed the Menshevik line were Jews, as against about a tenth of pro-Bolshevik delegates.[10] This can hardly have been accidental. But when one further considers that over a considerable period the Bund and the Mensheviks shared the same outlook in many important respects on party policy, we are entitled to conclude that we are dealing in each case with an interpretation of marxism which found a particularly responsive chord in Jewish tradition and temperament.

The revolutionary year, 1905, was the great watershed of policy for Bund and Mensheviks alike. Throughout the year the Bund within its area, which was not of course of decisive importance, worked to increase the impetus of revolution by the organization of trade unions, strikes and demonstrations, and within its limited scope, with success. So, of course, did the Bolsheviks and the Mensheviks. So did the progressive elements of the middle class, who probably played a bigger part in bringing about the concessions extracted from the autocracy in October 1905 than all the socialist parties put together. When the high hopes of 1905 were dashed by defeat and reaction, and the time came for the post mortem, Bund and Mensheviks alike drew the conclusion that one of the causes of the failure had been that the workers' movement in Russia was very far from being an organized mass movement, responsive to its social democratic leadership. This they regarded as necessary before strikes and unrest could culminate in a complete overthrow of the autocracy, when the workers would take their place as a real force behind the middle-class democratic order which, according to doctrine, must, as a first stage, replace the autocracy. Indeed the Bund could with justification claim that within its own, not admittedly very important or decisive, area, it had got very near to achieving something like a mass movement – there is no doubt that, with some exceptions, the strike movement was very much better controlled and organized by the Bund than by the Russian parties. After the inevitable reaction in which all social democratic organizations went through a period of extreme decline, a group of Menshevik leaders who remained inside Russia now became convinced that their primary task was to utilize such opportunities as the semi-constitutional regime set up in 1906 offered, in order to build up all possible forms of mass worker activity, and thereby develop that worker consciousness upon which alone they thought the party could be based. They were for the most part Jews – though their ideological leader was a Russian, A. N. Potresov, once a closer supporter of Lenin, but long since parted from him. It is not surprising that the Bund should have exercised a considerable influence on these Mensheviks.

This group has been frequently referred to under the abusive label of "liquidators" attached to them by Lenin, who accused them of wanting to liquidate the underground party. Lenin had drawn very different conclusions from the failure of 1905. He believed that the important task was to concentrate on building up the disciplined network of revolutionary leaders, who would direct the mass rather than carry out its directions, or help it to achieve its own aims. Ironically enough both were right – each from a different point of view. For, in so far as any political party played a part in bringing about the collapse of the monarchy in March 1917 it was the "liquidators", and many Bundists alongside of them: it was due at any rate in some measure to their activities in the so-called War Industry Committees after 1915 that worker unrest culminated in a revolution and the setting up of the Petrograd Soviet, which symbolized government by the masses (or anarchy – depending on one's point of view) at the critical first moment. So, what the "liquidators" liquidated in the end was the Russian empire – which was not what Lenin had meant at all. But Lenin, on the other hand, in November 1917, proved that he had created the kind of organization which could take government out of mass control and place it firmly under the control of his own party. So we are back again at the old question of what Marx really meant: should the impetus come from the workers themselves? Or should it, as Lenin said, be brought to them from the outside, by the professional revolutionaries?

But to return to the years after 1905. It is plain, in view of what happened in 1917, that the "liquidators" were very far from being the kind of pacific evolutionists which Lenin usually accused them of being – indeed, had they been so they would hardly have won much support from the essentially revolutionary Bundists. They were merely thinking of a different kind of revolution from Lenin's, though perhaps that was not realized at the time. Nor was it true that they wished to "liquidate" every kind of illegal underground party – no social democrat in his senses in Russia at the time would have advocated this as an immediate practical measure. But it was true that they were heartily sick of the kind of party organization which Lenin was engaged in creating around himself, with its conspiratorial intrigues, splits, unsavoury financial methods, and dishonest polemics against all those who disagreed with him. In fact, they wanted to create a new party organization of their own, and they very nearly succeeded. This was the point on which the Bund stood much closer to those Mensheviks, including their leader abroad, Martov, who were anxious at all costs to re-create a united party of all shades of opinion, including Lenin and the Bolsheviks. In this effort at reunification the Bund played a very big part, and on a number of occasions took the initiative in trying to bring it about. It was a laudable and logical enough intention – why, after all, if one is a marxist, should the party of the proletariat, which is agreed upon one and the same programme, be rent asunder by factional quarrels of a largely personal nature? From the point of view of the Bund there was a further motive: the Bund had been nominally readmitted to the nominally reunited party in 1906, on its own terms of autonomy. But until the reunion of the party became a reality, there was little chance of the Bund playing its full part in the social democratic movement as a whole. Whether from the point of view of the future of the Mensheviks these efforts at reunion benefited them more than Lenin, who was quite determined that there should be no reunion, is another question.

The Bund and the "liquidators" seem to represent a fairly characteristic aspect of the revolutionary outlook of the Russian Jew – in marked contrast to the Jewish participants in the populist movement, in whom it is very difficult to discern any characteristic which distinguished them from Russians, or Poles, or other nationalities. It was an outlook which drew its inspiration from the social democratic movements of Western Europe, especially Germany, and there were good reasons why a Jew should have been drawn towards it. One was the instinctive attraction towards something which seemed to be very different from the traditional Russian ethos with its undertones of pogroms, reaction, obscurantism, and Slav chauvinism. It was probably this attraction of the Western form of constitutionalism which drew so many Jews into the Kadet party. There, among the best elements of the Russian intelligentsia, the Jewish intellectual felt himself more than just an equal: he met men to whom, as Russians, Jewish emancipation was as dear as to the Jew who felt as alienated as any Jew from the Russian form of autocracy and reaction, and who realized that a people which kept a section of its population permanently deprived of rights could never itself hope to be free. The second reason which drew the Jew to this Western pattern of social democracy was the sense that in an ultimate workers' republic which would emerge there could be no room for racial or other discrimination. This was perhaps a stronger motive in the case of the Bundist than in the case of many Jewish Mensheviks, who often seem to have been very little conscious of their Jewish origin.

If these two motives, which were certainly present among Jewish revolutionaries, had been the only ones it is unlikely that there would have been many Jews in the ranks of the Bolsheviks at all. There was, however, a third factor, which often proved much stronger than the other two. It has already been stressed that all Russian social democrats remained revolutionaries, not evolutionists. In this respect they contrasted with the majority of social democrats in Germany, for example, who no longer regarded a proletarian revolution as inevitable or even desirable. But conditions in Russia, where the semi-constitutional regime was always liable to relapse into police rule, were very different. It was not therefore surprising that many Jews should have been drawn into the Bolshevik party, which certainly put revolution very much more in the forefront of its utterances, and which also provided the strong attraction which ruthlessness of method holds out to the impatient. And so it is not to be wondered at that we should find quite a large number of Jews in the Bolshevik ranks, though not so many as in the ranks of the Mensheviks. When it comes to assessing their relative importance or influence before 1917 the position is not so easy. No one really could rank anywhere near Lenin in importance in any party which Lenin controlled. Trotsky was perhaps an exception – but only in the period after the revolution, when he at last threw in his lot with the Bolsheviks. Among Lenin's lieutenants there were certainly a few Jews who mattered: Zinoviev and Kamenev, who probably did more than anyone to help Lenin to keep the Russian Social Democratic Party disunited and to create the small but reliable nucleus of the future Bolshevik party, were the two most important. But it could not be said that before 1917 Jews exercised any really decisive influence inside the Bolshevik faction, and certainly nothing like the influence which they had among the Mensheviks. In the history of social democratic ideology as a whole there are many Jewish figures of importance: Akselrod, Trotsky, Martov, and a whole host of lesser names – perhaps nine-tenths of the "liquidators" so called, for example. But Bolshevism, as it developed before the revolution, was essentially a Russian creation, and Lenin's creation at that, so much so that it is difficult to cite any name which should take its place beside his. So far as the work of organization was concerned, at the lower levels, Jews played an enormous role in Menshevism. In the building up of Bolshevism their role was not unimportant, but in no way comparable. For example, the general staff of nine set up by Lenin in 1912 at Prague, which marked the real beginning of Bolshevism as an independent revolutionary force, originally included two Jews, Zinoviev, and Schwartzman, of Vilna. But only Zinoviev played any significant part.

The position was very different after the revolution of 1917. Theoretically, if Jewish social democrats had been able to think out their fundamental principles and interest to their logical conclusion they would have worked to support a stable democratic government, to carry the war to conclusion, and to prevent the Bolshevik *coup d'état* of November 1917. This was the position advocated by Potresov and Plekhanov, and it found some, but not much, support among Mensheviks, and rather more in the Bund. But the times were confused, novel, bewildering and intoxicating, and little adapted to cool and logical judgement, let alone farsightedness. Thousands of Jews thronged to the Bolsheviks, seeing in them the most determined champions of the revolution, and the most reliable internationalists. By the time the Bolsheviks seized power, Jewish participation at the highest level of the party was far from insignificant. Five of the twenty-one full members of the Central Committee were Jews – among them Trotsky and Sverdlov, the real master of the small, but vital, secretarial apparatus of the party. In the first Council of People's Commissars there was, it is true, only one Jew, but that one was Trotsky, who was now second only to Lenin, and ranked high above his other colleagues in influence. But

Jews abounded at the lower levels of the party machinery – especially in the Cheka, and its successors the GPU, the OGPU and the NKVD. (In the issue of *Pravda* for 20 December 1937 there is a list of 407 officials of the NKVD, decorated on the occasion of the twentieth anniversary of the Cheka. Forty-two of the names, or about eleven per cent, are Jews, and the actual total of Jews may well have been higher, since many of them may be supposed to have adopted Russian names. How many of these Jews survived the purge of 1938 is another matter.) It is difficult to suggest a satisfactory reason for the prevalence of Jews in the Cheka. It may be that having suffered at the hands of the former Russian authorities they wanted to seize the reins of real power in the new state for themselves. Many of the enemies of Bolshevism, who tended to couple anti-Bolshevism with anti-semitism, argued that Bolshevism was a movement alien to true Russians and that it was a predominantly Jewish movement. The assertion was in fact untrue. In historical origin and in ideology Bolshevism is an essentially Russian movement, traditional and nationalistic, with a very thin veneer of international socialism. But to the ordinary Russian in the early years of the revolution the argument was quite likely to appeal. For the most prominent and colourful figure after Lenin was Trotsky, in Petrograd the dominant and hated figure was Zinoviev, while anyone who had the misfortune to fall into the hands of the Cheka stood a very good chance of finding himself confronted with and possibly shot by a Jewish investigator.

It was perhaps not surprising, in view of the very impulsiveness with which the Jewish socialist threw himself into Bolshevism under the stress of revolutionary fervour, that his fate inside the movement should subsequently have proved so tragic. The history of Bolshevism after the revolution is no part of this story. But one must recall the phases by which the Jews were edged out of their prominence as time advanced. There were, for example, many Jews on the left wing of the Socialist Revolutionary Party who were drawn into an ill-fated coalition with the Bolsheviks in the very early stages of the Bolshevik regime, and who six months later were fighting them in the streets of Moscow and Petrograd. The tragedy of the left socialist revolutionaries was that in their enthusiasm they accepted Lenin's demagogy at its face value – they believed in his promises of a revolutionary war, of land for the peasants and of democratic freedoms because they wanted to believe in them. The partnership between these somewhat quixotic idealists and the hard-headed and often quite cynical Bolsheviks was doomed from the start. It could not survive when once the essentially nationalist character of Bolshevism was revealed by the Treaty of Brest-Litovsk, beneath the veneer of international phrases with which it had come to power.

Or again, take the elimination of Trotsky, Zinoviev, Kamenev, and the countless Jewish Bolsheviks who fell with them during the 1920s, and the great holocaust of Jewish Bolsheviks which took place in 1937 and 1938. It is often said that these Jewish Bolsheviks were Jews in name only, that they were completely assimilated, that they did not consider themselves Jews, and that indeed they were social democrats who would have repudiated, and often did indignantly repudiate, any "bourgeois nationalist" leanings. This may be true – and yet it is hard to believe that such a high proportion of the victims of the aftermath of the revolution were Jews merely by accident. It is unlikely that conscious anti-semitism played a very big part, though it certainly played some. There is among Trotsky's papers in the Library of Harvard University an eye-witness account of the campaign against Trotsky and his followers from which it is clear that Stalin's agents did not hesitate to exploit latent Russian anti-semitism when it suited them. But on the whole anti-semitism was too much discredited in the first years after the revolution for it to be used more than furtively. The real cause lay deeper.

It has already been suggested that Bolshevism was essentially a national Russian, and not an international, movement. Several facts seem to support this view. In the first place, Lenin's doctrine derived quite as much from those traditional Jacobin elements in the Russian revolutionary movement as from Marx. It was necessarily these elements which came to the fore when once Lenin had turned his back on the Western European interpretation of marxism in terms of a party based on a conscious and active democratically controlled workers' movement – the interpretation for which the Bund and most Mensheviks stood. Again, the essence of Lenin's doctrine of organization was centralization, and centralization could only mean, in Russian conditions, control from Moscow, and so long as Lenin was alive, control by Lenin. This of itself, without any conscious nationalism – and certainly Lenin at any rate was personally free from any pro-Russian chauvinism – necessarily tended to give a Russian character to the control which was exercised. The Georgian communists, for example, discovered this to their cost – although the persons actually responsible for imposing the Russian straitjacket on them were a Georgian, Ordzhonikidze, and a Pole, Dzerzhinsky. Thirdly, when once the decision was taken by Lenin in March 1918 to impose upon his party the peace of Brest-Litovsk in place of a "revolutionary war" in the cause of world revolution, which had hitherto been avowed party policy, a blow was struck at internationalism. The cause of world revolution would not be abandoned – but henceforth Russia always came first. All these features became even more pronounced as time went on. It was against this Bolshevik nationalism that the Jew collided, and by it he was destroyed. The Russian Jewish revolutionary was as much the victim of the Russian revolution as its instigator. The revolution which he wanted to create was not the kind of revolution which in the end he helped to create. He was not of course alone – many of the best and bravest of the Russian revolutionaries suffered the same fate.

At the outset Witte's view was quoted that it was oppression which created the Jewish revolutionary. It is doubtful if this is the whole truth, though no doubt it was a part of the truth. In the main the Jewish revolutionary flung himself into the Russian movement fully convinced that in the brotherhood of international social democracy he could not possibly be anything other than an equal of the Russian, as indeed he was – outside the ranks of Bolshevism. Once inside the Bolshevik fold he readily jettisoned any claim to his national rights, for the most part only to perish in the end as a victim of a new kind of nationalism which he had not been able to foresee. Perhaps in the end the Bund was right in trying to allow for some national apartness, even if it ran counter to strict social democratic theory. Of course the Bund failed, but it is perhaps better to fail with integrity, than to succeed – only to discover that one has succeeded in the wrong cause.

1. *The Diaries of Theodor Herzl*, edited and translated with an introduction by Marvin Lowenthal (London 1958), p. 395.
2. Louis Greenberg, *The Jews in Russia*, vol. I, *The Struggle for Emancipation* (Yale 1944), p. 83.
3. On Perets see Ya. D. Baum, in *Katorga i Ssylka*, vol. 25 (Moscow 1926), pp. 97–128; on Utin see E. Tscherikower

in *Historische Schriften fun Yivo*, vol. III (Vilna 1939), at pp. 82–90 (in Yiddish).

4. N. I. Sidorov, "Statisticheskiye svedeniya o propagandistakh 70-kh godov v obrabotke III otdeleniya", in *Katorga i ssylka*, vol. 38, 1928, pp. 27–56.
5. Tscherikower, *op. cit.* pp. 152–72; N. A. Bukhbinder in *Istoriko-revolyutsionnyy sbornik*, vol. I, ed. V. I. Nevsky (Moscow–Petrograd 1924), pp. 37–66.
6. Lev Deych, *Rol' yevreyev v russkom revolyutsionnom dvizhenii*, vol. I (Berlin, n.d.), pp. 30–1.
7. *Iz arkhiva P. B. Aksel'roda* (Berlin 1924), pp. 31, 217–35, 215–16.
8. Quoted from *Revolyutsionnaya Rossiya* in *Vestnik Bunda*, No. 3, Geneva, June 1904, p. 22.
9. *Bol'shaya sovetskaya entsiklopediya*, vol. VIII, col. 98; *ibid.*, vol. XI, col. 531.
10. *Protokoly syezdov i konferentsiy vsesoyuznoy kommunisticheskoy partii (B). Pyatyy syezd RSDRP. May-iyun' 1907 g.* edited by Em. Yaroslavskogo (2nd edn, Moscow 1935), p. 659.

Bukharin's Way

This review of Stephen F. Cohen, *Bukharin and the Bolshevik Revolution: A Political Biography, 1888–1938*, Knopf (New York 1974) originally appeared in the *New York Review of Books*, 7 February 1974.

There are several reasons why Bukharin is unique among communist leaders as a subject for a biographer. In the first place there can be few, if any, leading communists of any nationality who, in the general consensus of those who knew them and worked closely with them, are invariably described in such terms as warmhearted, generous, and lovable. Brave scholars, gritting their teeth, have tried to do justice to Stalin out of a sense of duty. Trotsky, probably undeservedly, has aroused the romantic imagination of disappointed communists. To write about Bukharin calls neither for sacrifice nor for romantic self-delusion. Personality apart, Bukharin's unique importance in the history of Soviet Russia lies in the fact that he alone offered for that country a way forward radically opposed to the one adopted by Stalin. Trotsky, after all, before his routing by Stalin, had only put forward Stalin's eventual solution, but without drawing the logical conclusions that Stalin would draw.

Bukharin's plan was detailed, consistent, fully analysed, and based in every aspect, though not every detail, on Lenin's views as sketched by the dying leader at the very end of his active life. This is, of course, not to say that one can assert with any confidence that Bukharin's policy would have worked. This kind of hypothetical question is about as valueless as are the arguments adduced by some of our "communisant" academics to show that Stalin's policy was "realistic" or "necessary". The historian cannot say what might have been, since it is impossible to assess all the consequences that would eventually have flowed from a certain course of action had it been taken at a certain moment of time. On the other hand, human reason instinctively revolts against accepting the argument that a policy involving the massacre of tens of millions of innocent people and an internal upheaval of which the traces are fully evident over forty years later can ever be regarded as either realistic or necessary.

Hence the fascination of Bukharin. For disappointed socialists he offers a ray of hope. For Stalinists and neo-Stalinists the very fact that he existed is an uncomfortable fact to be suppressed and forgotten. The lickspittle left-wing intellectuals, who did such signal service to Stalin in bolstering the credibility of the preposterous show trials of the late thirties, devoted extra zeal to the assassination of Bukharin's character and to the suppression of his views. It is now no longer fashionable to defend the trials, so Bukharin, though not described any more as a spy and a traitor, becomes a simple-minded idealist with no sense of reality.

Certainly, a few reputable historians of Soviet Russia have, since the end of the war, told the truth about Bukharin. But their accounts have necessarily been short and incomplete. It has remained for a young historian (Professor Stephen Cohen is thirty-five) to put right some of the sins of the fathers, and to produce a full, fair, balanced, enormously well-documented, sympathetic yet not uncritical study of Bukharin's life and thought. I confidently predict that this magnificent book will come to be regarded by those whose opinions are worth listening to as one of the two or three really outstanding studies in the history of the Soviet Union of the past twenty-five years.

There is yet an additional reason why Bukharin is so uniquely attractive a subject for the biographer of a communist leader. In the course of 1936, a little less than a year before the arrest which was to culminate in his judicial murder, he was allowed to visit Western Europe – ostensibly on business connected with the acquisition of certain archives. During this visit he had long, frank, and detailed conversations about the situation in the Soviet Union and his own position with the late Boris Nicolaevsky and with the late Feodor and Lydia Dan. Some of the sensational (and subsequently confirmed) political information was published by Nicolaevsky at the time, in a form which carefully concealed Bukharin as the source, in the famous anonymous "Letter of an Old Bolshevik".

Reports of the other conversations were known for many years only to a few who could be trusted not to betray confidences which were likely to damage people who were still alive. But both Mrs Dan before her death and Boris Nicolaevsky felt it safe to publish (in 1964 and 1965 respectively) some of their records of these fascinating conversations, and also to reveal to those of us who were privileged to know them and to enjoy their confidence further details about Bukharin. This kind of authentic insight into the mind of one of Stalin's top victims cannot, so far as I am aware, be paralleled in the Soviet Union or elsewhere.

Nikolai Ivanovich Bukharin was born in Moscow on 27 September (9 October) 1888, like Lenin the son of a schoolteacher who rose in the public service by his own merits, and whose civilized influence on the boy's education was to be so evident in the man. Already a radical at school, the young Bukharin was formed as a revolutionary in the turbulent year of 1905, and became a professional Bolshevik, rising meteorically in the Moscow organization. Betrayed by Lenin's protégé, the police spy Malinovsky (a cause of prolonged friction between Bukharin and Lenin), Nikolai Ivanovich was arrested in 1910, escaped from his remote place of exile, and spent from 1911 until the revolution as a political émigré. Lenin's relations with him during these years were a curious amalgam of irritation and – something rare for Lenin – genuine affection. The passionate, almost loverlike quarrels between the brilliant young theorist and the Master during the war sound a little ridiculous today, particularly when one realizes that, with or without acknowledgement, Lenin in the end derived some of his most publicized views (on imperialism, for example) precisely from Bukharin. Bukharin's "semi-anarchist" views on the state (1916) become Lenin's in 1917 (Krupskaia to Bukharin: "V.I. asked me to tell you that he no longer has any disagreements with you on the question of the state"). All this is fully and sympathetically analysed by Mr Cohen.

Conflict between the theoretical and dogmatic Bukharin and Lenin, the practical and pragmatic tactician of revolution, who had little regard either for promises or for doctrine, was inevitable. There was also a strong ethical element in Bukharin which Lenin did not share, or for that matter understand. Although he never referred to the subject (except for an oblique reference in 1922, in a speech at the Comintern) it is a fair inference that Bukharin was aware of and profoundly shocked by Lenin's acceptance of large sums of money from the Germans. Perhaps it was this factor that made him such a passionate opponent of the pragmatically sensible, but to a true revolutionary repugnant, surrender at Brest-Litovsk in 1918. However, by the end of 1918, after a period of opposition as a leader of so-called Left Communism, Bukharin became more integrated into the new communist system, and reconciled to Lenin, of whom he remained a passionate admirer for the rest of his (Bukharin's) life.

By the end of the civil war he was the undisputed theorist of marxism in its Bolshevik form. His two major wartime works – *Imperialism and World Economy* and *The Economic Theory of the Leisure Class* – were published in full only in 1918 and 1919. In 1920 there appeared *The Economics of the Transition Period* and in the autumn of 1921 his *Historical Materialism*, which was beyond doubt one of the most influential works of the twenties in the whole vast literature of marxism. All these works together formed an outstanding contribution to the theory of twentieth-century marxism. They are very little read these days, at any rate by the adherents of the various shades on the left of the political spectrum. No doubt for both "Stalinists" and "Trotskyists" Bukharin's name is anathema for different reasons; while the more revolutionary extremists are repelled by the ethical, conciliatory, evolutionary attitude toward socialism which, under Lenin's influence, he firmly espoused.

It may come as a surprise to some readers to see the words "conciliatory" and "evolutionary" applied to Lenin at any period of his career. It is, of course, clear beyond dispute that the guiding principles throughout Lenin's active life were strife and conflict – class conflict, as he saw it in marxist terms, but at all events conflict between those who were right, that is to say himself and his supporters, and the rest, who were wrong. Almost from the age of seventeen, certainly from 1899 onward, when he first realized what he believed to be a real danger of the triumph in Russia of revisionism, he stood uncompromisingly for the inevitable, and much to be desired and worked for, violent, revolutionary transformation of society – going beyond Marx in this respect, perhaps.

In his revolutionary tactics and in his leadership of the new Soviet state, up till 1922, he stood for uncompromising conflict against political opponents and the clear separation of the sheep from the goats with which *Iskra* had in 1900 opened the campaign for the victory of what was to become Bolshevism. The peasants would for all time be led by the proletariat – if need be by force: thus Lenin in 1902, and right up to 1921, when the economic concessions, forced on the Bolsheviks by the threat of a general strike and the prospect of a peasant guerrilla war, were accompanied by stringent tightening of party control over the life of the whole country.

The New Economic Policy seemed to many Bolsheviks little more than a regrettable but necessary retreat, a temporary setback on the path of true Bolshevism, almost something of a trick, perhaps, to tide over a crisis in power. However, by the end of 1922 and early 1923, in those last articles which the dying Lenin, surrounded by Stalin's spies and cut off from, or deserted by, most of his friends, contrived to get published (including "On Co-operation", "Better Less But Better", "Our Revolution"), an entirely new doctrine was enunciated for the first time. We know from what Nicolaevsky tells us Bukharin told him in 1936 (and there can be no possible reason to doubt his account) that Bukharin had held frequent conversations with Lenin during the last months of the dying leader's active life.[1] Besides, as Mr Cohen's analysis proves beyond doubt, Bukharin's entire doctrine as it evolved after 1922 on the future course of Soviet Russia was little more than an expansion of Lenin's views, as sketched in embryo in these last articles.

The October revolution, Lenin argued, had been premature in the sense that power was seized by the proletariat long before social conditions were ripe for it. However, this could not have been helped; the Bolsheviks could not in the circumstances have acted otherwise than they did. The task now before the Bolsheviks was to undo the consequences which Marx, and every marxist, knew necessarily flowed from a premature seizure of power. The object now must be to create over a long period – generations, as Lenin described it, not centuries – in a predominantly peasant country, the social conditions which were essential to true socialism. The New Economic Policy, which was neither a ruse nor a temporary retreat in panic, but a policy embarked upon "seriously and over a long period", provided such an opportunity: the "commanding heights" of the economy remained under the control of the party, and all the essential preconditions for creating socialism were there.

For the peasants the answer lay in co-operative farming and

marketing. The co-operative system could in no circumstances be imposed by force. But the state and the party which controlled it could, by providing the necessary economic incentives and by demonstrating the superiority of state aid and co-operation over individualism, eventually bring the peasants to socialism by persuasion. But – and this Lenin emphasized again and again, as Bukharin would do until he was silenced – the essential condition for such a policy was to abandon the class war between the towns and the villages which had prevailed up to 1921 and which had been necessary in the early stages of the revolution. Nothing but peace between town and villages could provide the basis for the future socialism which was still to come in the Soviet state, according to Lenin. This peace had to be preserved at all costs and as a first priority, since it was only in a harmonious society that the peasant majority stood any chance of "growing into" socialism, and of acquiring the social consciousness which, in theory, should have been the foundation for the "socialism" which had in reality never been achieved after 1917, in spite of claims to the contrary.

Such, in rough outline, was the slender framework of theory upon which Bukharin was to build after 1923 a detailed, elaborate system of what, in more modern terminology, could be described as "socialism with a human face". The linchpin of his system was social peace – peace between classes, between town and countryside. This meant an end to the traditional exploitation of the Russian peasant, who had for centuries borne the brunt of all economic development in Russia. It also meant renunciation of the traditional class warfare of Bolshevik tactics. Bukharin, although in theory as much prone to accept talk of Bolshevik ruthlessness as any Bolshevik, was of a gentle temperament, averse in practice to the terror which he often advocated in theory, and never able to shake off the traditional ethics of a European socialist.

In time Bukharin added several new elements to Lenin's sketch of a policy. One was his theory of economic expansion and industrialization: following Lenin, this was based uncompromisingly on the need for a lasting peace between town and country. The peasant would in time "grow into" socialism. The process could and should be helped on fiscally: but one could not create socialism at machine-gun point, or, as the Left Opposition advocated, accumulate capital for industrial expansion by extracting it forcibly from the peasants.

The proper course, Bukharin repeatedly argued, was to encourage the peasants to increase their own prosperity, and to develop industry progressively: light industries to start with, so as to produce the many commodities which the peasants badly needed, and then, with the capital accumulated from the sale of consumer goods to the peasants, to develop heavy industry.

Stalin, whose prime concern after 1923 was to prevent the rise to power of Trotsky and his supporters, readily espoused Bukharin's doctrines. Bukharin's prestige as a theorist and as editor of *Pravda*, the fact that he had stood very close to Lenin after 1921 as well as his influence and reputation abroad through the Comintern (over which he presided) were all of inestimable value to Stalin in routing his "Left" opponents on the basis of the doctrine of "socialism in one country". Bukharin, for his part, gave Stalin invaluable service, using every dirty trick in the communist armoury to hasten the defeat and disgrace of Trotsky, Kamenev, and Zinoviev. Mr Cohen (with the intolerance of youth, perhaps) is somewhat censorious about Bukharin in this period, placing a verse from I Corinthians 13 on the importance of charity as an epigraph to the relevant chapter of his book. Yet Bukharin was, after all, a communist, reared in the communist tradition, with little sympathy for democratic niceties.

There are few, if any, examples of political chicanery which are not to be found in Lenin's career. It is easy to say (Mr Cohen does not say it) that when Stalin, having destroyed the Left Opposition with Bukharin's aid, promptly and quite unexpectedly started to dismantle the New Economic Policy and turned on Bukharin and his main supporters, Rykov and Tomsky, this was poetic justice. This is really unhistorical nonsense. Bukharin never doubted for a moment that after the Left had been routed, Lenin's policy would be fully implemented, and the foundations laid for a socialist future for Russia on the lines which Lenin had only had time to sketch. In order to achieve this the Left had to be defeated, and in terms of communist politics Stalin's way in the twenties seemed the only way. It was in the thirties that Stalin was revealed as the bloodthirsty maniac that he was, not in the twenties.

Of course, Bukharin was no democrat. He believed in dictatorship, in terror – in theory, at all events; he had no liking for it in practice – and in treating political opponents as enemies to be routed. Nevertheless, he stood for certain principles that belonged to the tradition of social democracy which probably still survived to some slight extent in Lenin, and were eradicated by Stalin. Bukharin believed firmly that the time for class war was over and that socialism could only be built on the basis of reconciliation and harmony. He expressed (long before the idea was developed by Preobrazhensky in exile and much later by Djilas) the fear that the commissars who controlled the resources of the state were in danger of becoming a new exploiting class. He even voiced some apprehensions (nowhere to be found in any published writing of Lenin's) that a communist party, enjoying monopoly of power and subject to no control whatsoever, was in danger of becoming corrupted.

There are innumerable instances of humanitarian acts by Bukharin, from his efforts to save the lives of the socialist revolutionaries put on trial in 1922, right up to the end when his influence was gone, and his life in imminent peril. Nadezhda Mandelstam has recently paid tribute to Bukharin – there are many more instances on record.

Above all, Bukharin should be remembered with respect and admiration for the enormous part which he played in helping to create a relatively free and varied marxist culture which survived until the thirties, the like of which has never been seen since. Bukharin's influence was exercised mainly through the Institute of Red Professors and through the Communist Academy, and through the Writers' Congress. A recognizable group of foremost scholars in history, literature, and law (most of whom perished without trace after Bukharin's fall) wrote important and original works, influenced and encouraged by Bukharin. Many of these works are very rare today. There is one work, by Ia. V. Staroselsky, on the Jacobin dictatorship, of which a copy was given by the author to the late Harold Laski (I have been unable to trace another copy in the major libraries in the United States). There is little doubt that this book, published in 1930, like many others including some works on Nechaev, and like some of Bukharin's own articles in the thirties, was intended as veiled criticism of Stalin. It is much to be hoped that as full a study as possible of this golden age in Russian marxist scholarship, which I understand is in train, will be available before too long.

The outstanding Russian marxist theorist of law, E. B. Pashukanis, wrote a preface to Staroselsky's book – Pashukanis was "liquidated" in 1937. The reason for killing him (he was criticized for heretical views, long recanted, on the withering away of the state) was plainly the fact that, as chairman of the Institute of Law of the new Academy of Sciences, he was, in the course of the summer of 1936, the guiding spirit of a group of lawyers working on the reform of Soviet criminal law in a more humane and liberal direction. There can be no doubt about Bukharin's involvement in this activity since, as he told Nicolaevsky, he was the main author of the civil rights section of the Stalin Constitution of 1936.

It may seem surprising that Bukharin, whose political downfall was complete by 1929, could have continued at liberty, active in the intellectual sphere as far as this remained possible, editing *Izvestia* and drafting the new constitution. But in the first place, Stalin was able successfully to assert his will over the party leaders only in 1936 and to inaugurate the great terror, the staged trials, and the judicial murder of leading oppositionists. For so long as he was unable to start the butchery of mid-1936 to 1938 he was content to allow all kinds of liberal fancies to flourish, either with the object of lulling the liberals, which meant the Bukharinites, into a false sense of security, or to let a hundred flowers bloom, like Chairman Mao, the better to lop their heads off when the time was ripe. Bukharin was not arrested until the spring of 1937: many members of the Central Committee, who, of course, paid with their lives, seem to have made a very belated if courageous stand to save Bukharin and something of the honour of the party. Bukharin was put on trial, with Rykov (Tomsky had already committed suicide) and nineteen others between 2 and 13 March 1938. He was sentenced to death, and on 15 March it was announced that the execution had been carried out.

The tragic fate of Bukharin raises a number of questions, the answers to which seem to me to be vital for the understanding of Soviet history and society. Stalin's motives in destroying him and his many important supporters in the party are clear enough. Since Stalin was determined to establish the kind of police state, ruled by terror and based on the conformity of the graveyard, which the Soviet Union became under his rule, it was essential for him to annihilate and defame all those communists who stood for social peace and some degree of tolerance and gradualism in economic policy. The usual arguments used to justify Stalin's action simply will not stand up – that the "kulaks" would "hold the country up to ransom", or that the rise of Hitler called for rapid industrialization in preparation for inevitable war. Evidence of "kulak" conspiracy is virtually nonexistent except in the imagination of Stalin's apologists.

Assuming that Stalin's methods of industrialization were more successful and faster than Bukharin's gradualism would have been (and who can tell?), the link with the rise of Hitler is completely unconvincing. Would Hitler have come to power, or come to power so soon and so easily, if it had not been for the bacchanalia let loose by Stalin, or for Stalin's direction of the German communists? No one can tell. Did Stalin, whose dearest wish after 1934 was to make a deal with Hitler, and who persisted in the face of all the evidence to believe in Hitler's pacific intentions toward Russia right up to the invasion of 21 June 1941, really ever believe that he was arming the Soviet Union against a Nazi attack?

It was, of course, Stalin's mastery over the party apparatus and his skill in manipulating it that made his victory over Bukharin and "the Right" possible, in spite of the very widespread support that they enjoyed in the country. But, as Mr Cohen rightly points out, this was not the only reason for Stalin's victory. The tradition of revolutionary extremism was very strong in the Bolshevik party, the tradition of all-out strife, of ruthlessness, of achieving the impossible, of storming the impregnable fortress and the like. This was indeed the tradition which had inspired Lenin – the tradition of Chernyshevsky, whose portrayal of the "new man" in the sixties, especially in his novel *What Is To Be Done?*, first started Lenin on his revolutionary career.

To these Bolsheviks the New Economic Policy and the talk of generations of social peace and of "growing into socialism" which Bukharin stood for seemed to be an aberration of the ailing Lenin, and a departure from everything that he had stood for hitherto – the latter was certainly true. There was, I believe, yet a third reason for Stalin's victory. Stalin appealed to what was most corrupt and degenerate in the party – the self-seeking careerist, the unprincipled sycophant, the new type of communist, totally indifferent to doctrine, whose horizon was limited to rising on the backs of those above him and treading on those whom he was in a position to betray. The fall of Bukharin was the triumph of a communist way of life which has not changed a great deal in its essentials to this day.

Why did Bukharin return to Soviet Russia in 1936 when he had the opportunity of staying away, and when he was in no doubt of the fate which ultimately awaited him? Primarily, perhaps, because his young wife and child were hostages in Stalin's hands. Bukharin also had a strong sense of responsibility for the many young intellectuals who made up an important part of his following, and may have had some hopes of saving them or shielding them. And, in contrast to Stalin, Bukharin was obsessed by the rising tide of Nazism and quite convinced that a clash was inevitable. In this coming clash he appears to have believed, and rightly, that a victory of Stalin's communism with all its faults held out more hope for the future than the darkness that would descend over mankind should Hitler win.

It was beyond doubt this fear of the rise of Nazism and the sense of the need to bolster communism, even Stalin's communism, as a defence against it that formed one of Bukharin's motives in agreeing to a minimum of co-operation with Stalin and his henchmen at the trial in 1938. Much nonsense has been written about Bukharin's "Confession". Dishonest or imbecile reporters, like Feuchtwanger or Ambassador Davies, leaned over backward to do Stalin's work for him, and to show that Bukharin's guilt had been proved. Koestler, in *Darkness at Noon*, invented the romantic theory of "last service to the party". The explanation, we now know, was much simpler. First and foremost was Bukharin's wish to purchase the lives of his wife and son – they spent twenty years in concentration camps, but they survived. Secondly, he did not confess – as several shrewd and honest observers noted at the time, and as Dr Katkov's illuminating study of the trial established beyond doubt in 1969 in a book which, until the appearance of Mr Cohen's, was the only serious study of Bukharin available.[2]

Bukharin at his trial made the minimal admission that his captors required and no more – the admission of general "counter-revolutionary" activity and membership in the bloc of "Rightists and Trotskyites": he denied every specific charge, such as wrecking activities, connections with German fascists, espionage activity on behalf of foreign intelligence services, and, the most grotesque charge of all, of forming a plan in 1918 to assassinate Lenin. His evidence, read in conjunction with the last article which he published, makes it clear that he was attempting to use the trial in order to outwit his captors, and to convey, in Aesopian language, something of the ideals to which he had devoted his life, and to sound his fears of Nazi ascendancy. It gives one a little satisfaction to be able to record that his attempt has in recent years been understood. Better late than never.

What is the significance of Bukharin for posterity? For those socialists to whom Stalinism has proved a disillusionment, and for those who see little to hope for from the various forms of violent revolution in which followers of Trotsky or Mao see the vision of a happy future, Bukharin offers the only alternative – a form of post-revolutionary revisionism. It is not surprising that voices are occasionally heard inside the Soviet Union echoing some of Bukharin's thoughts, if without acknowledgement. The attempt by the Czech communists to create something more civilized out of the wreckage of their Stalinist system was nothing but Bukharinism – even though this could never be mentioned without opening the floodgates of Soviet abuse and accusations of counter-revolution.

The fact that Bukharin has never been rehabilitated in the Soviet Union – beyond the grudging admission that he was not in fact a German or Japanese spy – need cause no surprise. To rehabilitate Bukharin, to permit, in other words, the open discussion and study of his works and his career, would be to remove the very foundations on which Brezhnev's police state rests, just as much as Stalin's did – arbitrariness, illegality, terror, albeit much reduced in extent, suppression of freedom of discussion even of marxist theory, party control of literature and scholarship (again reduced in extent as compared with Stalin, but real nevertheless), and a morbid fear of economic incentives. The rehabilitation of Bukharin may come – who can tell? If it ever does it will be a sure sign that real and substantial changes have taken place in the essential nature of the Soviet system of rule.

1. Boris I. Nicolaevsky, *Power and the Soviet Elite* (New York 1965), p. 12.

2. George Katkov, *The Trial of Bukharin* (New York 1969).

A Turning Point in the History of Socialism: The Kronstadt Rising

This article first appeared in *The Listener*, London, 4 June 1981.

On 17 March 1921, up to 50,000 crack Red Army troops stormed across the frozen waters of the Gulf of Finland to the island naval fortress of Kronstadt, there to overpower and defeat some 15,000 sailors and soldiers who had dared to challenge the claim of the Communist Party to rule dictatorially and alone. Some 8,000 rebels escaped to Finland. The siege had lasted ten days. Of those who survived the fighting, the great majority were either shot or sent to perish in the concentration camps.

This event, which appears in retrospect as a turning point in the history of socialism, made little impact outside Russia at the time. The leading Western European governments, Great Britain and France, and the USA were disillusioned with their incompetent, abortive and insignificant intervention in the Russian civil war, and never even considered support for the Kronstadt rising – support which might have brought the communist government down; at least, Lenin thought so. Communists outside Russia naturally accepted without question the Soviet party's assurance that the revolt was inspired by émigré counter-revolutionaries and led by White Guard officers, and that it had no popular support in the country.

Socialists, though somewhat shaken, for the most part consoled themselves with the hope that the first socialist state, as it was then believed to be, would in time get over its teething troubles and become more humane and liberal – as La Rochefoucauld says, we all possess the fortitude to bear the sufferings of others. Only the anarchists saw the Kronstadt events as the final indictment of communism – and, indeed, it was to a number of anarchist writers that we owed the first truthful accounts of the rising and its suppression.

For many years, this revolt of workers and peasants against Communist Party dictatorship remained unique: there were no communist-ruled states outside the Soviet Union. Inside it, the improvement in living conditions under the New Economic Policy inaugurated in March 1921 quietened protest for a time; while the ever-expanding forces of police terror, after NEP was reversed, ensured that rebellion remained impracticable, if not impossible. Since the expansion of the Soviet empire after the Second World War there have been left-wing revolts against the uglier aspects of communism in Hungary and Czechoslovakia, and there is one going on in Poland at present. It is therefore of interest both to re-examine the events in Russia in 1921 in the light of the considerable research that has been done on them in the past sixty years, and to enquire what parallels, if any, can be drawn between this remote episode and the struggles for a modest measure of humanity and freedom under communist rule which have taken place in the Soviet bloc.

The Kronstadt rebels always maintained that their movement was not the result of a conspiracy, but was a spontaneous explosion of protest against communist tyranny. Historical research bears them out. While émigré organizations were certainly looking for an opportunity to overthrow Soviet communist rule, there is no scrap of evidence of any links between the Kronstadt rising and any of these émigré groups. Historical research apart, if there had been any pre-arranged plan for a rebellion, it would have been crazy to time it for 28 February, about a month before the ice is due to melt in the Finnish Gulf. For, once the waters of the Gulf were free, aid from outside could reach the island fortress, and, moreover, the assault from the mainland by the communist forces would have been rendered extremely difficult.

The sailors' protest was in fact sparked off by strikes and demonstrations which took place in Petrograd towards the end of February, and which led the Kronstadters to hope that the movement which they initiated would spread to the mainland, and thence to the whole of Russia. The peasant rebellions then in progress in many parts of Russia, almost amounting to a guerrilla war, lent some force to this optimism. But the unrest in Petrograd was motivated more by hardships and starvation than by political discontent. It was put down comparatively easily by a combination of severe repressive measures and rushing supplies of food to the city.

The situation was quite different in Kronstadt. The fortress island was relatively isolated from the mainland: if once the authority of the local commissars were defied a major operation would be necessary to restore it, and this seemed to the rebels less likely than some kind of compromise on their demands. The leading element in the revolt was the sailors – some of them the same sailors who in 1917 had been among the most hotheaded supporters of the Bolsheviks, far outstripping the Bolshevik leaders in militancy. They had also distinguished themselves after the fall of the monarchy in March 1917 by a series of particularly brutal murders of their officers. The sailors and the large garrison, which numbered many members of the Communist Party in its ranks, loyally supported the Moscow regime so long as the civil war lasted. But this conflict came to a virtual end by November 1920. Communist methods of rule which had been supportable while the regime was in danger of defeat now became intolerable. Discontent was fuelled by what many of the peasant sailors had witnessed in their villages when they returned to them on leave.

On 28 February 1921, the crew of the battleship *Petropavlovsk* adopted a resolution which became the charter of the revolt. Its main demands were: the immediate re-election of the soviets by secret ballot and on the basis of full freedom of political agitation "in view of the fact that the existing soviets do not express the will of the workers and peasants"; freedom of speech and press for "workers, peasants, and for the anarchists and the left socialist parties"; freedom of meetings and free trade unions, and the formation of peasants' unions; liberation of all socialist political prisoners and of all workers, peasants, soldiers and sailors imprisoned "in connection with workers' and peasants' movements"; the setting up of a commission to review the cases of all who were detained in prisons and concentration camps; abolition of all special political departments (in the army, navy and transport), "since no one party can enjoy privileges for the propaganda of its ideas and receive money from the state for this purpose"; equal rations for all, except those engaged in work dangerous to health; abolition of all special communist detachments; full rights for the peasants to "do as they please with all the land" and to keep their own cattle, "provided they use no hired labour"; and the right of individual small-scale manufacture – again, without the employment of hired labour.

It is difficult to see this homespun programme of primitive communism as a "disguised appeal for the restoration of capitalism", as Soviet historians tend nowadays to describe it on the rare occasions when they refer to it – without, of course, reprinting it – though it is fair to say that Soviet historians of Kronstadt in the early thirties were much more objective. The aims of the rebels appear even more clearly from the pages of their newspaper, of which fourteen issues appeared, between 3 and 16 March. They rejected the Constituent Assembly because they were convinced that the communists would rig the election – this disproving any socialist revolutionary influence behind the rebellion, since the Constituent Assembly remained their big demand. The inclusion of peasant issues in the programme likewise tends to argue against Menshevik influence – the Mensheviks still at liberty had been active in the Petrograd strikes until their arrest.

As regards the communists, for whom the pages of their newspaper reveal a burning hatred, they were, in the rebels' view, entitled to stand for election to the soviets, since in a free election no one was expected to vote for them. Anarchist influence there may have been, since free soviets, the key demand at Kronstadt, are presumably compatible with anarchist rejection of government machinery.

The news of this defiant resolution sent the nominal head of state, Kalinin, accompanied by one of the chief commissars of the Baltic fleet, hurrying to Kronstadt on 1 March, where a great mass gathering was organized to receive them. After a rowdy meeting, punctuated by defiant critical personal comments about Kalinin and the commissar, who were, however, given a hearing, the *Petropavlovsk* resolution was put to the vote. It was passed overwhelmingly, against the sole dissenting votes of Kalinin, the commissar and another leading communist – in spite of the fact that there must have been hundreds, if not thousands, of members of the party in the crowd. The rebels now waited in a mood in which optimism alternated with a "victory or death" attitude. Their attempts to negotiate with the communist leaders in Moscow were spurned. After the rebels had rejected a peremptory demand for surrender issued on 5 March, military operations, which were to prove heavy in cost and effort for the communist regime, were started on 7 March.

If the *Petropavlovsk* resolution shows little appreciation of Rosa Luxemburg's maxim that "freedom is always freedom for the man who thinks differently", the rebels by their behaviour during the seventeen days of liberty were an object-lesson to all communists. Kronstadt was run by a Provisional Revolutionary Committee of naval ratings and clerks and workers. In contrast to the savagery with which the sailors had behaved towards their officers in 1917, the Kronstadt local communists were left unmolested, except that some of those who did not support the revolt were placed under arrest. The Committee took great pride in this, contrasting it in the pages of their rebel newspaper with the behaviour of communists when in power. Actually, around one-third of the local communists supported the revolt, and another forty per cent remained "neutral". The Kronstadt newspaper also published the communist charges against the rebels in all their absurd detail – another glaring contrast with Moscow communist practice. On the other hand, the rebels' abuse of leading communists, particularly Trotsky, who, as Commissar for War, masterminded the assault on the fortress, knew no limits.

It is easy to understand the panic which the news from Kronstadt engendered among the communist leaders, including Lenin. They were well aware that their support in the country had fallen to its lowest ebb since 1917, and they were not to know that the feverish attempts by the émigré organizations to get help to Kronstadt would come to nothing: they had to act before the ice melted. Moreover, on top of the widespread peasant unrest, there were serious opposition movements inside the Communist Party, particularly among the soviet and trade union communists, directed against the dictatorship from the centre. The Kronstadt revolt gave Lenin the opportunity, as he expressed it, to "put the lid on opposition" at the Tenth Congress of the Party which met while the rising was in progress.

As events turned out, the opposition groups were as terrified as Lenin at the prospect of being overthrown, and almost willingly submitted to the draconian measures which the Congress took to silence them. Not a single oppositionist spoke in defence of the Kronstadters, and many of them joined the 200 or more delegates to the Congress who went to Kronstadt to help to drive the reluctant soldiers across the ice. They knew as well as Lenin that freely elected soviets would have spelt the end of their own monopoly of power – in the soviets or in the trade unions. And, in the light of the theory of Leninism which had been victorious in 1917 by asserting the identity of "soviet" power with the power of the Bolshevik party, they were presumably acting consistently.

In those remote days of 1921 Bolshevism still stood in many minds for a glorious socialist future. By 1956, after the exposure of Stalin's reign of terror by Khrushchev, and after a record of abysmal economic failure in all areas except that of military expansion, the small communist parties directed from Moscow which had seized power in such countries as Hungary, Czechoslovakia and Poland could scarcely hope to command ideological support. They survive in power by the permanent threat that a revolt against Communist Party control would bring in Soviet tanks – as indeed happened in 1956 and again in 1968. If the communists succeed in retaining their nominal control in Poland, living as they do in uneasy partnership with a powerful Church and with private peasant property in land, it will be for the same reason.

The revolts against their communist regimes in Hungary and Czechoslovakia, and that going on in Poland, have certain features in common. They were and are in no conceivable sense based on rejection of the socialist system or on a demand for the restoration of private capitalism. They were and are, rather, the result of an effort to recover some of the idealism for making a better life which had impelled many of the Hungarian, Czech or Polish rebels to join the Communist Party, and a desire to remove what they saw as the ugly and intolerable features of communist monopoly of power. In all three cases – though in differing proportions – Communist Party members and non-communists have together supported the movement of protest. In these respects there is a parallel between the Kronstadt revolt of 1921 and the events in the Soviet bloc decades later.

The similarity between more recent events and the 1921 rising is probably closest in the case of Poland. For here, as in Kronstadt, though on a much wider national scale, workers and peasants are challenging the right of the Communist Party in its present form to act in their name. Like the Kronstadters, they regard this party as largely corrupt and inefficient.

Of course, the parallel, as almost invariably in political analysis, must not be pressed too far. For one thing, the countries of the Soviet bloc are virtually occupied countries, with imposed governments owing allegiance to a foreign power (and in the case of Poland, a hated foreign power). Nationalism, therefore, necessarily plays a very strong part in any movement against such a regime. There is no parallel here in the case of Kronstadt, where the most that can be said is that folk anti-semitism may have fuelled some of the rebels' venom against Trotsky. For another, in all three revolts in Eastern Europe a prominent part was played by intellectuals, which was hardly the case in Kronstadt. Again, in Kronstadt the future government which the rebels wished to see was to be based on a primitive kind of pluralism of left-wing parties. There was no demand for this or any kind of pluralism in the case of the countries of the bloc, and indeed it was reform of the Communist Party that became central to their demands – this is still strongly the case today among the many Polish communists who have joined Solidarity.

Yet the really important similarity lies in the implacable resistance of the Soviet Communist Party to any kind of attempt to force it to dilute its absolute monopoly of power. Lenin, from the time when he seized power, struggled with the full might of the security forces, the Cheka, against the growing popularity of the Mensheviks, which he did not feel strong enough to counter with legislation. As in Kronstadt in 1921, so in Hungary in 1956 and in Czechoslovakia in 1968, a party discredited by its broken promises had no hope of success by appealing to a sense of loyalty, and therefore resorted to force. From the battle across the ice in 1921 to the tanks in Budapest in 1956, or in Prague in 1968, there is a direct line of causation – to save its monopoly of power at all costs for a hated communist regime rather than to attempt to meet demands for reforms. If Poland proves fortunate enough – and, be it said, skilful enough – to avoid the fate of Hungary and Czechoslovakia, this will be a striking departure from traditional Soviet Communist policy.

Trotsky, As He Really Was

This article originally appeared in *Government and Opposition*, vol 17, summer 1982.

Trotsky's repeated failure as a political prophet does not seem to have damaged his reputation among his devoted followers. The very pivot of Trotsky's faith – that socialism in one country is doomed to failure unless supported by revolution in other countries – has been proved palpably wrong. The only reason why "socialist" countries like the Soviet Union or Poland, for example, survive at all is that they are able to bolster their own inefficient systems by vast loans and imports of food and technology from states where a free economy exists. In *The Revolution Betrayed*, in 1937, Trotsky foretold that a defeat of Germany by the Soviet Union would result in the crushing not only of Hitler, "but of the capitalist system"; while in the Soviet Union one of two things would happen. The first possibility was that a revolutionary party would take over which would restore freedom in the trade unions and the soviets, as well as the liberty of Soviet parties. It would purge the apparatus, abolish all privileges and limit inequality of payment to the minimum. It was a belated conversion to freedom by Trotsky. In 1921 the sailors and garrison of Kronstadt had risen and called for every one of these reforms. They were not only mown down as "counter-revolutionaries" with Trotsky's full support, and under his overall command, but his action was unequivocally justified by him years later in exile, on the grounds that failure to crush Kronstadt in 1921 would have opened the gates to "counter-revolution" – in plain words, would have put an end to communist monopoly of power. The second hypothetical future of a Soviet Union victorious in a war against Germany, according to Trotsky, was the victory of a bourgeois party, which would restore private property. Of course, all political prophets go wrong more often than not. But this particular failure reveals two characteristic weaknesses of Trotsky's power of analysis.

The first is the inability to grasp something which even Marx and Engels understood, – that political developments depend not only on material factors, but on moral considerations as well: the countries of Western Europe and the USA were not ultimately indissolubly linked with Hitler because he supported private capitalism (which, incidentally, he did not) but were opposed to him as posing a threat to the liberty for which they stood, and for which they fought the war that ultimately broke out. The second weakness brought out by this faulty analysis is the total failure to understand the real nature of the Soviet system. To the very end Trotsky justified it on the ground that, however perverted by Stalin, it was a socialist system. He failed to see (as some of his followers, like Preobrazhensky, pointed out long before Djilas) that under the guise of socialism, the Soviet system had grown into a system of privilege for a new ruling class of officials, whose control over the means of production and unrestricted power of dispensing rewards enabled them to exploit the rest of the country even to a greater extent than capitalists usually can. He also never grasped the real strength of the party apparatus which Lenin created and which Stalin perfected, the stranglehold which it had achieved over the entire life of the country, nor yet the way in which the whole system of government was subordinated to the one, overriding aim – the maintenance of the monopoly of power of the Communist Party apparatus.

The strange fact is that during the years before the revolution, when Trotsky was a staunch opponent of Lenin, he saw very clearly where the Bolshevik system of power would lead – to the ultimate tyranny of one man. Yet, having once joined the party (in August 1917) and become one of its leading and most influential figures, he seems to have devoted his great prestige and authoritative voice precisely to bolstering Stalin in his rise to sole power. Everything that he subsequently claimed to have believed in was sacrificed to the one aim of this monopoly of power by the Communist Party. He played a full part in the Bolsheviks' deception of their followers. One could compile a very long list of statements made in the early years when he was one of the top leaders of the party that for their blatant hypocrisy and dishonesty are matched only by Lenin's demagogy: "Long live the Constituent Assembly!" (7 October 1917) ". . . we shall guide the work of the Soviet in a spirit of justice and complete independence for all factions. The hand of the Praesidium will never oppress the minority" (23 September 1917, in the Petrograd Soviet); or the famous outburst (on 25 October 1917) confining the socialist parties "to the dustbin of history", when in fact they had won almost as many seats in the Soviet as the Bolsheviks, and would win many times the number of votes gained by the Bolsheviks a fortnight later in the elections to the Constituent Assembly; and repeated allegations, which he could not but have known were totally false, that the socialist parties during the civil war were "counter-revolutionaries".

No objective historian would deny Trotsky full credit for his work in organizing the Red Army and in achieving victory in the civil war. It was a formidable task, and his brutal ruthlessness in accomplishing these aims, in combat conditions, can, no doubt, be justified. His avowed intention in 1921 of applying the same methods as he used in the army to the trade unions and to labour generally was probably the beginning of his political eclipse – Lenin knew how to achieve much the same result without saying so. His support of Lenin in maintaining intact monopoly of power by the Communist Party, when the obvious solution to the pressing problems after the civil war was a coalition of all political forces, was unswerving. He stood by him in the hounding of the Mensheviks who fought for trade union freedom, and in the suppression of the Kronstadt rising. He backed him up at the Tenth Party Congress in 1921 over the silencing of debate inside the Communist Party and the elimination of all communist opposition groups. (He claimed later that these measures were intended to be temporary only: there is not a jot of evidence to support this contention.)

The hagiographers of Trotsky often tend to concentrate on the epic struggle against Goliath Stalin and to skate over the discreditable and abject instances in which Trotsky bolstered Stalin in his rise to power. (Mr Segal's book,[1] to be fair, does not omit these incidents, though he does lean over backwards to justify them.) According to his own account, he agreed with Lenin, who was dying, surrounded by Stalin's spies, and isolated from public affairs, that he would conduct a campaign against Stalin. Yet, at the Twelfth Party Congress, in 1923, with Lenin's explosive note on the national question in his pocket, which could have blown Stalin out of the water, he remained silent. Years later he claimed that he could have won, but did not wish to appear to be competing for Lenin's place. It is more probable that, along with the other Bolsheviks who helped Stalin in his rise to sole power, he was afraid to rock the boat for fear that the entire party might go under without Stalin's administrative skill in keeping it in power. Further, even more blatant, betrayals were to follow. In 1925 foreign dissident communists published an accurate text of Lenin's last notes (generally known as his Testament). They had in fact obtained the notes from Lenin's widow, Krupskaia. Trotsky, under threat of disciplinary action by the Politburo, published a statement branding the document as a "malicious invention" which was contrary to "Lenin's real will and the interests of the party". His disavowal of foreign opposition communists who had been expelled from their own parties for supporting him was a similar step.

It is, perhaps, fair to say that by 1926 Stalin's control over the apparatus was so effective that Trotsky had no hope of political survival – though it is also true to say that capitulation did not rescue him, and that resistance might have saved his honour. But it was certainly not the case in 1923 when he rescued Stalin from defeat. Moreover, his surrender to Stalin in 1926 greatly strengthened Stalin's authority both within and outside the country. It has often been said that Trotsky, as a newcomer to the party, did not really ever understand the power of the apparatus. But his early criticism of Lenin for creating this apparatus makes this argument untenable. The truth seems to be that he was a victim of the curse of his generation – the faith that anything can be justified in the name of an abstraction which is seen as the ultimate Heavenly City, the millennium, the one and only solution to all ills. In 1924, in one of his early capitulations to Stalin, Trotsky spoke words which have become famous, and which typify this perverted state of mind: "My party – right or wrong . . . I know one cannot be right against the party . . . for history has not created other ways for the realization of what is right." The blindness in this statement passes belief: it must have been obvious to anyone not hypnotized by an abstraction that "the party" which was supposed to possess this mystical power of historical rightness was little more than a clique controlled by Stalin, and able to pontificate on doctrine in the way best calculated to serve Stalin's ambitions. Even after his defeat, in exile in 1937, Trotsky obstinately refused to recognize what was obvious to nearly everyone else. Only "superficial minds", he wrote, could regard the struggle between him and Stalin as a power struggle: personalities and the greater skill of Stalin were irrelevant. What had happened was that while in Lenin's time Bolshevism was a mass movement, the masses had been pushed away, and "bureaucracy . . . conquered the Bolshevik party". Suppression of opposition parties in Lenin's time was merely an "episodic act of self-defence".[2]

None of this is borne out by the facts. Compared with Stalin's, Lenin's regime of the party was somewhat more democratic, but there was no period in its history when the "masses" participated in decisions. The "bureaucracy" of party officials was, in fact, composed overwhelmingly at its higher levels of old Bolsheviks who had joined the party before the revolution. The social composition of the party in 1927 was little different from what it was in 1921, in fact its proletarian component had slightly increased. As for suppression of the opposition parties, the evidence is overwhelming that as early as 1917 Lenin was determined (and was supported in this by Trotsky) to destroy the two socialist parties which rivalled him for power. Trotsky's real failure was his attempt to compromise, for the sake of preserving at all costs a figment of his imagination, "my party", with an opponent who knew how to use that party in order to destroy a dangerous rival.

One of Trotsky's adherents is reputed to have said: "Let's not forget that Russia is an Asiatic country: the way of Genghis Khan and Stalin suits it better than the European civilization of Leon Davidovitch." Certainly Trotsky retained some sense of kinship with European civilization – "*cette vieille canaille, l'Europe*", as he says in his diary in exile. But the pride and glory of European civilization are liberty, legal order, tolerance, pluralism, freedom of conscience; none of these played any part in Trotsky's scheme of things. He totally lacked the moral sense which Judaism and Christianity have imprinted on Europe (including, be it said, Russia) and which the movements with which Europe has been plagued like Bolshevism and Nazism have laboured to destroy. For lack of this moral sense he failed to see that only evil can come out of evil, that the resort to bad means can never produce good ends, however much these may be intended. Trotsky "speaks for humanity", proclaims Mr Segal, with much more rhetorical nonsense, in his final summing up. But it is not enough to "speak for humanity": if you lay claim to political leadership you have to preserve the lives and liberty of real men and women, not of an abstraction called "humanity". By helping Stalin to remain in power in the name of "the party", or "socialism", or some other unreal abstraction, Trotsky made it possible for him to carry his rule to its logical conclusion, and murder millions of men and women. Of course, no one could have foreseen the mass terror of the 1930s in 1923, or even in 1926 or 1927. But the risk inherent in naked, uncontrolled power is always there: it is the duty of responsible politicians to guard against it before it is too late.

Trotsky's language of passionate hatred no doubt won him many supporters at the time – words of moderation grate on revolutionaries' ears. His bile was particularly directed at the two facets of his own origins – the bourgeoisie, and the Jewish people. As he said in a speech of 29 June 1918, ". . . now let [the former ruling classes] clean [the dirt] which we are leaving behind, until such time as they join the working class in the pursuit of a common goal . . . Let every bourgeois house be marked as one in which so many families live who lead a parasitic mode of life, and we shall post yellow tickets on these houses." The "yellow tickets" foreshadow the rhetoric of Goebbels – after all, the methods and aims were the same. As regards the Jews, Trotsky did not deny his origin – he would have found it rather difficult to do so. But he refused, even in exile, to recognize that the Jews had any right to survive as a distinct people, or were the bearers of a valuable culture. "If the realization of communism should require the sacrifice of Jewry in its entirety, this would be the most beautiful mission that could ever fall to the lot of any people," he wrote in 1930.

One need not be blinded by Trotsky's brilliance, like Mr Segal, to see that he shone like a star among the drab figures who formed the Bolshevik leadership after Lenin's departure. He also had the great gift of welding supporters to his side whose loyalty nothing could shake. His friend Ioffe shot himself in 1927 as a gesture of protest against those who had reduced the party to such a sorry state that it could be brought to acquiesce in the expulsion and forced exile of Trotsky. In his farewell letter he wrote what he had many a time wanted to tell his friend but could not bring himself to do: that Trotsky's hope of ultimate moral victory lay only in the strictest refusal to compromise. But 1927 was much too late for this advice:

Trotsky's repeated compromises with an evil system and men before 1927 have denied him the moral victory which revolutionary followers, who have conveniently forgotten the true facts of Trotsky's career, have claimed for him.

Was his life a tragedy? Of course, as a human being he has much claim to our sympathy – martyred and accused of crimes he never committed, his reputation denigrated by falsification of history, his children murdered or driven to their death by Stalin's henchmen, and he himself, after years of troubled exile, murdered by an agent of Stalin's police who wormed his way into his household by particularly repulsive deceit. But tragedy is not merely a question of sympathy, however much merited. If we accept Hegel's definition of it, it must always be a conflict between two rights. But if we take Trotsky's career while in power – not what he wrote or said about it in exile – there is nothing to choose between him and Stalin, or any reason to suppose that had he been victorious in the conflict the Soviet regime would have turned out any better than it did. For they shared the same premise – monopoly of power for an all-powerful elite, subject to no independent or effective control. No amount of argument about "bureaucratic degeneration" and the like can alter this basic fact.

It is thus impossible to excuse Trotsky by the argument that he was defeated by an apparatus the strength of which he did not understand. He had been on the receiving end of Lenin's methods for years before 1917. Had he not written of Leninism, in the years before he embraced it, that its whole foundation was "built on lying and falsification, and carries within itself the poisoned element of its own disintegration"? He was content after 1917, as a leader of the Communist Party, to use these same methods to defeat both socialist opponents and communist critics. He fell a victim in the end to this same practice, now wielded by Stalin against himself. This is not the stuff of tragedy: it is the small change of dirty politics. More sympathy is due to the thousands of victims who went to their doom for supporting Trotsky in the belief that he stood for a better, nobler ideal than Stalin. No doubt Trotsky genuinely believed this too. But if one puts oneself forward as a revolutionary leader, with promises of a radiant future, one owes it to one's followers to have a clear understanding of the instruments which one employs. Trotsky's ineptitude in his assessment of Stalin (which Mr Segal deals with very fully) should condemn him in the eyes of posterity for having failed in this duty to those who accepted him as their leader. Trotsky sees him as a man of mean abilities, without originality, a bureaucrat who "grew out of the machine" created by Lenin, having previously poisoned the dying Lenin. "The truth was," writes Mr Segal, "that Trotsky's particular imagination could grasp personal character only as the feature of a system." But life is about men and women, not systems. In the end Trotsky fell a victim to his own obsessive preoccupation with abstractions. His flamboyant personality continues after death to fascinate revolutionaries for whom abstractions take the place of ideas, and illusions are a substitute for facts.

Forty-two years after his death, the mythology built around Trotsky still flourishes in innumerable small revolutionary groups that call themselves "Trotskyist". The Fourth International which he founded has adherents in some thirty countries. But there are now three "Fourth Internationals", each claiming to be the only true one, and there are further international groupings seeking to reconstruct the original Fourth International. There are also some such groups in individual countries. All these revolutionary fragments have minimal support in terms of membership, let alone electoral victory. But they have had successes in carrying into practice the very same revolutionary techniques by which Stalin successfully defeated Trotsky in Russia – intrigue, deceit and infiltration.

If Trotskyists ever succeed in winning power, it will be because ultimately the real force of communism – the Soviet Communist Party – is behind them, for all the abuse which the mother party may heap on them. Mr Segal, Trotsky's latest hagiographer (latest so far as I am aware), concludes, with unrestrained hyperbole, that his voice speaks posthumously for the poor, the hungry and those who are imprisoned by property in countries which proclaim themselves champions of personal freedom. This may well correspond to the beliefs of some of those who rally to the revolutionary call of Trotskyists, and, of course, to the hopes of the poor and miserable who support them. But in practice what Trotskyists are doing, where they are successful, is weakening the power of resistance to the advance of Soviet tyranny and oppression by undermining those countries which, for all their faults, are the world's only hope for the survival of liberty – the USA and the other countries of NATO. And not only liberty. In what country to date has a communist conquest brought anything in its train but a lower standard of living and economic inequality along with loss of freedom? Objectively, as the communists would say, the posthumous voice of Trotsky is really that of Stalin – *malgré lui*.

1. Ronald Segal, *The Tragedy of Leon Trotsky* (London 1979).
2. Leon Trotsky, *The Revolution Betrayed. What is the Soviet Union and Where is it Going?* translated by Max Eastman (London 1937), pp. 87–104.

LITERATURE AND IDEAS

Turgenev and Herzen: Two Modes of Russian Political Thought

This article was written in 1964.

What follows is the story of a quarrel. It took place about a hundred years ago, between two outstanding figures of that great intellectual Parnassus – nineteenth-century Russia – between Ivan Turgenev, the novelist, and Alexander Herzen, political journalist, revolutionary, essayist and memoirist. It was, of course, a quarrel about political issues, or rather about one particular burning issue – the political future of Russia. It was an issue which remained very much alive for a whole generation, and indeed, perhaps, for longer. Briefly, it concerned the future destiny of Russian society: was Russia, backward as she was when compared with the more politically, economically and socially advanced countries of Europe, simply destined to catch up, as it were, with her European elders and betters, and thereafter to develop along the same lines? Or, on the contrary, was there some specific, peculiar quality in the social and spiritual history of Russia which destined Russia for a path of future development, quite different from (and ultimately, of course, superior to) the pattern followed by, say, Britain, France or Germany? But before I deal with the dispute between Turgenev and Herzen on this subject, I should like to sketch, however briefly, something of the political atmosphere which predominated in Russian intellectual life at the beginning of the sixties of the last century.

The most momentous date in this decade was beyond doubt 19 February 1861 on which the imperial manifesto emancipating the peasants from serfdom was published. The reign of Alexander II had been inaugurated in 1855 with the promise of this tremendous reform. It was to prove only the first step on the long road of the economic and social evolution of Russia, which is not yet complete over one hundred years later. The freeing from bondage of some twenty-three million peasants and their families – the great majority of the population, in fact – was soon to be followed by reforms of the judiciary, the army and education, and by a system of local self-government. Politically Alexander's reform was to have the effect of stirring into consciousness the wider aspirations for freedom and progress among the Russian intelligentsia which had largely remained dormant throughout the dark and tyrannous reign of Nicholas I. This reign had been inaugurated in 1825 by the abortive revolt of the young intellectual nobility in arms – the Decembrists – the crushing of which virtually silenced all political expression, let alone activity, for thirty years. The accession of Alexander II opened the floodgates to the currents of political excitement which had been running underground. Much of this political thought was too unformed and too uncertain of itself for any definite formulation to be attempted. But two broad trends could already be discerned in the first years of the decade which were becoming increasingly antagonistic one to the other.

One trend, of which Nikolai Chernyshevsky was probably the leading exponent, saw salvation for Russia solely in a revolutionary upheaval which would completely transform society. His outlook was characterized by a distrust of reforms, and a bitter contempt for reformers and their liberal supporters. Although Chernyshevsky's actual participation in revolutionary conspiracy is a matter of doubt and controversy, there is no doubt of his influence on the minor revolutionary conspiracies which sprang up in the years immediately succeeding the Emancipation. It is also incidentally a matter of recorded fact that Chernyshevsky's outlook was one of the most important formative influences on the young Lenin many years later.[1] It may seem at first sight paradoxical that the most momentous step towards liberty in the history of the country should have been followed by the birth of revolutionary conspiracy – the first revolutionary movement, Land and Liberty, came into existence in 1862. But there were good reasons for it. The Act of Emancipation, when its complicated provisions became known, proved a shattering disappointment both to the peasants and to the intellectuals, for whom the fate of the peasant was the mainspring of their political aspirations. This was because the Act failed to fulfil the over-optimistic hopes that its preparation had engendered that in addition to personal liberty it would generously endow the peasant with land. There was another, and in my view, more important reason too. Nothing shakes the stability of an autocratic regime more profoundly than the moment when it becomes apparent that it is willing to make concessions to popular demand. Aspirations which seem hopeless while the regimes of tyranny are at their height begin to appear possible: the concession of an inch soon engenders the demand for an ell when once the magic of enduring autocracy is called in question.

The other political trend which emerged in the sixties is harder to particularize, because it was really a conglomeration of different political outlooks. What, however, all its adherents shared in common was that, unlike the radicals of whom Chernyshevsky was typical, they viewed the political future of Russia in terms of a deepening of the process of reform inaugurated in 1861. There were those to whom the primary task for the immediate future seemed to lie in the formation of an enlightened, rational, educated, and fully Westernized intellectual elite as the basis for the future "public opinion" or "pressure group" – to use modern terms – institutions which Russia still lacked. The leading representative of this view was Dimitri Pisarev. There were also some elements of a constitutional movement, on the Western European model. The adherents of this constitutional view hoped to influence the Emperor to complete his work of modernization by allowing Russia to develop representative institutions and a free public opinion. This movement never gathered real force, at any rate before the turn of the century. So long as Russia remained a predominantly peasant country constitutional ideas repelled the majority of the intellectuals, since they appeared to be of little value or interest to the downtrodden and suffering peasantry to whom they felt their primary moral debt. Then again, to complete the sketch of this non-revolutionary trend, there were the more conservative Slavophile traditionalists. These intellectuals rejected any kind of development on Western European lines for Russia, and claimed to see salvation in the traditional Russian institutions – including autocracy and orthodoxy. Indeed, a number of them regarded the absence in Russia of institutions firmly rooted in law and the prevalence of the arbitrary as a peculiar Russian virtue morally superior to the coldly legalistic and inhuman legal order (as it appeared to them) of, say, Britain.

The two protagonists, Turgenev and Herzen, do not readily fit into either of these rough sketches of intellectual trends which I have just attempted to trace. The older of the two by six years, Alexander Herzen was born in Moscow on 25 March 1812. He was in fact the illegitimate son of a wealthy nobleman, called Yakovlev, but was brought up as an openly acknowledged son in his father's very eccentric household, together with his gentle and timid German mother, who for all practical purposes was treated by Yakovlev as his wife. Alexander received the usual education of a young Russian nobleman and soon came into contact with the main intellectual currents of Europe of the time – especially Schiller, Schelling and the German idealists, Saint-Simon and the French utopian socialists, and Hegel. His career at the University of Moscow was interrupted by arrest and exile, not for revolutionary activity, but mainly on the suspicion of contacts with persons of radical views. In 1847 he left Russia for Western Europe. He was destined never to return. He was by now a very rich man, having inherited his father's fortune in 1846. After some years in France, Switzerland and Italy, during which he witnessed the revolutionary upheavals which began in 1848, he settled in England, in London, where he remained for over ten years. Here he founded a printing press and two free Russian periodicals – the *Polar Star* and *The Bell. The Bell*, which became the main vehicle for Herzen's political thought, circulated illegally but freely inside Russia and at any rate until 1863 exercised an enormous influence both through the opinions which it expressed and by the disclosure of facts suppressed by the censorship which Herzen learned from correspondents inside Russia.

Herzen was not a systematic political thinker, and his philosophy can perhaps best be sketched by outlining his main intellectual characteristics and preoccupation. He was a passionate lover of liberty – one of the deepest and earliest influences upon him was the legend of the Decembrists, and he solemnly dedicated himself at the age of sixteen (or so he afterwards claimed) to sacrifice his life to the liberation of Russia. But liberty to him always remained bound up with social justice. His travels in Western Europe, the failure of the revolution of 1848, the firm impact of Victorian England, where liberty and misery jostled each other side by side – all drove him to seek a solution for Russia which would avoid the, to him, repellent path of Western capitalism. This brought him very close to the views of the Slavophiles – like them, Herzen claimed to discern special virtues in the peculiar Russian tradition, and especially the peasant commune, in which he saw the main hope for a socialist future on specifically Russian lines which would show Europe the way which it had failed to find for itself after 1848. But, unlike the Slavophiles, Herzen had no use for religion, or for the Russian tradition of autocracy. He was essentially a rationalist, if an emotional and somewhat romantic rationalist. His writings exercised an enormous influence on the beginnings of the revolutionary movement in Russia – the slogan "Land and Liberty", in which the basic aims of the peasant were summed up by the revolutionaries until the advent of marxism, was coined by Herzen (with Ogarev). And yet he was not by temperament a revolutionary – he regarded revolution not, like Chernyshevsky, as the sole desirable aim, but as possibly inevitable though regrettable, and to be avoided if there were an alternative course. Perhaps the most attractive feature about Herzen was precisely this lack of commitment to a doctrine or "ism", in an age when such blind commitment was all too prevalent, and especially so among Russians. His discursive, sincere and moving record of his life, *My Past and Thoughts*, is one of the great monuments of Russian nineteenth-century literature, the record of a noble and tragic man, striving to the end to serve his people in the way that seemed best to him. The label "liberal" has been sometimes attached to Herzen, possibly under the influence of Lenin, who thus distinguished him from the "democrat" Chernyshevsky. The label is false – as indeed the quarrel, to which I am coming, will, I hope, show you. To be a liberal is to be one who thinks in terms of the growth of liberty within an order consisting of firmly rooted institutions, social and legal. The liberal process is a slow process, particularly where social justice is concerned. There are some who believe that it is the only sure process, if liberty is not to be engulfed and destroyed in the cataclysm which results when mankind seeks to accomplish social justice all at once. In this sense Herzen was never a liberal – "through socialism to liberty" remained his conviction, almost to the end of his life, though I think he began to doubt his faith towards the very end.

Ivan Turgenev, in contrast to Herzen, was primarily a creative writer – indeed some would adjudge him the greatest writer of Russian prose of all time. In his intimate letters there are several indications that political questions often repelled him and that he longed to escape into the realm of his pure art. But then, as now, a Russian writer could not cut himself off from the political reality which preoccupied all the active part of the society which he sought to describe. Turgenev, like Herzen, was a nobleman and a landowner, born on 28 October 1818 in the town of Orel. His childhood and adolescence were spent in the family estate, and Turgenev from an early age (unlike Herzen, whose youth was spent in Moscow) learned to know the realities of Russian village life and of serfdom, as well as of the arbitrary rule of the serf-owner which he could observe in the person of his tyrannical mother, who ran the estate. Ivan Turgenev studied in the University of Berlin and returned to Russia with the intention of entering the public service. But for this brilliant and socially successful young nobleman, who was beginning to make a reputation as a writer of distinction, and whose expectations of a future were considerable, the public service held few attractions. To a European and Westerner in temperament like Turgenev the constrictions of the Russia of Nicholas I became increasingly unbearable. In 1847, like Herzen, he left Russia for Germany and then for France, where most of the remainder of his life was to be spent. But unlike Herzen he never became an exile, and returned to Russia for short and longer visits on a number of occasions. Also, unlike Herzen, his departure from Russia was probably less a political act than the result of a desire to be near the Spanish singer Pauline Viardot, for whom he retained the closest attachment, possibly of a platonic character, till his death in 1883.

Certainly it is impossible to treat Turgenev as primarily a political thinker. And yet there is a consistency about his attitude to political problems which almost makes it possible to describe him as one of the few liberals, in the sense in which I have tried to define the term, in the history of Russian political thought. He had a sense of the importance of ordered and well-rooted institutions which few Russians have ever possessed. In a memorandum, only fairly recently discovered, which he wrote at the age of twenty-four, in 1842, as an exercise to qualify him for admission to the public service, he dealt with the question of serfdom from an angle which displayed a quite exemplary sense of the liberal view. He argued that the main defect of serfdom was that it prevented the development in Russia of legal order, on the basis of which alone the welfare of the country could flourish. So long as the peasants depended on the arbitrary will of the landlords, neither peasant nor landlord could develop a sense of law and order, and the landlords could not develop the sense of public service in running their estates which alone could lead to an improvement in agriculture. It was, I think, a remarkable and courageous perception of Russia's dominant social problem. Later, between 1847 and 1851, he developed his ideas in the masterly stories and sketches of village and peasant life, which were published collectively as *A Sportsman's Notebook*, in 1852. There is no doubt whatever that these sketches, which are a most unsentimental and yet moving and illuminating portrayal of Russian peasant life, exercised a considerable influence on the climate of opinion in which the Emperor's decision, after his accession in 1855, to put through the emancipation of the serfs took form. The *Sportsman's Notebook* was also Turgenev's only unqualified success with the radical intelligentsia, whom his liberalism and Westernism were in the future increasingly to antagonize or irritate. Indeed the quarrel with Herzen was far from the only one in Turgenev's life – there was bitter conflict with a number of others, including Dostoevsky and Tolstoy.

And yet such terms as "liberal" or "Westerner" are oversimplified and quite inadequate to describe the complex attitude of Turgenev to the peculiar problems of backward Russia. He was neither a blind admirer of Western Europe nor an advocate of indiscriminate imitation of its ways by Russia – though he was often to be accused of this by the over-sensitive Russian intellectuals. When Turgenev's most influential novel, *Fathers and Sons*, appeared in 1862 the radical intellectuals, almost to a man, treated it as an insult to all progressive thought and to Chernyshevsky in particular. This is the story of Bazarov, the medical student for whom Turgenev revived a forgotten term, the "nihilist", which won immediate currency as a term of abuse to be used against revolutionaries. Yet, as Pisarev was almost alone in perceiving, Turgenev's own sympathy (as we know from the revealing correspondence which passed between them) lay with Bazarov and the "sons", the determined and forthright materialists who took nothing on trust and who were determined to forge their own values for themselves.

Bazarov's early and pointless death from a virus infection contracted in the course of an autopsy, which he conducts just to keep himself in practice, his love for a woman which even in the throes of death he tries to reject as unworthy weakness, seem to me symbolical of Turgenev's sympathy and understanding for the plight of the reformers of the future in Russia: the endless morass of backward chaos with which they would have to contend, and the loneliness and human isolation in which they would have to live and die. But, like Pisarev, I remain in no doubt that Turgenev was on their side.

Turgenev and Herzen were temperamentally very different men, and were indeed never very close friends. I think Turgenev admired Herzen's generosity, his breadth of character, his sincerity and his humanity. But Herzen could never quite get over a certain contempt for the nobleman in exile, living in the train of Madame Viardot, the lion of French literary society, and the open admirer of European culture. It was not, for a man like Herzen, a serious life for a Russian intellectual. Herzen himself in London mixed very little with Englishmen, and spent all his time and energies on political activities and on contacts with other political émigrés. But in the spring of 1862 Turgenev visited London and spent many hours in political discussions with Herzen. The time was not propitious for relations between the two. For one thing, there had been signs of overt revolutionary activity in Russia in the course of the past year, which Turgenev regarded with open dismay as likely to arrest the process of reform on which the autocracy had embarked. Herzen, always equivocal on this issue, was also irritated by Turgenev's open disapproval of his close lifelong friend and collaborator on *The Bell*, Nikolai Ogarev, who was a much more extreme, Jacobin type of revolutionary than Herzen, and who at this period exercised a considerable influence over him. The publication of *Fathers and Sons* early in 1862 also served to exasperate Herzen's feelings towards a friend from whom he had been growing ever further apart. The result of the London conversations was the appearance in *The Bell*, between 1 July 1862 and 15 February 1863, of eight articles under the title "Ends and Beginnings". The articles and other matters of dispute led to correspondence between the two men, which lasted until April 1864, when the rupture of relations between the two took place. Relations were not resumed until 1867 and, certainly on Herzen's side at least, never recovered their former cordiality. We are concerned primarily with the difference of outlook which the articles and correspondence revealed. Yet the rupture was only in part due to this difference of opinion on a political question. In the course of 1863 and 1864 Turgenev received a summons from the Russian authorities to present himself for an examination into his political activities. He successfully resisted the order to return to Russia, and provided the authorities with a full, detailed and frank account of his activities and of his relations with politically suspect persons – including Herzen – over the past years. We now have the full text of his account as sent to the Russian investigating authorities. There is not a word in it that could fairly be regarded as reprehensible – there is no concealment of friendships, let alone denunciation of associates. After all, Turgenev had never been in any way connected with conspiratorial activity. He did not conceal his disapproval of the darker features of the Russian autocracy, but neither did he conceal his approval of the reforming activity of Alexander II. But for Herzen, who of course did not know the text of the account which we now have, the mere fact of treating with the authorities in this manner became an act of betrayal. He wrote a bitter attack on Turgenev and published it in *The Bell* on 15 January 1864, in which he referred to "a certain grey-haired Mary Magdalen (of the male sex) who wrote to the Emperor that she had lost her sleep, her appetite, her peace, her white hairs and her teeth through suffering at the thought that the Emperor did not yet know of the remorse which had overtaken her". It was an unpardonable attack, to which Turgenev reacted surprisingly mildly. Herzen's long reply, which ended relations, piled reproach upon reproach . . .

The argument in "Ends and Beginnings" and in Turgenev's letter in reply turns upon the question of the future of Russia's social and political development. In the course of his eight articles Herzen is concerned to contrast the "Ends" of Western Europe, which in his view has already passed the peak of its achievement and is sinking into bourgeois mediocrity, inhumanity and smug decay; and, in contrast, the as yet unexplored "Beginnings" of Russia, whose development has taken place quite outside the mainstream of European history, and whose potentialities for a more moral and socially just order are still unexplored. Herzen does not in these essays specifically reiterate his faith in the untapped potential for good of the Russian peasant, whom he regarded as socialist by instinct, but he had often used the argument before and would use it again, and it no doubt formed a part of the conversations in London with Turgenev earlier in the year. The decay of Europe, according to Herzen, has been precisely caused by the fact that, as he put it, "we have before us a civilization which has consistently developed on the basis of a landless proletariat, on the unconditional right of the owner over his property." According to Herzen, *The Times* a few days ago was congratulating Britain on its lack of interest in parliamentary debates, and "on the way in which workers died of hunger without a murmur" in contrast to their more turbulent Chartist fathers. Why should Russia go the same way? There was no law of conformity of development either in nature, or in history: "A mollusc does not strive to become a crayfish, a crayfish to become a trout, Holland to become Sweden . . ." Europe is old and decadent in its achievements – a hypocritical religion, and a liberalism which tolerates oppression and exploitation. Russia has achieved virtually nothing as yet, but has all before her: a kind of "cousin" in the Western European family coming late upon the scene, Russia will either achieve nothing, or will achieve something which will be peculiarly her own.

Herzen's articles are written with the passion which always characterized him. Turgenev's light banter in reply, though no doubt it contributed to the breach between the two men, nevertheless contains in essence a consistent view of Russia's destiny which he held all his life. (You will recall in this context the memorandum on serfdom to which I referred earlier, written twenty years before, which is already very similar in outlook.) "I am beginning to think," he writes to Herzen in November 1862, "that the so oft repeated antithesis between the West, beautiful on the outside and hideous within, and the East, hideous from the outside and beautiful within, contains a falsehood . . . Russia is no Venus of Milo . . . but a young woman no different from her sisters – except that she is a bit broader in the beam." Russia belongs to the European family, he writes a few days later; and "consequently, by the most immutable law of physiology, must travel the same road. I have yet to hear of a duck, which belonging to the species *duck*, nevertheless breathes with its gills, like a fish." What would you think, he adds, of a doctor who "having diagnosed all the symptoms of a chronic disease, declares that the trouble all stems from the fact that the patient is a Frenchman". Turgenev's banter obviously deeply offended Herzen, because his later letters take on a more serious, and defensive tone. (The quarrel was also exacerbated by some of the other causes of friction to which I have shortly referred, which supervened – the criticism of Herzen's friend Ogarev, and Turgenev's negotiations with the Emperor and the Russian police over his return to Russia, as well as other similar matters, such as Turgenev's refusal through caution to be published in *The Bell.*) Perhaps the substance of what Turgenev believed was contained in an earlier letter than the two from which I have quoted, dated 8 October 1862, which, although concerned with yet another disputed matter between the two, has a direct bearing on the argument with which I am concerned. Turgenev, in effect, in this letter is denying the basis of Herzen's faith – the superior instincts of the unspoilt Russian peasant – whom, of course, Turgenev knew at first hand, and Herzen knew hardly at all. "The role of the educated class in Russia," he writes, "is to transmit civilization to the mass of the people, so that they can decide for themselves what to accept and what to reject." He goes on to make a shrewd point: those who rely on the peasant as revolutionary material, he says, are in for disappointment: "The people, before whom you prostrate yourself, is conservative *par excellence*. Indeed, inside the peasant, tucked away with his sheepskin jacket, his warm, filthy hut, a belly stuffed to belching point and revulsion from any form of civic responsibility or self-reliance, are such bourgeois characteristics in embryonic form as will one day leave far behind them all the striking distinguishing marks of the Western bourgeoisie which you have depicted with such deadly accuracy."

The ideas and emotions which animated Turgenev in 1863 during his dispute with Herzen continued to ferment within him. No doubt the attacks on him for his supposedly uncritical admiration of the West, on his conduct in his relations with the Emperor as well as his criticism of the revolutionary radicals tormented him. At any rate, in 1867 there appeared his last novel but one, *Smoke*, in which his ideas on these subjects were systematically reformulated. *Smoke* is primarily a love story. The action is set in Baden-Baden, then a fashionable resort, in 1862. A young landowner, Litvinov, is awaiting the arrival of his betrothed, a simple, unspoilt Russian girl.

A chance meeting brings him in contact with his first love, Irina, who had been betrothed to him when he had been a student in Moscow. But Irina had failed him, she had been tempted by the prospects of the great fashionable world, to which her beauty and noble birth in spite of the poverty of her family offered admittance through a chance opportunity. Irina is now fashionably, but unhappily, married. The two fall passionately in love again, Litvinov breaks his engagement with his Tania, and arranges to fly with Irina. But at the last minute Irina once again fails him – she cannot face the break with the life which has grown indispensable to her, much as she hates it. Litvinov returns broken-hearted to his estate and after a few years once again finds his Tania. The two find happiness in their quiet marriage, devoting themselves to deeds of kindness and practical utility.

Summarized in this way it sounds banal. In Turgenev's hands the commonplace story acquires a magical beauty and inner depths of insight into the human predicament which make it for me one of the greatest of his great love stories. But its importance lies in the deliberate political overtones with which the author endowed it, which read very much like statements of his beliefs on fundamental issues – Westernism, and the Russian revolutionary radicals. With consummate skill Turgenev juxtaposes several of his convictions. Thus merciless satire on a group of rather worthless radicals who happen to be in Baden (and who are modelled on Herzen's friend Ogarev and on an actual Russian colony at the time in Heidelberg) is balanced by equally merciless satire of the brutish, reactionary generals and other dignitaries of the world of fashion who surround Irina. The moral that Turgenev is seeking to underline is that merely to see the radicals for what they are does not make a man into a reactionary upholder of all that is worst in Russian society. Again, the satire against Irina's world is extended to underline their aping of the worst features of French and German social life. This is in contrast with the long, but fascinating, speeches which Turgenev puts into the mouth of a somewhat mysterious but quite downright character called Potugin, who expatiates at great length on the ideas which Turgenev developed in 1862 in correspondence with Herzen. Again the moral is clear to see: to admire the West does not mean to accept uncritically for imitation by Russia all the features of French or German bourgeois life, but to recognize that the Western countries have advanced beyond Russia in the creation of certain institutions and a certain social order, and that Russia must, in order to advance, travel the same path, and cease – like Herzen and the Slavophiles – to glory in her backwardness.

Smoke was very badly received in Russia. Turgenev sent Herzen a copy, and used the occasion to renew the broken friendship. Herzen did not conceal his dislike of the novel, but he renewed the correspondence, if in somewhat distant terms. The old quarrel was not referred to. The last years of life which remained for Herzen were years of tragedy and frustration. He had suffered a number of family blows and bereavements. In politics he had begun to doubt his judgement and indeed his beliefs, and he felt that he was out of contact with the rising generation inside Russia, for whom his once great name no longer meant very much. The last, short entries in his diary which have come down to us are poignant and heartrending in their bitter despair and grief. In his last political writings, and especially in the three letters written shortly before his death to Bakunin, with whom he was now finally breaking, there are signs that Herzen had at long last come to believe that the gradual path of reform was to be preferred at all costs to the cataclysm of revolution; that his faith in the supposed socialist instincts of the Russian peasant had been misplaced; that even an oppressive state could not and should not be destroyed, but should be accepted as a stage through which all civilized societies had to pass, and could only be reformed by the perfecting of the individuals who composed it. But Herzen's political life and physical strength were exhausted. He died in Paris on 21 January 1870 and lies buried in Nice. Turgenev survived him for thirteen years.

I have suggested that Turgenev and Herzen each represented a mode of Russian political thought. I do not wish to imply by this that either of them had a systematic political philosophy, let alone that one was the antithesis of the other. There was indeed, in spite of difference in temperament, much in common between them. But there was one respect in which each approached the future destiny of Russia in a different way which is, I think, best illustrated in this conflict over "Ends and Beginnings". For Turgenev Russia always remained a backward member of the European family which had to overcome her backwardness before she could develop her true place in civilization. For Herzen Russia remained a repository of inner mystical spiritual gifts which would one day triumph over the forces of darkness which constrained and imprisoned them. Their two approaches to the problem of Russia's retarded development seem to me to have repeated themselves at the later stages of Russian political thought in a way which offers a parallel to this dispute of 1862. These parallels seem to me to justify the hypothesis which I have of two distinct modes of Russian political thought in relation to all important and quite real problems: granted that Russia was, as compared with the leading countries of Europe, backward in her industrial, economic, social and institutional development, what should be done about it? Was the answer quite simply that Russia had to make up for lost time, and catch up as fast as possible with her more advanced sister nations? Or were there certain inherent advantages in backwardness, a certain moral and spiritual superiority perhaps lurking behind the more distressing features of an apparently backward society, which would prove a blessing in disguise? And would enable Russia, provided she took the right course, to advance along a quite separate path of her own, and achieve in the end a different and indeed a far superior form of society as compared with the Western European capitalist form?

This was essentially the debate which took place in the last decade of the nineteenth century between leading political thinkers. The populist or *narodnik* revolutionary movement, whose activity culminated in the assassination of Alexander II on 1 March 1881, had exhausted itself as a revolutionary movement. This was due not only to the repressions which followed upon the assassination, severe as they were, but also to the realization that the murder of the Emperor had been a futile act which accomplished nothing. The intellectual populists of the nineties, sometimes called the "legal" populists, because they expounded their ideas within the permitted limits of censorship, did not advocate revolution. They were mainly concerned to argue that the development of the capitalist form of production in Russia was a historical impossibility. This was due to the lateness of Russia's entry into the race for markets: the foreign markets were already captured by the powers which had entered the race long before Russia, while the internal Russian market was quite inadequate to sustain large-scale capitalism. This they regarded as an undisguised blessing. They saw the right course of future development in agriculture based on the commune and in small-scale industry likewise grouped around the commune – the two together providing a healthy, satisfying and complete social order, particularly consonant with what they believed were the socialist instincts and traditions of the Russian peasant. They were optimistic for the success of this development because the autocracy – if for quite different reasons of its own – was determined to shore up the communal land system, which was in fact already showing signs of disintegration.

By this date marxism was already becoming a serious intellectual movement, at any rate, and for some years in the course of the decade we are now considering the main brunt of the marxist's argument was directed against the populists. Marxists, like Plekhanov and Struve, and later the young Lenin, argued that the disintegration of the commune was already a fact, and a welcome fact. They further contended that the historical process of development was the same in Russia as everywhere else – from feudalism to capitalism, and then to socialism. Capitalist development in Russia was therefore a welcome, and, they argued fiercely, a possible, course: it would come inevitably (Lenin even argued that it had already come) and everything should be done to speed it up. It would of course take a long time – though Plekhanov argued that because Russia was a latecomer in the capitalist race, the process would in fact be much speedier than it had been in Western Europe. As for backwardness, as Struve put it in 1894, in a phrase which became famous: "Let us acknowledge our backwardness and become apprentices to capitalism."

Now, of course, these were rational, internationalist, materialist, modern marxist determinists arguing against the populists, who were traditionalists in many ways, and had been strongly nationalistic. It may be said that there was nothing surprising or remarkable about the fact that they took up these diametrically opposite standpoints. But the human temperament is not quite as simple as that. Before very long the same, or a very similar kind of division seems to me to have taken place within the marxist movement itself. In 1903 the Russian social democratic movement split into two – the Bolsheviks, led by Lenin, and the Mensheviks, led by Martov. This is, of course, an oversimplification, because there were many trends in Menshevism, and a lack of unity among the Bolsheviks too. But it *is* true that there was always a broad division of the movement into two, which often seems to have been much more temperamental than doctrinal. And at the root of the division, in my view, was this eternal question of Russia's backwardness. After all, Russia in 1903, or for that matter in 1917, was not even remotely the kind of country that Marx had written about: the proletariat was still quite small, and the overwhelming majority of the population was made up of peasants. Full-scale industrialization still lay ahead, though a very remarkable start had been made. Logically, or at any rate in accordance with the logic of Marx, full-scale development of capitalism, and therefore of bourgeois democracy, had to precede socialism. This not only involved waiting a very long time, generations probably, but in the meantime – again, logically, and revolution has very little to do with logic – in the meantime, the social democrats would have to learn to co-operate with the bourgeois parties, to develop the mass worker movement, the trade union movement, and the like. To Lenin this prospect was repugnant – there are also many indications in his writings that he suspected that once the bourgeois system had established itself solidly in Russia it would be extraordinarily difficult to get rid of it. And so to Lenin, though of course in quite a different way from Herzen or the "legal" populists, backwardness became an advantage: it provided the ideal society in which a well-organized, disciplined conspiratorial communist party could strangle capitalism at birth, and then proceed to institute socialism. How far he succeeded I leave to others to judge. But, so far as the Mensheviks were concerned, they were on the whole more sceptical about the possibility of instituting a socialist order by dictatorship from above. Hence backwardness for them remained, as it was for Turgenev, something which Russia had to overcome broadly in the same way as it had been overcome in the Western European countries. In other words, they tended increasingly after 1903 when they broke with Lenin to lay stress on the development of workers' organizations, or some kind of co-operation with the semi-democratic, semi-constitutional regime set up in 1906, or longer-term aims of revolution, and so forth. In other words, they were becoming something like a Western social democratic party. They were, of course, never consistent or fully logical in their policy – that is probably why they were swept away so easily by Lenin in 1917. But that is another story.

I do not wish to overstress the parallel between 1863 and the 1890s, or the years 1903–1917 – there are innumerable differences of circumstance, doctrine and tactics. But the problem of Russia's backwardness was, and is, a real and continuing one. It was bound to underlie the eternal search for the right and true path of progress upon which successive generations of Russian intellectuals embarked. It is for this reason that I have ventured to deal with this quarrel of a century ago – between two of the greatest, the most sincere and devoted, and the most intellectually honest thinkers of the nineteenth century in Russia.

A Story of Incompatibility: Dostoevsky and Turgenev

This article originally appeared in *Adam International Review*, nos. 437–39, 1981.

There could have been no greater contrast than that between these two giants of Russian nineteenth-century literature. For Dostoevsky the spiritual message which he sought to convey was of first importance. Turgenev was above all and primarily a craftsman. There is a message to be found in his works – or in some of them – because no one could write with insight about nineteenth-century Russia without commenting on the burning questions which obsessed all Russian intellectuals. But Turgenev consciously rejected the role of propagandist, thus winning enemies both on the left and on the right of the political spectrum, who could not understand, or forgive, the fact that his concern was with human beings before political issues. Dostoevsky was a fervent Christian, a nationalistic, orthodox Christian. Turgenev was an agnostic, who frequently expressed regret that the certainty and consolation of religious faith were not possible for him. Dostoevsky's love of Russia was not only an intense passion, but an uncritical passion, heavily tinged with his belief that the Russian people were not only a "God-bearing" people, but had a messianic mission to perform in history. Turgenev's love of Russia was probably no less intense, but much more rational, tempered with critical evaluation of both faults and virtues – an attitude, described by one of his characters in *Smoke* as "odi et amo", which won him many enemies and unfair accusations.

There were other contrasts, too. If the keynote of much of Dostoevsky's work can be subsumed in the epithet "will", for Turgenev the equivalent is "fate" and "resignation". Much of Turgenev's life and work can indeed be explained in terms of a longing and admiration for the kind of all-consuming will which he himself lacked. This longing recurs repeatedly in his fiction, it is expressed in his admiration for Schopenhauer and probably underlay his belated flirtation with revolutionary activity for a short period in Russia in 1879. Dostoevsky, certainly from the period when he was working on *The Possessed* onwards, developed an obsessive hatred of radicalism in all its forms, which he believed originated in atheism. Turgenev rejected revolution along with all political violence and all dogmatic once-for-all solutions of human problems in favour of piecemeal, gradual reforms on liberal principles. But he had a deep admiration for all human beings who had the qualities of integrity and singleness of purpose, even where he disagreed with their views – such as Belinsky, Herzen, George Sand, or Lavrov, to name only a few. His friendship with the Aksakovs and Kireevsky, Slavophiles whose views he rejected, showed that this prevalence of human criteria over the political was not confined to his attitude to those of radical opinions. Finally one should perhaps mention the social gap that existed between the two men – Dostoevsky, the frequently impoverished son of a fairly humble army doctor, Turgenev the great aristocrat and heir to an estate of thousands of serfs. That this contrast in social status between the two writers rankled in Dostoevsky's heart is shown by contemptuous references in his correspondence to the other man's "aristocraticism", and the like.

The inevitable quarrel happened in Baden, in 1867. Relations until then if not cordial had been friendly, at any rate outwardly. Dostoevsky wrote after the quarrel that he never really "liked the man". Turgenev for his part occasionally upset the over-sensitive Dostoevsky by his satirical mockery, and, up to the period of his arrest, penal servitude and exile (1848–59) his comments on him suggest a dislike of what he saw as vanity and pretentiousness. Of Dostoevsky's writings, Turgenev expressly praised very few works – *Poor Folk* certainly, *Memoirs from the House of the Dead* and the first part only of *Crime and Punishment*. His letters to Dostoevsky during the first half of the sixties are warm, almost affectionate, and express concern for the efforts which Feodor Dostoevsky and his brother Michael were making to produce a literary journal. How sincere these letters were is another matter. Dostoevsky admired the more "Slavophile" of Turgenev's works – *A Sportsman's Notebook* and *A Nest of the Country Gentry* and apparently also *Fathers and Sons* ("apparently" because his comments are lost. But we know that Turgenev maintained that only Dostoevsky and no other had properly understood his hero Bazarov.)

The immediate cause of the quarrel was Turgenev's novel *Smoke*, which offended all sides in Russia by its merciless satirization of both the radicals and the conservatives (the "planters", as the author calls them), but especially by its attacks on the Slavophiles and its criticism of Russian faults from the point of view of a confirmed Westerner – views which Turgenev in effect admitted were his own. On 28 June 1867 Dostoevsky called on Turgenev who was living in Baden. He described what happened in a long letter of 16 August to the poet Maikov. He found Turgenev at lunch. "To tell you the truth, I never liked this man even before as a person . . . I also detest his autocratic, pharisaical way . . . of coming at you to embrace you, and then thrusting forward his own cheek for you to kiss." Dostoevsky in his letter made three charges against Turgenev. First, that he was an atheist. Second, that he hated Russia. He quoted a phrase from *Smoke* and said that it expressed the main thought of the book: "If Russia were to be sunk without trace there would be no loss or cause of excitement for mankind." Third, that he claimed to be a German. As Dostoevsky was leaving, he says, he made some derogatory remark about the Germans, to which Turgenev retorted: "In speaking like that you offend me personally. You must know that I have finally settled here, that I regard myself as a German and not as a Russian, and that I am proud of this." Dostoevsky added that he promised himself never to see Turgenev again. "He has offended me too much with his convictions." When Turgenev heard that the letter had been deposited in a documentary library for the benefit of posterity (we now know that it was not deposited by Dostoevsky) he wrote to the editor of the journal produced by this library giving his version of the incident. He denied that he had confided any of his innermost convictions to Dostoevsky, if only because he considered him a sick man who was not in full possession of his mental faculties. Dostoevsky had "relieved his spirits" with violent abuse of the Germans, but he, Turgenev, had had neither the time nor the inclination to retort.

It is improbable that either man was telling the whole truth. Turgenev, as has already been noted, was not an atheist, and on no known occasion claimed to be anything more positive than an agnostic. The suggestion that Turgenev "hated" Russia must appear palpably absurd to anyone who has read *A Sportsman's Notebook* or *A Nest of the Landed Gentry*, and is contradicted at every step by his whole life as we know it. He certainly admired Germany and was a Westerner by taste and inclination. But it would have been inconsistent with everything we know of his outlook for him to have declared that he now regarded himself as a German, and not a Russian. On the other hand, it is extremely improbable that one of Turgenev's argumentative temperament would have listened in silence to the diatribes of a man whom in his heart he probably disliked and perhaps somewhat despised.

For the next few years Dostoevsky brooded over his detestation of Turgenev whom, in the course of his work on *The Possessed*, he came to regard as one of the generation which by its radicalism, Westernism and rejection of Orthodox Christianity had brought Russia to the brink of disaster. The cruel satirization of Turgenev in the person of the "great writer" Karmazinov was the result. It is a merciless caricature, but like the most brutal of caricatures it contains elements of truth. Some of the physical traits can be recognized – the large fleshy nose for example, or the manner of speech. Other aspects of the description are so loaded with malice, and inaccurate malice at that, that they reflect more on Dostoevsky's obsessional frame of mind than on Turgenev's character – such as accusations of social climbing, intense snobbery, and complete lack of talent – "an old woman who has lost all the talent for writing she ever had". However, the satire on Turgenev's literary style – the description in *The Possessed* of the public reading by Karmazinov of his sketch "Merci" – reveals careful analysis and exploitation of the two works of Turgenev which even his greatest admirers would not regard as anywhere near his best – *Ghosts* and *Enough*. The satirization of *Ghosts* is of particular interest, since this was the study that Turgenev, at Dostoevsky's insistent request, wrote for the latter's journal, *Epokha*. Turgenev, who was of course deeply hurt by the satire on him in *The Possessed*, commented in correspondence with a friend that Dostoevsky had praised *Ghosts* to the skies in a letter to him. What Turgenev did not know was that at the same time, in a letter to his brother Michael, he was most uncomplimentary about both the story and its author.

The quarrel was never patched up. The two men met on at least two occasions before Dostoevsky's death in 1881. One was in 1879, in Petersburg, when Turgenev on a visit to Russia was fêted and idolized, especially by radical students – and, be it said, rather lost his sense of proportion in some of the things he said publicly to and about the radical revolutionaries whose violent activity he certainly did not approve. Turgenev seems to have been mistakenly convinced that all the radicals were trying to achieve was a constitutional regime – in fact, as the documents now available show, they were hell-bent on the violent destruction of the whole social and political order. In the course of a speech at a dinner, Turgenev made some optimistic remarks about the bright future which lay ahead for Russia. What he clearly meant was the grant by the Emperor of the constitution to the achievement of which he mistakenly believed the violence of the radicals to be directed. What Dostoevsky apparently took him to mean was revolution. An unpleasant scene, of which several descriptions exist, ensued.

The last meeting between the two men was, outwardly at any rate, more happy. It occurred in June 1880 during festivities lasting several days on the occasion of the unveiling of a monument to Pushkin in Moscow – the intellectual centre of the Slavophiles. Numerous speeches were delivered. Turgenev's relatively moderate appreciation of Pushkin, in which he doubted whether Pushkin had become a world poet, was coldly received. The highlight of the proceedings was undoubtedly Dostoevsky's speech, which was greeted with wild enthusiasm. His assertion that the Russian soul, as symbolized by Pushkin, strove towards the ultimate goal of achieving universal man struck a deep response from the Muscovite audience of intellectuals and students. At one moment in his speech, while praising the chastity and modesty of Pushkin's Tatiana, he linked with hers the name of Turgenev's Liza. Turgenev was visibly moved and blew Dostoevsky a kiss – according to some accounts he went up and embraced him.

But there was no question of a reconciliation. Turgenev was severely critical in a letter to his friend and editor Stasiulevich of Dostoevsky's speech. It was brilliant, he wrote, but totally false. Tatiana had been subtly described – but did only *Russian* wives remain faithful to their old husbands? And what is the point of this universal man? "It is much better to be an original Russian than a depersonalized all-man."

When Dostoevsky died Turgenev contributed twenty-five roubles towards a monument, but said or wrote nothing in public about him. In a private letter he pointed out what he regarded as elements of de Sade in Dostoevsky's writings. "And to think that all the arch-priests in Russia celebrated requiem masses for our de Sade . . ." The gulf which divided the two men continued beyond death.

The Triumph of Humanity in Turgenev's Work

This article was originally delivered as a lecture at the Turgenev Symposium at Yale University, 8–10 April 1983.

This paper is in substance an attempt to look at Turgenev's religious beliefs, as they appear in his writings. We have much evidence of his attitude to institutionalized religion: he respected, even envied, those who could find the consolation in it that was denied to him – as we know, for example, from his many letters to Countess Lambert. There is ample evidence in his correspondence of his distaste for the Church in Italy. Orthodoxy, on the other hand, held some attraction for him, partly because of the beauty of its service.

He attended the Russian Church in the rue Daru when he was in Paris, and the village church occasionally on his visits to Spasskoe. But the main appeal for him, I believe, lay in the human virtues which the Orthodox Church proclaims – humility, acceptance, submission. These are the keynotes of *Dvorianskoe Gnezdo*, for example – what Appolon Grigoriev calls Turgenev's protest against the predatory type of Russian in the name of the good, the simple and the humble. "Humility before the soil [*pochva*] and before reality arose in Turgenev's soul as the soul of a great artist, from the soil itself . . ." he says of Lavretsky. Portrayal of this Orthodox humility offers some of the most moving instances of Turgenev's works, and, not unnaturally, won him the admiration of the Slavophiles, whose doctrines, actually, were repugnant to him, and whose compliments somewhat embarrassed him. I am thinking, in particular, of Gerasim in "Mumu" who drowns his beloved dog because his mistress complains about it; or of Akim, in "Postoialy Dvor", who accepts with complete forgiveness ruin and degradation inflicted on him by his wife and her lover – both stories which were written around the same time, 1852–4, when he was living in exile in Spasskoe.

Probably the most complete example of this aspect of Turgenev's art is in "Zhivie Moshchi" which is now part of *Zapiski Okhotnika*. Although it was only published in 1874, it was probably first conceived, if not written, at the end of the 1840s or at the beginning of the 1850s, and was certainly based on fact. The bed-ridden Lukeria is simple and pious, with complete faith that heaven is her next destination. But the main emphasis in the story is not on piety, which is only incidental. The real stress is on Lukeria's humility, her delight in what natural beauty she can see from her bed of sickness, her undemanding contentment. The only thing she asks of the visiting young master is that he should persuade his mother to reduce the *obrok* on the peasants. It is unlikely that this saintliness of Lukeria, whose lover Turgenev may have been years before he encountered her smitten with illness, had remained forgotten in his mind until resurrected in written form for a symposium in aid of the victims of a famine in Samara government. It is more probable to suppose that it made a lasting impression on him, and that its influence was reflected in many of his stories and novels.

The young Turgenev may have been a traditional romantic atheist. In an early letter to Granovsky, from Berlin on 30 May 1840, he enthuses about Feuerbach, the modern originator of the materialist explanation of religion. A few years later, in reaction to reading Calderon's *La Devoción de la Cruz* he wrote the following to Pauline Viardot, which I quote at length because it shows the ambivalence of Turgenev's attitude to faith and to the humility and submission which in his view derive from it.

Calderon, he writes, is the greatest Catholic dramatic poet, just as Shakespeare is "the most human, the most anti-Christian". Calderon's "immovable, triumphing faith, without a shadow of doubt or even passing doubt, crushes you with the force of its grandeur and majesty, in spite of everything that is repellent and cruel in this doctrine. This denial, in face of the divine will, of everything that makes up a man's dignity, the indifference to everything we call virtue and vice with which grace descends on its elect – all this is a triumph for the human spirit. For the being that announces in this way with such daring his own nothingness raises himself at the same time to a state of equality with this fanciful Deity, whose plaything he admits he is. And this Deity is, moreover, the work of his own hands. Nevertheless, I prefer Prometheus, I prefer Satan, who stands for the rebellion of the individual. Atom as I am, it is I who am my master. I want truth, and not salvation, and I look to my intellect for that, and not to grace."

Humanity, truth, intellect – Turgenev retained his faith in all of these. But before long I believe this faith, while preserving the human element as its centre, began to acquire new aspects: goodness, kindness, love – in the sense of *agape*, not *eros* – the love that unites, not the love that delights, in the words of Bersenev in *Nakanune*.

"Yakov Pasynkov" was written in 1855–6, and most probably portrays in its main character something of both Belinsky and Stankevich, heroes of Turgenev's early youth. Pasynkov is poor and ungainly, but is near to saintliness in his sincerity, and in kindness and uprightness, devotion to the search for truth, and selfless dedication to his friends – his *agape*. There is virtually no story in "Yakov Pasynkov": its aim is to paint a picture of what to its author seemed the most admirable qualities that a man could possess. Pasynkov earns no laurels in his short life: the clear moral of the story is that what matters is not what you achieve in life, but what you *are* as a human being. It is also of interest to note that around the same time he wrote the Epilogue to *Rudin* at the insistence of his friend Botkin that he could not leave so unfavourable an impression of Bakunin, who had been imprisoned in 1855, as that presented by the main bulk of the novel, where he appears as a defeated and cowardly poseur. In the Epilogue, Rudin is redeemed by Lezhnev's *agape*, which helps him to see that what matters is not a man's achievement, but his quality as a human being. It is perhaps not too fanciful to see both in "Yakov Pasynkov" and in the Epilogue to *Rudin* the influence of Granovsky, who had died in October 1855, and whom Turgenev venerated. He may have known of Granovsky's belief, expressed in a lecture on Louis IX in 1850: "The great actors in history and the small . . . are alike bound by the duty to labour in the sweat of their brow. But they bear responsibility only for the purity of their intentions . . . Their actions enter history as mysteriously as a seed falls in the soil. The ripening of the harvest, the time of the harvesting, and the yield all belong to God."

Rudin seems to have marked a watershed in Turgenev's creative life. Although he had first thought of the theme of *Dvorianskoe*

Gnezdo in the autumn of 1856, it was not finished until two years later. The lecture on "Hamlet and Don Quixote", which had been in his mind for perhaps as long as ten years before, was written during an interruption in the writing of *Dvorianskoe Gnezdo* and after the completion of the novel, in December 1859. It is, so far as I am aware, the first clear, explicit statement of Turgenev's faith in the abiding, eternal value of *agape*. Let me quote the concluding lines of this marvellous lecture:

> The death of Don Quixote moves our heart with a tenderness beyond words. At this instant all the great significance of this personage becomes accessible to everyone. When his former armour-bearer, wishing to comfort him, tells him that they will soon once again be off on knightly adventures, "No," replies the dying man, "all that is over for ever and I ask forgiveness of all. I am no longer Don Quixote, I am now again Alonso the Good, as they used to call me once – Alonso el Bueno."
>
> The word is remarkable, the mention of this name, for the first and last time, overwhelms the reader. Yes, it is this one word that still has significance in the face of death. All will pass, all will disappear, the most exalted rank, power, all-embracing genius, all will vanish as the dust . . . But good deeds will not vanish in smoke: they are more permanent than the most radiant beauty. "All will perish," said the apostle, "only love [*liubov*] will remain."

The reference by Turgenev is presumably to the First Epistle to the Corinthians, Chapter 13, verse 8: "Charity never faileth; but whether there be prophecies, they shall fail; whether there be tongues, they shall cease; whether there be knowledge, it shall vanish away." The word "charity" in our Revised Version is the equivalent of *agape* in Greek, and of "love", *liubov* in Russian, which has no separate words for *agape* and *eros*.

The notion that only goodness survives the grave, that what matters in a human being is not his achievements or lack of them, but the purity and kindness, his *agape*, in his relations with his fellow men, occurs again in the last lines of *Osty i Deti*; as Bazarov's old parents pray at his grave: "Can it be that love, holy devoted love is not all-powerful? Oh, no! Whatever the passionate, sinful and rebellious heart that has been covered by the grave, the flowers that grow on it look on at us serenely with their innocent eyes. They do not speak to us only of eternal peace, of that great power of 'indifferent nature'; they speak also of eternal reconciliation and of the life everlasting." The last sentence, which echoes the Orthodox service for the dead, provoked an accusation from Herzen that Turgenev had become religious. I think it was true only in the sense that he had come to believe that the only eternal value of life was the love by which human beings are united one to another. The last coherent words which he uttered on his death-bed, as Prince Meshchersky heard them, when his mind was wandering and he appeared to imagine himself as a dying patriarch, giving advice to his daughter on bringing up her son, were: "It doesn't matter, so long as he is good, is good . . . is honest . . . Bring him up in truth, let him be loving . . ." Whether this view of love amounts to a religion is not for me to judge. But I am reminded of the fact that teachers of many faiths have told us that love is the central and abiding element of the way of religious life; and that Dante ends the *Divine Comedy* at the culmination of his ascent to Paradise with the overwhelming words: "My will and my desire were turned by love/ The love that moves the sun and the other stars."

The acceptance by Turgenev of love and goodness as an end in themselves, not for what they achieve in practice but as something that of themselves make up the element within us which is eternal – in religious terms, I suppose, which is God – is closely related to other aspects of his faith. It explains, in the first place, why he rejected the submission of the individual will of man to the divine will, the abasement before a God whom he himself has invented (as Feuerbach and Turgenev believed). This is, at any rate, how Turgenev, rightly or wrongly, understood the Catholic faith in 1847. In place of that, he accepted the humility and submission, the willing renunciation of Gerasim, Akim or Lavretsky. For this humility, I think, he saw as being brought into being by love, and not by fear. When, in June 1859, he read the *Pensées* of Pascal, it made an enormous impression on him as "the most frightening, the most disheartening book which was ever printed", as he wrote to Pauline Viardot. "This man tramples on everything which is most dear to you, throws you down in the mud, and then, for your comfort, offers you a religion which is bitter and violent and which brutalizes you (the word is his) – a religion which the intellect (that of Pascal himself) cannot fail to reject, but which the heart must *accept* by *contrition* . . . Human character is the opposite of this.

And I would dare add, Christianity is the opposite too – from the instant it has been reduced to the narrow and craven doctrine of personal salvation, of selfishness." (The last sentence is as he wrote it, if the letter is correctly transcribed by Granjard and Zviguilsky: Turgenev must have meant "from the instant that it has *not* been reduced, etc.")

Another aspect of Turgenev's faith which I believe to be closely related to his rejection of the omnipotent, cruel and severe God which he saw in the Church, or at any rate in the Catholic Church, was his obsession with nature, as a blind force, indifferent to the fate of man on earth, and engaged in the pursuit of its own, materialistic ends. The idea occurs repeatedly in Turgenev's letters and writings. It is the central theme of "Dovolno" – which Dostoevsky ridiculed so mercilessly in *Besy*.

I cannot be certain that this notion of nature is linked with what I believe Turgenev saw as the divine and transcendent element in man – his *agape*. But it seems to me likely that the idea of nature as remote and indifferent to the individual is not too far removed from the concept of a remote, indifferent and external God which he derived from his interpretation of Calderon or Pascal. Certainly, his view of nature recurs repeatedly in his letters and writings and obviously held a deep meaning for him. The underlying thought of "Dovolno" is the impotence of man in the path of all-devouring, indifferent nature. Since art is not an imitation of nature (where in nature are there to be found the symphonies of Beethoven?), it is a temporary consolation. Nature "creates, as she destroys, but is quite indifferent to what she creates, or what she destroys: she is concerned only that life should go on, and that death should not lose its rights." The only dignity left to man is to turn away, and say "enough". Turgenev then paraphrases Pascal's reflection (in *Pensées*, Paragraph 347) that man who is as insignificant as a reed when crushed by the force of the universe, is nevertheless superior to the universe because he knows he is being crushed, and the universe does not.

As I have said, we cannot be sure that Turgenev's views of man in relation to God and eternity and his picture of nature are related, though I feel that they are. We are on firmer ground when we come to consider Turgenev's views on love, since here the direct contrast between *eros* and *agape* comes into question. The theme which runs constantly through his work, from the beginning to the end of his creative life, is the degradation and enslavement which a man in love, i.e. in the throes of *eros*, has to suffer, in contrast to the sublimity of *agape*, when once, all passion spent, that can be attained. No doubt this attitude was influenced by his relations with Pauline Viardot where the sexual bond played at most little, and possibly even no part, but the unity of *agape* was unbroken, on his side at all events, from youth until old age.

A moving letter to Pauline Viardot, written at the end of 1870, when Turgenev was fifty-two, seems to me to epitomize what he felt for her: "... time goes slowly without you ... To the deep and unchanging feeling that I have for you there has become added some kind of impossibility of being without you ... When you are there my joy is serene ... Ah, dear friend, I have all the past twenty-seven years to treasure ... and it will be as it was for Burns's 'Joe Anderson my Joe' [*sic*] we will go down the hill together."

The physical side of love, in general, seems to have meant little to Turgenev – perhaps that was why he was able to respond so deeply to the appeal of the serenity of *agape*. There are references to casual sexual encounters in his correspondence ("No, my friend, at our years once in three months is enough," he wrote in February 1859, at the age of forty-one.) There are also hints of a somewhat senile sexuality in his affairs with Baroness Vrevskaia and with the actress Savina. What we do not find in Turgenev's life is the kind of all-consuming, all-devouring sexual hurricane that sweeps Sanin to oblivion in *Veshniia Vody*. The picture we get in that story of the sexual passion as indifferent nature, sweeping all before it, and concerned with the one object of continuing the species, derives from Schopenhauer's essay on "The Metaphysics of the Love of the Sexes". The story ends with the prospect of Sanin's redemption through *agape* – the forgiveness of Gemma, and his move to America to enjoy his declining years, all passion spent, in her proximity. The love of Sanin for Gemma which survives, which is eternal, is not the passion of a young man for a pretty girl, but the abiding love which is free from the restless drive of "indifferent nature" – the love of two human beings bound by sympathy, kindness and respect. A very similar idea is to be found in *Dym*, written some years earlier. The reconciliation with Tatiana with which the book ends has never struck me as artistically very convincing. But in terms of the contrast between *eros* (Irina) and *agape* (Tatiana), the incident bears out Turgenev's preoccupation with two kinds of love.

I believe that this commitment to the pre-eminence in life of human relations of love, undistorted by passion or by the impersonal forces of nature, determined much of Turgenev's attitude to other questions. Of course, man is frail, and Turgenev did not live up to his principles on all occasions. His repulsing of his daughter towards the end of his life, for example, when Paulinette's disastrous marriage had broken up, and she was forced to flee from her violent husband, does not make agreeable reading. But it can be said in his defence that while he showed little sympathy for her, he did provide her with some money; and that the last, pathetic appeal from her, which remained unanswered, was dated little more than four months before he died, when he was already very ill. There were also some other instances in his life which are quite inconsistent with the kind and loving behaviour which generally characterizes Turgenev.

It is not, in my view, too fanciful to discern a connection between this elevation by Turgenev of *agape* in human relations to the position of primary importance (which I believe should be seen as a form of religious commitment) and his general attitude to social and political questions. If once the way in which human beings behave one to another becomes the main criterion in determining supreme values in life, there is no room any longer for those instant, theoretical, all-embracing panaceas, designed to solve all problems at a stroke, which were so dear to many of Turgenev's fellow Russians. This is because these abstract, theoretical solutions are remote from the human beings who are affected by their results – whether it be revolution in France, revolt in Poland, or prospective revolution in Russia. The important matter in life for Turgenev is neither system, nor abstract formula or theory, but human beings in their interrelation with one another. The message of *Nov*, whose real hero is Solomin, is that revolutionary activity is of little if any value – true revolution means devoting oneself to practical service to the people – one must "raise the depths" of the virgin soil, as the epigraph to the book proclaims.

Let me close this rather too discursive discussion with the reflection that perhaps the lesson of Turgenev's faith is still alive in

Russia today. This is what an anonymous uncensored voice which came out of the Soviet Union in 1968 had to say, after rejecting socialism as the hope for a better society, because (in his words) "socialism alone doesn't make good men, good buildings, good anything . . . Then what is important? It sounds banal. Self-improvement. Individual effort. Study and thought for one's own moral development. The classical liberal virtues. Being honest and loyal and kind to the ten people closest to me rather than professing my good intentions to world history or social movements."

I think Turgenev would have approved of these words.

Michael Bakunin: Through Chaos to Utopia

This review of Arthur P. Mendel, *Michael Bakunin: Roots of Apocalypse*, Holt-Saunders (Eastbourne 1982) and Aileen Kelly, *Michael Bakunin: A Study in the Psychology and Politics of Utopianism*, Clarendon Press, (Oxford 1982) originally appeared in the *Times Literary Supplement*, 13 May 1983.

It was to be expected that the spate of material on Bakunin which has been made available in recent years should tempt further biographers. That indefatigable scholar, Arthur Lehning, has laboured hard to edit and publish the rich store of Bakunin documents which was acquired in 1936 by the International Institute of Social History in Amsterdam. This came mainly from the library of Max Nettlau, a scholar of independent means who devoted his life to the study of anarchism. He died in 1944, at the age of seventy-nine. He was the author, among many other writings, of a monumental biography in German of Bakunin, in three volumes, comprising over twelve hundred pages. Each page was written by him on wax paper and duplicated on an "auto-copier", and the forty copies so produced were sent to friends and major libraries, including the British Museum. After the reopening of the Institute, which the Germans had closed down in 1940, publication of Bakuniniana was embarked on, and seven fat volumes of *Archives Bakounine* have appeared since 1961.

Arthur P. Mendel started to write his book because he felt that E. H. Carr's biography did not sufficiently appreciate Bakunin's contribution to freedom: he finished the book convinced that no biographer of the anarchist aristocrat had adequately realized the threat which he posed to freedom, or the fact that along with passionate ranting about unlimited liberty, Bakunin, whether aware of the contradiction or not, was at the same time propounding "rigid authoritarianism". Actually, Carr, in his masterly biography, was alive to this inherent inconsistency in Bakunin's outlook. "Bakunin," he writes, "is known to the world as one of the founders of anarchism. It is less often remembered that he was the first originator of the conception of a select and closely organized revolutionary party, bound together not only by common ideals, but by the tie of implicit obedience to an absolute revolutionary dictator." But Mendel's main concern is to search for the roots of the crying inconsistency in Bakunin's political theories in the character of the man whose "anarchist, antinomian freedom was born not of the heroic strength and courage it seems to reflect, but rather of weakness, fear and flight". We are accordingly invited throughout the book, at all stages of Bakunin's troubled life, to pray in aid psychoanalytical explanations, such as narcissism and the "Oedipus link" with his mother. The case which Mendel makes seems convincing – how valid can be judged, if at all, only by specialists in psychoanalysis – insofar as this method is capable of being applied to subjects long dead.

The negative sides of Bakunin are well known. He seems to have lived his life in a dream world of his own making, like an overgrown child, afraid to face reality. He was tyrannical in his behaviour, anti-semitic, domineering, intolerant and meddlesome, with no sense of social responsibility. He borrowed money whenever he could, with little prospect – or, for that matter, intention – of paying it back. The charge of dishonesty by which Marx secured his expulsion from the international in 1872 was untrue. But there are enough discreditable episodes in Bakunin's career which were genuine.

Yet, by itself, this catalogue gives an incomplete picture of the man, because it leaves out of account his extraordinary power of charming and fascinating, if only for a time, those with whom he came in contact. He would also act nobly on occasion. In Dresden, in 1849, after the failure of the attempted insurrection, he could easily have escaped. But, as he wrote later, "I could not bring myself to desert poor Heubner", a fellow insurgent who would not abandon his post even when all was already lost. This cost Bakunin over ten years of prison and exile.

He was a most powerful orator, in spite of the barrier of having to use languages foreign to him. He exercised an enormous influence over would-be intellectual revolutionaries, romantics like himself, intoxicated by the appeals to violence and destruction, and little concerned with the improbability and the patent inconsistency of the promised utopia.

Both his latest biographers, Arthur Mendel and Aileen Kelly, are fully aware of the discreditable aspects of Bakunin's career, and devote much space to them. Both, like Carr before them, agree that his theoretical writings are riddled with inconsistencies, interesting for psychological reasons only. But where Professor Mendel calls Freud in aid, Dr Kelly is concerned with "utopian psychology". The passage of time has probably put Bakunin in perspective: the riddles in his career have been solved, so far as the facts are concerned. His theoretical writings tend mostly to appeal to those who are emotionally drawn to them, rather than to those who are intellectually converted. He has thus become a subject for the psychologist, rather than the political philosopher – or perhaps, the political philosopher must, like the two authors with whom I am concerned, turn psychologist in order to interpret this extraordinary man.

But the mythology which surrounds Bakunin's life, and which was first circulated by his early admirers, is not dead. Thus, Kelly takes Lehning to task for reasserting, in his "extensive introductions and commentaries to the volumes relating to Bakunin's activities in the International, Bakunin's inventions", enshrining them as the one true version of the events, and omitting "the evidence which subsequently discredited the denials of Bakunin and his henchmen". Her indictment of Lehning for selective and misleading use of Bakunin's correspondence to bolster Bakunin's version of his relations with Marx seems convincingly established on the basis of letters quoted by her from the volumes of the *Archives Bakounine* concerned. Since the facts relating to Bakunin's secret Alliance are too well established to be seriously disputed, Kelly attributes to Lehning "the genuinely Bakuninist faith that it is possible by an effort of will to transform reality into what one would wish it to be."

There are two episodes in Bakunin's career which have given rise to much speculation. One is the long *Confession* which he wrote while in the Peter and Paul Fortress in 1851, after being requested by Nicholas I to do so. Max Nettlau regarded it as an act of subtle deception, which is the view accepted by the Bakunin mythologizers. Professor Mendel, who devotes a good deal of discussion to this controversial document, seems to come to the same conclusion as Carr – that it was a voluntary act, and was in the main an accurate autobiography. Dr Kelly does not address herself to the question. Whatever the truth about Bakunin's motives, the *Confession* did not win any favours from Nicholas for Bakunin. It was only after the Tsar's death that his successor, Alexander II, was persuaded by Bakunin's mother (whom on occasions her son vilified in terms which are as inexplicable as they are embarrassing) to replace imprisonment by exile.

The most remarkable episode in Bakunin's life was probably his relationship with the fanatical terrorist, Nechaev, the prototype of Peter Verkhovensky in Dostoevsky's *The Possessed*. Nechaev, inspired by Karakozov's attempt to assassinate Alexander II in 1866, and intent on fomenting revolution by organizing the students to put Bakunin's ideas into practice, founded a small revolutionary group in 1869. Nechaev was the first Russian revolutionary to spell out "the full implications of the principle that the end justifies the means in revolution" and to act out his belief in real life. The conspirators of 1881 who killed Alexander II could, with some justification, claim that all attempts to persuade the government to reform had been exhausted by the time they acted. It was not until Lenin's revolutionary principles were put into practice that these "full implications" of Nechaev's theory became evident. He made contact with Herzen, Ogarev and Bakunin in 1869, completely captivating the last two. Herzen suspected him from the first. Bakunin was taken in by Nechaev's totally mendacious account of the extent of his almost non-existent revolutionary organization. He helped to obtain for him part of a fund which Herzen (who died in January 1870) had held for revolutionary purposes, and gave him a certificate of membership (numbered 2771) of a fictitious World Revolutionary Alliance, which Nechaev on return to Russia used to intimidate his group. To some extent the fake certificate enabled him to persuade his fellow members to murder the student, Ivanov, ostensibly because he was suspected of betrayal, actually with the aim of binding the group together by the bond of a crime in common.

Arrived in Geneva, Nechaev continued to lie and cheat in his wonted manner, stealing letters for the purpose of blackmail, weaving fantasies of revolution and the like. On 2 June 1870,

Bakunin wrote a long letter to Nechaev (it runs to over thirty printed pages in Volume IV of *Archives*), breaking off relations with him. Bakunin's motives for this have been much discussed. Lehning attributes the break to ideological disagreement. Mendel thinks it was due to injured vanity because Nechaev had treated him with contempt, by using methods against him that were only justifiable against political enemies. Kelly devotes a long chapter to a discussion of the subject: it is the most illuminating treatment of the question to date. The letter of 2 June, incidentally, revealed (as first pointed out by Confino) that Bakunin was not, as was generally supposed, the author of the notorious *Catechism of a Revolutionary*, made public at the trial of Nechaev after he was extradited for the murder of Ivanov. But Kelly seems to be right in arguing that Bakunin could well have had a hand in, or an influence on, it. She also argues most convincingly that the cause of the breach could not have been Bakunin's revulsion against Nechaev's methods – indeed, as she shows, letters written by him after the break of 2 June 1870, comparing Nechaev to Belinsky, or justifying the murder of Ivanov, disprove this. She attributes the rupture with Nechaev to envy, to the realization that his own "pursuit of the millennium" in politics called for Nechaev's means, but that he, Bakunin, lacked the strength and resolution to employ them – "a Rudin, impotently yearning to embody his ideal of unreflecting action". This is, by the way, not too far removed from Professor Mendel's contention that the clue to Bakunin is to be sought in his weakness.

Dr Kelly owes much of her interpretation to Turgenev's *Rudin*. Bakunin (in spite of the author's occasional denial) was Turgenev's prototype for Rudin. The two had been intimate friends for some years as students in Berlin. But Turgenev was kind-hearted and charitable, and was persuaded by his friends to excuse Rudin's character by the regime of Nicholas I, which left Russia's young intelligentsia, for lack of any opportunity to participate in the kind of public service they yearned for, to flounder in the morass of theoretical speculation – the superfluous men. Dr Kelly is neither kind-hearted nor charitable so far as Bakunin is concerned. She sees him as an awful example of what happened when the pursuit of wholeness, imbibed in his youth from German idealism, took possession of an "introverted, divided and unfulfilled personality".

She concludes that:

> Bakunin's vision of the unified human personality of the distant future may differ from the marxist one in its rhetoric and the immediacy of its appeal, but it comes from the same philosophical stable and imposes the same constraints on the choice of means. Given that the use of force is the only way yet devised of eliminating the tension between the individual and the whole, the proponents of the ideal of the unity of civil and political society are constrained by their own logic to propose a dictatorship which submerges the first in the second as a means to the goal of the ideal society. Our century has seen how the means tend to become the immediate end, the goal recedes to a distant future, and eventually the despotism which was to lead to paradise becomes instead a "desperate simulation" [the phrase is Kolakowski's] of paradise itself.

There is one aspect of Bakunin's writings which has perhaps not received the attention it deserves: the accuracy of his forecast of the course of the revolution in Russia, even if he was nearly half a century out in his timetable. He believed that revolution was more likely in a backward country like Russia, and that the peasants would play the decisive role in bringing it about. (It was indeed a peasant army which decided the issue in Petrograd on 27 February 1917, and again a peasant army which helped Lenin to power eight months later.) The method of revolution, according to Bakunin, was to be total anarchy. But the chaos must be controlled and guided by a secret, all-powerful elite, operating within it. (All this along with constant denunciations of "Jacobins" and of all organs of authority.) And lastly, Bakunin's vision of Russia, liberated from Tsardom and enjoying the happiness of freedom, heading a commonwealth of Slav states, likewise freed from Austrian or Turkish tyranny, has become, in caricature, the Soviet bloc.

The Last Years of Alexander Blok

This is an unpublished lecture.

I hope it may not appear over-presumptuous that a mere student of the Soviet political scene like myself should venture to discuss a poet, and a poet as great and difficult as Alexander Blok at that. My justification is that Blok's acceptance of the revolution in "The Twelve" and his subsequent years of comparative inactivity present something of a political as well as of a poetic problem, and certainly became a matter for political debate both inside and outside Russia. And Blok himself somewhere speaks of "the indivisibility, without fusion, of art, life and politics". Let me pose this problem in its boldest form: in 1918 Blok produces the greatest poem of the revolution, perhaps the greatest poem of any revolution. Three years later, in 1921, he dies, after a period of almost complete silence. What does this silence imply? Does it mean that Blok changed his mind when he saw what the revolution had brought in its train?

In the Russian emigration, between the wars, the view was much canvassed that Blok had bitterly repented of writing "The Twelve", and had indeed died of remorse. Many will, of course, remember something of the consternation that Blok's poem caused in Russian intellectual circles in 1918, among those – the majority – who did not accept the October *coup d'état*. The Merezhkovskys were the leaders of the anti-Blok movement, particularly Madame Merezhkovsky, Zinaida Gippius, whose close friend Blok had been for many years. She sent him a volume of bitter poems; Blok drafted a prose reply, which he never sent; but he sent her instead a poem written on 1 June 1918. In the last line of this poem he speaks of the banner of the International waving high above the two of them, like the dawn above the dark cliffs. In a memoir of Blok, which she wrote when she was already in emigration, Zinaida Gippius describes her last meeting with Blok – in a crowded Petrograd tramcar. Let me quote a few sentences from this passage to show how charged with emotion their relations became because of "The Twelve":

> One day in a tramcar. Someone stands up and says, "How do you do." A voice that cannot be mistaken for anyone else's. I lift up my eyes – it is Blok. His face under his cap is somehow long, dry, yellow and dark. "Will you give me your hand?" Slow words spoken with an effort . . . I extend my hand to him and say: "Yes, personally, only personally – not socially." He kisses my hand, and after a silence, "Thank you." Then more silence. "They say you are going away?" To which I reply: "Well – one either has to go away from here or die. Unless of course one is in your position . . ." A long silence on his part, then he pronounces with particular gloom and very distinctly: "One can die in any position." Then suddenly he adds: "You know I love you very much." To which I say: "You know I love you too".

It was their last meeting. It must have happened in late 1920, or early in 1921.

It was no doubt this sense of shock that a poet so well loved by his friends could have identified himself with the Bolsheviks – for so it appeared – that gave rise to the "remorse" theory. Thus the poet Georgy Ivanov says in so many words that Blok died of remorse. The following passage is his account from *Peterburgskie Zimy*, or rather from the edition of this fascinating volume of memoirs which appeared in New York in 1952. Strangely enough the passage on Blok is not found in the original edition, which came out in Paris in 1928. Here it is:

> Blok paid with his life for having created "The Twelve". This is not a fine phrase, but the truth. Blok understood the mistake of "The Twelve" and was horrified . . . Like a sleepwalker who suddenly awakes he fell from a height and was killed . . . Here is a short account of the facts. The doctors who were treating Blok just could not determine what he was suffering from. At first they tried to sustain his rapidly ebbing strength, which was failing without cause, and later, when again from an unknown cause, he began to suffer unbearably, they injected him with morphia . . . A few days before Blok's death a rumour went around Petrograd that Blok had gone off his head. This rumour

> undoubtedly came from literary circles which were close to the Bolsheviks. Later many variants appeared in Soviet periodicals of Blok's death-bed madness. But none of them mentioned the following most significant detail: the dying Blok was visited by . . . the Director of the Petrograd State Publishing House, Ionov. Blok was already unconscious and in constant delirium. The delirium was always the same: "Are all the copies of 'The Twelve' destroyed? Was there not one other left? Liuba, go and have a good search, and burn them, burn them all." Liubov Dmitrievna, Blok's wife, patiently repeated that all copies had been destroyed. Blok would quieten down for a little – and then begin once more.

Ivanov does not say from whom he heard this story.

It is incidentally not quite true to say that the doctors could not diagnose Blok's disease. His doctor, Dr Pekelis, has written an account of Blok's illness, from which it is clear that Blok suffered from endocarditis – though it is true that there was also present a severe psychopathic condition.

There are two other accounts of Blok's last days and of his death, which do, to some extent, bear out part at least of the story Ivanov tells. Blok's aunt, Madame Beketova, wrote a short, personal biography, published in Petrograd in 1922. In it she says that Blok's mind began to be clouded – he became extremely irritable, gloomy and apathetic and not fully conscious. "The psychoasthenia became more severe, and finally took on the sharpest form." For some time before his death he hardly spoke. The two stories are not quite inconsistent, and are indeed not dissimilar. But, unless Madame Beketova wrote her biography at the bidding of the party authorities, which I find hard to believe in the comparatively free conditions of literature which still prevailed in 1922, then it would appear that the rumour current just before Blok died that his mind was wandering was not very far from the truth. The other account which I have been able to trace was published, also in Petrograd, by Chukovsky, in 1924. Chukovsky's account is based on a letter which he received from a young girl who was present in the Blok household during his last weeks. By the beginning of August, she writes, Blok was unconscious almost all the time. At night he became delirious, and cried out in so terrible a manner, that, writes this correspondent, "I will never forget it so long as I live." This too is not inconsistent with Ivanov's account. Such evidence as there is, therefore, does not preclude the possibility that remorse was one of the factors that drove Blok to his death. But, in the case of a poet, I think that the real evidence for a problem of this nature must be sought in his works and his utterances. It is upon the basis of a poem said to be by Blok that Peter Struve put forward the suggestion that Blok ended his life in a state of remorse for "The Twelve". Struve was among those who took up an attitude of severe moral condemnation of Blok for having written this poem. In 1921 he published in his newly revived *Russkaia Mysl* a note on "The Twelve" in which he says the following:

> A man and therefore a writer can take up various attitudes to vice, sin, beastliness and low vulgarity: he can accept them with indifference, as part of the process of simple portrayal and representation; he can idealize and exalt them; and lastly, he can approach them with a hierarchically aesthetic valuation, placing them in the proper relation with other sides of poetry and reality. Only this last attitude is aesthetically correct and religiously lawful.

Struve then goes on to say that Blok, in "The Twelve", tends to waver between the three attitudes, and hence falls into cynicism and blasphemy. He ends with the following sentence:

> One is involuntarily reminded of the prophetic confession by Blok himself that he belongs to some accursed race of men, to the "children of Russia's terrible years", in whose exalted hearts there is always some fateful emptiness.

Struve sent the article to Blok, who copied it into his diary and underscored heavily the sentence: "The fateful emptiness in their exalted hearts", but he did not make any written comment. I am not sure that I agree with Struve's judgement on the moral duty of the poet: I am quite certain that Blok would never have agreed with it, or even understood it – so remote is it from his own conception of the poet's function.

Years later, apparently in 1932, Struve published another article on Blok, which I have been unable to trace, and which does not appear in the detailed bibliography of his works prepared by his son, Gleb Struve. But it would seem that in this article Struve reprinted a 28-line poem by Blok, which he said had been written by the poet on 19 July 1920. Struve refers to this article and to the poem in an addendum which he wrote to a little book by N. A. Tsurikov, called *Zavety Pushkina, Mysli o natsionalnom vozrozhdenii Rossii*, which was published in 1937. By 1937 Struve unfortunately could give no clue to the origins of this poem – which does not appear in the ostensibly complete edition of Blok's poetry in the two volumes edited by Vladimir Orlov, and published in Moscow in 1946. Nor is it referred to by Mochulsky in his beautiful and sensitive biography of Blok. However, Tsurikov reprints the poem, from Struve's manuscript presumably, and it is certainly a very beautiful and moving poem. It is also deeply religious. But it does not use religious symbols in Blok's characteristic manner. It is religious in the simple way of a soul in anguish. If indeed this poem is by Blok, it certainly shows the poet at odds with his past, and longing for the consolation of religious faith. The last two lines are:

I am ready to drain the whole cup,
If only I could wipe out the past.

This could be a "penitential poem" as Struve calls it. I think it could also be a cry of despair from a man whom destiny had made the mouthpiece of a national cataclysm, and who would, if he could, find peace and wipe the past from his mind. I hope that someone more expert on the subject of Blok than I can claim to be will be able to throw some more light on this poem.

Now let us look at the Bolshevik versions of the mystery of Blok's silent years. Lenin does not appear to have referred to Blok, but Trotsky wrote about him at length in his *Literature and the Revolution*. "Of course," says Trotsky, in a graphic sentence, "Blok is not ours. But he rushed towards us. He rushed towards us – and disintegrated." He explains Blok's failure to accept the revolution in its entirety – wholly and unreservedly – by the fact that he was rooted in the traditions of his class. This sounds rather silly, or perhaps old-fashioned one should say – like something from Feuerbach. It was particularly silly in the case of Blok, who had for years before the revolution, as well as after the revolution, painted the life of the bourgeoisie with an emotional loathing; and who broke with his most intimate friends like the Merezhkovskys because they were not prepared to join him in repudiating all bourgeois values.

Indeed, it is I think very essential to remember this almost physical loathing for the middle class, and for the civilization of the bourgeoisie which dominated Blok for many years before he wrote "The Twelve". Later on he was to explain it in semi-sociological, semi-mystical terms in his article "The Collapse of Humanism" to which I will return later. It was an outlook which linked Blok with the Slavophiles, with Dostoevsky and with Bakunin. It helps us to understand not only the quality of his earlier patriotic poems, but also it explains "The Scythians", which he wrote in 1918 under the impact of imminent renewal of the German invasion, and of the Left Socialist Revolutionary call for a great peasant uprising against the invader in the name of world revolution. It must also not be forgotten that Blok had played a large part in the activities of the commission which investigated, in a series of interrogations, the fall of the Tsar's regime. The impression which the evidence assembled by this commission left upon him is not likely to have enhanced any sense of allegiance he may have had to the old order.

But apart from these ritual marxist fetishes, Trotsky understood perfectly well the real nature of "The Twelve". Blok, he says, had to choose. A "drawing room poet could have chosen to go on chirping poems complaining about the difficulties of life under the Bolsheviks. But Blok was infected by the epoch, and he translated it into his own inner language."

Now I think this is true – that is why "The Twelve" is such a great poem. Trotsky, incidentally, was quick to notice what the angry anti-revolutionary intellectuals did not all notice – that "The Twelve" was not a very flattering picture of the revolution. Of course it was not. It showed a medley of the familiar hooligans and prostitutes of the Petersburg streets, whom Blok had used as symbols in his poetry for years before the revolution. But in "The Twelve" these property figures come to life with a dionysiac quality which they had never possessed before; it was as if the "cranberry juice" of the clown in *Balanganchik* had become real blood now that Blok's earlier forebodings of the revolution had become reality. It was the figure of Christ at the head of the Red Guards that Blok's friends could not forgive – even if they could understand how, in the language of Blok's symbolism, that figure came to be there.

"I will not forgive. Your soul is innocent," wrote Zinaida Gippius. Like Struve, she required of the poet that he should restrain his poetic impulse to describe, to portray reality by a moral judgement on that reality. But she realized that Blok was innocent in soul, because he was incapable of such an approach to the poetic act.

Let me turn to Blok himself. For Blok had much to say about "The Twelve" and about his own relation to the revolution. There is no doubt that for the remaining years of his life, after writing "The Twelve", he was much haunted by this poem, this monumental, dramatic "*chastushka*", as Mandelstam called it, "immortal as folklore is immortal". Blok wrote this poem in the course of three weeks – between 8 and 29 January 1918 (Old Style), that is to say during the troubled and rather violent days which followed upon the dispersal of the Constituent Assembly on 6 January. On the day he finished the poem in draft he records in his notebooks: "A terrible noise, growing within me and all around . . . Today I am a genius." "The Twelve" was published on 3 March 1918 in the Left Socialist Revolutionary paper *Znamia Truda*. I have already referred to the storm which its appearance caused. "If only it were not for the Christ," V. G. Korolenko said in August 1918. "It is after all such a true and such a terrible picture. But the presence of Christ speaks of the author's Bolshevik sympathies." Some time later Blok told Gumilev, who criticized the ending of "The Twelve" for its artificiality, "I don't like the end of 'The Twelve' either. I should have liked the end to be otherwise. But the more I looked into it, the more clearly I saw Christ." So far as we know, Blok maintained to the end that "The Twelve" had been written in a state bordering on possession. In a note on the poem, written in April 1920 – that is to say three months earlier than the penitential poem quoted by Struve – Blok gives this well-known description of his poetic activity:

> It was in January of 1918 that I for the last time surrendered myself to the elemental force [*stikhiia*] no less blindly than in January 1907 or in March 1914. The reason why I do not recant what I wrote then is because it was written in tune with the elemental force. For example, while I was writing and after I had finished "The Twelve" I could hear for several days on end, physically, with my ears, a great noise all around – a composite noise (most probably the noise of the collapse of the old world). Therefore those who see a political poem in "The Twelve" are either very blind to the meaning of art, or are sitting up to their ears in political dirt or are possessed by great malice whether they be friends or enemies of my poem.

At the same time it would be untrue to deny all relation of

> "The Twelve" to politics . . . In the sea of human life there is a small creek . . . which is called politics . . . The seas of nature, life and art were in ferment, and the spray rose above them like a rainbow. I was watching the rainbow when I wrote "The Twelve". That is why a drop of politics has remained in the poem. Let us see what time will do with all this. Perhaps all politics is so dirty, that one drop of it will muddy and corrupt all the rest; or perhaps this drop will not kill the sense of the poem . . .

Whatever Blok may in the end have come to believe about his poem, of one thing there is no doubt: he never wavered in his intense conviction that the poet is the inspired vehicle of the spirit of his age, borne aloft by the elemental force which is stronger than himself. In his lecture on Catiline, delivered in May 1918, Blok has this to say with reference to Catullus, and his poem "Attis", in which Attis bitterly laments the religious fanaticism which led him to rob himself of his virility:

> In my view, the subject of this poem was not the personal passion of Catullus, as is usually asserted. The opposite is the case. The personal passion of Catullus, like the personal passion of every poet, was saturated with the spirit of the epoch; its destiny, its rhythms, its dimensions, just as the rhythms and dimensions of the poet's verses were inspired by his period. For, in the poetic perception of the world there is no divorce between the personal and the universal. The more sensitive the poet, the more indissolubly he feels at once both that which is his own, and that which is not his own. Therefore, in an epoch of tempests and perturbation the most tender and intimate strivings of the poet's soul are likewise filled with tempest and perturbation.

Then, years later, in his memorial speech on Pushkin, delivered in February 1921, six months before his death, Blok describes the activity of the poet, the "son of harmony". The poet has three tasks, says Blok. He must first liberate the sounds from the elemental chaos, which has neither beginning nor end, in which music dwells. Then, he must transform those sounds into harmony by giving them form; and then, at last, he must bear this harmony into the outward world. Blok could never understand the conception of the poet as a pure craftsman. His cold, but polite, contempt for Gumilev springs immediately to mind. His last literary essay, entitled "Without

Divinity or Inspiration" was a bitter and rather irritable attack on the Acmeist poets in general and on Gumilev in particular. It only saw the light of day in 1925, in a volume of literary essays by various hands published in Leningrad.

The turbulent weeks of January 1918 proved to be the last occasion when the spirit of the age possessed Blok to write great poetry. (I exclude "The Scythians" written soon after, in February 1918, because that was a Left Socialist Revolutionary pamphlet, rather than a poem.) But his remaining years of life, though almost barren of poetry, were by no means inactive. It was during these years that he wrote three or four of his more important essays, in which his somewhat fanciful vision of the destiny of mankind is expressed in the most musical prose. "The Intelligentsia and the Revolution", written about the same time as "The Twelve", is the best known of these – the credo of the devotee at the mystical altar of "revolution". It is a bitter, satirical attack on those intellectuals who have failed to discern the mighty spirit of the revolution behind its outwardly unattractive form. What has the intellectual to be afraid of? He has nothing to lose – unlike the bourgeoisie, which has a bedrock of family, capital, position and title, "like the dung beneath a pig". Yet, "it is as if a bear had stepped on the ear of the Russian intelligentsia: petty fears, petty little words . . . How shameful to pronounce the beautiful word 'comrade' in inverted commas!" The essay, which caused almost as much consternation as "The Twelve", ends with the famous sentence: "Listen to the Revolution – listen with all your body, all your heart, all your consciousness." Stripped of its imagery, this essay reads to me almost like a credo of those Left Socialist Revolutionary romantics to whom Blok, so far as he ever had any political allegiances, felt closest.

To the same year, 1918, belongs the long lecture on Catiline, to which I have already referred. It is based on some very singular notions on this episode in Roman history, inspired by Ibsen's juvenile work "Catilina" which William Archer did not include in his edition of Ibsen's collected works, and describes as "of little or no inherent value". In this brilliant, if rather highly-coloured lecture, Blok seeks to draw a parallel, a symbolical, rather than an historical parallel, between contemporary events in Russia and the conspiracy of Catiline. Then as now, the old world was going down before the new world which the birth of Christ was soon to herald. In Catiline's time, says Blok, "there arose that wind, which grew into a tempest which destroyed the old, heathen world. Catiline was caught up by the wind which blew before the birth of Jesus Christ, the herald of a new world." And so Catiline, though his conspiracy failed, becomes a kind of "Roman Bolshevik", as Blok calls him. But the symbolism does not end there for Blok. Catiline's conspirators also had their Blok, no less than the Red Guards of Lenin. This was Catullus, who, like Blok, was filled with the music of the age, the music of the crash of the old world and the advent of the new. This music, Catullus, according to Blok's original theory, expressed in his poem "Attis" to which I have already referred. "Do you hear it," asks Blok, "this uneven, hurrying step of the doomed men, the step of the revolutionary, the step in which the tempest of fury reverberates, and resolves itself into broken, musical sounds? Listen to him – *Super alta vectus Attis celeri rate maria / Phrygium nemus citato cupide pede tetigit* . . ." You may think, as I do, that all this is rather exaggerated and I suspect rather bad history. But that is not the point. Its interest lies for us in the dominant idea of Blok's last years – that the advent of Bolshevism was a cataclysm, a kind of Spenglerian mutation of human life on earth, which could be paralleled only by the birth of a new order and the death of the old, which happened in Rome in the year AD 1. This idea is most fully developed in another lecture which Blok delivered in November 1919, "The Collapse of Humanism", and one in which a number of critics have seen a marked similarity to the views of Spengler, with which Blok is unlikely to have been familiar. This lecture is difficult to understand, and even more difficult to summarize – it is small wonder that the practical Maxim Gorky who heard the lecture was completely bewildered by it. "I couldn't understand: was he distressed or pleased by the fact of the downfall of humanism?" Gorky noted in his diary. Blok's theme is, very roughly, as follows: for four centuries, from the mid-fourteenth to mid-eighteenth, Europe developed under the sign of humanism, of which the ruling idea was the free individual personality. But the crisis of humanism came with the emergence of a new motive power – the masses. This happened about the time of the French revolution. The nineteenth century loses its unity of culture, it rapidly becomes mechanized and the spirit of music deserts it. Culture, which is musically a unit, and which dwells beyond historical time, gives way to civilization, in which there is no music. The "civilized" nineteenth century, in the bad sense, of course, has thus lost that equilibrium which is essential in order to remain close to the "musical essence" of the world. Having deserted civilized humanity, the spirit of music returned to that elemental force (*stikhiia*) in which it was born: to the people, to the barbarian masses. "Therefore," says Blok, "it is no paradox to say that the barbarian masses have become the guardians of culture, since they possess nothing but the spirit of music." The old world is already going down in the flood of the music of the barbarian masses. The issue is already decided. The "civilization" of humanism is already conquered by the mighty new movement. "Throughout the entire world," says Blok, "the tocsin of anti-humanism is sounding . . . man is getting closer to the elemental force; and therefore man is becoming more musical." The process of the collapse of humanism takes time: thus the ancient world was already conquered when Christ was born, though the Roman Empire still lasted for several centuries thereafter.

It is easy to see now why Blok was so hurt by the reception of his poem "The Twelve". It would have been impossible for him to understand how any question of moral approbation of Bolshevism, which his critics read into "The Twelve", could enter into the matter at all. The figure of Christ in the poem was to him part of his symbolism. It may be also that something of the symbolism of the year AD 1 in Rome crept into "The Twelve", because Blok thought in symbols. "Love and hate" (*odi et amo*) was another symbol, echoing Catullus, which Blok used for his own emotional state in relation to the revolution – both in a conversation with Zamiatin, and in an essay on Wagner, written in March 1918. "*Odi et amo – Quare id fieri fortasse requires Nescio; sed fieri sentio et ex*," wrote Catullus to a Roman courtesan. But for Blok, there is no personal passion for the poet which is not at the same time linked with the spirit of the age, the "*stikhiia*", the elemental force, of the new world coming to cast down the old.

I have mentioned an essay on Wagner which Blok wrote in March 1918 and which I think throws an important light on Blok's attitude to revolution. It is called "Art and Revolution" (also the title of one of Wagner's essays), and the subtitle is "On the creative work of Richard Wagner". Wagner's art, says Blok, is closely linked with the Communist Manifesto – the "Ring of the Nibelungen" was conceived and executed at the end of the forties and the beginning of the fifties of the nineteenth century. "It is linked," writes Blok, "with that great revolutionary tempest which then swept over Europe. The wind for that tempest was sown by the rebellious Russian soul in the person of Bakunin. Bakunin, that Russian anarchist with a burning faith in world conflagration, who was so much hated by the realist politicians (including Marx) . . ." How, asks Blok, was Wagner the artist saved from destruction, when the worst fate of all befell him – the adulation of the bourgeoisie, and the consequent popularity? Even the Emperor William had a motor siren fitted to his limousine which played the Wotan *leitmotiv*. Wagner survived because he bore within him the burning unity of love and hatred, which the bourgeois cannot stand. Blok refers with enthusiasm to Wagner's essay "Art and Revolution" where at one point Wagner refers with hatred to Christ as the "wretched son of a Galilean carpenter"; and yet elsewhere he proposes to erect an altar to Christ. There, cries Blok, is the real poison of love and hatred in one, the poison, as Blok calls it, which permeated all Wagner's work. It was this poison which made Wagner immune from death under waves of bourgeois adulation. In this poison lies Wagner's strength – his certainty of survival.

This somewhat hysterical essay is very illuminating on one aspect of Blok's mind, though at the same time a little terrifying. Remember that it was written at the very height of Blok's revolutionary fervour, when he was pouring out his innermost feelings in poetry and prose, like a man possessed. It shows, to my mind, an emotional attitude to revolution which is far removed even from that of the Left Socialist Revolutionaries, let alone the cool mind of Lenin. The Left SRs were romantic and unrealistic, but even they envisaged the revolution as a means to a more or less concrete end. Indeed Maria Spiridonovna and Natanson both believed that the turn of their party would come when the Bolsheviks had shown the sterility and even bankruptcy of their ideas. But in this outburst of Blok's there is something of that pathos of destruction for its own sake, which was indeed so dominant both in Bakunin and Wagner. "*Die Lust der Zerstörung ist zugleich eine schaffende Lust*," wrote the young Bakunin, in words which Blok, I think, would have echoed. As for Wagner, the close identity between Wagnerian musical language and the subconscious forces drawn upon by the Nazis is very fresh in all our minds. I think that this essay, which is not closely paralleled in any other of Blok's writings so far as I am aware, lifts the curtain for a moment on a very significant aspect of Blok's emotional love and hatred of revolution for its own sake – the destructive force, hateful yet at the same time an elemental force which must inevitably sweep all before it. And after that? I wonder if Blok ever thought of what would come after the revolution in concrete terms? I will return to this later. For the moment let us return to the more material plane.

Of course, to those who move in a more material plane, the language of symbolism is not always readily apparent. The witty Zinaida Gippius expressed this in a note on Blok in her diary, dated 24 October 1917. "With Blok and with Boria [Andrey Bely] . . . it is only possible to converse in the fourth dimension. But they don't understand this, and therefore enunciate words which sound pretty abominable in the third dimension." I have purposely refrained from quoting some of the pretty abominable things that Blok did say in connection with the revolution for the first year or two after, precisely because I think they would give a wrong impression of the real man. In his enthusiasm for the revolution he was often prepared to condone or dismiss lightly some fairly unpleasant aspects of the revolution which naturally appalled Zinaida Gippius. After all, the "barbarian masses" fulfilling their historical, or "musical", destiny, could hardly be expected to be gentle and selective in their methods – there are incidentally some Hegelian historians of the Russian revolution in the West to whom any dwelling on the petty little blemishes of a great historic cataclysm, allegedly as inevitable as Niagara, still today seems as futile as it did – once – to Blok. But to return to Blok. The fourth dimension, as Zinaida Gippius called it, was a very real thing to him. He felt beyond doubt or hesitation that he was the vehicle for the music of the birth of a new age. That is why I am not myself concerned about Blok's "remorse" over "The Twelve": a man does not feel "remorse" because he has experienced an earthquake. And attempts to apply the kind of moral judgements that Struve applied to Blok in 1921 seem to me rather a misunderstanding of symbolism in general and of Blok in particular.

Blok remained active until shortly before his death. He threw himself into the work of popularizing literature and the theatre for the masses – hating it, but doing it conscientiously and with determination. He edited Heine and Lermontov, he wrote a very bad play called *Ramses*; this play was written at Gorky's suggestion that a series of dramatical "historical pictures" should be prepared with the object of educating the masses. He took part in the founding and activity of the Free Philosophical Association, and became the first President of the Petrograd Branch of the All-Russian Union of Poets. He prepared editions of his own works, and continued with abortive efforts to finish his poem "Vozmezdie", almost to within weeks of his death. We have ample evidence of the stifling effect which the life of a literary bureaucrat had on the poet. By the end of 1920 he had completely lost the will to live, although the first physical symptoms of his illness, endocarditis, did not appear until April 1921 according to his diary and to the recollection of his aunt, Madame Beketova. Friends who saw him in Moscow on his visit there in May 1921 speak of him as already not of this world. His last weeks on earth were weeks of terrible suffering and he died in a delirium on 7 August 1921.

"Blok," says his biographer Mochulsky, "did not die of disease, but because music forsook him, because he could no longer breathe, because he wanted to die. His death was as mystical as the whole of his life had been." But even without invoking mysticism, I do not find very much difficulty in understanding why the will to live had forsaken Blok by 1920. After all, Blok does not stand alone among the many romantic revolutionaries to whom the "elemental force" of 1918 was the music of history, and the bureaucratic corruption, the loss of all revolutionary honour of 1920, was the end. The whole Left Socialist Revolutionary movement, or those members of it who did not forego their individuality by joining the Bolsheviks, virtually committed suicide of one kind or another. Some, like Steinberg, committed mental suicide by the language of mild conformity, followed by exile; others committed moral suicide by joining the ranks of the Cheka. On a simpler, less exalted plane than Blok, they were caught up by the mystique of the revolution, of the new era: their exaltation was cast down when bureaucracy, dishonesty and corruption inevitably began to replace the élan of 1917, inevitably, because a minority government determined to keep in power, and which is not wanted by the population, has no alternative but to go through all the phases Lenin's government went through towards the conclusion of the Civil War.

And so Blok, the inspired medium, the possessed *vates* of the revolution, grew silent and died: the depression was of a measure with the exaltation, and it cost him his life. Blok's death was not in my judgement a death of remorse: on the contrary it personified the death of the revolution which Blok thought he discerned as an historical force in 1917, and which by 1920 had led to an ugly, rather shoddy, very corrupt, somewhat dishonest bureaucratic satrapy, with Lenin fast becoming the satrap. How could this not be reflected in Blok, the man veritably possessed with the revolution? From mid-1920 onwards, a different note begins to sound in the diaries and in the letters, or at any rate in those portions of them which the Soviet authorities have seen fit to publish. Here is the entry for 18 April 1921: "Life has changed (it is a changed life, but not a new life, not a *vita nuova*), the louse has conquered the whole world. This is already an accomplished fact, and all will now be changing in the *other* direction, and not in the direction which was our life and which we loved." No one who knows a line of Blok's bitter attacks on the bourgeoisie can suppose that he is here lamenting the old social order: he is lamenting a revolution which has gone sour, which came in as a lion and was going out as – a louse. But in any case all doubt is removed when one turns to one of the last things Blok wrote, his speech "On the Function of the Poet" delivered on 11 February 1921 for the anniversary of Pushkin's death. A few days earlier, on 5 February 1921, he had written what was to be his last, or perhaps last but one, poem in the visitors' book of the Pushkin House in Petrograd. The speech is built around Pushkin's attitude to the "mob" (*chern*). By the word *chern*, says Blok, Pushkin certainly did not mean the common people – he meant the bureaucrats. The poet must have *pokoi i volia* "quiet, and his own free will" – for it is characteristic of Blok that he used this word *volia*, with its undertones of anarchy and peasant risings, of Pugachev and Bakunin. Pushkin, whom he quotes, had spoken of *tainaia svoboda*, "inner freedom". But *pokoi i volia* are also taken from us, says Blok. "Not the external quiet, but the creative quiet. Not infantile freedom, not freedom to indulge in playing the liberal, but the creative free will, the secret freedom. And the poet dies because there is nothing left for him to breathe: life has lost its meaning." He ends with a warning: "Let the bureaucrats beware of an even worse description than *chern*, 'mob', when they are preparing to force poetry along some direction of their own, affronting the secret freedom of the poet and preventing poetry from fulfilling its mysterious purpose."

Yet one more passage must be quoted, because I think here Blok was expressing what most of his audience felt: "Over Pushkin's death-bed sounded the infantile babblings of Belinsky. This babbling seemed to us to be the complete antithesis of, and completely inimical to, the courteous voice of Count Benckendorff. It seems still to be such to us. It would be too painful for all of us, if it were to become apparent that this was not so; and even if it is not quite so, let us go on thinking that it is so." Benckendorff – the symbol of cold, inhuman bureaucracy, hated by any self-respecting *intelligent*; Belinsky – the symbol of the revolution of the future, the hope and idol of every *intelligent*. Could it be that Blok was beginning to fear that Belinsky on closer acquaintance was but Benckendorff writ large?

To my mind, this is Blok's farewell to the whole revolutionary mystique, the faith in revolution as an end in itself, which possessed generation after generation of the Russian intelligentsia from Belinsky onwards – Pushkin certainly was never affected by it – and led them to destruction, like the Gadarene swine in the epigraph to Dostoevsky's *Possessed*. In one of his last letters to Chukovsky, Blok writes with that mixture of love and hatred of his country which dogged him all his life: "I have now neither soul nor body, and everything aches . . . And so after all, this dirty, own mother of mine, Russia, has gobbled me up as a sow gobbles up her young." Blok had drunk deeper of this mystic draught of revolution, had made himself the sounding board for what he heard as the music of the new age. Is it a matter for great wonder that with the death of the revolution, Blok should have died too?

Or perhaps one could put it another way. I suggested earlier that the real force which drew Blok irresistibly towards the revolution was its destructive aspect – in other words, not what the revolution was going to *do*, but what it *was*, its being, not its becoming. Now the Russian revolution, like every revolution, spent its force in a very short time. What followed after was the lawlessness, bureaucratic, corrupt comings and goings of some kind of daily political and social life. Intrigue and inefficiency at the top, apathy below, would not be an unfair description of Russia in 1920. But it is quite irrelevant to my context whether the Bolsheviks were doing the right things or the wrong things in 1920. My point is that they were in the nature of things no longer revolutionaries, but the government. But think of the effect on Blok, the exalted visionary, whose whole emotional being had been centred upon this great cleansing destructive tempest. The tempest had come and gone – what was there left for him to live for? If a man lives his whole life waiting and longing for a cataclysm, it is perhaps inevitable that he should perish with that cataclysm. So Blok had lived for revolution, for that final *Götterdämmerung*, when the cleansing waters of the Rhine would rise and submerge the ruins of Valhalla. The revolution had come and gone – leaving Blok spiritually empty and unprepared for the aftermath. The music which had poured out through his whole being was now silent. In the new world, so terrifyingly like the old, Blok had nothing to live for. He was too great and too sincere in his emotions to find refuge in pretence. Death was the only possible answer.

"We have killed Blok, all of us," the excited Zamiatin shouted to Gorky over the telephone on 7 August 1921. But I think he was wrong. Blok willed his own death long before it happened, when he linked his very being to the future revolution.

Alexander Solzhenitsyn: Conscience of Western Civilization

This review of Alexander Solzhenitsyn, *The Gulag Archipelago, vol. II, 1918–1956: An Experiment in Literary Investigation, Parts III–IV*, translated by Thomas P. Whitney, Harper & Row (New York 1975), was originally published in the *New York Review of Books*, 13 November 1975.

"There are times, in my opinion, when one has to lower the tone, take the whip into one's hands not just to defend oneself, but in order to go into the attack in a much cruder manner" – so wrote Dostoevsky to Strakhov, over one hundred years ago, when embarking on *The Possessed*. I am not here concerned with the relative literary stature of Dostoevsky and Solzhenitsyn, though the comparison between the two writers is made from time to time; nor am I concerned with comparing the monumental *Gulag Archipelago* with *The Possessed* in terms of the relative achievement of each work in teaching us to realize the evil that men do to each other in the name of ideals, or obsessions, such as "socialism" or "revolution".

But there is one striking parallel between the two works which is very relevant to my discussion: neither is concerned with economics or with the class struggle or with "social forces" (whatever these may be), which have become the accepted language of so many of us who have written about revolutions since Feuerbach and Marx created a new language for us. Dostoevsky and Solzhenitsyn are concerned with unfashionable matters, so embarrassing to modern man, like sin and God and repentance. They see problems in terms of what goes on inside men, not in the environment outside them. Small wonder that Solzhenitsyn has aroused such indignation not only in the ranks of the KGB and its numerous allies, which was to be expected; but, more surprisingly, among many of those who disapprove of the evils of communist rule as much as he does, and have themselves suffered as much from it, but who use a different language when they attempt to describe it.

In many ways this present episode in Russian intellectual history takes us back to the year 1909, and the publication of a short volume of essays entitled *Landmarks* (*Vekhi*). The seven authors of this volume included former marxists, like P. B. Struve and S. L. Frank, and other leading intellectuals and historians. The theme that bound these disparate thinkers together was their merciless exposure of the failure of the Russian intelligentsia, of whom, of course, the authors were leading members, to realize that in their pursuit of false and abstract materialistic political aims, they were leading the country to a disaster for which they would all be to blame. Although the views of the seven authors are widely different in many respects (a fact which makes this volume of essays, nearly seventy years later, still one of the most stimulating products of the Russian intellect), the basic thought common to all of them was well defined in the Preface by M. Gershenzon. This was, he wrote, "the recognition of the primacy both in theory and in practice of spiritual life over the outward forms of society, in the sense that the inner life of the individual . . . and not the self-sufficing elements of some political order is the only solid basis for every social structure".

The scandal caused by the publication of *Landmarks* will scarcely seem credible to those unfamiliar with the intellectual life of pre-revolutionary Russia. The volume ran into five editions in a short time. It provoked violent attacks from the Kadets, from the socialist revolutionaries, and from innumerable individuals. The leader of the Kadets, P. N. Miliukov, toured Russia in order to denounce *Vekhi* at a series of public meetings. Lenin wrote a particularly obtuse attack on the volume, which probably in part explains the book's popularity today among the unofficial Soviet intelligentsia as well as the regular attacks on it by the Soviet establishment.[1]

This account of the past is not merely of historical interest. It is very relevant to understanding the intellectual position of Solzhenitsyn. Indeed, in a recently published essay Solzhenitsyn draws explicitly, and with approval, on the position enunciated so dramatically by the authors of *Vekhi*. This essay, entitled "The Smatterers", has recently been published in English in a volume entitled *From Under the Rubble.*[2] As Max Hayward points out in an illuminating introduction (which one could have wished a good deal longer), the very title suggests a reminiscence of a second volume published in Moscow by some of the *Vekhi* authors in 1918, and immediately suppressed (it was called *De Profundis*, of which the Russian is "*Iz glubiny*" which echoes "*Iz pod glyb*", the Russian title of the recent volume). In his essay "The Smatterers" (one of his three contributions to the volume), Solzhenitsyn analyses *Vekhi* with praise and understanding, and indeed the central theme of *Vekhi* – that solutions to man's problems do not lie in systems or in the elimination of enemies, but in the moral position of individuals – is the core of Solzhenitsyn's faith. Without understanding this faith one cannot appreciate the significance of *Gulag Archipelago*.

This faith is summed up by Solzhenitsyn when, towards the end of his book (pp. 615–16) he records the lesson which he learned from his life in camp:

> Gradually it was disclosed to me that the line separating good and evil passes not through states, nor between classes, nor between political parties either – but right through every human heart – and through all human hearts . . . Since then I have come to understand the truth of all the religions of the world: they struggle with the *evil inside a human being* (inside every human being). It is impossible to expel evil from the world in its entirety, but it is possible to constrict it within each person.
>
> And since that time I have come to understand the falsehood of all the revolutions in history: they destroy only *those carriers* of evil contemporary with them (and also fail, out of haste, to discriminate the carriers of good as well). And they then take to themselves as their heritage the actual evil itself, magnified still more.

This is, incidentally, also the faith of a whole group of *samizdat* intellectuals inside Russia for whom Solzhenitsyn is now the free spokesman, notably G. Pomerants, who writes in a fairly recent essay: "The most important movement now is within the systems, from the letter to the spirit, and not just a simple change of symbols – such as, 'We have exchanged marxism for Christian orthodoxy, so now we need worry no more.' "[3]

Indeed the importance of the second volume of *Gulag Archipelago* is that one of its main objects is to reveal how Solzhenitsyn's present faith evolved during his sojourn in the concentration camps.

An enormous intellectual era separates the publication of the two volumes in English. Volume I appeared very soon after Solzhenitsyn's dramatic forcible expulsion from his native Russia, from which he had never contemplated voluntary emigration (slanderous rumours to the contrary, spread by the KGB, notwithstanding). It was written and hidden in Russia, but copies were safely preserved abroad. Publication was only authorized by Solzhenitsyn after the KGB had managed to secure the copy hidden in Russia, driving an innocent woman to suicide in the process. Volume I, which dealt with Solzhenitsyn's original arrest and confinement in the camps of the Soviet Far East, was – as everyone knows – one of the most harrowing and vivid accounts ever written in any language of human suffering and degradation. It destroyed once and for all, if only by the white heat of its sincerity, any lingering suspicion that any honest person might have had (I ignore the intellectual streetwalkers who only believe what they consider it profitable to believe) that the many accounts already available of Stalin's regime might have been exaggerated.

In the interval between English Volumes I and II a vast literature has grown up on the subject of one of the most extraordinary geniuses of our time. He himself has published extensively – lectures, interviews, broadcasts, an autobiography. He has become the most vocal opponent of the United States policy called "détente", and his activity culminated with a visit to the US on the eve of the Helsinki Conference during which Dr Kissinger's advice to the President not to receive Solzhenitsyn for fear of offending the Soviet authorities may yet prove to have done more to expose the more humiliating and illusory aspects of so-called "détente" than the millions of words spoken and written on this policy of the Nixon era which has survived the downfall of Nixon.

However, the influence of Solzhenitsyn on United States policy is a separate and fascinating issue on which it would not be right to digress here, but which will, I very much hope, be the subject of serious study before very long. What concerns us here is the new illumination which Volume II of *Gulag* throws on the political philosophy of Solzhenitsyn, in the context of the enormous amount of new material which has seen the light of day since Volume I became known to the world at large.[4] And, closely connected with this question, the importance of Solzhenitsyn in modern Russian intellectual history – meaning of course, the storm of discussion which Solzhenitsyn has raised both among émigré intellectuals, and among *samizdat* writers inside Russia. The reactions of the KGB hacks are predictable and of no particular interest, except as a source of disinformation spread by numerous KGB agents in the non-communist world.

Let me remind readers that the term "second volume" is somewhat misleading. There are in fact seven volumes in the Russian text. The first three of these were published in English translation as Volume I in 1974. The present Volume II consists of volumes three and four of the Russian text, published in Paris last year. The last three volumes, due to appear in Russian in Paris very shortly, will eventually form Volume III of a forthcoming English edition.[5]

Volume II of *Gulag* is in only a limited sense a sequel to Volume I: it is rather a continuation of the main purposes of the whole work – to tell the awful story of an epoch in Russian history, which must never be forgotten, and to pay the moral debt owed to the great majority who did not survive by one who did. Readers of Volume I will not require to be told that it is written with the same white heat of emotion, that its harrowing descriptions achieve heights of the descriptive writer's art which have rarely been equalled, let alone excelled. Much of the work is necessarily historical, since one of its main objects is to show that the concentration camp and its horrors, the brutality, the cynical exploitation of human misery, and the trampling on the elements of justice stem from Lenin, and were only developed on a larger scale by Stalin. The exposure of Lenin as the true author of "Stalinism", though by no means new to those familiar with the works of Western historians of the past thirty years, has proved a sensitive and controversial issue among Solzhenitsyn's Soviet and émigré critics, as will be seen below.

The historical first quarter of the book deals with the origins of the system, the first major concentration camp of Solovki, and the extension of the system of extracting at minimum cost their labour from expendable human beings in the construction of the White Sea–Baltic Canal. (One hundred thousand perished in this enterprise: when Solzhenitsyn visited the canal in 1962 it was virtually deserted. Such is the perfection of "socialist planning".) The major part of the book deals with the camp system and, more widely and analytically than Volume I, with the interrelation between the forced labour system and the corrupt nature of Soviet life and government as a whole. From first to last the work breathes moral indignation – at Lenin, at the sycophantic and dishonest authors (headed, of course, by the most venal writer in the history of Soviet literature, Maxim Gorky) who wrote down the official account of the White Sea Canal project knowing it to be all lies, and at the officials who carried out monstrous instructions. But Solzhenitsyn also has high praise for those who succeeded in preserving their integrity to the end (normally their death) even in the camp – and indeed gets very near to stating that only those were corrupted inside who were already corrupt when they came in – which is hard to believe, but who are we to argue with him?

Not all of *Gulag* II's facts by any means will be familiar to Western historians, since many of them have been culled by meticulous and detailed questioning of survivors inside the USSR and by some archival material. (How *did* he get access to it?) Besides, even the familiar facts take on a new vitality when put through the prism of Solzhenitsyn's style – much as Gibbon's prose will never be superseded by whole libraries of lesser writers' accounts of the late Roman Empire. (It should, perhaps, be observed that Solzhenitsyn is not entirely free from the irritating tendency of so many Russian émigrés to dismiss all the work of Western historians of Soviet Russia – which, on the whole, has been one of the major achievements of modern historical scholarship – as little more than a regurgitation of Soviet propaganda.)

On the whole, Solzhenitsyn has not been too well served in the past by the translators of his major works – on this subject readers may wish to refer to the meticulous analysis by Alexis Klimoff which will be found on pages 611–49 of the invaluable reference volume cited in footnote 4.

Of course, those who can read *Gulag* in the original will sympathize with the difficulties which face the translator – the irony, the superb use of words with mathematical precision, the slang. The use of camp slang, and of current Russian phrases which derive from camp slang, is not merely a device to add verisimilitude.

It is Solzhenitsyn's belief that the Russian language has been completely defiled by official expressions which are demanded of the Soviet writer, and which are false (this form of literature is quaintly called "socialist realism"). Hence, he writes (p. 489), "From the thirties on, everything that is called our prose is merely the foam from a lake which has vanished underground. It is foam and not prose because it detached itself from everything that was fundamental in those decades." Only camp slang can get back to those "fundamentals".

Mr Whitney's translation certainly preserves the irony. He has taken most meticulous care over the slang, searching out the exact meanings which in numerous cases Solzhenitsyn leaves unexplained for his readers. If it sounds somewhat inappropriate at times (at any rate to an English reader) this may well be due to the fact that prison slang does not in the USA or Britain fulfil the same role in the development of language as in the Soviet Union. It is, I think, as a stylist that Mr Whitney is least successful, and one would certainly not suspect from his version that we are discovering a writer of Russian prose of quite outstanding distinction. My impression throughout was that the translation is meticulously accurate. The one chapter which I checked against the original confirmed this view. I found five mistranslations or inaccuracies, but only one is of any importance. This is the use of the term "vermin" for the Russian *tvarei* on page 601. "If these millions of helpless and pitiful vermin still did not put an end to themselves" etc. – where in the Russian Solzhenitsyn clearly writes "helpless and pitiful creatures", the normal meaning of *tvar* in Russian, in which no (singularly inappropriate) tone of contempt is implied as is implied by the word "vermin". I repeat, this is an impression only. A much more detailed analysis, based on a complete comparison of texts, will no doubt be made in due course.

It is perhaps natural that those who were, or still are, devoted followers of the theories of Marx, and who are fully aware of the atrocities which have been committed in Russia and elsewhere in their name, should look to "betrayal" by Stalin as an answer, and idealize Lenin. Trotsky was a good example of this approach, though one need have no illusions about the kind of atrocities that

Trotsky would have committed had he and not Stalin won in the contest for power in which he was so pitifully outwitted.

The case for Lenin is perhaps stronger. No historian who knows any of the facts could disagree with the view, now almost universally accepted, that Lenin created the instruments of rule (or misrule) which enabled Stalin to carry out his purposes. (Roy Medvedev, in *Let History Judge*, got very near to ignoring even this, which to my mind much reduces the value of a work which has many points of merit.) But it has sometimes been argued that Lenin had certain built-in moral restraints which would have stopped him from going to the lengths to which Stalin went. Not having observed these moral restraints during Lenin's active life, I incline slightly more favourably to the argument that Lenin would not have needed to use so much violence as Stalin because he had moral authority, and Stalin had none.

The most convincing argument in Lenin's favour is the one which is supported by Bukharin's political *credo*. This is, that Lenin towards the end of his life, when already disabled by his illness, virtually turned away from the system which he had created, though maintaining that "historical circumstances" had forced the Bolsheviks in 1917 into the un-marxist policy of trying to build socialism before social conditions in the country were ripe for it. Lenin now, in 1922 and 1923, foresaw a long period of social peace and relaxation of force in order to build, by persuasion, not compulsion, the social conditions without which socialism could only end in tyranny. This view, if it is the correct interpretation of Lenin's last thoughts, as Bukharin believed, was a complete reversal of his practice while he remained in full control of affairs up to the spring of 1922.

Roy Medvedev in his latest book, excellently translated and sensibly annotated, still seems to maintain the view (shared by Trotsky and his followers) that Lenin's rule retained (while he was in power) the elements of "democracy" without which socialism is for Medvedev unthinkable.[6] It is a view that I find difficult to reconcile with the known facts, before 1917 as well as later.

To Solzhenitsyn this entire discussion would, no doubt, appear pointless, since his whole approach to the problem of the just society is based not on the existence or absence of this or that safeguard or law or practice but on the moral beliefs and behaviour of the individuals who make up that society. Let me try to summarize, as I see it, Solzhenitsyn's faith, as it is now discernible from *Gulag* II, as well as from such writings as his essays in the volume entitled *From Under the Rubble*, from his well-known "Letter to the Soviet Leaders", and from a less well known, only recently published omitted chapter of the *First Circle*.[7]

In the first place, it is central to Solzhenitsyn's view that the evils associated with Stalin's period of rule were inherent in the materialist doctrines associated with Marx and with Lenin, and therefore were inherent from the start in the revolution of 1917. This was so for at least two reasons: first, because the doctrines of both Marx and Lenin were based on the false premise that the good society was only prevented from coming into being by the malevolence of certain individuals and classes who were the implacable enemies of the earthly utopia, whose elimination was therefore the first essential step toward progress, and whose continued survival impeded that ever-elusive progress. (Although, so far as I know, Solzhenitsyn does not say so in his writings, the same premise underlay the Jacobin reign of terror.) And secondly, because of the fallacious belief that the nature of human life is determined wholly by external social and material factors. This message runs like a thread of scarlet through the terrifying pages of *Gulag* II.

In truth, Solzhenitsyn argues (closely echoing *Vekhi*), the determining factor lies always within the individual without whose regneration no improvement is ever possible in any society. In Russia this must take the form of "Repentance and Self-Limitation", which is the substance of the title of one of the essays by Solzhenitsyn in *From Under the Rubble* – repentance for the past and self-limitation of future ambitions. The call for "repentance" has offended some of Solzhenitsyn's Russian critics, who argue that the Russians have not necessarily inflicted more misery and suffering on others than, say, Germany or the great empires of the past. Solzhenitsyn does not dispute this, but argues that repentance is the necessary preliminary to moral regeneration.

The second call, for "self-limitation", lies at the core of the much-criticized "Letter to the Soviet Leaders". The idea that a nation should seek to improve the quality of its life by accepting voluntary limitations on economic growth and territorial expansion may well be criticized as idealistic rather than practical. But

Solzhenitsyn might well retort that the more "practical" view has led to a threat of the destruction of our natural environment and indeed of life on our planet, thanks to the "marvels" of modern science.

Solzhenitsyn attaches the greatest importance of all to the rejection of the "rubble" of over fifty years of lies and falsehood, from under which some spiritual life is only now beginning here and there to emerge in Soviet Russia. The late Boris Pasternak was, in my opinion, the first to venture into the Herculean labour of what Confucius once called "the rectification of names" – the purification of the Russian language from the generations of abuse with which the propagandists and the literary hacks had polluted it. *Dr Zhivago* was such an act of purification: the Soviet thought-policemen were quick to recognize its danger, even though, unlike Dostoevsky and Solzhenitsyn, Pasternak never attempted "whip in hand" to go over from defence to the attack.

The conclusion, in practical terms, which Solzhenitsyn draws for his fellow Soviet citizens is that the time has come for them to resist acceptance of official lies, to refuse co-operation with the authorities, and to struggle for the truth by all means open to them. This, he maintains in *Gulag* II, was virtually impossible under Stalin, but is possible now. Solzhenitsyn does not call for martyrdom – our Greek word, which embodies the idea of "witness" by self-sacrifice and which in the Russian equivalent is derived from the notion of "intense sufferings". I think his call is far nearer to the traditional Orthodox idea of *podvizhnichestvo*, the valiant and open performance of acts of faith for the glory of the faith. He also contends that Russians should resist the temptation to emigrate and should stay on in order to carry on the good fight inside. (It will be recalled that Solzhenitsyn did not "emigrate", but was arrested and forcibly put on the plane by seven KGB stalwarts.) Solzhenitsyn's fanatical demand for the *podvizhnichestvo* which completely rejects emigration has led him to criticize severely many of the Soviet émigrés, who feel that their emigration was as much forced upon them by the repressions and threats of the Soviet authorities, which left them with no alternative, as Solzhenitsyn's own departure from the Soviet Union. In the case of Soviet Jews, Solzhenitsyn has expressed sympathy with those who genuinely seek a new home in Israel, and wish to be associated with Israel. But he has not concealed the fact that he regards the Soviet Jew who has no intention of settling in Israel, but uses his ostensible Zionism as a means of escaping from the Soviet Union to the United States of Europe, as one who has betrayed his duty *as a Russian*.

Solzhenitsyn's counsel of uncompromising perfection has aroused a storm of hostile criticism both among the Russian émigrés, and inside Russia. He has been accused of setting a standard which the ordinary Soviet citizen cannot reasonably be expected to follow: and he has been accused of hypocrisy in that, it is alleged, the standard which he demands of others is not the one which he strictly followed while he was in Russia. I regard it as well nigh indecent presumption for those of us who still live under the protection of the rule of law to discuss what those who live under arbitrary tyranny may or may not be expected to do in resisting it. I admire beyond measure the courage of those who do resist: I would never presume to condemn those who have found that they were unable to do so.

But the allegation of hypocrisy seems to me, on the evidence, to be unfair. Nowhere does Solzhenitsyn suggest that he has not at times been subject to the weakness or lack of resistance which he condemns in others. In Chapter 12 of Part 3 in *Gulag* II the reader will find a full and frank account of how the author was persuaded or outwitted into acting as an informer while in camp, though in fact he never did inform; and how he was only saved from pressure to continue in KGB employment after he had left camp – since the KGB seldom, if ever, releases an agent once recruited – by the genuine plea that he was in the throes of a dread disease (the cancer from which he, miraculously, recovered). In his autobiography recently published (in Russian) in Paris he does not spare himself in discussing the occasions when, in spite of his beliefs, he displayed a weakness toward the authorities which he later regretted.[8]

We shall understand nothing of Solzhenitsyn and of the Russian tradition to which he belongs if we persist in seeing him as a straightforward anti-communist for whom the destruction of communist rule would be the solution of all Russia's problems. To go back to *Vekhi* again, a leading theme of these essays was the "apostasy" – as Struve called it (*otshchepenstvo*) – of the radical and socialist intellectuals who saw the destruction of the autocracy as the be-all and end-all of their aim; and who had become "apostates" or "heretics" within a sick body which it was their duty to seek to heal and not merely to destroy. The tradition goes back much further, to Vladimir Soloviev, whose writings had a profound influence on the *Vekhi* authors. Writing in 1884 (on "Judaism and the Christian Question") he stressed that the true prophet, both in the Jewish and in the Christian traditions, does not rise up in revolt against the spiritual and secular powers, but pursues these powers with his expositions and exhortations and thereby carries out his true calling not be separating himself from his society, but by identifying with it.

It is surprising that this strange and disturbing genius, who falls into none of the familiar twentieth-century patterns – anti-communist, democrat, even saint, who if a rare figure is still a recognizable one – should have aroused controversy and misunderstanding. For many he can be summed up as a "Slavophile" – but only for those whose sense of history is weak. Certainly, like the authors of *Vekhi*, Solzhenitsyn shares some beliefs in common with the Slavophiles of the mid-nineteenth century: Orthodoxy, a belief in the importance of the Russian tradition, a critical attitude to the devoted materialism of Western civilization. Like the Slavophiles, he has been critical of the suitability of a democratic form of government for Russia – debating on this subject with academician Sakharov for whom, in spite of their quite different approaches to Russian problems, he entertains, or entertained when *From Under the Rubble* was published, feelings of the highest respect.

But there were two characteristics of the nineteenth-century Slavophiles which seem to me to be quite alien to Solzhenitsyn. While recognizing the importance of the distinctive nature of the Russian tradition, he does not display the Slavophile romantic and unhistorical veneration for the supposed virtues of the pre-Petrine tsars of Muscovy. And secondly, while it is true that stress on the importance of legality, rule of law, and the like is a comparatively rare feature in his writings, it is certainly not the case that like, say, K. S. Aksakov, he dismisses all law as something formal, Germanic, alien to the Russian soul, as something which would destroy the mutual trust which should exist between tsar and people. This was an important part of Slavophile faith.

However, Solzhenitsyn, in his autobiography, expresses something bordering on contempt for the importance which Chalidze attaches to the exercise of constant pressure on the Soviet authorities to force them to observe their own law.[9] Besides, whatever admiration he may ever have felt for this courageous young man has been finally extinguished by Chalidze's emigration to the USA, which for Solzhenitsyn is the sin that cannot be forgiven.

Yet, on occasions Solzhenitsyn has openly recognized the vital importance of the rule of law in any society. In an extract from the forthcoming third volume of *Gulag Archipelago* of which he authorized advance publication, entitled "The Law Today", he strongly criticizes the hypocritical façade of laws, courts, and decrees behind which the Soviet authorities exercise their completely arbitrary rule.[10] If he stresses this theme much less than such authors as Sakharov or Chalidze, it is because for him the primary emphasis always remains the moral regeneration of the individuals who form a society, in the first instance, by the rejection of the lie which Soviet life tries to force upon its citizens at all times.

A recent perceptive essay on the "neo-Slavophile" movement among Russian dissenters includes Solzhenitsyn in this group, without, of course, identifying him with its many and varied manifestations – such as often extreme anti-semitism.[11] This is not the place to refute in detail the slanderous and totally untrue allegation, which I have occasionally met with in addressing Jewish audiences, that Solzhenitsyn is "an anti-semite". Suffice it to say that the charge is not borne out by the evidence; and that Solzhenitsyn is fully alive both to the sufferings that Russians have inflicted on Jews and to the contribution which Jews have made to Russian culture.[12] But Solzhenitsyn has in this respect suffered both from the ignorance of his accusers, and from the sin by association, in certain respects, with some of the "neo-Slavophiles". Those who are determined to see Solzhenitsyn as an anti-semite will no doubt be reinforced in their prejudices by the fact that in his rogues' gallery of Gulag torturers Jews play a very prominent part. Is he to be blamed for recording a fact of history, when the evidence shows that a very disproportionately large number of Jews, until the Great Terror of the thirties, did indeed serve in the ranks of the Soviet secret police? Incidentally, the one, single camp commandant whom Solzhenitsyn praises in this book was a Jew. I doubt if Solzhenitsyn is ever more concerned with a man's nationality than he is with his qualities as a human being. But then neither is he inhibited from asserting what he believes to be the case – that a Jewish Russian is different from an Orthodox Russian, with centuries of Russian tradition behind him. But that is a long way from anti-semitism.

It should be obvious by now that Solzhenitsyn's philosophy is not easy to summarize, and is even harder to label. Undoubtedly, much of the difficulty of understanding him is accounted for by the fact that the language and terminology of his writing are usually quite out of harmony with the materialistic jargon of modern social analysis. Nor, as recent American audiences will have realized, is he much given to compromise or tact where principles in which he believes are involved. Not for him, therefore, the hypocrisies of Helsinki or the delusions of "détente", as they appear to him. At present his disillusionment with what he sees as the failure of the Western democratic systems to stand up for freedom and against tyranny is profound. As he wrote recently in reply to Western critics who accused him of lack of enthusiasm for the Western democratic system: "Thus, I have not only 'not' spoken out against Western freedom: I repeat, we prayed to it as our only hope. But now we see that for thirty years freedom itself has voluntarily yielded position after position to violence."[13] It is also true that his fanaticism often leads him to exaggeration, to an overstressing of communist gains since the end of the war, to an inability or unwillingness to recognize that there have been some gains in the cause of freedom, some resistance to creeping tyranny; to an inability to see that others might conceivably be pursuing truth and virtue in ways very different from his own. An uncomfortable man? Of course. But one whom we can only ignore at our peril, for his message is of vital relevance to our age, and he has suffered for the right to proclaim it. Clearly the time has not yet come to assess the importance and influence of a man who, I venture to predict, is destined to rank as one of the most remarkable human spirits of this generation, and certainly one of the few men of this stature who has been born and lived entirely within the Soviet period of Russia's troubled history.

1. [see pp. 68–92 above. (ed.)]
2. A. Solzhenitsyn and others, *From Under the Rubble* (London 1975).
3. G. Pomerants, *Neopublikovannoe* (Frankfurt 1972), p. 333, footnote.
4. For an excellent anthology of critical essays on Solzhenitsyn and his work and much bibliographical detail, see *Aleksandr Solzhenitsyn: Critical Essays and Documentary Materials.*

Ed. John B. Dunlop, Richard Haugh and Alexis Klimoff. 2nd edn, 1975.

5. [vol. III, translated by Harry Willetts. (New York, London 1978). (ed.)].

6. Roy A. Medvedev, *On Socialist Democracy*. Translated and edited by Ellen de Kadt (New York 1975).

7. The Russian text was published in *Vestnik Russkogo Khristianskogo Dvizheniia*, No. 114 (Paris–New York–Moscow 1974), p. 203.

8. A. Solzhenitsyn, *Bodalsia telenok s dubom* ("How the calf butted against the oak tree") (Paris 1975). [There is an English translation: *The Oak and the Calf*, translated by Harry Willetts (London–New York 1979). (ed.)]

9. Valery Chalidze, *To Defend these Rights*. Human Rights and the Soviet Union (New York 1974).

10. See *The Times*, London, 13 February 1974.

11. John B. Dunlop, "The Eleventh Hour", *Frontier*, No. 2, vol. XVIII (London 1975).

12. For a well-documented discussion of the attitude to Jews in Solzhenitsyn's writings, see Roman Rutman, "The Solzhenitsyn Question", in *Soviet Jewish Affairs*, No. 2, vol. IV (London 1974).

13. A. Solzhenitsyn, "The Artist as Witness", *Times Literary Supplement* (London 23 May 1975).

INDEX